Most accounts of Je
1832) deal with him
utilitarianism or libe
book deals with a les
important aspect of h
namely his theory of the ways in which the
institutions of government should be
organized so that they might function as
efficient and yet responsive guardians of
the community's interests. It thus focuses
on his programme for the executive and
judicial branches of government rather
than for the legislature and the electorate.

By exploring the evolution of his ideas in a
number of fields, it seeks to explain how he
gradually built up a stock of principles,
concepts, rules and legal expertise which he
was able to combine brilliantly into a
comprehensive and prescient constitutional blueprint covering the
executive and judicial branches in unprecedented detail. Dr Hume suggests that
eighteenth-century political thought was
richer in ideas about government than has
usually been allowed, but that Bentham's
special qualities of mind enabled him to
widen and deepen those ideas much further
than his contemporaries could have
foreseen.

In the second half of the nineteenth century,
Idealist and other critics of Utilitarianism
built up a stereotype of Bentham which
represented him as simple-minded, crude
and insensitive in argument, and ignorant
of social and political life. *Bentham and
Bureaucracy* shares the modern approach
which rejects that stereotype, and sees him
as no less complex, subtle and well-informed
a thinker than most of his critics.

BENTHAM AND BUREAUCRACY

Cambridge Studies in the History and Theory of Politics

EDITORS

Maurice Cowling   J. G. A. Pocock
G. R. Elton   J. R. Pole
E. Kedourie   Walter Ullmann

BENTHAM
AND
BUREAUCRACY

L. J. HUME
Reader in Political Science
The Australian National University

CAMBRIDGE UNIVERSITY PRESS

CAMBRIDGE

LONDON   NEW YORK   NEW ROCHELLE

MELBOURNE   SYDNEY

Published by the Press Syndicate of the University of Cambridge
The Pitt Building, Trumpington Street, Cambridge, CB2 1RP
32 East 57th Street, New York, NY 10022, USA
296 Beaconsfield Parade, Middle Park, Melbourne 3206, Australia

© Cambridge University Press 1981

First published 1981

Printed in Great Britain by
Western Printing Services Ltd, Bristol

British Library Cataloguing in Publication Data

Hume, L. J.
Bentham and bureaucracy.
(Cambridge studies in
the history and theory of politics)
1. Bentham, Jeremy. 2. State, The
I. Title
320.1′092′4   JC223.B5   80–41999

ISBN 0 521 23542 1

JC
223
B5H854

TO THE MEMORY OF MY PARENTS

Frederick Roy Hume
and
Alice Clare Hume, née Stapleton

485589

CONTENTS

PREFACE

This work has been in preparation for many years, although for several of those years I was not aware that it was to be a volume of this kind. During its preparation, many people have contributed to it in various ways, and I am grateful for their help.

It was made possible in the first place because the Australian National University granted me study leave in 1967 and 1975 to examine Bentham's manuscripts and printed materials in London and other places. The University has also provided me with other facilities and opportunities. In particular, successive heads of the Department of Political Science have encouraged me to persevere with a topic which, it must be conceded, is not central to the work of the Department.

In the course of my research on Bentham, I made very heavy use of the Library of University College, London, and I want to thank the Librarian of that institution, Mr J. W. Scott, and those of his officers who had to deal with my many requests for help and information, especially Miss M. Skerl, who guided me through the Bentham Mss. for the first time in 1967. At University College, too, Professor J. H. Burns and other members of the Bentham Committee gave me direction and advice when I took my problems to them. I also drew extensively on the resources of the British Library (for both printed works and manuscripts), the Goldsmiths' Library of the University of London and the Public Records Office in London, and the National Library of Australia in Canberra. For shorter periods I was able to consult manuscripts of or relating to Bentham in La Bibliothèque Publique et Universitaire at Geneva (Dumont Papers), in the Cornwall County Record Office at Truro (Carew-Pole Muniments), at Althorp (Spencer Papers) and in the Library of the Royal Botanic Gardens, Kew (George Bentham Papers). I am conscious of the help and courteous attention that I received at each place.

As the years have passed, the members of my family, my colleagues and many of my friends have grown accustomed to the presence of Jeremy Bentham as my constant if invisible companion, and they may even have come to accept him. He has been a more obtrusive figure for my wife, for she has sometimes had to act as my unpaid research assistant and has more often had to manage in the periods when he made excessive demands on my time or seemed likely to defeat me entirely.

Because I have been writing about Bentham for so long, many typists have worked on parts or versions of my draft. I must mention in particular Mrs Judy Rix, who typed the bulk of the final draft as well as some earlier material; Mrs Lyn King, who coped with my earliest efforts when I was uncertain about the shape of my future argument; Miss J. Collins and Mrs P. Naylor, who typed the first substantial drafts of the opening chapters; and Miss Ellen Ruffles, who helped to incorporate my afterthoughts and to attend to the consequent tidying-up.

I am listing below certain formal acknowledgements for material reproduced in the text. I want, finally, to acknowledge certain intellectual debts, going back more than thirty years, to some of my former teachers: to Professor P. H. Partridge, who first introduced me to the study of political thought; to Mr J. L. Mackie, who first convinced me that what the text-books said about Bentham was not necessarily true; and to Professors S. J. Butlin and J. A. La Nauze who, by precept and example over a number of years, tried to convince me of the merits and the possibility of exact scholarship.

L.J.H.
Canberra
May 1980

ACKNOWLEDGEMENTS

I wish to thank the following for permission to quote copyright material:

The Bobbs-Merrill Company Inc. of Indianapolis for passages from Schwab's Introduction to d'Alembert's *Preliminary discourse to the Encyclopedia of Diderot*, and from H. Paolucci's translation of *On crimes and punishments* by Beccaria.

The Athlone Press, London, for passages drawn from H. L. A. Hart's edition of Bentham's *Of Laws in General*.

The Librarian of University College, London, for quotations from and references to the Bentham Manuscripts in the College Library.

The Keeper of Manuscripts at the British Library, for quotations from and references to the Bentham Manuscripts lodged in that institution.

The Editors and publishers of *The Journal of Accounting Research* and *The Bulletin of Economic Research* for permission to use material which appeared in articles by me in those journals.

LIST OF ABBREVIATIONS

B.L. Add. Mss.   British Library Series of Additional
Manuscripts.

Bowring (i, etc.)   *The works of Jeremy Bentham. Published
under the superintendence of his executor,
John Bowring* (11 vols., Edinburgh, 1838–43),
vol. 1, etc.

C.W.   *The collected works of Jeremy Bentham.*
General Editor, J. H. Burns (London, 1968–).

G.B.   George Bentham (Jeremy's nephew).

J.B.   Jeremy Bentham.

Lambert   *House of Commons Papers of the Eighteenth
Century*, ed. by Sheila Lambert (Wilmington,
Delaware, 1975).

S.B.   Samuel Bentham (Jeremy's brother).

Stark   *Jeremy Bentham's economic writings*, ed. by
W. Stark (3 vols., London, 1952–54).

U.C. (iv, etc.)   The Bentham Mss. at University College,
London, Box iv, etc.

I

INTRODUCTION

This work is an essay in the history of ideas, the report of an inquiry into the sources and evolution of Jeremy Bentham's ideas about the functions, structure and activities of government. Its starting point is the programme for the organization of government that Bentham set out in his *Constitutional Code*, which was the last and in a sense the culminating major product of his many years' work on jurisprudence and codification.[1]

The *Constitutional Code* is in some respects a repellent work. Its arrangement is obscure and its language is obsolete and contorted. It represents, nevertheless, a remarkable achievement.[2] It far surpasses in comprehensiveness and in attention to detail the many Constitutions that were drafted during Bentham's own lifetime, in North and South America, in France, in Norway, in Spain, in Portugal and elsewhere in Europe.

In particular, the five chapters relating to the Executive display these qualities and other important ones as well. They are much more extensive and go into much more detail than the material that Bentham's contemporaries provided for this branch of government: their 250 pages of double-column print contrast strikingly with, for example, the couple of score of Articles in the French Constitution of 1791, the 4 Sections in the Constitution of the United States of 1789, the 33 Articles in the Greek Constitution of 1822 or even the 100 Articles in the Spanish Constitution of 1812. And Bentham's chapters possess a theoretical consistency and sophistication and a prescience that are quite unusual among constitutional draftsmen at any time or in any place.

Bentham's account of government's functions is much closer to the twentieth-century pattern than to that of his own lifetime. He allocated to it a sparse but positive role, giving a relatively large weight to the domestic (social and economic) functions that

British and other governments were only cautiously and hesitantly assuming in the 1820s and 1830s. He thus foresaw and advocated the multiplication of functions that in Britain fell within the scope of the Home Office and the Board of Trade and that came to be a dominant feature in nineteenth-century administrative experience.

He similarly foresaw and advocated many of the changes in the structure and organization of the Executive that were adopted to cope with the new responsibilities: the establishment of central government departments for health, education and other social services, the concomitant recasting of the system of local government, the rationalization of control of the armed forces, the replacement of a multitude of financial authorities by a single department of finance (the Treasury), and the substitution of hierarchically-organized and single-headed ministries for boards as the typical administrative agencies. Similarly his Civil Service was to be organized on modern not on early nineteenth-century lines, for it was to consist of officials remunerated wholly by salaries, and recruited, promoted and disciplined according to carefully prescribed, formal and quasi-objective methods. And the working relations, the obligations and many of the working conditions of the officials were also prescribed in great detail. Central to the working relations were the correlative notions of superordination and subordination – hierarchy – which Bentham insisted must operate throughout the whole governmental system. The obligations included the keeping of a complex set of records and accounts (in which fourteen different kinds of books were named in a section occupying twenty-one pages of one of the chapters) and the observance of a set of 'Rules of Deportment by Functionaries towards non-Functionaries'. The treatment of working conditions extended in one direction to 'Architectural Arrangements' and in another to the sorts of tribunals that might consider charges of misconduct against officials.

Bentham's treatment of the Judiciary was less novel than his treatment of the Executive, but it displayed many of the same qualities. It too was very detailed and extensive, occupying eleven chapters of the Code and extending to such matters as the time of sittings, the provision of courts and the character of their furniture and equipment, and the form of the judges' robes. It also ran parallel to the treatment of the Executive over considerable areas, for it sought to rationalize the structure and operations of the Judiciary along the same lines and by the same means. Bentham saw the Executive and Judiciary as two co-ordinate 'departments' of a single governmental structure and he wanted to apply the same criteria to each of them, and as far as possible to arrange them according to the same pattern.

As significant as the detail was the inner coherence of Bentham's Code. Most constitutions have been the work of conventions or committees, and have been enriched or disfigured by the outcome of contests and bargains among the competing interests and philosophies. Bentham's was the product of a single controlling mind, it proceeded according to a single mode of analysis and it expressed a single philosophy.[3] And the analysis and the philosophy were made explicit in the Code itself, for Bentham included in it a great deal of material that normally does not find a place in formal constitutions. To the conventional contents of a constitution – which he called the Enactive articles – he added a mass of Expositive, Ratiocinative and Instructional articles in which he explained and defended the Enactive provisions. He thus provided a theory of as well as a programme for the organization of government.[4]

In his theory and his programme he treated the Executive and the Judiciary as both bundles of offices and masses of individual employees. He analysed the offices separately and linked them to each other through relations of command and obedience – the right to command and the duty to obey. The individuals participated in the system through their occupancy of particular offices and their possession of the relevant rights and obligations; they were related to each other through the same system of command and obedience and the sanctions (including reward) that existed to enforce obedience. Thus it may be misleading to say that Bentham was making provision for a modern Civil Service: the use of that phraseology may imply the existence of a corps to which individuals belong in a way that shapes their lives and outlooks, to which and to other members of which they feel a sense of loyalty, and in which loyalty and other informal sentiments and relationships influence the working of the system. It was certainly not Bentham's intention to create a governmental machine of that kind. He knew about informal relationships and their ability to pervade an administrative agency, but it was precisely his aim to eliminate such forces and to make the working of his Executive depend entirely on the formal relations of command and obedience.

He analysed and prescribed for each office in terms of a standard set of categories which summed up a great deal of his theory. The broad categories were:

Number in an office, or Grades of offices
Functions, or fields of service
Relations with other offices and authorities
Term of service
Attendance
Remuneration
Location (i.e. recruitment or appointment) – locable who,
                                        located how
Securities for appropriate aptitude

These were complemented by standard ways of treating the several categories, and above all by a detailed classification of administrative functions into the following main groups:

(a) Functions relating to persons: Locative, Dislocative, Self-suppletive, Directive;
(b) Functions relating to money or other things: Procurative, Custoditive, Applicative, Reparative, Transformative, Eliminative, Inspective or Information-elicitative;
(c) Functions relating to persons, things and occurrences: Statistic or book-keeping, Registrative, Publicative and Report-Making;
(d) Functions relating to persons, things, and arrangements: Melioration-suggestive[5]

He carried his reflections on many of these matters to the point where he was able to express them as administrative rules or principles, notably 'individual responsibility', 'uniformity in management', 'unity of authority', 'the principle of publicity', and the 'junction-of-interest-and-duty prescribing principle'. In these ways – and however grotesque and obscure the language – Bentham was providing a comprehensive account of administrative activity, that is of the matters to which the designers or directors of any organization must attend and of the ways in which they ought to handle those matters.

On these grounds it seems fair to say that Bentham was providing a substantial and coherent theory of organization and management. He was assuming throughout that one common

task faced those persons at the head of a government, and that
it was identical with the task faced by those in charge of any
administrative or productive agency. That task was the deployment of human and material resources within the agency as
effectively as possible, with maximum efficiency and at minimum
cost – or in his own and oft-repeated phrase 'Official aptitude
maximized, official expense minimized'. He was assuming that in
all but the simplest and smallest administrative units, the optimum
deployment of resources would not be achieved spontaneously
but must be actively sought. And he was assuming that successful
management did not depend solely on personal talent or flair, but
that it must be promoted through the design of the agency itself,
and that its requirements could be expressed in rules and principles. He believed that in the *Constitutional Code* he had provided
a blue-print which was not only suitable for government but was
also adaptable to the requirements of all other substantial organizations.

We can discern in his blueprint two persistent themes and
purposes: making the process of decision making as rational as
possible, and making the subordinate officials and other resources
completely, quickly and economically responsive to the super-
ordinates' commands. His particular observations and recommendations found a place in his scheme because he expected
them to contribute to one or the other of these processes, or to
both together. This is as true of, for example, his treatment of
architectural arrangements as of the statistic function. Each is
designed to maximize the flow of information to the super-
ordinates and thus place them in a position to detect and punish
disobedience and to adapt their policies and decisions to changing
circumstances and varying performances; each is designed to give
the subordinates the optimum working environment in which to
exercise their talents or 'aptitudes' in the service of the organization and in accordance with the directions of the superordinates.
At a more general level it can be said that the whole structure
consists of a system of communications, a system of discipline,
arrangements for scientific recruitment and a hierarchical pattern
of authority. But once again these different components are not
independent, for communications and hierarchy and perhaps
even the mode of recruitment contribute to the maintenance of
discipline, and discipline in its turn makes them work well.

Once Bentham's scheme has been described, I believe there is little room for doubt that it closely resembles the orthodox theory of organization and management which established itself in the first two or three decades of the present century: the theory which we associate with the notions of 'scientific management' and 'principles of administration'. It resembles that theory in objectives, devices, principles and above all in spirit. It shares with it the objective of exploiting resources scientifically through the careful analysis and study of activities and actions to find the 'one best way', a systematic division of labour, the design and construction of systems of rewards and penalties to operate as precise incentives, attention to the layout of buildings and equipment, close control over movements in stocks and the prevention of waste of all kinds, the limitation of initiative and discretion on the part of the individual worker and the centralization of information and authority at the top. It shares with it, too, a belief that the appropriate course of action can be summed up in rules and principles, and reliance on a formal structure of hierarchically-arranged authority and on rules and the means of their enforcement.

These general points can be illustrated in two examples drawn from the classical literature of management theory. The first is Henri Fayol's list of the fourteen 'principles of management which [he had] most frequently had to apply': division of work, authority, discipline, unity of command, unity of direction, subordination of individual interests to the general interest, remuneration, centralization, scalar chain (line of authority), order, equity, stability of tenure of personnel, initiative, esprit de corps.[6] Some of these reproduce almost exactly Bentham's thoughts in almost his own words. Very few do not appear in some form in his reasoning and even some of the exceptions – stability of personnel, initiative – turn out to be so qualified by Fayol that they do not differ greatly from Bentham's doctrines. Perhaps only in relation to 'esprit de corps' is there a real difference between them. The second example is Luther Gulick's list of the functions of the executive of an organization: planning, organizing, staffing, directing, co-ordinating, reporting, budgeting.[7] Again, some of these are covered explicitly and most of the remainder implicitly in Bentham's standard set of functions. Among the less-obvious ones planning and organization are both comprehended within what Bentham calls the Melioration-suggestive function, which is the activity of proposing reforms and improvements in 'persons, things, money, instruments of statistication, registration and publication, ordinances and consequent arrangements', in short in any and every aspect of the organization.[8] Co-ordination may be the absentee from Bentham's list, for it seems that he took so strictly hierarchical a view, and left the subordinate officials so little discretion, that he did not separate out co-ordination from the general directive function.

It can be conceded that Bentham did not anticipate all the detailed conclusions of scientific management or all the 'principles of administration' that had been accumulated by the 1930s. He did, however, develop an approach that could accommodate scientific management and the principles, that did in fact include some elements of both of them, and that covered (even if sketchily and sometimes crudely) all the ground claimed for classical organization theory in its heyday. The scheme set out in the *Constitutional Code* comes much closer to being a complete version of that theory than do, say, the writings of Charles Babbage who is commonly regarded as a precursor of it.[9]

It is also true that Bentham's scheme was markedly bureaucratic, in the sense of that term popularized by Max Weber. As in Weber's ideal-type, Bentham's functionaries were to be subject to authority only with respect to their official obligations; they were to be organized in a clearly defined hierarchy of offices each of which had a clearly defined sphere of legal competence; the office was to be filled by a free contractual relationship and on the basis of technical qualifications possessed by the candidates and tested by formal examinations; the officials were to be remunerated by fixed monetary salaries and were to treat their official duties as their sole or primary occupation; there was to be a system of promotion; the officials were not to own or to be allowed to appropriate the means of administration; and they were to be subject to strict and systematic discipline and control in the conduct of their offices.[10] Bentham's proposals diverged from the ideal-type only by retaining a novel scheme for the sale of offices within the arrangements for recruitment and promotion, by providing less security of tenure in the last resort, and by placing a ban on retirement pensions (which he called 'pensions of retreat').

The comparison with Weber's analysis leads on to a more general point. Bentham's programme for government was an exercise in rational-legal authority, in which every act, activity and office was legitimate only in so far as it was authorized by rules of law formulated and enacted by a legislator, and in which loyalty and obedience were owed not to individuals as such but to individuals endowed with authority by law. Bentham did not match Weber's achievement in looking at bureaucracy from the outside and in seeing it as just one of a number of possible modes of organization. Yet he did in a sense perceive the nature of bureaucracy and the conditions of its existence, and he sensed its growing importance in European life. The theory of bureaucratic organization had emerged fully in his work.

These characteristics of the *Constitutional Code* pose a challenge to historians of ideas to explain how Bentham was able to reach these points in his thinking. The problem has two aspects, one relating to the general evolution of ideas and the other more specific to Bentham. The general aspect can be illustrated by reference to Fayol. The latter published his little treatise in 1911 and it was regarded almost immediately as a major contribution to the subject. In the words of a recent commentator, 'he was the first of the modern management writers to propound a theoretical analysis of what managers have to do and by what principles they have to do it'.[11] How was Bentham able to work to substantially the same position eighty or ninety years earlier? The more specific aspects of the problem relate to a distinctive feature of Bentham's general philosophy and modes of reasoning, his commitment to a thoroughgoing individualism and nominalism which denied the reality of all but individual persons, acts, events and experiences. Given his individualism, how was he able to create a system in which abstractions and collectivities – the office as distinct from the official, the chain of responsibility and the system of communications as distinct from particular rules and prescriptions – were recognized and came to play a large part?

The answers to those questions are not and cannot be simple. The student of Bentham's thought enters a Hegelian world, where everything is connected with everything else in multiple ways, and where particular themes and notions appear and re-appear in many contexts in any of which they may display new aspects or be subtly transformed. Bentham's ideas about government must accordingly be traced through, and disentangled from, his thinking about many other subjects, including jurisprudence, prison-management, the poor law, the naval dockyards, education, religion and parliamentary reform.

Nevertheless, the rudiments of answers can be given fairly shortly. The essential clues can in fact be found in one of the earliest and best-known assessments of Bentham's character and significance, the essay that Hazlitt published in his collection entitled *The Spirit of the Age*. After identifying Bentham as primarily a 'jurist', Hazlitt went on to deny that he was an original thinker:

> Mr. Bentham's forte is arrangement...He has methodised, collated and condensed all the materials prepared to his hand on the subjects of which he treats, in a masterly and scientific manner; but we should find a difficulty in adducing from his different works (however elaborate or closely reasoned) any new element of thought, or even a new fact or illustration...[In his discussion of utility] his merit is, that he has applied this principle more closely and literally; that he has brought all the objections and arguments, more distinctly labelled and ticketed, under this one head, and made a more constant and explicit reference to it at every step of his progress, than any other writer.[12]

Hazlitt underestimated the extent to which Bentham did produce new structures of thought and new facts or illustrations, but his assessment drew attention to four important points. These were Bentham's concern with the law, his utilitarianism, his sensitivity to and willingness to take over the ideas of others, and his superb capacity to explore systematically and exhaustively any notion that he took seriously. It was, as Hazlitt suggested, his contribution to as well as his blight upon utilitarianism that he clarified and set out in a systematic way the implications of what had been more often a commonly accepted standard of judgement than a formal doctrine. He proceeded in the same way in his consideration of government, seeking to state rigorously what had been formulated only loosely, seeking to translate into operational programmes what he encountered as mere aspirations. In this process, his own utilitarianism was of great importance; not only his acceptance of 'the greatest happiness' as the supreme moral value, but also his never-ending efforts to relate means to ends in a rational way, to treat all institutions and arrangements as means to the supreme end, to condemn and discard the inferior means and to shape everything else to serve it more efficiently. And it was equally important that he was a 'jurist', educated in law and committed to it as a mode of social control. His interest in the law led him to the study of a body of writings on legal and quasi-legal issues, in which he found general ideas about government and many of the standard eighteenth-century ideas about administration and administrative reform. His own approach to the law gave heavy weight to problems of judgement, the judiciary and punishment, and this made him especially sensitive to administrative issues and brought him up against specific administrative problems. His utilitarianism and legal bias together encouraged him to immerse himself in the theory of the modern state as it then stood, and to try to perfect the theory.[13]

The general answer to our questions is, then, that Bentham evolved his ideas about government and administration by working simultaneously in two directions. He gradually translated and elaborated certain general theories into a number of principles and devices that could be applied to government and applied in an administrative setting. At the same time he selected, modified and restated administrative principles and devices in order to reconcile them with his general theories, and tried to provide them with an adequate institutional basis. As Hazlitt suggested, very few of the ideas that he took up at either level were wholly new. He found them in the thinking of his contemporaries, as part of the climate of opinion. Equipped, however, with his extraordinary capacity for systematic analysis and his extraordinary pertinacity, he built them into a structure that his contemporaries had not known and probably did not even envisage.

The process of building that structure was a very long one, extending over most of his working life. It was never his principal concern, but was always incidental to the grand work of codification on which he saw himself as almost continuously engaged. Yet it is possible to see in it several distinct phases and a definite progression, as his varying approaches to codification encouraged him to deal successively with different aspects of government and to deal with them in greater or less depth.

The material 'prepared to his hand' by his predecessors and contemporaries was already pretty voluminous. Some of it was to be found in formal works on political philosophy which have come down to us as part of the 'great tradition', including those of Hobbes, Locke, Montesquieu and Hume. More of it was in the less famous but influential writings which are known to have attracted or repelled Bentham, such as those of Helvétius, Beccaria and Blackstone. And other instalments were in more ephemeral or more narrowly-based discussions of social policy and institutions: exercises in codification or reform of the judiciary; tracts or pamphlets dealing with various aspects of police, oeconomy, Cameralism or the emerging subject of political economy; compilations such as the remarkable 'Instructions' that Catherine the Great issued to her Legal Commissioners in 1767–68; and legislation, Parliamentary debates and Government reports on legal and 'economical' reform, of which the most impressive were the reports of the Commissioners for examining the Public Accounts of 1780–82.

These diverse sources yielded a fairly common assumption that the Government must accept responsibility for promoting economic progress, social welfare and social order. There was, it is true, considerable debate and uncertainty about the economic role of government, and these were greatly stimulated by the publication of Smith's *Wealth of Nations* in 1776. But they related to the strategy rather than to the responsibilities of government, and they left intact the interest in preventive police – especially in the 'metropolis', where the problems arising from urbanization and the expansion of a commercial economy were most apparent – and the interest in devising suitable policies and institutions for the idle, the impotent poor and the criminal.[14] Those attitudes were accompanied by increasing disillusionment with the performance of government and many of its existing practices but also by an assumption that administration could be rendered more pure and more efficient if only the problem were tackled in the proper way. Running through the different works and subjects were two general themes and attitudes. One was utilitarianism, in the sense of a propensity to measure the value of institutions by their contribution to particular and narrowly-conceived objectives. The second was rationalism, expressed firstly in an expectation that one could make institutions more efficient by imposing on them uniformity, simplicity and clarity, and secondly in a programme and a preference for legal-rationalism. The programme did not exist complete in any one place when Bentham began his studies, but its elements were scattered about in the familiar doctrines of sovereignty and in the numerous schemes for codification and judicial reform.

Bentham proceeded to absorb these ideas into his own thinking in three main phases. In the first he adopted and embraced the philosophy of legal-rationalism, which provides the common thread running through his jurisprudence, and drew from it some immediate implications for the nature of government and the character of its operations: the primacy of legislation in government and in society, the legal status of government as a trust, the nature of governmental powers and similar points. In the second phase he produced more detailed material about institutions and processes as he explored some of the notions to which he had committed himself (such as crime, punishment, reward, indirect legislation), and began to speculate about the principles and instruments of enforcement and the conditions on which these could be made to work. At the same time he carried further his attempts to fit government into his account of law. Finally, he sought to apply his principles and more particular ideas in a practical way, by drawing up detailed plans for concrete institutions, ranging from prisons to naval dockyards.

These phases were not not quite distinct chronologically, but they can be associated more or less closely with particular periods of his life. The first was practically complete by 1782 and most of its fruits are in the four major works that he had written by that time: the *Fragment on Government*, the *Introduction to the Principles of Morals and Legislation*, the *Comment on the Commentaries* and *Of Laws in General*. The second followed closely on it and was substantially the work of the 1780s, in the essays on reward, punishment and indirect legislation and in the large body of material (mainly in French) in which he tried to provide a sketch of a general and all-comprehensive code.[15] The third phase overlaps both of the others, for his efforts to apply his principles to real institutions – to design real institutions to fit his principles – began in the 1770s and continued in the 1780s. But it was in the last decade of the century that he made most rapid progress here, drawing up elaborate, detailed and markedly bureaucratic schemes for preventive police, pauper management, judicial organization and the dockyards, and similar but less elaborate ones in other fields, and adding to some of them extensive commentaries which contained substantial bodies of speculation about management.

The outcome was that by 1802, when Bentham's life was thrown into confusion by the collapse of the Panopticon project,[16] he already possessed most of the elements that he was later to put into his programme for the Executive and the Judiciary in the *Constitutional Code*. Some points were missing or weakly formulated, but these were a relatively small part of the total. One important thing was lacking, however, and that was any clear impulse to build the elements into a comprehensive scheme.

That impulse was not supplied finally until the early 1820s, when the emergence of revolutionary movements and new regimes in Spain, Portugal, Greece and elsewhere encouraged Bentham to believe that someone would soon commission him to draft an all-comprehensive body of laws which would include a constitutional code. In the meantime he occupied himself with a multitude of different subjects which do not obviously have anything in common. Some of them were, in a quite technical sense, legal subjects, such as evidence, juries and the law of libel. Others were apparently remote from the law, such as parliamentary reform, religion, education, language and the political economy of colonies. The twenty years between 1802 and 1822 (when his drafting of the *Constitutional Code* got seriously under way) therefore seem at first sight a barren period. But in a number of ways those years contributed significantly to both the form and the content of the *Code*. What he wrote then had more unity, and was more concerned with constitutional law and administration, than a simple listing of the titles and subject matters would suggest.

The unifying element was his ambition to track down, delineate and find antidotes to sinister influence within the political and social system. This informed not only what he wrote about parliamentary reform but also much of his work on law, religion and even language and logic. In this way he oriented himself towards constitutional law and ultimately a constitutional code, and worked towards the admission of abstractions and 'fictitious entities' into his account of political and administrative life. Bentham himself sometimes saw not only his Parliamentary Reform Bill but also his work on the Church and on some technical aspects of the law (e.g. libel law) as instalments of a future constitutional code; and he was undoubtedly right, because that is the way he handled the issues. It was also important that in some of these works he was speculating about modes of generalization while in others he was developing broad themes, notably the theme of responsibility; between them these would determine the shape of his constitution and the provision that he must make for the Executive. And in some of them, too, he was including a good deal of administrative material as he tried to put into detailed form his plans for restructured institutions such as the Church or the judiciary. This served to keep fresh in his mind the patterns that he had devised in the 1790s, to demonstrate that they were indeed applicable outside the particular contexts for which he had devised them, and occasionally to fill in gaps which remained in his thinking. In the period immediately before he started to draft the *Constitutional Code* he was already trying to bring together many of his thoughts on the Executive in a work provisionally entitled 'Thoughts on Economy as applied to Office: Aptitude Maximized, Expense Minimized.'[17]

In the early months of 1822 'Thoughts on Economy' had to compete for Bentham's attention with an earlier and still more ambitious project, the realization of his ever-present dream of producing a complete code of laws. Among the new constitutional regimes, he seems to have looked first and most confidently to Spain and the Spanish ex-colonies as potential patrons of his work. Later, he turned to Portugal – which seemed, while constitutional government survived precariously there, to have given him the commission that he had sought – and then to Greece. But his published *Codification Proposal* was addressed to *all* nations professing liberal opinions, and he was prompted by events in Naples and Norway to see encouraging prospects there. The opportunities were apparently abundant. The subsequent story has been told by Halévy and others.[18] The potential patrons dropped away one by one, and Bentham came to concentrate on the *Constitutional Code*, although he had not represented this in his published or unpublished 'offers' as the first part of the pannomium that he would complete.

The drafting of the chapters relating to government followed more or less as a matter of course. It proceeded through the incorporation, systematization and refinement of the material that Bentham had accumulated during the previous 50 years. The process was not completed, however, without a good deal of storm and stress, as may be seen in the successive redrafts of the material that has survived in a readily identifiable form.[19] But on the whole, the problems that Bentham was wrestling with at that stage concerned form rather than content: the relation between the Constitutional and other codes on which he continued to work, the location of the 'rationale' or 'reason-giving' material which he believed must accompany the 'enactive' provisions in any satisfactory legislative document, and the taming of his own verbosity. Perhaps the last major problem of content was the reconciliation of the bureaucratic treatment of the Executive and the Judiciary with the general emphasis on elections and recall that characterizes the *Constitutional Code* as a whole. To state the matter in Bentham's terminology, the *Code* was mainly about 'locability' and 'dislocability', to be effected through an electoral system, and only secondarily about 'punibility', to be effected through rules and their enforcement; whereas in the chapters relating to government the emphasis is switched from dislocability by the electors to punibility, and this is what stamps on them their bureaucratic character. In Bentham's own mind the two approaches seem to have been reconciled through the very extent of his commitment to elections, and his faith in their power to discipline behaviour either directly or at a distance.

We can summarize this brief chronological account by recognizing three major stages in which Bentham evolved his bureaucratic programme and his conception of the functions of government. In the eighteenth century he collected others' ideas, absorbed them into his own thinking and restated them in terms acceptable to himself, and tried to apply them to specific institutions. In the 1820s he extended his principles and his devices to cover the whole of government. In the intervening years he developed his own ideas in ways which made that task seem necessary and fruitful, and which permitted him to embark upon it. The whole process can reasonably be described in Hazlitt's words, as the masterly collation and condensation of the materials prepared to his hand. But it was much less simple and straightforward, involved more work on the materials and in the preparation of categories to accommodate them, and resulted in a more original structure than Hazlitt imagined.

In subsequent chapters, I propose to describe the process in more detail, arguing and illustrating points that have appeared here as simple assertions. In order to do so, it is necessary to begin at Bentham's own starting point, that is the notions and doctrines that he had available to him when he turned his mind to the structure, operations and functions of government. These will form the subject matter of the next chapter.

GOVERNMENT IN EIGHTEENTH-
CENTURY THOUGHT

In the second half of the eighteenth century, a large and rapidly growing body of ideas bearing upon government was available to anyone who might want to develop a systematic view of the subject. It was to be found in the assumptions underlying contemporary practices in government and some other institutions, and in those aspects of political thought which historians have classified as individualism and the theory of the modern state.[1] These two closely related modes of thinking, whose foundations had been laid in the sixteenth and seventeenth centuries by Bodin, Hobbes and a host of lesser thinkers, had become by the middle of the eighteenth century a standard approach to problems of government. They were still being extended and developed and, while retaining most of their original character, were being made to yield new and far-reaching conclusions about institutions and their workings.

Individualism and the theory of the modern state were a commentary on and a response to the several processes that most clearly differentiated the modern from the medieval world: the centralization of legal authority and military power within the territories of any one government, the concomitant decay or destruction of corporate privileges and autonomous jurisdictions, and changes in the position of individuals as they ceased to be subject to local or corporate authorities and thus ceased to be constrained or protected by intermediate authorities between themselves and the state. In the beginning, the attention of theorists had been directed especially to the legal and psychological foundations of the new political and social relationships. As the new relationships became more firmly established, more familiar and more widely sought by both individuals and governments, so the corresponding theories first permeated the thinking of political philosophers and publicists, and then expanded beyond the foundations to cover the construction and working of institutions and arrangements. The eighteenth-century fruits of this development were a mass of plans for novel policies and establishments designed to complete the structure of the modern state and both to respect and to exploit the newly-recognized independence of individuals.

The nature of the original theoretical response to modern relationships had been summed up most clearly and completely in the *Leviathan* of Thomas Hobbes. The doctrines of *Leviathan* encompassed individualism and the theory of the modern state, presented the two in an integrated form, and provided a rudimentary blueprint for the investigation of institutional and policy issues by later thinkers.

By treating mankind as naturally asocial and without obligations, Hobbes generalized and legitimized the growing independence of individuals and at the same time provided the centralized state with its *raison d'être*. In his world of independent individuals, social order could be established only as conscious social control, and the state was the indispensable instrument and source of that control. He justified and filled out his account of the asocial individual in his theory of human behaviour, built around individual appetites and aversions and culminating in the will or act of willing, and in his theory of moral language which treated good and evil as synonyms for, respectively, the objects of the appetites and the objects of the aversions of any individual.[2] He performed a like function for the state by endowing it with – insisting that it must possess – a will like an individual, and by adopting and extending the theory of sovereignty; that is, the theory of an unlimited, indivisible and permanent authority possessed by the state and exercised typically in the issue (and enforcement) of commands in the form of laws.[3]

In setting out his understanding of sovereignty, Hobbes made it clear that the sovereign's exercise of the legislative function was what distinguished him from other elements in the state, and that legislation must displace adjudication as the primary function or the essence of government. The sovereign's law, the expression of his will, was the immediate instrument of social control.[4] He complemented this view with the rudiments of a theory of law and legislation, and some account of the relationships between the sovereign and other authorities within the state.[5] He adapted and refined his command theory of law by allowing for the adoption of existing laws or other forms of tacit command, by insisting nevertheless on promulgation as a condition of a real and operative law, by recommending that each law be accompanied by 'a declaration of the causes and motives for which it was made', and by recognizing that each law must (on his own theory of behaviour) include some element of punishment or reward to make it effective.[6] The last point meant that punishment and reward must be viewed in a utilitarian way as means of inducing obedience, not as retribution or an expression of community values or attitudes. He admitted that the law must be interpreted in the course of its administration but he insisted that the interpreter or judge must be authorized by the sovereign to perform that function. The judge, like all other authorities in the state, must be subordinate to the sovereign.[7]

Hobbes completed his outline of the state's institutions with a sketch of some of these other authorities and their activities and policies. He envisaged the appointment by the sovereign of public officials ('ministers', in the sense of subordinate agents) to care for the finances of the state, to lead and care for its army, to instruct the people in their moral and political duties, to maintain order and to execute judgements, and to represent the sovereign abroad. He also envisaged that the sovereign would make some provision for the maintenance of the poor and would have an economic policy which might involve the regulation of property and of domestic or foreign trade, for these were all aspects of 'propriety [which] belongeth in all kinds of commonwealth to the sovereign power'.[8] He was careful to distinguish the officials engaged in these *public* tasks from the servants employed in the household of a monarch or even the officers of a parliament who were employed 'for no other purpose, but for the commodity of the men assembled', arguing that 'they that be servants to them in their natural capacity, are not public ministers; but those only that serve them in the administration of the public business'.[9] He was here making the important distinction between the incumbent and the office, in this case between the personal needs of the sovereign and his powers and functions. He condemned the ancient practice of trying to provide for the sovereign by a permanent endowment of land or income.[10] He was also hostile to the 'farming' of taxes to contractors, to the grant of monopolies as a method of raising revenue and to the payment of some sorts of officials (especially the judiciary) by fees instead of salaries.[11] He envisaged that the sovereign would purchase most of the services it required, and would raise the money it needed by variable taxes. The ability to impose such taxes, he thought, was one of the sovereign's attributes against which there could be no legitimate objection on the part of subjects.[12] In these ways Hobbes was already taking the theory of the modern state beyond its foundations in sovereignty or legal supremacy, and into the area of government and administration. Although he did not venture very far into that area, he went far enough to establish that it was a legitimate object of political speculation and that indeed political speculation must cover it in order to complete the theory of the state.

In the course of the next century, political philosophers and publicists increasingly accepted the theory of sovereignty and many of its implications for institutions and arrangements. The propositions that Hobbes had advanced provocatively in 1651 became the axioms of a considerable band of writers on politics, and on its eighteenth-century satellites oeconomy and police. They were sometimes reshaped and juxtaposed with ideas derived from other (possibly rival) thinkers, such as Locke or Montesquieu, but they were still recognizable in their new settings. They figured prominently in the work of the popularizers and synthesizers of the second half of the century, such as Sir William Blackstone, Catherine the Great (in her *Nakaz* or Instructions to her Legal Commissioners) and the German publicist J. F. von Bielfeld. These and other writers had gradually followed and then outstripped Hobbes in examining the policies, institutions and functioning of the state, but the legal doctrines pervaded their thinking about all the other matters. On the one hand those doctrines prescribed a set of tasks to be performed in order to perfect the state and to realize the opportunities presented by its accumulation of power. On the other hand they provided a way of thinking – what one might describe as the elements of a theoretical model, cast in terms of command, obedience, enforcement and other legal categories derived from sovereignty – that could be applied to the constituent parts of the state as well as to its whole structure.

In these extensions to Hobbes's account, the Executive received a share of attention, but it was rarely their principal subject matter, and it was never discussed as a self-contained topic. The fundamental issue was still the state's monopolization of legal authority, so questions of law, the judiciary and legal reform attracted more attention, and attracted it earlier, than the subordinate matter of administrative reform, except where the latter seemed to be the necessary means to the former or a substitute for it. And as we might expect, discussion and controversy were provoked more often by problems and obstacles than by what was happening smoothly and quickly. The consequence was that the most ambitious programmes and the most thorough consideration of principles were clustered around the issues which proved most difficult to resolve, and they were produced in countries where the transition to the modern state was arousing most opposition. This meant that the most thorough and sophisticated discussion of legal unification and administrative reform was the work of writers from Prussia, Austria and sometimes France. In those countries, despite their monarchs' pretensions to 'absolutism', the real power of their central governments was limited by a plurality of legal systems and legal authorities, and by the entrenched privileges and immunities enjoyed by the Church, the nobility and provincial communities.[13] In compensation, their governments sought to rely more heavily on the civilian officials clustered around the monarch, but these too proved to be uncertainly loyal and efficient: the officials' social alliances, together with practices such as 'venality' (the sale of offices) and the 'farming' of taxes to contractors, made it difficult for governments to dismiss their servants, to discipline them or to do without them.[14] To move from any point towards the modern state in the Continental monarchies seemed to require the reconstruction of the whole system of government, and programmes of reform tended to be correspondingly ambitious and to focus on the consideration of principles.[15] In England, the monarchy was weaker in relation to the other participants in government than on the Continent, and the civilian officials may have been fewer and less thoroughly organized, but the central government as a whole was stronger. The English legal system had long been centralized and unified, the local authorities had been pretty effectively subordinated to the centre, and venality and farming in public finance were no longer important.[16] The British government and the British com-

munity were therefore able to undertake and to think about
reform in a piecemeal fashion.[17] But where events made the need
for action seem more urgent or seemed to require more far-
reaching reforms – as, for example, during the War of American
Independence or in relation to the government of India – the
English discussion became more sophisticated and was cast more
often in terms of principles and general propositions.

The eighteenth-century apologia for centralized authority included most of Hobbes's thinking about the fundamental relationships between individuals, society and the state. It included a
version of the individualist theory of behaviour which represented
mankind as '[loving] variety and change...desirous of doing the
most with the smallest possible fatigue, being stimulated or curbed
by the certainty of either good or evil' and as refusing to 'be
released from the sway of that universal principle of dissolution
which is seen to operate both in the physical and the moral uni-
verse, except for motives that directly strike the senses'.[18] It
followed, as Hobbes had argued, that in the absence of a sovereign
men could not generate their own social order or law; that in
Blackstone's words, 'unless some superior were constituted, whose
commands and decisions all the members are bound to obey, they
would still remain as in a state of nature, without any judge upon
earth to define their several rights and redress their several
wrongs'.[19] This meant that any body of men constituted a genuine
society, with defined rights and obligations, only in so far as they
possessed a superior to whose commands they were all obedient
and responsive. At the same time it implied that law-making
'must be the exclusive preserve of the sovereign'.[20] Autonomous
jurisdictions and enclaves of privilege appeared on this view to be
not merely inconveniences to sovereignty but incompatible with it
or at least subtractions from it. As Catherine put the point in her
compendium, 'in the very nature of the thing, the sovereign is
the source of all imperial and civil power'.[21] All legitimate
authority must be either delegated authority, or the authority of
the sovereign itself; all social rights must be created and maintained by the sovereign's law.

A closely related point was that legislation was habitually treated
as the first and controlling function of government, sometimes
explicitly but more often implicitly. Blackstone stated it explicitly,
arguing that 'wherever that power resides, all others must con-

form to, and be directed by it, whatever appearance the outward form and administration of the government may put on'.[22] Bielfeld was more typical in simply listing it first among the eight functions of government that he recognized, and in treating the others as derived from and complementary to it.[23] The older view, which had represented adjudication as the fundamental task of the prince, was now quite pushed aside. It had been undermined by the advance of the concept of a state-of-nature, in both Hobbes's and Locke's versions. Medieval thinkers had been able to conceive of the prince as primarily the judge of his people because they were taking for granted the existence of a people with an established law; once modern theorists began to discard law along with other social phenomena in order to create their model of the 'natural man', they could not escape the necessity to erect and give priority to a legislator in order to re-introduce law into their model of society. The apotheosis of the legislator was a necessary not an accidental part of their thought. Locke had been among the first to acknowledge the necessity;[24] his eighteenth-century disciples found no dependable way of escaping from it. The strongest challenge to it came from Montesquieu's doctrine of the separation of powers,[25] but that did not always displace or destroy the idea of legislative supremacy. The two doctrines could even be combined in a single argument, as in John Adams's defence of the separation of powers in American government: for Adams, it was precisely because the legislative power was 'naturally and necessarily sovereign and supreme' that the Executive had to be given some independent basis and means of defence against it.[26]

Along with these aspects of the theory of sovereignty, the eighteenth century inherited and accepted its stress on will as the source of law. This too was a product of the individualist mode of thinking which allowed for no motive force in behaviour or institutions except will, and which required all social phenomena to be interpreted and stated in terms of will, preferably a single will. The eighteenth-century theorist who most thoroughly assimilated the voluntarist outlook and made it a central part of his doctrine was of course Rousseau, but he was only the crest of a wave of voluntarist thinking which caught up the more democratic along with the more monarchist of thinkers.[27] The unqualified doctrine was stated clearly (if not without subsequent contradiction) by Bielfeld and Blackstone. Bielfeld *defined* law as 'the expression of the will of a superior, by which he imposes on those who are subject to him, the obligation to act in a certain way'.[28] The notion of will ran through Blackstone's chapter 'Of the Nature of Laws in General' in which he set out his general legal and political philosophy. It determined his understanding of both natural and positive law. The former was the will of God; the latter must be the product of 'one uniform will' – the sovereign – to which the other members of the community had consented 'to submit their own private wills'.[29] Writers who were more suspicious of monarchy or more seriously committed to natural law tried, like Rousseau, to tame or re-locate the sovereign will but could not do without it. Beccaria avoided defining law as a product of will, but re-introduced the idea in a nominally democratic (or social-contract) form when he began to discuss the legitimacy of law. He found that its legitimacy – its 'natural and real authority' – depended on 'the common will of all', 'the united wills of living subjects' which were expressed in the oath or compact of allegiance to the sovereign.[30] Denis Diderot seemed sometimes to go further in repudiating the link between law and will; for example when, in his commentary on Catherine's *Nakaz*, he defined positive laws as 'only corollaries of natural laws'.[31] But at other times he adhered to the voluntarist view quite strictly, notably in his article on 'Representatives'. He there identified the function of representation with the expression of will, and correlated different forms of government with the extent and the ways in which wills were expressed. He contrasted a despotism in which there is no representation and 'the will of a single person makes the law' with firstly an absolute monarchy in which the sovereign makes laws that 'are, or at least are deemed to be, the expression of the wills of the whole nation which he represents', and then with a range of other systems extending to a direct democracy in which there is again no representation but 'the whole people retains the right of making known its wills in general assemblies composed of all the citizens'.[32] This may strike the twentieth-century reader as no more than orthodox democratic thinking, but its effect was to confirm in contemporary thought the position of will as the source of law and of the social arrangements that only law could create.

The primacy of legislation in government and of will in legislation led naturally to the view that the judiciary must not intrude, directly or indirectly, on the legislator's territory. The eighteenth-century exponents of this doctrine did not usually go as far as Hobbes in demanding the subordination of the judge to the legislator, but they tended to take a more restrictive view of the propriety of interpretation. At this point the separation of powers worked with rather than against the considerations flowing from sovereignty. Montesquieu had neatly (if perhaps unintentionally) run the two together, arguing that 'there is no liberty, if the judiciary power be not separated from the legislative...were it joined with the legislative, the life and liberty of the subject would be exposed to arbitrary control; for the judge would then be the legislator'.[33] The part of Montesquieu's argument that was taken up and repeated by others was the last part, the fear that the judge might turn himself into a sort of legislator. The consequences were stated bluntly by Beccaria: 'judges in criminal cases cannot have the authority to interpret laws', the sovereign remains 'the only legitimate interpreter of the laws', and the function of the judge is confined to determining 'whether a particular man has or has not committed an unlawful act'.[34] Punishments must also be prescribed by the law, not determined by the judge.[35] Catherine was able to take over all of this as received doctrine.[36] In England, William Eden echoed it in rebuking English judges for sometimes forgetting that 'they are not authorized to interpret the penal laws; and that they are entrusted with the execution of them by a Legislature actually existing, and alone competent to such interpretation'.[37] Monarchists and democrats could again join together in resisting any threat that the judiciary might offer to the sovereign authority of the legislator.

In their treatment of all the points so far mentioned, the eighteenth-century authors were still substantially reproducing Hobbes's theory of sovereignty. They were, however, commonly attracted by two other sets of ideas which could not easily be combined with or absorbed into the concept of sovereignty and which consequently left a residue of ambiguity in their thinking. These were firstly the English notion of government as a trust and its Continental equivalents, and secondly vaguer ideas about the social and the physical environment in which law must operate.

J. W. Gough has described at length the history of the idea of trust and its variants in English politics and their connections – sometimes close, sometimes remote – with the precise notion of a trust in English law and legal theory.[38] Despite the difference between English and Continental law to which Gough refers, the French terms 'dépôt' and 'dépositaire' and their equivalents in other European languages (usually translated into English as 'repository' or 'depository') carried much the same meaning for Continental writers as 'trust' did for the English. The idea became one of the commonest in eighteenth-century political rhetoric. It was employed freely by democratic thinkers, and by those (such as Catherine the Great and the English Whigs) who were prepared to experiment with constitutional restraints of one kind or another without committing themselves fully to a democratic point of view.

One model, provided by Montesquieu, was that of the French parlements which should 'promulgate the new laws and revive the old ones', and should in Catherine's version 'remonstrate, if they find anything in them repugnant to the fundamental Constitution of the State, etc.'[39] The English translator of the Instructions, who avoided the word 'repository' and wrote instead of a body 'to whom the care and strict execution of [the] laws ought to be confided' was close enough to Catherine's and Montesquieu's thought.[40] Beccaria and Diderot seem to have had in mind a different model. For Beccaria the sovereign was 'depository of the actual wills of all', which implies an authority to employ (not merely to preserve) what he had received, but to employ it conditionally.[41] For Diderot, too, sovereigns were 'dépôts' or 'dépositaires' of power, or power itself was 'un dépôt'; these assertions do not make sense except on the assumption that the power was to be exercised conditionally 'for the welfare of the State'.[42] Diderot brought out still more clearly the idea of restraints in his comment on Catherine's 'depository of the laws', for he spoke there of the possibility that the 'dépôt' might be 'violated' by the sovereign and inquired what the 'dépositaire' should do in these circumstances.[43] At that point he was not far away from the Whigs' understanding of a political trust, although the Whigs thought of the monarch himself as the trustee and did not need to ask what should be done if the trust were breached. As Burke put it in one of his classic formulations:

[All] political power which is set over men and...all privilege claimed or exercised in exclusion of them, being wholly artificial and for so much a derogation from the natural equality of mankind at large, ought to be some way or other exercised ultimately for their benefit... [Such] rights or privileges or whatever else you choose to call them, are all in the strictest sense a *trust*; and it is of the very essence of every trust to be rendered *accountable*; and even totally to cease when it substantially varies from the purposes for which alone it could have a lawful existence.[44]

One function of the idea of trust or dépôt was thus to impose limits on the exercise of power by the sovereign. Where the idea was accepted, even half-heartedly or in a restricted context as by Catherine, it was no longer easy to treat sovereignty as unlimited or indivisible in the fashion of Hobbes or Bodin. But less damage was done to some of the underlying social assumptions than might appear at first glance. In particular, will was left intact, as the motive force for the whole system, although it might now be represented as operating indirectly through the trustee in some or all matters, instead of directly on all parts of the system. For this reason it was possible to turn the concept to the service of the modern state. It accustomed people to the idea of delegated power, of power exercised on behalf of a superior and exercised on conditions laid down in precise terms by the superior. In this way it was available to form one of the intellectual foundations of hierarchy, when that was seen as one of the state's needs.

The outcome of speculations about the relationship between law and its environment might be better described as incoherence rather than ambiguity. Sharply different views emerged, and although they were sometimes adopted by the same person there was little real prospect of harmonizing them. The *locus classicus* of these speculations was *The Spirit of the Laws*. In his first chapter in 'positive laws' (Book I, Chapter 3) Montesquieu summarized the things which the laws 'should be in relation to', that is, the things to which they should be relative, and to which the draftsman or sovereign should adapt them. Those things included 'the nature and principle of each government', 'the climate of each country' and the quality of its soil, and the occupations, the industries, the religion, 'riches, numbers, commerce, manners and customs' of the inhabitants.[45] In the body of his work, and constituting its most famous and original aspect he devoted a long series of Books to 'the law in relation to' most of these topics.

Although the topics often served him merely as springboards for quite different points that he wanted to make, the general tendency of his argument was to confine the discretion of the legislator by indicating things – physical things or social things – that he must take into account or that might constitute boundaries beyond which he could not usefully go. There were, if Montesquieu could be believed, effective limits if not legal limits to what the sovereign's will could accomplish.

In so far as the limits were set by the physical circumstances of climate, population and economic resources, they could perhaps be accepted by most of the partisans of sovereignty, though the doctrinaire Helvétius rejected Montesquieu's whole 'endeavour to explain, from physical causes, an infinite number of political phenomena, that are very naturally explained by moral causes'.[46] The real division of opinion was on the treatment of customs or manners. The social assumptions of the theory of sovereignty required that these should be the product of law; to treat them as determinants of law was to strike at the foundations of the theory. This point was grasped by some but not all of those who wanted to retain an effective notion of sovereignty.

On one side of the divide stood Montesquieu and Catherine the Great; on the other Diderot, Helvétius and David Hume. Montesquieu in fact allotted a role to the laws in the formation of the 'esprit général' or common character of any society,[47] but in the passage which Catherine paraphrased he distinguished sharply between law and custom and argued that 'it is very bad policy to change by law what ought to be changed by custom'.[48] Diderot totally rejected the argument when he encountered it in the *Nakaz*. 'Customs are the product of laws', he replied; 'customs are good when the laws that are observed are good, bad when the laws are bad'.[49] Helvétius had already presented the same line of argument at greater length and in a more extravagant form. In opposition to Montesquieu, he maintained that the moral qualities of the people in any state, their happiness, their ideas and the superiority of one state over another all depended on the laws established by the legislator. According to him, 'no change in the ideas of a people is to be hoped for, till after a change in its legislation...the reformation of manners is to be begun by the reformation of the laws'.[50] He therefore proposed that morality should be 'blended with policy and legislation' in such a way that

'the moralist is to indicate the laws, of which the legislator insures
the execution, by stamping them with the seal of his authority'.[51]
These were large claims for the power of legislation. But the more
sober and discriminating Hume made claims for it that were only
a little less grand, when he was setting out his grounds for
believing 'that politics may be reduced to a science'. 'So great is
the force of laws, and of particular forms of government,' he
argued, 'and so little dependence have they on the humours and
tempers of men, that consequences almost as general and certain
may sometimes be deduced from them, as any which the mathematical sciences afford us.'[52] Hume, Diderot and Helvétius were
following through more faithfully than Catherine the logic of the
argument about sovereignty. Unless it is complemented by an
assumption that law is an enormously powerful means of social
control capable of 'reforming manners' and of acting independently of 'the humours and tempers of men', the theory that a
society can be wholly ruled by and kept in dependence on the
sovereign's laws must collapse. But logic did not always prevail.
It was clear that Montesquieu and Catherine had solid grounds
for believing that in practice laws would have to be adapted to
existing customs and that customs might change independently
of the laws. It was unlikely that customs could always be explained away as the products of law, in the way that Helvétius
proposed to explain them. So the relationship between law
and customs remained an awkward, undigested element in the
eighteenth-century theory of the state's legal foundations.

Most of the ideas which have been described above were
presented by their authors as discrete and sometimes incidental
remarks, in the course of a discussion of other and usually more
concrete topics. But some writers understood that the reforms they
were proposing could be made to hang together in a certain
way, and that they added up to a distinctive form of political
organization and of government. They had an explicit notion
of the modern state, though they did not yet employ that
name.

Two of the more remarkable descriptions of the notion were
stated in the form of imaginary historical reconstructions of
English society, in which accounts of the modern state were projected back into the past. One of them appeared in J. L. De
Lolme's influential study of the English constitution and govern-

ment. De Lolme took as one of his principal themes the early
unification of England and the early establishment of the Crown's
authority over the nobles; he based on this his explanation of the
different course of constitutional development in England and in
other countries, especially its close neighbour France. Writing of
political conditions in the thirteenth century he claimed that:
'England was not, like France, an aggregation of a number of
different sovereignties; it formed but one state, and acknowledged
but one master, one general title. The same laws, the same kind of
dependence, consequently the same notions, the same interests
prevailed throughout the whole.'[53] De Lolme was drawing attention in that passage to a real contrast between France and
England, and to real tendencies in the medieval English kingdom,
but he was greatly exaggerating the extent to which the kings'
ambitions had been realized. In the exercise of historical imagina-
tion he was outstripped by Blackstone, who projected the modern
state back to Alfred's England. Blackstone represented Alfred as
re-modelling the constitution by forming 'out of its old discordant
materials. . .one uniform and well-connected whole'; as 'reducing
the whole kingdom under one regular and gradual subordination
of government, wherein each man was answerable to his immediate superior for his own conduct and that of his nearest neigh-
bours'; as placing 'all under the influence and administration of
one supreme magistrate the king'; as becoming 'a general reservoir, [in whom] all the executive authority of the law was lodged,
and from whom justice was dispersed to every part of the nation
by distinct, yet communicating ducts and channels'; and as
collecting 'the various customs that he found dispersed in the
kingdom [which] he reduced and digested. . .into one uniform
system or code of laws, in his dombec or *liber judicialis*'.[54]
Again, this was not unrelated to Alfred's actions and policies, but
it made them appear much more successful and self-consciously
coherent than they were in fact.

While De Lolme's and Blackstone's descriptions cannot be
taken seriously as history, they reveal the criteria that the two
men wanted to apply to both the past and to contemporary
society. De Lolme approved of the kind of state that he believed
thirteenth-century England to have been, just as Blackstone
approved of Alfred's England as he painted it. Each author was
using his reconstruction of the past as the basis of a critique of

other and more recent societies. And their critiques were substantially the same. They were taking as their model of a properly
organized state one in which the community was directed and
managed through a single, unified body of legislation acting
uniformly on its individual members, and in which government
consisted of legislating and of actions to support and enforce
legislation.

A similar but in some respects more interesting model of the
state was set out in the 'Memorandum on Municipalities' that
Du Pont de Nemours drafted for Turgot in 1775.[55] This was
explicitly a critique of and a programme for contemporary society.
In diagnosing the ills of France and of French government, it
employed much the same criteria as Blackstone and De Lolme:
unity, clear relationships of authority and subordination between
the central institutions and the subjects of the state, and a responsiveness of the whole state to the sovereign's commands. Turgot
wanted 'the component parts of [the King's] dominions' to have
'a regular organization and known relationships',[56] and he wanted
to have for that purpose a uniform, comprehensive and hierarchical set of authorities (the 'municipalities') linking each part
with the centre. Du Pont described these as constituting 'a chain
along which the most distant parts might communicate with [the
King]' and their intended function was clearly the same as
Blackstone's 'ducts and communicating channels'.[57] The outcome,
Turgot hoped, would be that the King 'could govern like God by
general laws', and would neither be frustrated by the sectional
loyalties centred on the provincial Estates, nor required to engage
in a multitude of detailed administrative tasks to effect any one
of his purposes in the community.[58] According to Du Pont, Turgot
hoped to create a similar and parallel system for the administration of justice.[59]

The most interesting feature of Turgot's memorandum was that
it tried to give institutional content to its criteria and to satisfy
them in institutional terms. In this respect it belonged with the
large body of eighteenth-century literature directed to showing, in
more detail and more systematically than Hobbes, how the legal
supremacy of the sovereign might be made effective and how it
might be exercised in practice. Some of this literature was concerned, like the memorandum, with the structure and institutions
of the modern state, some with the law itself as an instrument of

the sovereign's will, and some with the purposes for which the enhanced power and authority of the sovereign might be employed or (in other words) the functions of the state.

The eighteenth century employed two general guides in determining the functions of the state: natural law and utility or the public welfare. These provided permanent points of reference throughout the discussion, but they were not able to carry it very far. Each was liable to become merely a form of words, not a genuine criterion; it is difficult, for example, to find much content in Bielfeld's proposition that 'if natural law tells us what is just, political science ['la Politique'] teaches us what is useful'.[60] Natural law was designed to provide, and did provide where it was taken seriously, boundaries to the sovereign's discretion, but it did not offer much help to those seeking positive guidance. Utility did not set initial limits of the same kind, but it entered into contemporary thinking in another and more important way. It focused attention on – or was the product of a focusing of attention on – the rational adjustment of means to ends in society. People were asking regularly of any policy or arrangement 'what purpose does it serve' or 'how well does it serve that purpose', or they were seeking regularly to justify policies and arrangements on the ground that they best served some defined purpose. This utilitarian mode of thinking and arguing came to be widely employed and widely accepted. But it too had to be filled out, and the notion of utility had to be given some definite content, before it could be of much help in fixing the scope and content of the sovereign's laws.

With hindsight we can see that in the long run the centre of the discussion was being occupied by political economy. The classical economists brought to view the existence of market forces, and they purported to demonstrate that those forces could achieve certain social objectives and could form obstacles or set limits to the achievement of the state's objectives through law. In a further development of the argument the free market, and the purely contractual relationships on which it rested, could be represented as a model for first the whole economy and then society as a whole, and the legitimate sphere of the state and its law could be confined within very narrow limits. Even in its weaker and less dogmatic form, political economy provided a powerful challenge to those who favoured an active state. Its challenge had in some way to be met and answered, if its conclusions were not to hold the field.

It is, however, anachronistic to see political economy as having that kind of significance or as occupying that place in the discussion before the end of the eighteenth century. Older and quite different ideas, some of them associated closely with the modern state, still commanded respect. There was little dissent from Hobbes's principle that the instruction of the people must be among the principal tasks of the state, and Beccaria gave it a distinctive eighteenth-century character by arguing that 'perfecting education' was 'the surest but most difficult way to prevent crimes'.[61] Moreover, political economy had barely established itself as an independent body of knowledge. Until late in the century it had not fully separated itself from the two related fields of police and oeconomy, and it had to compete with police (of which it might reasonably have been regarded as an outgrowth or branch) as a source of advice about the social and economic functions of the state. In order to understand or describe eighteenth-century thinking about these matters, it is better to begin with police than with political economy.

Leon Radzinowicz has written of 'that strange word police' and of its elusiveness in eighteenth-century discourse.[62] In the present context, it can most usefully be seen as defined by its primary purposes, which were commonly identified as security or public health, and cheapness or plenty. In its origins, and even as it operated in the eighteenth century, it had strong connections with municipal administration – the administration of towns. Nicholas de Lamare defined it explicitly in those terms – 'the public order of each town' – and Bielfeld made a sharp distinction between the police of towns and the police of country areas, and had very little to say about the latter.[63] Many of the things that were included under the headings of public order and public health, for example the inspection of butchers' shops or the paving and lighting of streets, were clearly functions of local authorities. The pursuit of 'plenty' contained much that had the same character and displayed a markedly local outlook – the outlook of a relatively isolated community, forming a narrow and largely closed market, dealing mainly in perishable goods, depending on limited sources of supply, and liable to be assailed by famines, by the activities of traders' rings and forestallers, and by the dishonest

practices of traders who stood in no fear of outside competition.[64]

By the middle of the eighteenth century, however, police was
being seen more often as a matter for the central government and
its categories were being re-interpreted in national terms or were
being stretched to cover problems having a national dimension.
In one of its aspects, it was 'preventive police', concerned with the
prevention of crimes and the maintenance of order. In another,
it was concerned with the provision of social assistance and the
maintenance of public institutions, including poorhouses, bride-
wells, hospitals, houses of correction and gaols. Some of these
had a charitable or humanitarian basis, but they could also be
seen as instruments of preventive police, helping to keep potential
criminals off the streets, encouraging in them habits of industry
and discouraging idleness, providing alternatives to crime for the
destitute. The institutional form of police was the subject of a
large body of literature in the eighteenth century, in the general
works like Bielfeld's and Lamare's, in studies dealing with particular institutions or classes of institutions (poorhouses or gaols),
and in others dealing with some aspect of public affairs to which
the institutions might be related.

Oeconomy had a shorter history than police and a less well-
defined subject-matter. It was concerned more especially with
problems of public finance and in general with the domestic
economy of the central government. But its boundaries could also
be extended, to cover the resources and the obligations of the state
(the community) as well as those of the government, especially
where (as in physiocracy) questions of public policy and public
finance were intermingled. In their wider forms, police and
oeconomy overlapped.

The Empress Catherine summarized the content of both bodies
of thought in two supplements that she added to her Instructions
in 1768. She thus gave a convenient account of how the functions
of government were viewed at that time. She directed that police
should be understood to cover the maintenance of public decency;
the prevention of robberies; precautions against fires; the collapse
of buildings and other accidents (which were sometimes referred
to collectively as 'calamities'); the preservation of public health;
the regulation of weights and measures; the protection of supplies
of foodstuffs; the relief of the sick and impotent; and the pro-

vision of relief for the able-bodied poor.[65] She defined 'the oeconomy of the state' narrowly, as the 'expences, revenues and publick management of the finances...otherwise termed the direction of the Exchequer'[66] but in practice went outside that definition in her selection of topics for discussion. Her working notion of oeconomy included population policy, the encouragement of agriculture, the expansion of trade, the improvement of internal communications (canals, roads, bridges and ferries), and the development of crafts and manufactures and of the technical and scientific knowledge on which they depended. In the end she worked around to new definitions in which she distinguished between the domestic economy of the state (essentially public finance) and its 'political oeconomy' which 'comprehends the whole body of the people and affairs and a distinct knowledge of their situations, their ranks and their occupations'.[67] To a considerable extent Catherine (and those on whom she was drawing) carried over into the discussion of national police and political economy a paternalism in social matters and an inclination towards dirigisme in economic policy that they had inherited from 'the police of towns'. But those attitudes were not universal, and sometimes – and even in Catherine's account – they were held in a qualified form. For example, Catherine stressed the need to strive and plan for a 'balance...on our side' in foreign trade, but wanted for internal trade 'a circulation which has no obstacles, nor shackles which restrain it'.[68] Here and elsewhere, those who were writing within the tradition of police were slowly recognizing that national problems and local problems could not be understood or treated in the same way, although they might have the same names.

Classical political economy can be interpreted as an amalgamation of oeconomy with some of those problems and categories of police which had been translated from a local to a national level. The process of amalgamation can be seen at work in the intellectual development of Adam Smith himself. One of the places where he rehearsed his ideas for his masterpiece, *The Wealth of Nations*, was in the lectures delivered at Glasgow University in 1762–64 but collected and published long after his death as *Lectures on Justice, Police, Revenue and Arms* and *Lectures on Jurisprudence*.[69] Most of his discussion of political economy was a part – the largest part – of his account of police; the remainder came in his account of public revenue. In his lectures on police, he spoke in the traditional way of 'cheapness or plenty', but interpreted this in national terms as 'the most proper way of procuring wealth and abundance'. He had thus discarded the presuppositions of the narrow, closed market, and was able to proceed smoothly to a formal inquiry into the nature of wealth – 'wherein opulence consists...[and] the natural wants of mankind which are to be supplied' – and the causes of the wealth of nations.[70] It was then a short step from here to the discussion in *The Wealth of Nations*, which proceeded independently of the concept of police. At that point, or perhaps a little earlier on the publication of Steuart's *Principles of Political Oeconomy*, political economy had emancipated itself from police, and had succeeded or absorbed oeconomy.

Steuart's book was published in 1767, at almost the same time as Catherine's Instructions; Smith's was not published until 1776. The *Wealth of Nations* made an immediate impact, and almost immediately began to win converts to the cause of freedom of international trade. But the emancipation of political economy from police did not mean that it immediately eliminated the attitudes and doctrines of police from the thinking of contemporaries, or that thereafter all discussion of the functions of government was concentrated in or about political economy. Smith pressed his case for free markets on a narrow front, and qualified it in various ways. The most important of his qualifications was his admission that the state should provide (or arrange for the provision of) 'public institutions', including some form of public education. And the progress of utilitarian attitudes left his conclusions provisional, liable to be overturned as new public needs became apparent, or as new information became available about the working of the market in general or about particular markets. It was possible, long after Smith had written, to accept his case for freedom in international trade, and still to demand that the state be active in other ways. Most people continued to believe that there must be public provision for the relief of the poor; as J. R. Poynter has shown, in the long and anxious debate about the English Poor Law, the 'abolitionist' case was rarely put earlier than the generation of Malthus.[71] The demands for internal communications, for protection against calamities, for public education and for certain public health measures were hardly affected at all by the new authority of the political economists.

All of this speculation about functions and policies assumed that in practice there would exist an effective system of sovereign-made law laying down uniform conditions for economic and social life. That was as true of the writings on political economy which advocated free trade and mobility of resources as of the writings on police which advocated the creation of poor-houses and hospitals. Neither policy could be implemented successfully unless local privileges (to tax, to regulate or simply to disobey) could be and were over-ruled by the central authority. Many of the publicists grasped that point and tried to make sovereignty more than an assumption or aspiration by carrying further their inquiries into jurisprudence. Their purposes were to identify and then to establish the conditions in which law would in fact issue from a central source, in which all members of the state would stand in the same direct relationship to the sovereign, in which the sovereign's law would be easy to administer and enforce and in which it would in fact regulate and direct individual behaviour. They sought to achieve those purposes by formulating criteria for the arrangement or construction of the law, for its composition and finally for certain aspects of its content, especially its pro-visions relating to offences, reward and punishment. Their choice of subjects and their principles continued to resemble those of Hobbes, but this was one of the points at which they began significantly to outstrip their great predecessor.

The first and in some respects fundamental part of their pro-gramme was the 'codification' or transformation of law into a single, comprehensive and consistent corpus. This was of course one of the points on which an alliance between the publicists and the practitioners of 'enlightened government' could most easily be effected, because several governments (for example, those of Russia, Prussia, Austria and some of the Italian states) were already moving towards codification. It was fundamental to the reform movement for two reasons: in practice, the central authorities in most countries could establish their legal supremacy only by substituting their own law – and usually their own courts and systems of legal administration – for the feudal customs and the laws administered by the multiplicity of estates, corporations and provincial governments which operated within their terri-tories;[72] and other legal reforms could most easily be carried through as part of such a general re-casting of the whole body of law. But the theorists and publicists did not greatly stress such practical considerations when they were explaining the benefits of codification. They referred more often to the intellectual criterion of consistency and absence of contradiction, or 'the connection and agreement that [should subsist] between' particular laws.[73] In this form the codification movement reached as far as England, which did not face the same problems of creating order out of legal chaos as did the more heterogeneous states such as Prussia or Austria. The notion of consistency was taken up and applied by Daines Barrington, in his influential work, the *Observations upon the Statutes*. Barrington, however, perceived that he was advocating not a code on the Roman or Prussian model, but a more limited revision and consolidation of statutes, and opportunities for more frequent revisions and repeal in the future.[74] Both he and William Eden occasionally referred to the aggregate of statutes as a 'code'.[75]

In the countries where the practical problems were more severe, the notion of codification had correspondingly more emotional force behind it, as can be seen in Diderot's reactions to Catherine's project for the codification of Russian law. Diderot welcomed the idea that Russia should have a code, but he regretted still more the fact that France was still cursed with the multiplicity and diversity of laws inherited from ancient times and that she seemed to be 'condemned never to have a code'. He was particularly critical of Charles VII whom he blamed for this state of affairs, contending that the King had preserved and legitimized the customary laws when he might have replaced them with 'a uniform and general law'.[76] It is evident that there was more behind Diderot's bitterness than a mere preference for consistency as an intellectual value.

The second important element in the programme of legal reform was a demand for clarity and simplicity in the drafting of laws. Most of the relevant doctrine was supplied by Montesquieu in his chapter on 'Things to be observed in the composing of Laws': 'The style ought to be concise'; 'the style should also be plain and simple'; 'the words of the laws should excite in everybody the same ideas'; 'when the law has once fixed the idea of things, it should never return to vague expressions'; 'the laws ought not to be subtle'; 'when there is no necessity for exceptions and limitations in a law it is much better to omit them'; 'there ought to be a certain simplicity and candour in the laws; made to punish the iniquity of men, they themselves should be clad with the robes of innocence'.[77] Beccaria, Eden and Catherine followed Montesquieu closely on this matter – Catherine almost word for word.[78] It became part of the climate of opinion that the laws should be 'clear and perspicuous' (Blackstone), 'simple and easy of comprehension' (Necker).[79]

The underlying rationale again had two aspects. Simplicity and clarity were seen as further means of preserving the supremacy of the sovereign legislator, this time against the incursions of judicial interpretation. As Beccaria argued, one of the best ways of confining the judiciary to its proper role seemed to be 'a fixed code of laws, which must be observed to the letter [and] leaves no further care to the judge than to examine the acts of citizens and to decide whether or not they conform to the law as written'.[80] Simplicity and clarity would make it easy to reduce the judge's task to that level. At the same time they were expected to help maximize the impact of the law on the subject, by reducing or eliminating the possibilities of misunderstanding and evasion of the law's provisions.

It was understood, however, that the style and the arrangement of the law could not alone ensure its maximum impact. In order to be an effective instrument of social control it had to include what Beccaria called the 'tangible motives' of reward and punishment,[81] and theorists strove with some success to translate and extend Hobbes's simple recommendations into more detailed and more general principles. Montesquieu again led the way by raising, and providing tentative answers to, a whole series of questions about the definition and classification of offences, the effectiveness of punishment and of different forms of punishment, the 'proportions' between crimes and penalties, the best forms of trial-procedure and how far particular procedures or particular forms of getting evidence might be legitimate.[82] Bielfeld, Beccaria, Eden and others took up these questions, and adopted, rejected, amplified or modified Montesquieu's answers.

The standard approach to these subjects was summed up by Beccaria. On the topic of punishment, he expressed his conclusions in these words: 'In order for punishment not to be, in every instance, an act of violence of one or of many against a private citizen, it must be essentially public, prompt, necessary, the least possible in the given circumstances, proportionate to the crimes, dictated by the laws.'[83] His thinking, however, was not focused exclusively on punishment. He was always ready to agree that reward might be an alternative or a complement to punishment, and he also believed that human nature 'is much more securely regulated by obstacles than by prohibitions'.[84] The outcome of these further considerations was a doctrine that 'it is better to prevent crimes than to punish them', and that prevention did not necessarily depend on direct prohibition but might be approached indirectly.[85] Beccaria drew these ideas together in the proposition that the statesman's task was to find 'the means of uniting our own interest with that of the public'.[86] He was there coming very close to Hobbes's remark that 'where the public and private interest are more closely united, there is the public most advanced',[87] and the thought was expressed again and again in different words by other eighteenth-century writers including Helvétius, Hume, Catherine, Burke and Jacques Necker.[88] In addition to these general reflections about punishment and reward there was much more, in Beccaria's works and elsewhere, about more particular matters, such as secret accusations, torture, the death penalty, whether duelling and suicide should be classed as crimes, the classification of offences and the promulgation of laws.

The popular jurisprudence of the eighteenth century included another component, which appeared to be a purely legal point but which began to introduce new considerations into the theory of the sovereign state. This was an elementary classification of laws (or of commands having legal force) according to the degree of their generality. It was probably derived from the attempts of Locke and others to prevent arbitrary government by demanding that the legislator should 'decide the rights of the subjects by promulgated standing laws'.[89] In the eighteenth century this became a demand that laws should be 'always general' in their terms and perhaps in their objects, that they should contain 'nothing private but should relate wholly to the common good', and that they should be expressed as rules.[90] Most of the synthesizers and popularizers stated this point in one form or another. But some of them began to recognize that not all of the sovereign's commands could or would be rules, and that unless the command theory of law were to be abandoned it must be made flexible enough to accommodate the non-rules. Montesquieu and Bielfeld acknowledged that 'ordinances of police' need not be rules although they were made by or on behalf of the sovereign; they treated those ordinances as a sort of quasi-law.[91] Catherine, who extended their distinction into a more abstract, tripartite classification of law, went further and found a place for more obviously administrative acts and activities, including 'that Order by which all affairs are to be carried into execution, and the different instructions and institutions which relate to them', and injunctions 'made upon some emergency and what is only occasional, or relates to some particular person'.[92] In this process of refining the notion of law, sovereignty and legislation were gradually broadened to incorporate at least some form of executive action, and to draw administration into legal theory and to assimilate it to legal processes.

The discussion was brought closer to the Executive in the further consideration of two aspects of sovereignty, the processes of law or decision making, and those of law-enforcement. The sovereign which aimed at social control needed to identify and discriminate among problems and potential subjects of legislation. It needed equally to have means of distributing the rewards and penalties prescribed in its laws. Attempts to show how these needs could be satisfied led ultimately into questions of procedure and organization.

The standard recipe for decision making was to accumulate and to deploy knowledge effectively. We have encountered a hint of this in the Empress Catherine's definition of the political branch of oeconomy, which called for a 'distinct knowledge' of the people's 'situations, their ranks and their occupations'. Similarly Bielfeld assumed without question that it was among the first duties of officials to acquaint themselves with, and to find means of informing themselves about, the problems and the subject-matters for which they were responsible: 'without a perfect knowledge of the country on which he is working, the Treasury official would be bound to take only unsound measures'.[93] Turgot believed that the King of France should be given 'an account of the whole of France by provinces, districts and parishes, in which the description of each place would be accompanied by its map; such that if someone mentioned a village in your presence, you could see in a moment its position, recognize the roads or other works which it was proposed to undertake, know which individuals had property there, and know the character and the income of their estates'.[94] Necker also wanted to collect and analyse information for the King on a wide range of subjects, including population, the production of various commodities, wages, communications, hospitals and paupers, exports and imports, public revenue and the number of officials. He proposed that the information should be arranged in summary tables and in 'separate books' to which the reader of the summaries could be referred for more detailed information. 'This collection,' he wrote, 'would be of very great use to active ministers.'[95]

To supply information of that kind was the aim of the practitioners of 'political arithmetic', which was one of the intellectual movements out of which political economy had developed. In the second half of the eighteenth century their art had established itself as a useful aid to government. Bielfield, who was rather critical of some of the methods employed by particular statisticians and of some of the claims for accuracy made on their behalf, nevertheless thought it worthwhile to devote a chapter of his book to a discussion of the subject, and he concluded that it yielded information that was accurate enough for the needs of government.[96] To some extent, then, the task of improving the 'intelligence' of government could be reduced to the development and application of the techniques of the political arithmeticians. But both Necker and Turgot saw that this would not be enough, and that to employ those techniques successfully would require changes in the government itself. Turgot proposed that the new municipalities should collect and transmit the necessary information; to have them perform that task was one of the main reasons why he wanted to establish them. Necker proposed to tackle the problem at the other end, at the centre rather than the periphery, by establishing a new central agency, 'a separate board, solely destined to collect a multiplicity of interesting informations, and to class them in a clear and easy method'.[97]

In the discussion of law enforcement, the balance was shifted still more towards questions of organization or structure, although techniques were still seen as important. Three aspects of enforcement were considered at some length: the prevention of crimes, the discovery of criminals or at least suspects, and the judicial processes of hearing, judgement and sentencing in accordance with the law.

As we have seen, reformers had been impelled towards judicial re-organization as part of their ambition to destroy enclaves of privilege and jurisdiction outside the control of the sovereign. The creation of a single system of law had to be complemented by the establishment of a system of courts, dependent on the sovereign, which would administer that law and no other. The impulse was expressed in a practical way in the attempts of Maria Theresa, Frederick the Great or Turgot to create a new judicial structure. Another sign of its strength was Bielfeld's argument, resolutely maintained in the face of the facts, that seignorial justice was really subject to Royal justice and did not involve absolute jurisdiction because 'that would be inconsistent with the very principles of sovereignty which we have established'.[98]

The common pattern favoured by the reformers was hier-archical, like Turgot's municipalities. But programmes often pressed beyond structure in that narrow sense to the courts' pro-cedure, to the qualifications, tenure and appointment of the judges and sometimes to the conduct and tenure of the officials serving the courts. Frederick's plan was notable for covering all these matters in some degree, and for trying to bring under control the fees payable to courts and their officers.[99] (Fees were a source of grievance to litigants; but they were also a source of judicial independence of the sovereign.) Even in England where, as in relation to most aspects of the modern state, the problems of unifying the system were less onerous than elsewhere, there was some interest in these matters. Eden, for example, was interested in revising the courts' procedure in criminal matters.[100] Black-stone offered a reasoned defence of the existing system, but the form of his argument acknowledged the reformers' efforts to find a procedure that would reduce both the length and the number of suits before the courts.[101]

The prevention of crimes and the discovery of criminals were the main tasks of preventive police. The operations of this branch of police were being widely described and discussed throughout the century. Thus de Lamare in his *Traité de la police* gave a truly voluminous account of the methods employed by the police of Paris in the early eighteenth century; Bielfeld incorporated similar information, but in a much more easily assimilable form, in his chapters (vol. I, chs. VII and VIII) on the police; Sir William Mildmay provided a summary of French practices for English readers in his little book *The Police of France*;[102] and other English writers such as John Fielding and Jonas Hanway discussed conditions in England more directly.[103] Those works made people familiar with the techniques developed by the authorities of Paris and other big cities for the prevention of crimes. These can be summarized as exposure to public view, surveillance, records and inspection: the lighting of public streets at night, the publication or dissemination of information, the patrolling of streets and public places by day and by night, the requiring of innkeepers and lodging-house keepers to keep registers of their guests and to submit reports to the authorities, the requiring of pawnbrokers and dealers to keep registers of transactions and customers, and the regular inspection of registers to ensure that they were being maintained and to collect the information that was being recorded.[104]

These were the measures by which it was hoped to realize the potential of law, and to make it in fact as well as in theory an effective instrument of social control. They clearly implied a body of officials, a police *force*, to administer them. In England it remained a principal question at issue whether such a force should be established by the Government. This was a settled question over most of the Continent, so firmly settled that Bielfeld simply assumed that the head of the police would be of 'Cabinet rank' (though not necessarily or invariably a member of the Cabinet).[105]

In discussing decision making and law-enforcement, eighteenth-century thinkers were thus led to confirm and adopt Hobbes's perception that the theory of the modern state must encompass the agencies through which the state operated as well as the legal foundations of its operations. If the central government were to be genuinely sovereign, it could not rely on its monopoly of legal authority but would have to possess a set of servants and institutions that would obediently execute its will. Experience had shown that many of its inherited institutions and practices, and even some of those that had been devised in the sixteenth and seventeenth centuries, were not well adapted to its purposes: they were simply inefficient or provided too many opportunities for obstruction and disobedience. In order to perfect its legal authority, it must replace them with others, more obedient and more efficient.

But the recognition of those truths was not confined to the institutions of law and order where we have so far identified it. Eighteenth-century governments, stimulated by their growing authority and sanctioned by the fashionable doctrines of police and oeconomy, were reaching out ambitiously in a number of directions and making heavier demands on their financial and administrative resources. Experiments in social policy and in economic regulation were jostling with foreign and colonial adventures for attention and oversight. Almost everywhere, however, performance was lagging behind ambitions and targets, especially in the crucial fields of revenue collection and borrowing where many governments still had to rely on masterful tax-farmers to do a major part of the work for them. It was again apparent that legal authority could be translated into effective power only through obedient and efficient agencies which did not yet exist in sufficient numbers or in a sufficiently highly-developed form. So alongside the plans for legal reform there grew up a mass of proposals, critiques or concrete reforms concerned with other, more clearly administrative, devices and institutions. One of the most extensive (and best documented) reforms was that undertaken by the new Prussian monarchy, but many other European governments took some steps in the same direction. Administrative reforms usually found a place in the programmes of enlightened governments. English governments were as usual more piecemeal in their approach but not entirely inactive. Many English Ministers could plausibly claim to have initiated reforms or removed abuses in the revenue departments or elsewhere, among them Walpole, Henry Pelham and George Grenville. The war with the American colonies helped to get under way the Economical Reform movement of the 1780s, which produced a much more extensive and thoroughgoing crop of reforms than ever before in England, although it did not differ much in motive or approach from what had been said or done during the previous fifty years. But what was actually accomplished was always much less than was canvassed, advocated and described in utopian programmes.[106]

It is probable that the new thinking about institutions was influenced by contemporary practices and innovations in factories and workshops and by the corresponding 'production economics' part of political economy. It certainly shared with industrial practice and production economics an interest in the rational

adaptation of means to ends or (in more concrete terms) the more
efficient use of resources. But it also shared many characteristics
and assumptions with the legal speculation described above.
It viewed any institution much as legal theory had come to view
a body of law, and as the theory of sovereignty had always represented the well-ordered state: firstly, as satisfying the requirements
of simplicity, clarity and consistency; and secondly as a set of
individual elements, each obedient to a will at the centre, and
controlled by that will through the processes of law-making and
law-enforcement.

The demand that administrative arrangements should be
simple, clear and consistent is one of the most familiar themes in
this group of writings. 'A more simple, regular and accordant
system'; 'a systematic simplicity and uniformity'; 'uniform, constant and steady management'; 'a simple and regular method';
'a precise and regular order'; these and similar phrases recur
frequently in the literature, providing criteria on which existing
arrangements might be judged and on which new proposals might
be justified. The most elaborate form of this mode of thinking
consisted in mechanical analogies, in which the administrative
system was seen as a machine whose different parts must be
shaped, fitted and balanced to form a harmonious whole.[107]

The analogies between well-ordered state and well-ordered
administration relate to most of the state's features. The demand
for unity and universal jurisdiction in the state was matched by
demands that the administration should be focused and dependent on a single point. The assumption that the state imposed
order on a mass of self-interested individuals by means of law was
matched by an assumption that the head of a government or an
administrative agency could most conveniently discipline its self-
interested employees by means of rules. It was assumed of the
administration, as of the state, that the rules must be backed by
motives or incentives, consisting of some mixture of rewards and
penalties. And it was understood that rules, penalties and rewards
were of little use unless they could be effectively enforced, and
that they must be complemented by other measures for that purpose. In practice, the measures favoured by judicial or administrative reformers resembled strongly the devices of preventive
police. In sum, the reformers treated the institutions of government as fundamentally a legal structure, as a community which

(like the larger community in which it was located) must be regulated and controlled by legal methods. The legal methods to which they turned were those which they had discovered to be appropriate to the sovereign state. This dependence on law, and on law of that particular kind, gave the administrative reform movement a strongly legal–rational character.

As in speculations about the state, it proved relatively easy to formulate the ideal of a wholly unified and dependent administration, but a good deal harder to show how to remove sources of independence and obstacles to unity. Bielfeld stated the ideal with his customary clarity. He wanted an administration in which the head would be able to have his plans put into effect 'without being frustrated or thwarted by the opposing activities of more junior officials...[and in which] the limits of each person's authority would be precisely defined and all the radii of the circle would focus on a common centre'.[108] But he, and others who shared his vision, saw that this would require a fundamental restructuring of many existing departments and agencies. They saw that they would need to build loose congeries of more or less co-ordinate offices and bodies into definite structures, and transform more or less independent agencies into branches of larger organizations. Only then would it be possible to create a 'central point, a point of direction and of combination',[109] within any system whether it embraced a single department or a whole government.

Many plans of this kind were prepared, especially in the field of financial administration. They directed attention to four main points: the designation of a central element or chief office to which the other elements would be responsible; the responsibility of the branches to inform the chief office of their proceedings and to surrender to it the control of any resources which came into their hands; arrangements for co-ordination or supervision at the centre; and the possibility of an intermediate structure between the chief office and the smallest or most outlying branches. Out of them came some additional principles or organizational preferences, as well as quite detailed proposals on some points. In Britain, the centralization of cash balances became an official (and ultimately successful) policy in the 1780s. One of the principal measures which enacted it gave legal recognition to the important bureaucratic principle (which we found to be

foreshadowed by Hobbes) that the official rights and obligations of
office-holders should be distinguished from their personal rights,
and that the continuing office should be distinguished from its
temporary occupant.[110] In the more complex administrations,
such as finance, the idea of an intermediate structure between the
centre and the periphery found considerable support, and this
generally took the form of a hierarchy in which each layer
reported to and through the one above it. In some cases it was
appreciated that this procedure would be facilitated by the introduction of standard forms and techniques which would permit
aggregation and comparison.[111]

It was also sometimes appreciated that the system would work
only if the 'central point' were organized to receive and assess the
information flowing to it. Bielfeld provided a general plan for
this purpose, specifying eight separate departments among which
the functions of government should be divided, and (for the larger
states) a Council (Cabinet) to which the heads of the departments
would either belong or have access. He proposed that the Council
should meet regularly four times a week, and that each department should have a definite responsibility to submit reports to the
sovereign and the Council on the more important matters falling
within its duties.[112]

Bielfeld's discussion of these relationships drew attention to an
unresolved issue in the organization of an office, especially its top
layer. It arose out of the common practice in the eighteenth and
earlier centuries of resting final authority and responsibility in a
'college' or board. In the second half of the century the practice
was breaking down and was being subjected to critical scrutiny,
but it continued to survive and to possess defenders especially
among the German Cameralists.[113] In Britain certain boards were
quietly being replaced by individuals in fact though not in name,
but a reforming Comptroller of the Navy (Charles Middleton)
who regarded his board as desperately unsatisfactory never found
a way of getting rid of it.[114] Bielfeld came down strongly in more
than one place in favour of having an individual rather than a
board at the head of any organization and he tried plausibly to
maintain that principle by insisting that the Council was only
advisory to the king and was a funnel between him and the
several departments, and that if the king were inactive there should
be a prime minister. But, at the same time, he was willing to allow

that foreign affairs might be conducted by a triumvirate.[115] His position here might be compared with that of Necker, who knew and quoted the arguments against collective responsibility but nevertheless sometimes preferred it to individual responsibility on the ground that no single man of sufficient calibre could be found.[116]

In some respects the arguments about hierarchy or collective responsibility were unrealistic because they were paying no attention to sources of independence in the system that precluded any rigorous re-structuring of offices or functions. The most important of these were the survival of the revenue-farms, the practice of selling offices, and the system of remuneration by fees, which secured cheapness in administration at the cost of making the officials' incomes independent in the short run of the will of the employing government. These were the more immediate problems. Each practice found some critics and few defenders, but the criticism of the first two often lacked bite, perhaps because where they were well-established they seemed almost inescapable.[117] Most schemes for reform, whether narrow or broad, included some provision to pay officials by salaries rather than fees, and this principle made steady headway as the century advanced.

It is also true that most schemes for reform included a set of rules which was supposed to provide the framework for the institution, to prescribe the duties of the officials and often to prescribe their procedures and their relations with each other. The most remarkable individual example of the species was the 'Règlement' of the Prussian General Directory by King Frederick William,[118] but 'regulations', 'rules' or standing 'instructions' were nearly always made the basis of reform and of the future conduct of the institution. It reached its most explicit legal form in the reports of the (English) Commissioners for examining the Public Accounts (1780), who demanded that 'no office should be holden but by legal tenure'.[119] The rationale of this approach was that it made 'the administration of public affairs' independent 'of the humours and education of individual men' (David Hume) and connected the public interest 'with institutions that may render it permanent, and independent of men and circumstances' (Jacques Necker).[120] But in most cases it was presented without explanation or justification, as though it needed none.

The primary purpose of rules was to specify how the functions of the department or agency were to be performed, by describing duties and activities and sometimes by prescribing hours of attendance or prohibiting practices inconsistent with or detrimental to the officials' duties. Their second function was to provide for their own enforcement, by specifying penalties and rewards (including possibly salaries or adjustments to salaries), and by establishing means of detecting breaches of the rules. On the whole, the first function was performed more efficiently than the second, but the importance of the second was well understood and it was often discussed and often tackled. The standard measures were records or accounts, reports, inspection and publicity; that is, the officials were required to keep records, and to submit themselves and their records to inspection. These were substantially the same as those that the police of Paris and other cities had devised, in order to detect crime and criminals through the records they imposed on inn-keepers, pawnbrokers and the like. Sometimes (and often in agencies concerned with financial administration) these devices were identical with those that were required to enable an organization to perform its basic functions adequately, and so they did not have to be separately provided. In other kinds of organization, it was recognized that separate provision had to be made. Praise and prescription of records, inspection and reporting as instruments of control are to be encountered in nearly all eighteenth-century writings on administration, including those of the Cameralists, the reports of the Commissioners for examining the Public Accounts, Howard's study of English prisons, the works of Necker and other critics of French administration, Charles Davenant's critique of English Excise administration and Thomas Gilbert's plan for the reform of the English Royal Household.

The purpose of most of these devices was to provide the managers or directors of an organization with information about their subordinates' behaviour and its results, and in particular about failure or misconduct. The managers were then expected to take whatever action was best calculated to correct the situation. At one point, however, the public was enlisted in aid of, or possibly against, the managers. The publication of rules, lists of official duties or reports was intended to alert members of the public to the real obligations of officials, to permit them to measure performance against obligations, and to equip them to report shortcomings and ultimately to demand that obligations be met and failures corrected or punished. This theme had been present from the outset in the practice of police, for example in the regulation of markets. In the 1780s it found a most enthusiastic spokesman in Necker. Unusually among public officials, Necker admired and respected public opinion, as well as trying to use it. (As he valued it as a corrective to the frivolity and irresponsibility of the Court at Versailles, it was presumably the opinion of the Parisian bourgeoisie that he had in mind.) He believed that in France (though not elsewhere) social attitudes had created 'a tribunal...before which every one who attracts public notice is obliged to appear' and that 'public opinion as from a throne distributes praises and laurels, and establishes or ruins reputations'. He also believed that the authority of public opinion was beneficent: 'it is the ascendancy of public opinion that opposes more obstacles in France to the abuse of power than any other consideration whatsoever'.[121] He was giving a much larger role to public opinion (and perhaps foreseeing more clearly the character of democratic politics) than most of his contemporaries and predecessors. But he could reasonably have claimed to be doing little more than drawing out, in new circumstances, the implications of their use of publicity. His defence of his own most considerable attempt to influence public opinion – the publication of his *Compte Rendu au Roi* – was partly anticipated in some remarks of Bielfeld's on the importance of presenting a clear and comprehensive account of the State's finances.[122]

Some reformers and designers of institutions went into considerable detail in describing the kinds of records or the arrangements for publicity or for inspection that they believed to be desirable. Bielfeld went so far as to specify the shape of the paper on which reports were to be submitted, and the arrangement of the reports on the page (a very minor but not pointless detail).[123] He also covered more important matters, including visits of inspection by senior officials to the provinces, the form of Council records and who was to keep them, and the powers and functions of a body of auditors. He set most of this out in quite extensive models for two Ministries, those for Finance and Foreign Affairs, and for a Council Office.[124] Bonvallet des Brosses went into similar but more systematic detail in describing the form of the tables in which information must be submitted by the various subordinate offices in his projected 'Caisse Nationale', the pattern of communications among the separate offices, and a network of committees which would provide a form of inspection. These were atypical but not isolated examples.

There remain some aspects of the administrative reform movement that cannot so easily be related to legal categories or interpreted as the application of a legal model to the Executive. They were concerned with the quality of the resources, and primarily with the quality of the personnel, available to any branch of the government. This was not a matter that could easily be stated or solved in legal terms, although law was eventually required to play a part in imposing the preferred solution. The problem was seen to arise especially in the process of recruitment. The prevailing modes of recruitment in all Western countries were the sale of offices – venality – and patronage. Attitudes to venality have already been mentioned. Throughout the eighteenth century, the exercise of patronage was the cause of a good deal of disquiet to those who took a utilitarian (efficiency-oriented) view of the Executive. At the turn of the century, Davenant was denouncing 'spoils' and the influence of faction in the English revenue service; in the 1760s Bielfeld was listing the qualities necessary in senior officials and urging the importance of choosing officials who possessed those qualities; in the 1780s Necker was condemning abuses of patronage, introducing some changes in the system in the financial departments, and stressing (like Bielfeld) the need to choose competent men, not flatterers or clients of some great or small patron.[125] But there was an indeterminate quality in much of what was said on the subject, and it often lapsed into nothing more than moral exhortation. This had its importance, because it served to disseminate utilitarian criteria, and so to prepare public opinion for a more thorough application of them, but it could not easily be translated into practical measures. Bielfeld's discussion, for example, was quite lively and provided quite good advice, but its core was a single and rather special issue – whether or not the senior posts should be reserved for men of noble birth. (He argued that they should not.)[126] Necker took some practical steps by trying to exclude outsiders from the exercise of patronage and to concentrate it in the hands of senior responsible officials;[127] but he too had little more to offer the senior officials except good advice. There was, however, a current of opinion during the century in favour of recruitment on the basis of formal qualifications. This flourished particularly in Prussia, where the establishment of University chairs in 'Cameral science' in 1727 and of civil service examinations in 1770 are usually taken to be landmarks. In British thinking, it apeared in a mature form right at the end of the century, in Lord Wellesley's despatch justifying his creation of a College at Fort William for the training of Indian Civil Servants.[128]

The view of the Executive which emerged from all these reflections and recommendations can be stated in three main parts. It was a view of government in society, which made the Executive a subordinate and dependent part of the structure of government, subordinate to the sovereign legislator for direction and supervision. It assigned, however, a substantial set of responsibilities as well as very great authority to the government as legislator, and by extension to the Executive as agent for the legislator. The scope of these responsibilities was being questioned in the last third of the century, but they had not yet been significantly whittled down. The third part of the collective or aggregate view was that it was appropriate to supervise and regulate the Executive in the same way as the government regulated society, that is with commands and directions supported by a battery of rewards, penalties and devices designed to maximize the information and the powers of direction of those at the top. Where it was necessary to depart from the legal model, it was supposed that this could be done best by treating the Executive as a set of resources to which efficiency-oriented criteria could be applied.

In this way, most of the elements of the bureaucratic model, founded on legal-rationalism, had been brought to light. Few or no attempts had been made, however, to present them together in a consolidated account and few people recognized organization and management as subjects that might be discussed separately or in a systematic way. There were general studies by the Cameralists (with whom Bielfeld is sometimes classed) but these were on the whole too ambitious and too indiscriminate in their coverage to provide a thorough study of the Executive. Turgot's 'Memorandum on Municipalities' presented an integrated view of government but it covered only one aspect of the subject. At the level of details, there were also gaps and weaknesses. Often the recommendations were pious aspirations rather than operational programmes. Even in their most impressive forms, for example in the list of tables devised by Bonvallet des Brosses for his Caisse Nationale, one might doubt whether they were really carefully enough designed to be the instruments of control that they purported to be. Nevertheless, there had been accumulated a large mass of materials, in which most of the relevant problems had been pin-pointed, many solutions had been offered and a general method for finding solutions had been adopted and had been brought to view in a very clear fashion.

3

THE FOUNDATIONS OF BENTHAM'S THOUGHT: THE *COMMENT*, THE *FRAGMENT*, THE *INTRODUCTION* AND *OF LAWS IN GENERAL*

It is never easy to say when a man first develops a thought or adopts a set of values, but it seems clear that Bentham worked out the bases of his own position between about 1769 and 1782. He was admitted to the Bar in 1769 at the age of twenty-one, and in the same year (according to Bowring) read thoroughly the works of Montesquieu, Helvétius, Beccaria and Barrington. Soon afterwards he settled into the life of a private scholar and semi-professional author and translator.[1]

For a time, law and public affairs had to compete with botany and other physical sciences for his energies and attention, but within a few years the legal and political studies prevailed over the scientific. He embarked on the systematic study of offences and punishment not later than 1772, and on his critical analysis of Blackstone's *Commentaries* not later than 1774. From these topics he moved in one direction to explore the foundations of law and its social functions, and in others to begin investigating a series of more particular topics, including reward, procedure, evidence and penal policy, and to start constructing a model penal code. A great deal of that work remained unfinished in 1782, but it is nevertheless appropriate to see that date as marking a turning-point in his intellectual life. He had by then drafted four sub-stantial works, although only one had been properly completed: the published *Fragment on Government*; the incomplete *Comment on the Commentaries* from which the *Fragment* had been derived; the *Introduction to the Principles of Morals and Legislation*; and the sequel to the *Introduction* which is now known as *Of Laws in General*. He had also sketched out for himself the outlines of a programme of future work which was designed to build on the foundations that he had laid down in those works and which in its fully developed form was to occupy him for most of the rest of his life.[2]

In this period of thirteen years, he immersed himself in the kind of literature and the kind of thinking described in chapter 2. The issues and the body of writings were unfolding while he was himself at work. Of the four famous books that he read in 1769 the earliest (*The Spirit of the Laws*) was twenty years old and the most recent (Barrington's *Observations upon the More Ancient Statutes*) barely three. Bielfeld's *Institutions Politiques*, Steuart's *Political Oeconomy*, Catherine's *Nakaz*, Mildmay's *The Police of France*, and Blackstone's *Commentaries* were all products of the 1760s. Eden, Howard, Hanway and Adam Smith published in the 1770s when Bentham was already working on his own projects. Necker's apologia, the Reports of the Commissioners for examining the Public Accounts and other administratively-oriented writings came still later. He read all of these, and others on similar subjects: the codes and digests recently issued by the Governments of Prussia, Austria, Tuscany, Sardinia and Poland; Halhed's *Code of Gentoo Laws*; Coxe's *Account of the Prisons and Hospitals in Russia, Sweden and Denmark*; other works on the police of the Low Countries and on politics in Sweden; Chastellux's *De la Félicité Publique*, and *Hermes* by James Harris. His earliest publications – the *Fragment* (1776) and the *View of the Hard-Labour Bill* (1778) – were contributions to and interventions in the ongoing debate that was concerned with the nature of the modern state, its instruments and its conditions.

In participating in that debate, Bentham was also sharing in the outlook – the assumptions, objects and range of interests – that had dominated it from Hobbes onwards. He accepted both the individualist theory of behaviour and the theory of sovereignty as starting-points for his own reasoning. He agreed that, in a world of self-interested individuals, the foundation of social and political order must be sovereignty, and the standard of right and wrong must be traced to individual motives and experiences. He assumed further that sovereignty must consist in the ability to legislate or command and to enforce commands, that the operations of government must be essentially legal in character (and so must be describable and explicable in legal terms), and that enforcement must depend on the law's forms, its sanctions and the institutions devoted to its execution and administration. To that Hobbes-like set of assumptions he added, in the eighteenth-century fashion, a belief that government must be a trust conducted on behalf of the subjects or citizens of the state.

He believed no less firmly, however, that most of those conditions of good order and sound policy were still unsatisfied, in Britain and in the rest of Europe. The intellectual task that he set himself was to look for ways of satisfying them, and thus of completing and perfecting the institutions of the modern state. This meant looking for ways of perfecting the legal and other instruments available to the sovereign–legislator, of ensuring the supremacy of legislator and legislation among the authorities and activities of the state, and of providing or at least drawing attention to the principles and other conditions necessary to permit (or require) the sovereign to fulfil its trust. It was in that sense, and on those grounds, that he was a reformer. In this respect his attitude was indistinguishable from that of the multitude of other publicists and projectors such as Montesquieu, Helvétius, Beccaria and Eden. But his thinking was distinctive in two ways. The range of his interests was unusually wide, for he was equally ready to apply his mind to problems of specific institutions, to the fundamental principles of government and jurisprudence and to intermediate questions such as the law of evidence and legal procedure. Secondly, he assumed that all such issues were inter-dependent and that it was necessary to push much further into the most general ones, the principles of jurisprudence, if one were to make any progress with the rest. He became a jurist because he believed, with a long line of earlier thinkers, that law and jurisprudence provided the key to politics and social relations and to the solution of their problems.[3]

In this formative period up to 1782, he was working simultaneously at a number of levels. But, apart from the few and narrow questions tackled in his pamphlet on penal policy, it was only at the most general level that he had substantially completed his investigations. The results were set out in the four major works which form a more or less separate and complementary group among his writings. Their functions were to declare his commitment to the ideal and the theory of the sovereign state, and to purify and clarify the theory in the form in which he understood

it and adhered to it. So he proceeded to sum up what his predecessors had said, for example about sovereignty or utility, and
to show how those doctrines excluded other propositions with
which Blackstone and others had carelessly and confusedly combined them. The work of clarification, however, took him beyond
that point, important as it was. It led him to fill in gaps, or to
discard errors that he discerned in the accepted versions of the
doctrines, and to draw out some of their implications. In these
ways he began to determine and partly to develop his approach
to issues at other levels, and sometimes to build into his general
theory certain ideas that he had derived when thinking about
concrete problems. It was also important that he employed in his
investigations a relatively self-conscious methodology and set of
techniques. It is significant that in the early 1780s when he was
naming the four people who had most influenced his work on
codification, he included two – d'Alembert and James Harris –
whose contributions had consisted in techniques of inquiry.[4]

His methodology had indeed a good deal in common with that
which d'Alembert had set out in his manifesto, the 'Preliminary
Discourse' or Preface to the first volume of Diderot's *Encyclopedia*.[5] It showed the same sort of 'adjustment of the rationalist
spirit of Descartes to the empiricism of Locke and Newton' as
R. N. Schwab finds in the thought of the Encyclopedists.[6] It drew
from the rationalists an assumption that consistency, unity and
order are characteristic of all phenomena and all knowledge, and
from the empiricists a hostility to *a priori* metaphysical demon-
strations and a belief that knowledge is derived from clear,
distinct and simple sensations of individual objects. Bentham,
however, did not follow or agree with d'Alembert or the other
leading Encyclopedists on all points. His application and interpretation of the common stock of ideas reflected in particular his own
interests in the physical sciences, which were focused mainly on
botany and chemistry. He greatly admired, for example, the work
of Carl Linnaeus which d'Alembert was inclined to dismiss as
tainted with a metaphysical spirit of systems.[7]

At the core of Bentham's methodology was the empiricist
doctrine that what we know consists ultimately of simple individual objects or entities: 'the only objects which have any real
existence are those which are corporeal...That which is styled a
corporeal object is one single and entire corporeal thing.'[8] On this

ground he habitually denied any real existence to groups or collectivities beyond the existence of their individual members, and any real existence to universals or abstract terms. For the same reason his favourite theoretical technique was analysis or decomposition, the breaking-up of apparently complex things into their simple components. The reliance on decomposition was of course characteristic of the whole empiricist school with which he (together with d'Alembert) was aligning himself. It had added point for him because of his interest in chemistry and his participation in the translation of a work by the Swedish chemist and mineralogist, T. O. Bergman.[9] He described his own object and procedure in jurisprudence to be the 'decomposition of a law, a sort of mathematical chemical process' and he supposed that chemists might 'imagine the difficulty he must have found in getting the several elements to detach themselves from one matter and chrystallize apart'. Reinforcing the analogy with chemistry, he added that the procedure required 'somebody who should be to law what Bergman is to Chemistry' for its complete success.[10]

He recognized, however, that, although he might deny the real existence of complexes, groups and abstractions, he could not banish them entirely from discourse, even his own. His solution was the point that he attributed to d'Alembert. It was to treat them as 'verbal or fictitious entities' which might serve as a convenience in discourse or argument but could always be reduced, at least in principle, to real entities. So incorporeal objects could be 'nothing but so many fictitious entities' and must be 'either one or several corporeal objects considered in some particular point of view'.[11] The validity of particular fictions must be judged by their utility or convenience; but it must always be possible to pierce the veil that they interposed between fact and understanding, and to obtain 'a clear perception of the real state of things'.[12]

Two other features of his methodology that he shared with d'Alembert were a keen interest in language, including grammar, and a concern with classification as a further technique available to the theorist or as a particular application of his fundamental technique of analysis.[13] The aspect of language that interested him was its efficiency, that is its efficiency as a means of expressing and conveying ideas, especially the commands that must be the real content of the laws. The ideal that he set for himself in matters of expression consisted of 'precision, perspicuity...conciseness and uniformity'.[14] He believed that these conditions were to be achieved mainly by adopting a terminology that matched the simplicity or analytical structure of entities. But he maintained that jurisprudence did not yet possess a satisfactory terminology, and he accepted as part of his task the provision of a 'new language', or at least those parts of the language that were still missing. He justified this 'word-coining' on the grounds that it must be undertaken by 'whoever would write a fundamental book on any subject that belongs to the moral department of science', and by referring to the practice of Linnaeus and other scientists.[15] But a suitable terminology was only the first condition of success. The second was to adopt it and to use it properly. This meant using it consistently and uniformly. He described how he sought to keep to those standards in his own work by a 'steady and, as far as attention could hold out and the capricious tyranny of language would admit, unviolated resolution of employing throughout the same words to signify the same ideas'.[16]

His reference to Linnaeus in his defence of word-coining points to the fact that there were points of contact between language and classification in his thinking. He thought of the two processes of classifying and of word-coining as proceeding together, through the recognition of similarities and differences among phenomena and the discarding of inappropriate and misleading names, including names which were inappropriate because they failed to recognize real distinctions or implied false ones. In other words, despite his apparent commitment to an empiricist view of the world as consisting entirely of particulars, Bentham did assume that reality (including social phenomena such as laws or offences or 'the several powers subsisting in a state') had a certain structure, and that it was the function of classification to uncover the structure and to display the *classes* of objects and possible relations among them. Similarly it was one of the functions of analysis to deal in classes, for it was the technique through which classification must proceed. But Bentham had in mind a special kind of analysis, in the application of which he regarded himself as a pioneer anticipated only by James Harris. It was what he called the method of 'analytical exhaustion' or '[analysing] a subject upon an exhaustive plan'. He described it as consisting in the subdivision of any class of things into two groups such that 'every thing that comes under the common name and belongs not to the one [group] belongs to the other'. This operation could be repeated an indefinite number of times. Its point was to ensure that nothing would be left out or be counted twice, and that classes would be genuinely exclusive; he complained that these criteria were simply not satisfied by most would-be classifiers, who proceeded un-systematically by 'examining such of the objects comprised under [any] class as they happened to meet with on their way' and by 'looking over the names of such articles as they could think of'. Only by adopting his method, he argued, would the theorist or the legislator obtain 'an exhaustive view of the objects' that he must take into account or bring under control.[17]

Classification and analysis were therefore vital, but they were the instruments not the distinguishing characteristics of the kind of speculation at which he was aiming. His notion of theory reflected and illustrated still more clearly the rationalist aspect of his thought. He believed that the theorist must transcend the mere accumulation of facts through the application of knowledge and intellect to the facts, just as (he said) Linnaeus had done.[18] Theory or speculation must acquire the form of a science, and that consisted in 'a set of consistent principles and connected rules'.[19] To formulate and display the principles and the rules were the purposes which classification and analysis were supposed to serve.

Up to that point, Bentham's methodological reasoning was general in scope. Its propositions might apply to any field of study. To them, however, he added a few points that applied particu-larly to the field in which he was primarily interested, namely legislation and law. The first of these points was closely connected with his regard for principles and rules, although its source seems to have been as much political as philosophical. It was a plea for 'reason-giving' in legislation, that is for adding to the law 'the principles and subordinate reasons on which the several provisions of it have been grounded'.[20] Bentham supposed that this was something which 'nobody [had] ever thought of doing before', although as we saw in the last chapter Hobbes had proposed something of the sort. It had far-reaching implications for the form of law. His second law-oriented point was his demand for a 'logic of the will', by which he meant a body of philosophical reasoning, analogous to the logic of Aristotle and his successors,

but concerned with 'sentences of volition' or 'sentences of imperation' and 'sentences of interrogation' instead of the 'sentences of
assertion' to which the traditional logic had confined itself.[21]
At this point his interest was not strictly in language or modes of
expression; he saw logic as concerned with mental operations –
the traditional logic with the operation of the understanding, the
logic of the will with the *faculty* of will. He put forward this
demand because he believed law to be 'the most considerable
branch, – the most important application' of the logic of the
will.[22] His final point was a summary of the conditions of sound
and realistic action, in the triad 'knowledge, inclination and
power'.[23] His immediate purpose was to apply this to legislative
activity by inquiring whether a given legislator possessed these
qualities and, if not, how or whether he might be equipped with
whichever of them that he lacked.

It was only at or near the end of Bentham's formative period
that he found it possible and necessary to put forward his views
about techniques and methodology. It would be wrong to represent him as beginning in 1769 with the whole set of these ideas
fully-matured. He himself maintained that he worked out his
techniques, such as analytical exhaustion, 'little by little', and that
seems wholly plausible.[24] But a substantial part of what he was
doing in the early 1780s was describing procedures that he had
been employing, and formulating and making explicit the fundamental stock of rationalist and empiricist propositions that had
always served as his methodological premises. They had already
significantly contributed to and conditioned the achievements of
the four major works that were more or less complete by 1782.

His first and fundamental achievement in those works was to
adopt and re-state the theory of sovereignty. Most of what he said
on that subject is to be found in the *Fragment on Government* of
which, as F.C. Montague remarked many years ago, 'the true
scope...may best be expressed by calling it an essay on sovereignty'.[25] Here two things were equally important for the future
development of Bentham's thought: the meaning that he gave to
sovereignty, and his acceptance of the underlying social and
psychological theories that made society and the social order
depend on legislation and the legislator. On both sides he introduced some qualifications into his account, but these proved to be
relatively trivial or indeterminate.

His commitments and assumptions can be seen most clearly in his definitions of and comments on a series of familiar concepts, including 'political society', 'law', 'rights' and 'duties'. He found these being employed by Blackstone, his target and victim in the *Fragment on Government*, and he offered his own definitions as a way of exposing the confusions in Blackstone's arguments. Most of his own argument turned on his treatment of political society, which he equated with 'state of government' and contrasted with 'state of nature' or 'natural society'.[26] He visualized political society as consisting of two classes of persons, on the one hand a 'governor or governors' and on the other hand a set of undifferentiated 'subjects'. As in the modern state, the relationship between governors and subjects was direct and the power or authority of the governors fell on all subjects alike. The governors had the usual attributes of sovereignty. Their authority was 'though not infinite...indefinite'.[27] They operated through expressions of will and these expressions were laws if they were explicit 'commands' or 'parole expressions', and quasi-laws or fictitious commands if they were tacit.[28] The governors were differentiated from subjects because, and in so far as, the other members of the society were 'in the habit of paying obedience' to them.[29] The habit of obedience, together with the expressions of will to which it was a response, marked the distinction between political and natural society. In other words, in the absence of a supreme governor, of will and of obedience, political society would not exist; these were the things that constituted it. Moreover they determined its general character, for the key relationships of rights and duties were also created by will and obedience and – in this case – by a liability to punishment in the event of disobedience. Rights and duties were correlatives; a right was an ability to enforce performance of a duty; and a duty to do something existed when one was liable to be punished according to law for not doing it. '[Without] the notion of punishment,' Bentham asserted, '(that is [without the notion] of *pain* annexed to an act, and accruing on a certain *account* and from a certain *source*) no notion can we have of either *right* or *duty*.'[30]

At one level, it may be said, these were definitions which simply identified the terminology that Bentham intended to employ. As we shall see, Bentham himself sometimes argued along these lines. But at another level they were propositions about society.

They expressed a belief that will and obedience – not the tacit adoption and acceptance of socially-created norms and values – constituted the bonds holding a society together. And they represented rights and duties as the products of will, as sustained by sanctions and as therefore dependent on the existence of a sovereign ('governor or governors') to create and maintain them. This mode of thinking disposed Bentham to treat all structures, institutions and stable relationships as essentially legal ones, and to seek to analyse them in legal terms or by establishing a legal basis for them.

It has recently been pointed out that while Bentham adopted the theory of sovereignty, he provided in the *Fragment* and other early writings a more subtle analysis of the concept than he has usually been credited with. He showed that it must be a complex condition and that it might be compatible with limitations of time or scope.[31] But in his hands these modifications did not serve to break down the fundamental notion, or begin its transformation or absorption into an alternative doctrine. Their function was to make it a matter of fact, a variable condition which could be recognized in some situations but not in others and which might exist more completely in some situations than in others. They made it possible for Bentham to maintain the doctrine in the face of certain empirical objections to it and to do so without emptying it of content. For example, he was able to admit the existence of dual or imperfect jurisdiction in the form of an individual 'conceived to obey and not to obey at the same time, so as it be with respect to different persons, or as we may say, with respect to different *objects of obedience*';[32] and yet this admission left intact the fundamental notions of command and obedience. He was thus enabled to treat sovereignty not only as an instrument of analysis but also as the basis of a programme. In so far as it was a variable it might be created, sought, defended or extended. In that form it provided the foundations for the whole of his subsequent theory, which became an account of the conditions on which a utility-oriented sovereignty might exist and be perfected, and an attempt to realize those conditions.

Just as Bentham qualified his theory of sovereignty, so he sometimes backed away from an identification of society with the sovereign state. He hinted or admitted in a number of places that a social structure and social relationships might exist independently of the sovereign's law. One of those places was his original distinction between a state of government and a state of nature: his description of the latter implied a definite grouping and social relations, for it included a 'habit of conversing' among the several individuals in that state;[33] his definition of the former suggested that it depended ultimately on an extra-legal force, the habit of obedience. Elsewhere he recognized the family as an autonomous institution, and admitted the existence of rights, powers and duties that were not created by the sovereign's law.[34] He classified the duties and rights derived from the sovereign as *political,* and distinguished these from religious and moral duties to which he thus conceded an independent existence. In each case, however, he failed to follow up those hints and qualifications and left the non-legal relationships as at most a shadowy appendage or an illegitimate rival to the legal structure stemming from the sovereign.

One of the reasons why he failed to integrate the legal and the non-legal was that his social and psychological theories gave him no basis for doing so, even when the prospect appealed to him. Consistently with his methodology, the version of the individualist theory of behaviour to which he adhered was an unusually clear and systematic one. In social life, only the individual person was real, and the only real interests were those of individuals; in human behaviour, only individual experiences, motives and acts were real.[35]

Certain of the elements that he introduced into his account of pleasures, motives and sanctions have sometimes been seen as the germs of a different kind of theory. These were pleasures (or pains) that had an obviously social dimension, such as the pleasures of amity, good-name, benevolence and power. Their real function, however, was to confirm his individualism by completing the reduction of social phenomena to individual terms. These quasi-social pleasures remained individual phenomena, existing only as individual experiences. There was no reason to suppose that, when they occurred, they would persist or that they would fall into any particular pattern. They might be used, as Bentham used them, to explain specific acts and relationships, but they could not serve as the basis for predictions about future behaviour, the design of stable institutions, or the generation of habits or customs. They did not supply any ordering principle independently of the sovereign's law, although the sovereign's law might exploit them in the interests of order. In describing pleasure and pain as our 'sovereign masters' he was not indulging in showy rhetoric but was expressing his real understanding of the springs of human action.[36]

With this set of intellectual tools it was difficult for him to make anything of social behaviour outside a legal structure and he rarely did so. The 'habit of conversing' that he postulated as a constituent of natural society remained unanalysed and almost completely undescribed. His few references to natural society suggest a rather Hobbesian form of freedom and equality, in which the only identifiable sort of intercourse is the invasion of others' natural liberty: 'As yet then, you and I and everyone are at liberty. Understand always, as against the law: for as against one another this may be very far from being the case.'[37]

At the point where it was most important that he should give an account of habit and custom, he evaded the issue and left it unresolved. That point was of course where he introduced the 'habit of obedience' as the basis of political society; he needed then to account for such a phenomenon, and yet to show that it was not one of a family of habits which might provide a social structure independent of the sovereign. He moved some way towards those objectives by applying his individualist techniques to the notion of a habit: it was, he said 'but an assemblage of acts',[38] and could therefore be no more than the sum of its parts, a mere description of behaviour which could properly exist only in the past. But he wanted at times to speak of habits or customs in quite a different way, for example to refer to them as a 'disposition' or as having some 'influence' on future behaviour or as setting limits to the efficacy of law. He was aware that he was involving himself in contradiction by using those expressions, and tried to provide a solution:

Strictly speaking, habit, being but a fictitious entity, and not really anything distinct from the acts or perceptions by which it is said to be formed, cannot be the cause of any thing. The enigma, however, may be satisfactorily solved upon the principle of association, of the nature and force of which a very satisfactory account may be seen in Dr Priestley's edition of Hartley on Man.[39]

But that uncharacteristically feeble and evasive piece of argument really solved nothing. His treatment of the relationship between sovereignty and custom remained as unsatisfactory as that sup-plied by his predecessors and contemporaries. The status of the habit of obedience – his answer to the question whether it was the product or the source of sovereignty – was left entirely obscure.

His discussion of the family as an institution and of extra-legal duties provides, paradoxically, some additional evidence of the extent to which his thinking was dominated by the categories of the sovereign state. He seems to have regarded the family as a natural institution, and was therefore anxious to maintain that it was not political or part of the political system. But in trying to establish its institutional character, he found in it the character-istically political phenomena of command and obedience, and he had to look for some other way of distinguishing it from a political society. He did so by adding to his notion of political society a second characteristic or criterion, that of a capacity for 'indefinite duration'.[40] This permitted him to argue that a family could not be a political society because it tended to dissolve as its subject-members grew to maturity. It left unimpaired, however, the assumption that command and obedience constituted the typical (perhaps necessary) form of social action and interaction. He reinforced the assumption by his references to the family feelings of 'affection, gratitude, awe, the force of habit and the like', for he saw these as important only in so far as they tended to prolong the 'habit of obedience' beyond the period of physical dependence which was its original source.[41]

Command and obedience reappeared similarly in his analysis of non-political rights and duties. He was willing to speak of a duty (and thus of a right) only when he could relate it to a demand emanating from an identifiable source, and to the likeli-hood of punishment following upon the neglect or rejection of the demand. So religious duty was 'created by punishment... expected at the hands of a person *certain*, – the Supreme Being'; and moral duty was created in a similar fashion by the expectation of 'various mortifications resulting from the ill-will of persons uncertain and variable, – the community in general: that is, such individuals of that community as he, whose duty is in question, shall happen to be connected with'.[42] He insisted that where the demand and the sanction were absent, there could be no duty but only a 'sentiment'. He was describing, then, not moral and

religious orders distinguishable from the political and legal order
of command and obedience, but three orders operating in the
same way and distinguishable only in the sources of the commands which activated them. The functioning of the sovereign
state served as the model for all the duties of which he was aware
or which he was prepared to recognize, and all were to be
analysed and understood in quasi-legal terms.

To install the sovereign as the *model* for all social phenomena
was not, however, to establish it as their *source*. The implication
of Bentham's argument was rather that there might exist in any
community several different sets of commands and duties, those
of the political sovereign, of the Supreme Being, of one's family
(or more particularly one's father) and of other members of the
community capable of administering sanctions. This was in accord
with his analysis of sovereignty, as he seems to have been aware.[43]
But it raised the possibility of conflict between the different commands and between the different authorities from which they
were issuing, and his perception of that form of conflict was much
less clear or at least less clearly expressed. There exists some
evidence, in his early writings on religion, that he was aware of the
possibility of conflict, that he was granting primacy to the political
sovereign, and that he was treating other demands and duties as
illegitimate if they competed with those of the sovereign.[44] He did
not, however, argue the case for primacy in the major works,
although a claim to it was perhaps implicit in the 'indefinite'
nature of the authority that he attributed to the Supreme Power
in a government.[45]

The form of his argument therefore left the sovereign in an
insecure and ambiguous situation. But Bentham did not tarry over
these problems. For him, as for the student of his thought, they
were aspects of the background which were important but did not
require urgent attention. His immediate concern was with the
part of social life that he had classified as 'political', and more
particularly with the nature and the use of the legal weapons
available to the sovereign. Most of the rest of what he had to say
about government was incidental to, and by implication from, his
discussion of those issues.

In arguing that the sovereign was the source of political duties
Bentham did not mean that it was the proper judge of right or
wrong or of how its legal weapons ought to be used. On the con-

trary, he maintained, the principle of utility provided an objective standard to which the sovereign, like everyone else, ought to defer and which ought to determine its commands: 'To say, that a thing is politically right and at the same time morally wrong, or morally right and at the same time politically wrong is to talk nonsense...Ethics and law must not be inconsistent.'[46] It was this conviction that led him into moral theory and determined his approach to it, for in practice he identified ethics with utilitarianism. He believed that the principle of utility was neither 'novel', nor in need of justification; it had been Beccaria's and Helvétius's principle and 'before it was Helvétius's it was in some sort everybody's'. The task for the moral theorist was not to discover or establish it but to apply and 'to pursue it'.[47] So Bentham himself offered a quite perfunctory defence of the principle and its claims, but a much more elaborate account of the meaning of utility, the application of the principle and the ways in which it could and should be taken into account by the sovereign. The resulting body of doctrine – the bulk of the *Introduction to the Principles of Morals and Legislation* from chapter III onwards – functioned as a set of moral demands on the sovereign and a guide to the methods by which it might meet those demands. At certain crucial points it served to fill out and to direct Bentham's analysis of the legal instruments themselves.

His ultimate ambition was, and always remained, to provide sovereigns and communities with a code *in terminis*, that is a concrete body of law. But he could not complete that task immediately. He found that he had to undertake an ever-increasing amount of preliminary work in defining his objectives more precisely and defining more clearly the conditions on which they could be achieved. The principal source of that need was his conception of the character of a code. He was not satisfied with the political criteria and goals which had given birth to the codification movement, namely the synthesis and reconciliation of diverse bodies of law, or even the assertion of the sovereign's supremacy in the making of law. He accepted those criteria, just as he accepted that the code should be precise, concise, perspicuous and utility-oriented. But he demanded also that it should be 'complete and regular' and 'grounded on natural and universal principles':[48]

In a map of the law executed upon such a plan there are no *terrae incognitae*, no blank spaces; nothing is at least omitted, nothing un-provided for: the vast and hitherto shapeless expanse of jurisprudence is collected and condensed into a compact sphere which the eye at a moment's warning can traverse in all imaginable directions.[49]

In order to construct such a plan and map, he had to acquaint himself with the boundaries and all the principal features of the area it was supposed to cover, with the relationships and ordering principles among the several parts and features, and with the means of perfecting the latter. He could not find a satisfactory account of any of these matters in the writings of his predecessors and contemporaries; his original work in jurisprudence was an attempt to discover them for himself. He was unable to work out his position in all respects and it was this circumstance – rather than a psychological drive 'to be always running from a good scheme to a better'[50] – that interrupted and delayed publication of the *Introduction to the Principles* and *Of Laws in General*. But these imperfect works were complete enough to reveal his answers to many, and the most important, of his questions.

He concluded that the topography of a code must be supplied in the first place by a theory and a classification of offences. This belief explains why the theory of offences was one of the subjects that he began to study in the early 1770s. His view was that '[every] law turns an act into an offence: and one law creates but one offence: so many offences, so many laws: for every law there is an offence: for every offence there is a law'.[51] It followed that 'the division of offences is in fact the division of the whole law', and that 'a complete analysis of all the offences that can be treated includes a complete account of everything that can be done in the way of law'.[52] As the last point implies, Bentham assumed that the theory of offences must be (or must at least include) a 'censorial' theory stating what kinds of acts ought to be designated offences. This meant that the theory must be based on, and must be a systematic application of, the principle of utility; indeed to provide a natural basis for the theory of offences was one of his chief reasons for extending his jurisprudence into ethics and for employing the principle of utility.[53]

Bentham developed this part of his theory in the long chapter of the *Introduction to the Principles of Morals and Legislation* entitled 'The Division of Offences'.[54] He grouped offences into five principal classes. The first four were based on the identity of the victim of the offences: Private Offences were offences against individuals, Self-Regarding Offences were offences against one-self, Semi-Public Offences were offences against groups and corporations within the community (a category whose presence in the analysis sometimes troubled Bentham), and Public Offences were offences against the community as a whole or public institutions. The fifth class consisted of multiform or heterogeneous offences which could not be fitted into the other classes but might 'be detrimental in any one of the ways in which the act of one man can be detrimental to another'.[55] It included offences by falsehood (including forgery and perjury), and offences against trust (that is, trusteeship, where definite legal rights and obligations had been created). Bentham then divided the broad classes into divisions or genera according to the aspect of the victim that was damaged by the offence, and the divisions into branches or groups. The pattern was set by the treatment of Private Offences. Bentham assumed that an offence was damage to, or wrongful invasion of, the attributes of individuals. These attributes were person, property, reputation and condition; by the last, Bentham meant status or role in a relationship, and he specifically mentioned rank or title, marriage and the family, the relationship of master and servant and membership of a profession. Since offences and the law were co-extensive, the law must be a set of barriers against invasions of person, property, reputation or condition and their various derivatives.

While the theory of offences provided a catalogue of the laws, it did not constitute an exhaustive account of a code. There were inter-relationships among offences and among laws that did not appear immediately from an enumeration of them, and there were other aspects and components of individual laws besides the creation of an offence. These all had to be investigated and stated separately.

An important source of the inter-relationships was the fact that to create an offence – for example, to forbid a certain act – was not to prevent that act. In order to have any force, a law must include or have joined to it some motive to observe it, in the form of a sanction. But to prescribe a sanction was in turn only to make a *prediction* of reward or punishment, not to ensure its realization:

Let the law stop here...what has been done by the law as yet amounts to nothing: as an expression of will, it is impotent; as a prediction, it is false. The will of the legislator concerning the matter in question has indeed been declared: and punishment has been threatened in the case of non-compliance with such will: but as to the means of carrying such threats into execution, nothing of this sort hath as yet been made appear.[56]

Bentham concluded that the only course available to the legislator in these circumstances was 'to go on commanding as before' and 'to issue a second law requiring some person to verify the prediction that accompanied the first'.[57] The outcome of this line of reasoning was that the prevention of a given offence must involve not just one but a cluster of laws; one law directed to the potential offenders and others directed to those persons concerned with the detection, apprehension, sentencing and punishment of actual offenders. The 'subsidiary' laws might be joined with the 'principal' (offence-denominating) law in a single statute, or they might be stated elsewhere. A particular law might be principal in relation to one offence but subsidiary in relation to another. But some laws, including 'all laws relative to the course of judiciary procedure' would require some principal law to give them meaning and set them in motion; Bentham classified them as 'adjective or enclitic laws'.[58]

The code, then, while consisting of individual laws, was something more than the sum of its parts. Bentham expressed this by analogy; by analogy not with organisms, but in the eighteenth-century fashion with physical constructs such as pyramids and machines.[59] These physical analogies met his needs precisely because they enabled him both to recognize the total structure and to see the individual parts as existing and surviving independently of each other. Moreover, the notion of the machine permitted him to bring out a further aspect of a code and to demonstrate its capacity for change and improvement:

In a body of laws as in every complex piece of mechanism a great part of its perfection depends upon the facility with which the several parts of it may be altered and repaired, taken to pieces and put together. But such a system if constructed upon a regular and measured plan such as that appears to be which we have been attempting to sketch out, would not only have the advantage of every other which remained untouched, but alterations, whenever any were made, would give less disturbance to it: provided that such alterations, as often as they were made in point of form, were accommodated as they easily might be to that of the original groundwork.[60]

Another line of reflection about the relationship between offences and laws brought Bentham to the conclusion that a rational code must abandon the distinction between penal and civil law, at least in its conventional form.[61] His fundamental point was that if there were to be a body of law about property and other matters commonly dealt with in 'civil law', it must have the same character as other law and must therefore create offences and prescribe sanctions like penal law. His inference was that the civil and the penal branches were 'inextricably interwoven', and that in 'every law (at least in every law that is comparatively speaking of any importance) there is one part which is of a penal, and at the same time another part which is of a civil, nature'.[62] The residual distinction between penal and civil was either a distinction between kinds of law books, or between the 'imperative' aspect of a law and the 'expository' or 'circumstantiative matter' that it needed if it were to be intelligible. This expository matter might be peculiar to a given law, or it might relate to several or many laws. In the latter circumstances, 'a quantity of circumstantiative matter applying alike to divers parcels of penalizing matter, might instead of being placed contiguous to each, be placed contiguous to none, forming on the contrary a kind of independent parcel of itself'.[63] There might therefore be a civil branch of the law, or even a civil code incorporating all the expository matter detached from individual laws, but these could not exist in a self-contained form independently of the penal law, for 'the civil branch of each law...is but the *complement* of the penal'.[64]

In developing this argument, Bentham suggested more than once that the only genuine or effective law was one that prescribed punishment as a sanction.[65] Elsewhere, however, he took a different view. He regarded punishment as the most efficient and generally applicable sort of sanction, but like Beccaria he was prepared to concede a secondary role to reward (or remuneration) and to the prevention rather than the punishment of offences. He disparaged reward as 'too weak to act alone' and as incapable of sustaining 'the business of government' for half an hour; but he allowed that it might serve as 'an occasional subsidiary force' and might be relatively useful in providing a motive for 'acts of a positive kind'.[66] He attached more importance to prevention. To cover the sorts of things that Beccaria had included in his chapter on 'How to Prevent Crimes', Bentham developed the concept of 'indirect legislation', which he defined as 'the several ways of preventing misdeeds otherwise than by punishment immediately applied to the very act which is obnoxious'.[67] It might use either reward or punishment as a sanction, but it would normally attach these to some act other than the one that the sovereign aimed to prevent. It was close to, and in a sense incorporated, the principles and practices of preventive police.

Bentham believed that the whole topic of sanctions required a much more intensive treatment than his predecessors had given it. He tried to provide the basis for such an inquiry in the chapters in *An Introduction to the Principles of Morals and Legislation* dealing with pleasures, motives, sanctions and punishment, but he thought of them as merely a beginning.[68] He had already done a good deal of work in a separate Theory of Punishment, and he envisaged going on to write chapters or essays on reward and indirect legislation, but he was not able to fit these into the manuscript of *Of Laws in General* before he stopped work on it. He moved a little further from a purely 'punitory' approach to law by introducing what he called 'occasional appendages' of a law. He defined these as 'remedial' laws and as subsidiary laws 'contributing still further to obviate the mischief which it is the object of the principal law to provide against'.[69] They were distinguished from preventive police or indirect legislation by the fact that they were concerned with the consequences of an offence ('the mischief') rather than the offence itself and only came into action after the offence had been committed. Bentham divided them into three classes: compensative, therapeutic or catapaustic, and metaphylactic. These were concerned with, respectively, making '*compensation* for what [mischief] is past, to cure, that is put a stop to, what is present, and to guard against what might otherwise be to come'.[70] He envisaged further chains of subsidiary laws dealing with the procedure appropriate to each class.[71] The topic was potentially an important one, but Bentham did not do more than locate it and open it up in *Of Laws in General*.

Another idea which Bentham adopted from popular eighteenth-century jurisprudence was the distinction between general and particular laws, but he developed this until it became almost unrecognizable. He followed Catherine rather than Montesquieu or

Blackstone in treating particular laws or mandates as no less properly laws than general rules might be.[72] If a document or statement was an expression of will, if it was directed to a person or persons, if it had a definite object (an event or act to be brought about or prevented) and had some force or sanction to achieve its object, it was a law irrespective of its generality or particularity. It might be a statute made by Parliament or it might be a regulation, order or instruction issued 'by a magistrate the most conspicuous part of whose power is of the judicial kind – or of the executive kind – or by one whose legislative power is derived'.[73] But the distinction between particular and general was important, Bentham maintained, because it pointed to a distinction between different sorts of legal *powers*:

Correspondent to the distinction which respects the laws themselves is that which respects the power of making them. The power of enacting particular laws, the power as it may be called of imperating *de singulis* is one sort of power: the power of enacting general laws, that is of imperating *de classibus*, of making laws in general terms is, as we shall see, another and a very different sort of power.[74]

The point of the distinction, his reason for making it, was to draw attention to a peculiar disability from which he believed general legislation suffered, namely an inability to determine the individual things, persons or acts that must be included within the classes mentioned in the general rules. Bentham was here applying his individualist or nominalist philosophy even more rigorously than he usually did, and was denying that individual persons or events necessarily belonged naturally to classes or were naturally covered by general terms: they might have to be 'aggregated' or assigned to classes. To be completely effective, therefore, the power of legislating had to include not only the power of imperating *de classibus* but also an aggregative or accensitive power.[75]

Bentham subsequently analysed the accensitive power at some length.[76] He divided it into five kinds, relating respectively to persons, things, acts, places and times. The most important of these, and the one about which he had most to say, was the accensitive power relating to persons. He made it broader than the assignment of individuals to classes; as he expounded it, it came to include the 'investment' of persons to conditions (e.g. matrimony), their investment with rights or powers and their appointment to offices. For many purposes it could be referred to as an 'investive' power, which would be flanked by a disinvestive power.

The result of Bentham's speculations about the generality of laws was therefore a fairly elaborate analysis of the power of imperation. He absorbed this in a more general account of legal powers, both public and private. Imperation became one of the two categories of public powers that he recognized. The second category was the power of contrectation or impressive power, which Bentham characterized as power to use or dispose of things, and power over the bodies or 'passive' faculties of persons as distinct from their minds or active faculties.[77] It included the application of the punishments or other physical sanctions prescribed by law, and for that reason the power of imperation rested ultimately on contrectation. Both imperation and contrectation might exist as private powers, the former in a limited and subordinate form but the latter more widely as 'the power which a man exercises over the land he walks over or cultivates: the bread he bakes or eats: the coat he wears or brushes: the child or the servant he feeds, beats or reprimands'. Any of these powers might be held as beneficial or fiduciary powers; in the former case, for the benefit of the power-holder himself; in the latter for the benefit of some other person or persons, and to be styled a trust.[78]

Bentham expressed a large part of his legal theory in a powerful image in which he likened legislation and the tasks of a legislator to a state of warfare in which the enemy was 'political mischief':

[The] legislator is the commander: the moral and religious sanctions his allies: punishments and rewards (raised some of them out of his own resources, others borrowed from those allies) the forces he has under his command: punishments his regular standing force, rewards an occasional subsidiary force too weak to act alone: the mechanical branch of legislation...the art of tactics: direct legislation a formal attack made with the main body of his forces in the open field: indirect legislation a secret plan of connected and long-concerted opportunities to be executed in the way of stratagem or *petite guerre*.[79]

The ideas that he summarized in that paragraph represented in themselves a substantial contribution to the theory of the modern state, because they were focused on the means by which the state's legal supremacy could be translated into action and hence into social control. But they constituted only part of his thinking about the state. They were supplemented by, and led on to, a series of more concrete things that he managed to say about its activities and institutions.

The bridge between the two sets of topics was provided by his fundamental assumptions about sovereignty and society. They dictated that the state's activities must be operations on and with the law and that its institutions must be the products of will and law. The institutions must also, like any political society, depend for their continued existence on command, obedience and enforcement and must operate through these forms of behaviour. For this reason, any one part of the system of government must be analogous to any other part and to the political system as a whole: the judge's relations with the officials of his court must resemble, and must be sustained in the same way as, those of a Minister with his officials and those of a sovereign with his subjects. Moreover, the distinction between public and private law and legal phenomena was for most purposes unimportant. Any general propositions about the topics of civil law – powers, rights and condition – might be applied indiscriminately to public or private law. Government could only be accounted for and analysed in legal terms, and the established body of legal analysis could easily be extended to cover any aspect of the state. In practice, Bentham chose to extend it at a number of points. We have seen one minor example of this in his concept of indirect legislation, which accounted for and legitimized preventive police as an activity of government. More important examples were provided by his treatment of powers, including powers held in trust, and offences. He proceeded to develop from these bases some pretty clear ideas about constitutional law and about the powers and functions of government and its basic structure, and ultimately to form some notion of the Executive.

In a much-quoted letter written to Lord Shelburne in July 1781, Bentham explained that he regarded the constitutional branch of the law as the one that should be tackled last by the reformer, and that he was only just coming to give it serious consideration.[80] It seems that he was being a little unfair to himself, or falsely modest. It is true that he had not yet tried to bring together into one place or one scheme the various points he had made about government, or tried to discuss the principles of constitutional law at length. But he had convinced himself that constitutional law

was a proper and necessary part of his system and he had begun
to deduce some of its general characteristics and even a few of its
details.

The link between constitutional law and his treatment of
private law was provided by the concept of trust. Despite his own
claims that his youthful attitudes amounted to a sort of unthink-
ing Toryism,[81] his commitment to the Whiggish notion of government as a trust was already deep-seated in this formative period.
It determined his understanding of the objective to be achieved
through constitutional law, which was to make the government –
the trustee – act invariably in the interests of the beneficiaries, its
subjects.[82] And, because he had already developed a general
theory of trusts, he was able to proceed quite rapidly to form a
view of what a trustee-government would be like and how it
might best be regulated and disciplined.

In his general discussion of trusts, he distinguished among those
bodies according to the nature and number of the beneficiaries:
'1. an assignable individual or individuals; 2. a subordinate class
of persons individually unassignable, or 3. the public at large:
trusts may accordingly be distinguished into private, semi-public
and public trusts.'[83] He reinforced the analogy between public
and private bodies by insisting that the principles applicable to
private trusts must be equally applicable to public ones, for
'public powers differ no otherwise from priviate fiduciary powers
than in respect of the scale on which they are exercisable: they
are the same powers exercisable on a different scale'.[84] He
concluded that there must exist a body of constitutional law,
resembling an instrument setting up a trust and covering 'the
designation of persons invested with public trusts, and of the
powers they are invested with'.[85] As a body of law it must meet
the criteria that he had established for law in general, and it must
operate in the same way as other branches of the law. It must,
unlike the rather random collection of principles, conventions and
statutes known as 'the British Constitution', be comprehensive,
uniform and integrated, a code like every other branch of the
general code. It must have both a civil and a penal aspect,
imposing duties, creating offences and marking out the punishments to be inflicted for the neglect of duties and the commission
of offences.[86] And it must consist of the optimum combination of
rewards and punishments and of direct and indirect forms of

legislation.[87] The forms and devices that enabled the government to regulate the community could and must be employed in the regulation of the government itself.

Besides formulating this notion of constitutional law, Bentham had also begun to apply it and to give it content in a tentative way. He did so most clearly in his analysis of public offences. He defined many of the sub-divisions of this class as offences against trust: against judicial trust, against fiscal trust, against sovereign trust, against military trust and so on. Some of these were offences that might be committed by members of the public through interference with the trustees in the performance of their duties, but others might be committed by the trustees themselves. The law of public trusts must guard against both kinds. The trustees' offences fell into two branches, breach of trust or abuse of it. In either branch they must arise through 'some deficiency in the three requisite and only requisite endowments, of knowledge, inclination and power'.[88] Bentham indicated, in the *Fragment on Government*, a few ways in which offences based on deficient 'inclination' might be discouraged: in particular, general measures having a liberal or radical tendency, such as 'frequent and easy *changes* of condition between govern*ors* and govern*ed*'; 'liberty of the press'; and 'liberty of public association'.[89] These detailed measures and his more abstract reflections and definitions amounted to much less than a constitutional code or any part of it. They did, however, represent a start on the identification of the points that a code must cover and of the many places where they might arise.

Bentham's analysis of offences, and especially of public offences, also made a significant contribution to his ideas about the responsibilities or functions of government. In general, his view of those responsibilities was cautious, defensive and closely related to contemporary ideas about police. Part of it emerged in his treatment of private and heterogeneous offences. This assigned to the state the role of maintaining and protecting personal safety and the existing rights and possessions on which his analysis focused attention. It envisaged little in the way of initiatives or positive activity on behalf of the community. Its negative tendency was reinforced by Bentham's hesitant attitude to self-regarding offences, which he seems to have included for the sake of completeness rather than out of any conviction that the community should notice or prohibit such actions.[90] His discussion of public offences modified that approach and contributed to a more rounded and positive view of government. It was based, like the analysis of private offences, on the aspects of the victim that might suffer damage, but here the victim was the community and its agencies, and the damage would consist in obstacles to the government's performance of its functions and to the community's achievement of its objects. Bentham accordingly provided a list of eleven of these functions and objects. It included a group that was primarily defensive – external security, justice, the preventive branch of the police, protection of the public wealth, the public force – but that nevertheless included a possibly open-ended responsibility to protect the community against physical 'calamities' as well as against human offenders. A second group belonged with the more expansive views of police and oeconomy that were accepted by some of Bentham's contemporaries. Its significant items were the enlargement of population and of the national wealth, and the positive increase of the national felicity.[91] For the most part, Bentham avoided committing himself to a precise view of the government's role or its proper lines of action in dealing with these matters. In all cases its role and its policies were subject to the dictates of utility and might change as new information or new techniques became available. But he was least cautious in dealing with the positive increase of national felicity. He indicated there that the government must at least take some responsibility for education, the care of the sick and insane, the maintenance or housing of the poor and an indeterminate number of other fields of social policy.[92] He moved a little further into the same area when he began to talk about compensatory and other remedial procedures as 'appendages' of a law. By introducing those categories of action into his theory he opened up another potentially wide field of governmental activity although he seems not to have discerned the implications of his point at that time. It is probable that on balance he did not want any marked extension of the existing functions of the state, except possibly in the area of social policy which he saw as a new branch of governmental activity; but he interpreted those functions in a fairly generous way, and he gave no indication of wanting to cut them back except in relation to self-regarding offences.

Like his discussion of offences and appendages, his analysis of legal powers turned out to incorporate a considerable political content. On the one hand it permitted him to account for and to legitimize a variety of governmental and even political activities. On the other hand it helped him to work towards and to justify the view of the structure of government that he favoured.

The fundamental point here was his claim that all the 'possible powers in a state [were] reducible to...the power of contrectation...and the power of imperation'.[93] That classification of powers superseded, in his theory, the orthodox division of activities into legislative, judicial and executive. It eliminated the class of judicial powers, identifying the acts of the judiciary as the exercise of either imperative or contrectative powers. It also cut across the familiar distinction between legislative and executive. Although imperation obviously resembled legislation and contrectation resembled the execution and administration of laws, the correspondence was not exact. Imperation absorbed many acts and activities that would ordinarily be thought of as administrative, especially instructions to subordinates and appointments to and dismissals from offices, which Bentham could classify as accensitive or investitive acts. (He was here drawing out the implications of his refusal to identify law with rules.) Under the same headings, he was able, finally, to go beyond *governmental* powers and to show that other 'powers in a state' were susceptible to the same sort of treatment. He interpreted the notion of investment to cover not only the appointment of officials by members of a government, but also the appointment or election of members of the government or the legislature. It was on this sort of ground that he regarded the source of the notion – the distinction between the *de singulis* and the *de classibus* modes of imperation – as affording 'a clue without which it would be scarce possible for us to find our way through the labyrinth of constitutional jurisprudence'.[94] The whole discussion of powers both illustrated and vindicated his assumption that all the operations within a state were legal phenomena and could be described in the terms supplied by his legal theory.

In rejecting the orthodox classification of powers, Bentham was simultaneously, and consciously, undermining the conventional characterization of the structure of government as a set of three more-or-less co-ordinate branches, the Legislature, the Executive and the Judiciary. He did not seriously object to the division into branches, and indeed he continued throughout his life to refer to those three branches or 'departments' of government. But he wanted to deny that any one branch had exclusive control over, or was confined to, any one class of powers, and he wanted to deny that the different sorts of powers or the three branches were or should be 'separate', that is independent and co-ordinate.[95] He wanted the powers and the branches alike to be different instruments for translating the sovereign's will into behaviour. His theory of powers achieved those objects. For the reasons outlined immediately above, it left the Judiciary with no distinctive powers at all, and the Executive with a mixture of imperative (legislation-like) and contrectative powers. And it represented contrectation as complementary, and as such subordinate, to the imperative act which expressed the sovereign's will.

Having undermined in that way the doctrine of the separation of powers, Bentham was free to adopt and to present the alternative eighteenth-century view of the relations between Legislature and Judiciary. He did so with only a few variations. He permitted the sovereign–legislature to express its will in either of two ways: by conception when the sovereign itself formulated and issued the 'mandate'; and by adoption when someone else had originated it. In the form of pre-adoption, adoption covered both the delegation of law-making authority and the confirmation of proposed laws; in the form of susception, it covered the confirmation of laws already issued.[96] It accounted satisfactorily for all the species of laws which Bentham's definition permitted judges and officials to make, and re-asserted the authority of the legislator over the whole process of government.

Bentham applied these ideas in some more detailed comments on the Judiciary. He introduced them to deal with the problem of judicial interpretation. He followed Beccaria and other Enlightened thinkers in opposing 'the licentiousness of interpretation' and in condemning it as a usurpation of the sovereign's authority. He believed, however, that interpretation could not be eliminated altogether and must be regulated instead. His solution was to condone it when it arose from genuine gaps or obscurities in the law, but to impose on the interpreting judge a duty to propose to the Legislature an amendment that would remove the blemish.[97] This was a variant of devices that Bielfeld and others had proposed in slightly different circumstances.[98] Bentham added that the judge's amendment should become law unless it was specifically disallowed by the Legislature. His scheme vested the initiative in the judge, and required a very small degree of participation by the sovereign Legislature. But it fell within the scope of adoption and left the formal authority of the Legislature undisturbed.

Bentham was, as yet, less interested in the Executive than in the Judiciary. But he had formed some notion of what the former should be like and of its place in the scheme of government. That there should be an Executive, and that it must be complex and possibly extensive, followed from his account of contrectation and was taken for granted in his theory of public offences. In order to carry out the simplest instructions of the Legislature, he argued, a judge 'must be provided with a variety of assistants: which assistants must for certain purposes be of various ranks, occupations and descriptions: witnesses, registers, court-keepers, jail-keepers, bailiffs, executioners and so forth'.[99] Similarly in his discussion of public offences he assumed that the government would maintain a large number and a wide range of establishments many of which would have a productive or commercial character. They included establishments adapted to the service of the public force (arsenals, dockyards, magazines), to the care of public wealth (public roads and harbours, post-offices, packet-boats, market-places) and possibly to the various branches of national felicity.[100] These institutions were among the particular targets of offences against the state, and formed part of the machinery of government as he understood it.

He was aware, too, that such establishments and groups of officials must have, in terms of his own theory, a regular structure and a legal basis. He made the point clear in writing about the judges' assistants, many of whom, he contended, 'must begin to act in their respective characters even before the matter is submitted to [the judge's] cognizance' and must '[on] this and other accounts...have their duties prescribed to them by the law itself'.[101] The point was a very small one in his total argument, but it was a significant one. It showed him to be already committed to the ideal of legal regulation of the Executive, and to be employing the rudiments of the notion of a bureaucracy built around abstract offices ('respective characters') which were to be defined by their legally-created powers and duties.

The final element in his concept of the Executive was an attempt to define within a small space its share of the total powers and activities of government. He described these as:

1. exercise of investitive power
2. issuing of executive laws
3. issuing of executive orders *ad individuos*
4. duties of office, i.e. obediences at large (not comprehended under the former classes) as in receiving money, making up accounts, going on military expeditions, along with the subordinates: inflicting punishments, exercising [...] powers of procedure, i.e. doing what is ordained to be done by laws compensative, catapaustic or metaphylactic.[102]

This list confirmed that the Executive must have a share of both imperative and contrectative powers and activities, and it represented a first attempt to split these up and to give a coherent account of distinctively administrative activities. It also left unchallenged the supremacy of the Legislature, for the contrectative powers had necessarily to be set in motion through imperation, and the Executive's imperative powers could easily be made subject to adoption or supervision by the Legislature.

The nature of Bentham's achievements in the four early works can now be summarized. His starting-point had been a picture of simple forms of interaction between a sovereign and a mass of individual subjects, in which the sovereign commanded and the subjects obeyed, and in which the sovereign's commands were directed to the subjects' needs and sought simultaneously to counter and to exploit their impulses. As he analysed commands and their impact on the community, the picture became much less simple. He revealed that commanding included different activities, could take on different forms, could operate on the community – could exploit motives and impulses – in different ways and that it required the support of yet other activities. The subjects' needs, or the form in which they presented themselves to the sovereign, could be classified to produce distinct and recognizable functions of government. The functions and the multiple activities implied the existence of a considerable institutional structure, parts of whose shape and some of whose bases Bentham could already discern. As he introduced the additional elements into his account, he became aware of and tried to depict some of the relationships among them. Finally, he saw that law could be turned against itself, or at least against its sources and those who enforced it, and that commands regulating and binding the agencies of government could be devised in the form of constitutional law.

These judgements, it must be stressed, relate to the development of Bentham's own thinking, not to his contribution to political thought. Although he was already an innovator in legal theory, he was in these early works a consumer rather than a producer of political thought, and especially of thought about government. Here at least, Hazlitt's assertions can be accepted with little qualification, for very few of Bentham's ideas were not already familiar to his contemporaries. But he used those ideas in two ways, one of which did add something to his original stock. On the one hand, he was reconciling others' ideas, or matters of common observation, with his own fundamental legal categories, making those ideas or observations his own, and placing himself in a position to employ them easily in the future. Important examples of this kind of process were his successful absorption of a multitude of activities under the two headings of imperation and contrectation, and especially his derivation of the notion of accensitive power to account for the particular activity of appointment and dismissal. These achievements were of value, but mainly to his own development as a thinker. On the other hand, he was giving to some ideas a more rational or systematic form than they possessed when they reached him. He was showing what law must be like if it were true, as de Lamare had said, that it consisted in the four points to command, to prohibit, to permit and to punish. He was beginning to show what the law relating to government must be like if it were true that government was a trust, and what the Executive must be like if it were to be equal to serving the Judiciary and the Legislature. In these respects he was ceasing to be a consumer and was becoming a producer, if only in a modest way.

At nearly every point, however, he had left unsettled questions, principles that were too general to provide practical guidance, lists of activities and functions that were illustrative rather than exhaustive, mere sketches of structures and relationships, details without a context and plans without details. He was not unaware of these deficiencies. In the revealing letter that he wrote to Lord Ashburton in 1782, he indicated that he was continuing to think about some of the unsettled questions and the gaps, and that he hoped soon to dispose of them. His immediate projects included a plan for a complete code in which the parts would be set out and their relationships shown, an essay on indirect legislation, and another on reward.[103] These were among the materials in which he was able to carry forward his discussion of government in the next few years, fitting additional observations and concepts into his categories, and teasing out additional implications and conclusions from his stock of principles.

4

FURTHER EXPLORATIONS IN
JURISPRUDENCE

While Bentham was still building up his stock of fundamental principles, he was already beginning to think about some of their applications to particular situations. The first fruits of this style of thinking were some writings about religion, the little pamphlet entitled *View of the Hard-Labour Bill* (a commentary on a preliminary draft of what became the Penitentiary Act of 1779), a sketchy plan for a Board of Shipbuilding to stimulate inventions and experiments in naval architecture, and a similar plan for an Office of Intelligence to collect information about the merits, defects and operations of existing laws.[1] The essays on religion displayed the awareness of the political significance of churches, liturgies and doctrines that was so prominent in Bentham's later writings on that subject. The three institutional schemes were not, in contemporary terms, very distinguished essays in institution-building, but they served as pilot studies or exercises for the construction of the more complex institutions that Bentham later undertook, and in the meantime they led him to think carefully about some of the principles and devices of preventive police. He did not, however, persevere with these topics once he began serious work on the introduction to his code. And when, in 1782, he laid aside the manuscript of his incomplete masterpiece, he did not return to them but concentrated instead on the three essays that he saw as its natural sequel. They occupied him intermittently for much of the rest of the decade, and intensively in its middle years.

In the end, he left the three essays unfinished too, although versions of them ultimately appeared in the French editions of his works that Etienne Dumont published in 1802 and 1811.[2] But he worked very hard on them during the 1780s, and incorporated in them a good deal of new thinking. Like the works out of which they had evolved, their focus was primarily legal but they assumed and implied important notions about politics and government. They enabled him to extend and clarify his understanding of constitutional law and the role and status of government in society, to introduce some new elements into his account of government's functions, and to say a good deal more about the sovereign's modes of operating on society and on its own servants and about the modes in which the community could act on the sovereign. His reasoning on these subjects flowed on into, and in some cases was only completed in, his important but largely neglected writings of the 1790s.

As befitted a sequel, the three essays were conceived as a continuation and elaboration of the lines of argument developed in their predecessors. But in their political aspects, these arguments were enriched and supplemented by other bodies of thought and other attitudes. Bentham derived some of these from the *View of the Hard-Labour Bill* and the other essays of the 1770s, but others were new. The more important of the new materials were a set of ideas about political economy (which he seems to have studied closely for the first time in the 1780s), and perhaps a greater body of information about real conditions and problems in both government and economic life.

From the early 1770s onwards Bentham had been living on the fringes of politics and administration and had been acquiring some knowledge of industrial practices through the employment of his brother Samuel in the naval dockyards. He seems to have been brought closer to such matters, and to have been encouraged to consider them as throwing up intellectual problems of administration and management, through his association with Lord Shelburne and his circle during the 1780s, and in the course of his visit to Samuel in Russia in the middle of the decade. Shelburne was a leading figure in the Economical Reform movement which was at its height when Bentham first became attached to him in 1781. His own special contribution to it, as Secretary of State and Prime Minister in 1782–83, was to help to guide it from a concern with corruption ('influence') and with simple economies, to a concern with administrative efficiency.[3] He was also unusual among eighteenth-century politicians, as Derek Jarrett has pointed out, in cultivating political relations with the Dissenters, and this had 'brought him into contact with a whole network of people in

the Midlands and in the north of England who were in the fore-
front of industrial and technological development'.[4] Bentham may
have been influenced by his attitudes and may have shared some
of his acquaintances; there is a little concrete evidence of these
things in the facts that, encouraged by Shelburne, he was reading
the works of Necker,[5] and that he was able in the next decade to
find his way around the world of craftsmen and industrialists as
he embarked on the construction of his model penitentiary. The
effects of the visit to Russia are much clearer. Samuel, while
nominally an army officer, was in practice an estate manager,
supervizing farms and industrial establishments, and he was also
engaged in developing his own mechanical inventions. Jeremy
necessarily saw this work at close quarters and – despite his dis-
claimers – was occasionally drawn into it, engaging labour on
Samuel's behalf, writing letters, scraping together money and
dealing with urgent issues when Samuel was absent.[6] These circumstance, and experiences probably stimulated his interest in
political economy, and shaped the way in which it entered into
his thought. He was as impressed by its theory of production
(including the notion of the division of labour, and the strong
emphasis on capital as a factor in production), as he was by the
theory of markets and exchange. Its doctrines were among the
things that caused him to re-shape (but not, I believe, fundamentally to alter) his conclusions about the functions of government; but they also subtly pervaded his thinking as an extension
of utilitarianism, in the sense of the rational adaptation of means
to ends. The theory of production became a classic example of
the translation of general utilitarian precepts into more detailed principles and guides to action in particular sorts of
situations.

The setting for most of Bentham's new theory, including his
theorizing about political economy, was provided by his essay on
the *Corpus Juris* or general character of a code of laws. Something
must be said about the structure and the drafting of that work,
which was complex and is still in some respects obscure. In
Dumont's version it was entitled 'Vue Générale d'un Corps
Complet de Législation', and it was later translated into English
as 'General View of a Complete Code of Laws'.[7] Bentham
possibly did not decide on a final title for it in the 1780s, but at
one time he considered calling it 'Projet d'un corps de loi complet

à l'usage d'un pays quelconque', and he usually referred to it as 'Projet'.[8] As these various titles imply, it was intended to be a comprehensive account of the scope, subjects and principles of legislation, a prelude to the concrete comprehensive code of laws that he hoped finally to complete. In its scope and purposes, and sometimes in its content, it resembled Catherine's *Nakaz*, but it tried to cover the same sort of ground in a more sophisticated and more systematic way. Bentham experienced great difficulty in deciding on a structure for it, and his drafting ran through at least two complete plans, which he labelled respectively 'Projet-Matière' and 'Projet-Forme', and numerous smaller variations. The published 'Vue Générale' was closely related to the 'Projet-Forme' series of Mss., but these did not incorporate all that he had drafted in earlier versions. The latter sometimes contain points of significance for government.

The 'Projet' provided Bentham with his main opportunity to develop his understanding of constitutional law and its relationship with other bodies of law. He reiterated his earlier view that it was the third and last major branch of the law, together with penal and civil law.[9] But that division was an analytical one, referring to the aspects of law and not to its arrangement. He envisaged that the comprehensive code would be, or could be, arranged in a series of particular codes, some of which would apply to all members of the community while others applied to those in particular situations and relationships. Among the latter group he mentioned a Procedure Code (applying to judicial procedure), a Military Code and an Ecclesiastical Code. He did not quite succeed in locating constitutional law within this scheme. He thought of it, at this stage, as a cluster of codes rather than a single Constitutional Code, but he experienced difficulty in deciding how many members the cluster should have or what they should be. Most of the time he had three in the cluster, dealing respectively with 'political law', finance and political economy;[10] at various other times he considered adding to or associating with them military and ecclesiastical law, codes for police and municipal affairs, and finally parliamentary procedure ('political tactics' in his terminology).[11] But the laws relating to police, finance and political economy tended to dissolve and be dispersed to other parts of the system when he tried to say something about them. He was probably hampered here by an assumption, inherited from Catherine the Great and others, that these three topics were legal categories into which laws must somehow be fitted. The tendency of his argument was to show that they were not. But he was not quite ready to accept that conclusion, and they survived as awkward and undigested elements in his treatment of constitutional law.

It was clear that the centre of his constitutional system must be the projected Political Code, but the chapter assigned to that topic in the latest version of the Projet-Forme was rather thin.[12] Its thinness disguised, however, some real progress that he had made in determining the character of constitutional or political law. He had put some of the relevant points in a chapter on 'Politique' which he had discarded at a late stage in his drafting. Other points, and in some respects more fundamental ones, were to be found in his discussion of civil law.

He made civil law the vehicle for his constitutional ideas because he continued to believe that constitutional law was about 'property in trust', and that its foundations must be laid 'in the Private Civil Code'; and more precisely that they must be found in those parts of the Civil Code dealing with domestic and other 'conditions' or 'states'.[13] He now argued that a condition, as a legal entity, was constituted by and could be reduced to the rights and obligations attached to it and the means of acquiring those rights and obligations:

The domestic or civil state is only an ideal base around which are ranged rights and duties, and sometimes incapacities...To know a state is therefore to know separately the rights and the obligations which the law has added to it: but what is the principle of union which binds them together, to make the factitious thing which is called a *state*, a *condition*? It is the identity of the investitive event with respect to the possession of that state.[14]

It followed that a condition or (in constitutional law) an office or authority could be known only through a description of the rights and duties attached to it and of the means of acquiring it. Bentham's model for the analysis of any condition consisted of five points: '1. methods of acquisition; 2. methods of losing; 3. rights; 4. duties; 5. incapacities if there be any'.[15] This became accordingly the pattern for the constitutional code, with the addition of 'an exposition of the formalities which ought to accompany the exercise of the powers attached to these offices,

in those cases in which they are exercised by political bodies'.[16]
He thus confirmed that 'offices' (not persons) must be the units
recognized in constitutional law, that these must be treated as
prior to the persons who occupied them and as the source of the
occupants' powers, and that the law must be an account of the
offices, their powers and the relationships among them.

The aspect of constitutional law that he chose to investigate
most thoroughly in his 'Projet' was the nature of powers. He did
not advance beyond generalities, but he succeeded in filling out
what he had said on the subject in *Of Laws in General*. He made
it possible to do so by splitting up imperation and contrectation,
and by employing together his two distinctions between *de singulis*
and *de classibus* on the one hand and between powers over persons
and powers over things on the other. He described a government's
powers in three stages or levels of generality: elementary political
powers; powers of the second order, or powers modified and
applied; and powers of the third order, or powers determined by
the name of the office. He regarded the elementary powers as
fundamental, and the others as reducible to them. In their simplest
and most succinct form, the elementary powers were:

1. Immediate power over persons
2. Immediate power over the things of another
3. Immediate power over public things
4. Power of command over persons taken individually
5. Power of command over persons taken collectively, or over
   classes
6. Power of specification or classification
   1. With regard to persons
   2. With regard to things
   3. With regard to places
   4. With regard to times
7. Attractive power. Power of granting or not granting rewards[17]

He supposed that these elementary powers could be sub-divided
indefinitely and that they could be possessed 'in chief, or in rank
more or less subordinate'.[18] He could make little of the powers of
the third order, viewing them as of use only in relation to particular countries. The powers of the second order were the more
familiar elements of political discourse, that is legislative, judicial
and executive powers. Bentham discussed these mainly to show
that they could in fact be reduced to elementary powers, and to
demonstrate again that most of the supposed executive powers

were really legislative or judicial and that the 'term executive power presents only one clear idea – it is that of one power subordinate to another, which is designated by the correlative appellation of *legislative power*'.[19]

Those speculations about powers and offices in 'Projet' served to show more precisely the topics that might be covered by constitutional law. They did not dictate or indicate how the several topics might be covered. Bentham was able to move towards clearer or fuller ideas about filling in his legal categories by appealing to some of the other bodies of reasoning that were newly-devised or that he had not drawn on fully when he was drafting *Of Laws in General*. His treatment of the functions of government was one of the chief beneficiaries of this process.

His work in political economy pushed him towards a narrowing of government's functions, but in the end it left most of his original view intact. Unlike many later liberals, he did not regard political economy as a master-science or as providing a model for all social relationships. He saw it as a branch of jurisprudence, a body of principles relating to a particular branch of legislation or of the business of government.[20] It was the branch concerned with abundance, which was one of the four 'subordinate ends' into which he now decomposed utility.[21] The fundamental question that he asked in his economic studies was how abundance (output) might be promoted, and in particular what kinds of action by governments would help to promote it.

He gave his first answers in a manuscript which now appears to be lost, and which (like the chapter on 'Politique') he discarded at a late stage from his 'Projet-Forme' series of chapters.[22] Those answers were that the volume of output depended mainly on the factors of production and the ways in which they were combined, and that governments could do a little, but only a little, to increase it. In arriving at that conclusion, Bentham brought two sorts of argument to bear on the issues. One was the standard case for free trade, consisting of the virtues of competition and the interdependence of buyers and sellers in a market. The other (not foreign to the advocates of free trade such as Adam Smith, but with deeper roots in Bentham's own thinking) was a further application of the method of analysis or decomposition: the dissolution of an economic community into its individual members and their interests, together with the judgement that each individual was the best judge and protector of his own interests. Translated into economic terms this meant that the wealth of the state was the sum of the wealth of individuals, and that each individual must know better than any government how to do his own work and promote his own wealth. In particular, Bentham held up to scorn the idea that a government could know or judge as well as an individual capitalist what would be the most profitable lines of employment for capital. Nevertheless he found some tasks that governments might or possibly should perform. The most substantial of these was assistance for infant industries ('industries naissantes'). Those that he favoured most strongly were the promotion and dissemination of knowledge and the encouragement and protection of inventors by patent laws and in other ways.[23] The role that he found for the government was thus located on the fringes of the economy, and consisted in being helpful but not interfering.

This argument was subject, however, to a general qualification which was present in his conception of political economy but which twentieth-century observers are apt to overlook because they approach the subject in a different way. The modern approach to economic policy and to the economic role of the state is to ask how governments should intervene in and regulate the more-or-less concrete institutions and activities that we think of as 'the economy'. Bentham's question was not about the economy but about 'abundance'; that is, not about a certain area of social life but about certain grounds for intervention. But his theory provided him with three other sets of possible grounds for the regulation of any institution or activity. These were the other 'subordinate ends', namely security, subsistence and equality. It followed that when considerations of 'abundance' yielded no case for the regulation of some trade or industry, considerations of security (such as public health or the prevention of crimes) might produce a very strong case.

As it happened, Bentham was developing at about the same time a body of theory dealing with the conditions of security, and this suggested a number of grounds for intervention. It was the product of his speculation about indirect legislation and preventive police. In this part of his work he assumed that a well-ordered or secure community must be an effectively-policed one, and that effective policing required that the individual members of the community should be carefully identified, watched and guided into harmless occupations and amusements, and required that their rights and transactions should be carefully recorded and made accessible to proof. In his pursuit of those objects, he collected and listed all the measures of preventive police that he could find in the literature. He covered here most of the practices and devices known to Lamare, Bielfeld or Mildmay: the establishment of a regular guard or police force; the licensing of activities or trades; the lighting or clearing of lurking places; the keeping of records relating to travellers and their movements; the regulation of dealings in weapons, poisons, 'pick-lock keys' and gaming instruments; the dissemination of information about 'sharpers' tricks', prices and poisons, and about criminals and the offences that they committed; the establishment of standards of quality or quantity, and of marks attesting to the reaching of those standards; and the banning of improper advertisements.[24]

These devices did not go beyond his characterization of police in *Of Laws in General*; their significance was that they showed how many things he was prepared to contemplate, if not necessarily to recommend, that a government might do in its work of 'police for the prevention of offences', 'police of public amusements' or 'police for recent intelligence and information'. They showed, in particular, a willingness to contemplate quite extensive intervention in the economy in the form of the licensing of activities, the distribution of information and the setting and regulation of standards. But they did not amount to a definite programme of intervention; they represented instead a sort of armoury of weapons which governments might employ from time to time as security came to be threatened in various ways. Moreover, security itself was, like abundance, only one of four needs competing for the attention of governments. In the event of a conflict between the requirements of abundance and those of security, the final decision could be determined only in the standard utilitarian manner, by a weighing of the happiness to be attained or forgone by adoption of the respective courses of action. No general formula (such as 'laissez-faire') could foreshadow or predict the answer in any given case. This point is in fact well illustrated in the chapter on political economy that eventually found its way into the 'Vue Générale'.[25] It turned out not to relate at all to the content of economic policy or the scope of governmental action. It was concerned with the question whether economic legislation required, and should be gathered into, a specific branch of the comprehensive code. Bentham's negative answer was not a commitment to (or against) laissez-faire, but was simply a declaration that laws relating to the economy 'if there be any such' would be found in other parts of the code.

Although the theory of indirect legislation had such far-reaching implications for the state's functions, Bentham was not seeking guidance about that matter when he began to draft his essay on the subject. In his eyes, indirect legislation was focused rather on the techniques of government, the means of establishing social control. That continued to be the principal issue to which the argument of the essay was directed. The bulk of it was an analysis of and a commentary on the 'means of preventing offences' that he had gathered together in his lists of the devices of preventive police.

As Bentham had originally conceived the techniques of social control, indirect legislation was to be complemented by reward. Reward might even be regarded as a branch of indirect legislation, and at least shared with it the principle of uniting interest with duty – a principle that Bentham had formally adopted in drafting his *View of the Hard-Labour Bill*.[26] But in practice the two subjects tended to diverge, for the reason that he had mentioned in *Of Laws in General*: reward was more efficient as a means of inducing services than of preventing offences, while the prevention of offences was the more important task for a legislator. He was able to find some minor uses for reward in the work of regulating the community, notably as a means of encouraging the arts, sciences and inventions that would promote abundance.[27] But as a contribution to the theory of social control, what issued from reward was quite overshadowed by Bentham's analysis of the means of preventing offences in 'Indirect Legislation'.[28] His analysis took the form, as it so often did, of a classification of the various measures; in this case, a classification based on the different ways in which the measures might impede the commission of an offence or deter a potential offender. The most important and widely-applicable categories were to take away the power to commit an offence, to reduce the temptation to commit one, to facilitate knowledge of the fact of an offence, to increase the difficulty of escape by an offender, to diminish the sensibility of a potential offender to temptation, to increase the 'responsibility' (that is liability to punishment) of a potential offender, and to give more people an interest in preventing offences.[29] The whole classification and its accompanying commentary were a sort of manual of preventive police, summarizing for inexperienced or ill-informed governments the approaches that were widely employed, and providing guidance on their relative effectiveness and the circumstances in which they might most appropriately be used.

In elucidating the powers, functions and techniques of government, Bentham was examining different aspects of the impact of government on the community. But this did not exhaust his interest in government. He was almost equally interested in its internal organization and management and the community's impact on it. He now viewed this in terms of preventing 'misrule' or 'abuses of authority'. 'Misrule' was formally equivalent to the 'breach of trust' and the 'despotism' that he had referred to in his major works, but it was much more than a formal category. It was a ubiquitous tendency, engendered not only by the natural inclinations of governments but also by a mass of vested interests that encouraged them to follow those inclinations. He described these forces most clearly in his early writings on religion. As James Steintrager has remarked, these writings reveal him to have been fully aware of 'the cause of opposition to reform that he was later to term interest-begotten and office-begotten prejudice', and in particular to have been aware of the ways in which the political authorities and the Church gave each other mutual support in imposing obligations on the community and in discouraging opposition from the community.[30] Accordingly he looked for ways of counteracting all such forces and arrangements, as well as for techniques for improving the internal efficiency of governments.

He looked for and found them mainly in the places where he had sought enlightenment about the government's impact on the community, namely in his speculations about indirect legislation, reward and political economy. The most fruitful of these proved to be indirect legislation. In his essay on that subject he discovered many devices that could be used as weapons against misrule. Some of these were scattered through the chapters in which he discussed the several principles of indirect legislation, and he then gathered most of them together in a separate chapter on 'General

Precautions against Abuses of Authority'. He had worked them out sufficiently early to permit him to apply them directly to constitutional law in his drafts for the political sections of his 'Projet'. He provided there both an extensive analysis of misrule, and a slightly sharper and more radical account of the precautions against it. But the former did not get beyond his working papers and the latter was in the chapter on 'Politique' that he eliminated from his final plan for the 'Projet-Forme'.[31]

His precautions were, in general, adaptations of the devices of preventive police to official life. In his terminology, most of them were means of increasing the liability of an offender to punishment, or means of facilitating knowledge of an offence. As he went about the work of adaptation, his notion of official life itself became more complex. He saw, and stressed, that there were two sorts of abuses or problems: those stemming from the inadequate control of the sovereign or supreme power over his subordinates, from their disobedience and failure to execute his will; and those stemming from the misbehaviour of the supreme power itself.[32] In the course of this argument, he experimented with a new approach to supremacy, in which he suggested that it referred only to the relations among the different institutions and persons within the government, one of whom must be supreme and the others subordinate. This permitted him to make the point, which had always been implicit in his definition of a political society, that the sovereign was dependent on the people and on their obedience.[33] In the end, however, he did not organize his discussion of precautions around the distinction between the abuses committed by the supreme power and those committed by the subordinates. While he recognized that some rules or devices might apply exclusively to the head of state, he thought that most would be equally useful in protecting the people against the supreme power and in enabling the supreme power to subdue and keep in order its subordinates.[34] So he cast his analysis of precautions in general terms. But as he proceeded with it, the distinction began to reappear.

Some of his precautions were directed to the ways in which governments should organize themselves. Bentham found something to say for both 'dividing power into divers branches' and 'distributing particular branches of power each among divers sharers'.[35] The first point was a plea for a departmental structure of government, in which the legislators, the judges and the military would be distinct persons. The second pointed to the advantage of the collegial mode of administration. These were surprising doctrines in view of Bentham's hostility to the separation of powers and his insistence (in the essay on indirect legislation as elsewhere) on individual responsibility as a vital weapon against misconduct. They clearly troubled Dumont, who took some care when preparing the material for publication to add explanations and distinctions which reconciled it with Bentham's views about responsibility and the separation of powers. It is likely that Dumont was right, and that Bentham intended the division of power to be no more than a separation of *functions* which would leave undisturbed the supremacy of the Legislature, and that he intended to apply the collegial principle to the Legislature but not to administration. But these remain rather puzzling parts of his argument, for he indicated or hinted at the relevant distinctions rather than stating them in his usually incisive manner. He supplemented these proposals by suggesting that officials should be moved frequently from one location to another so that they could not build up local connections which might corrupt or protect them, that the power of appointment to any office should be separated from the power of dismissal, and that the exercise of power by subordinates should be made subject to 'rules and formalities'. He had in mind here two sorts of rules: 'the one limiting the cause for which such or such a power shall be exerted; the other the formalities to be observed in its exertion'.[36] It is not clear why he regarded these as a form of *indirect* legislation, but he included them consistently in his drafts and his plans for the treatment of that branch of legislation.

A second set of precautions consisted of various forms of information and publicity, including the 'setting of marks...upon all public stores and other articles of property that are occupied in trust'[37] and the 'publicity of state proceedings'.[38] The proceedings of the state that were to be publicized were the fees payable for official transactions, the duties of officers, public accounts, judicial proceedings, proposed legislation, the reasons on which measures were grounded and 'a view of the data referred to by those reasons'.[39] It was at this point that he began to introduce the activity of the community into his account of government. The policy that he was advocating was what is now known as 'open government', and he was treating the participation and at some points the initiative of members of the community as an indispensable part of its working.

The community's participation was required firstly in order to bring to the notice of the sovereign any abuses of authority – any forms of disobedience – committed by his subordinates. For this purpose Bentham proposed that members of the public should be allowed and encouraged to send information and petitions to the relevant authorities. He took a particular interest in the acceptability of anonymous information (less as evidence of misbehaviour than as a warning to be on the alert for evidence) and he argued in general that 'the channel of communication' between ruler and ruled must be kept 'as free and unclogged as possible'.[40] He was thus far viewing the people as agents of the sovereign, and as means of enhancing its power over its own servants. He also advocated, however, liberty of the press and rights of assembly and association, which would enable the people to share their information with each other and make their views and preferences known to the government.[41] These proposals amounted to a reiteration of the conditions of freedom in government that he had earlier advocated. He carried his argument a little further by speculating tentatively about the use 'in certain cases' of the device of the secret ballot, and about measures against bribery and the corruption of electors.[42] In these respects the people would no longer be acting on behalf of the sovereign but would be acting on their own behalf against the sovereign. He now believed that privileges and liberties 'which are conceded by the wisdom and generosity of the rulers of a community are certainly not as secure as those which are extracted from their impatience or relinquished by their fears'.[43]

In the same series of writings he employed briefly and unobtrusively an important theoretical innovation. This was a subtle reinterpretation of the Whigs' notion of 'influence'. When Dunning, Burke or other Whigs complained about influence, they meant the use of Royal patronage to manipulate the Legislature and thus to disturb the balance of the mixed constitution. Bentham was not interested in maintaining the mixed constitution, but he was perturbed by the growth of the Executive's power at the expense of the Legislature's. His first response to it (apparently in 1780) was to try to incorporate a general notion of influence in his theory by treating it as a particular kind of legal power and thus finding a place for it in his legal categories. But he distinguished it from other powers in a way that set it somewhat apart from the operations of the legal structure: its distinguishing feature was that its methods and instruments were not reserved to government by law but were such 'as persons in general are not prohibited from applying'. (The 'power of punishment', by contrast, did belong to government, for the use of any of its methods by private individuals 'would constitute an offence'.)[44] This opened the way for him to look at it as a set of forces operating or arising outside the legal structure. He took that additional and significant step in the course of preparing his abortive chapter on 'Politique' for the 'Projet'. Instead of trying to analyse it as a legal phenomenon, he began to inquire directly into the sources and possessors of influence. He named as its sources, for example, the ability of a patron to appoint clients to or to dismiss them from desirable offices, the ability to free them from obligations to serve in undesirable ones, the ability (derived from wealth or other advantages) to perform other discretionary services for them, or the possession of a reputation for wisdom. Any of these things, he thought, could act as a non-legal 'source of motives' or a means of determining behaviour. He then recognized five classes of persons who might possess influence: women, servants, persons in a superior position, persons in an inferior position and the clergy.[45] Apart from these points, which appeared in his draft as a series of jottings rather than a connected text, he made little of the subject at that time, but it added another, and more directly political, dimension to a theory which up to that time had been conducted almost exclusively in legal terms.

In setting the community to work either for or against the sovereign, Bentham was seeing misrule as essentially the 'abuses of authority' which he highlighted in the title of his chapter in 'Indirect Legislation'. That was probably the predominant strain in his thinking in the 1780s, but another element was present too. He recognized that 'the trustees of the people [might] swerve from the line of their duty' either by choosing the wrong objective or 'by making a wrong choice with regard to the means'.[46] Accordingly when he began to specify forms of misrule, he took account of deficiencies in knowledge and ultimately deficiencies in power, including the resources available to the sovereign. He listed among the sources of misrule 'ignorance on the part of persons in office', 'improper choice of persons to fill offices', 'want of active talent', 'want of judgement and firmness' and finally 'mis-management through negligence – through bad judgement or misapplication'.[47] These ideas were linked with important ten-dencies in his thought in other and sometimes productive ways.

His interest in the knowledge – and ignorance – of rulers had already appeared in the *View of the Hard-Labour Bill* and in his plans for the Office of Intelligence and the Shipbuilding Board. The last two of these were intended to collect and sift information that would facilitate decision making. He hoped similarly that the prison-administrators envisaged in Blackstone's and Eden's draft Penitentiary Bill would collect statistics relating to crimes and criminals and would thus furnish '*data* for the legislator to go to work upon...[forming] a kind of political barometer by which the effect of every legislative operation relative to the sub-ject may be indicated and made palpable'.[48] He was here sharing, as we saw in chapter 2, a common eighteenth-century attitude or prejudice; and in his own theory it was closely connected with the logic of the will. He followed James Harris in believing that 'a sentence of interrogation is a particular species' of a sentence of volition, and he accordingly recognized within the logic of the will a subdivision 'which concerns the forms of interrogation [having a more particular regard] to the...business of collecting verbal information: a process subservient to the business as well of the legislative as of the executive departments'.[49] The logic of the will provided a theoretical base (a mode of legitimation) for the information-collecting activities that he favoured, and for his con-demnation of official ignorance.

His interest in talent, judgement and misapplication led him in a different direction. In stressing those points, he was beginning to view government as a set of resources which would only yield the best results if one paid attention to their quality and to methods of combining and using them. This opened the way to a new form of interaction between the theory of government, political economy and the theory of reward, for an important theme common to reward and political economy was precisely a concern with resources and their management.

The theory of reward had failed to make a major contribution to the control of the community because it was limited in practice to situations in which services were being supplied. Bentham found a new role for it by focusing it directly and exclusively on such situations. He made it an analysis of the means by which, and the terms on which, services could be secured, and thus gave it an economic (or market) orientation rather than a legal one. His essay on reward tended to become a manual for any person or institution (including a government) who wanted to secure or control services; that is, typically, an employer of labour. In that form it became a complement to his production-economics. When the two were put together, the theory of production and the principles of reward constituted a wide-ranging account of the use of measures in enterprises and activities, a general guide to maximizing output or to performing tasks at minimum real costs.

Production-economics contributed the major or fundamental parts of the combined theory. It was essentially a classification, in which the principal headings were the kinds of ways in which output might be increased or a work might be performed more economically, such as:

> to increase the number of men capable of working;
> to increase the amount of work done;
> to increase the effect of work;
> to increase the volume of productive capital;
> to employ capital in the most advantageous ways.[50]

He broke some of these down further into several sub-headings or specific methods. Thus he identified nine methods of increasing the effect of labour, and another nine methods of increasing the volume of productive capital. The former group consisted of an increase in the dexterity and knowledge of workmen, the saving of time spent in comings and goings, the invention of machines, the use of the cheapest form of power, the simplification of inter-mediate processes, the saving of materials by re-using them or using them simultaneously in other processes, the use of cheaper substitute materials, the improvement of the quality of materials without making them dearer, and a reduction in the cost of trans-port. Bentham's plans for increasing the amount of work done included the bringing of the idle ('fainéants') and other spare resources into productive employment, and the use of 'attractive' methods (that is, incentives or rewards) rather than coercive methods to ensure diligence. Among the possible attractive measures, he mentioned favourably piece- or task-work systems of payment.[51]

The principles of reward extended and completed this argument by dealing more exclusively and at greater length with the remuneration of labour. Bentham tried to catalogue the different sorts of things that would function as remuneration, to indicate the issues and alternatives facing the potential remunerator, and to provide rules for his guidance. He devised in the end two sets of rules, for he felt constrained to draw a distinction between ordinary rewards (including wages) on the one hand and salaries on the other, and to treat each kind separately.[52] The special characteristic of salaries, in Bentham's view, was that because they were fixed over some period, they could not function as a reward for performing any services but must be a reward for accepting a post or office. Because of this peculiarity, the rules for ordinary rewards could not apply to them without qualification.

The ordinary rules expressed a general attitude and sometimes led to more specific conclusions. The attitude was predictably a utilitarian one: that reward was and must be judged as an instrument, a mode of influencing behaviour, and that the 'matter of reward' consisted of scarce resources, which should be husbanded and should not be distributed gratuitously or as an expression of gratitude for actions that had already been performed. The conclusions included the propositions that employers should seek alternatives to money as a form of reward, that rewards should be so exactly proportioned as to provide enough but no more than enough incentive to produce the desired result, and that they should include provision for penalties for failure or non-performance. If these points did not provide a perfectly clear guide to action, they did firmly point towards some and rule out certain other courses and practices. For example they sanctioned, and provided a rationale for, the systems of piece-work and bonuses that he had recommended in his work on political economy;[53] and they repudiated one traditional approach of governments to reward, namely that which sanctioned the discretionary bestowal of honours and favours on persons who had performed great or little services. (Bentham would have required at least a regular *scale* of such honours and benefits, so that a general or diplomat or court favourite would be able to calculate rationally how hard he must exert himself in order to qualify for a step in the peerage or whatever else he might aim at.) He provided further guidance of the same kind in his rules for salaries. After repeating his advice to seek economy and to unite interest with duty, he went on to counsel employers to make the real the same as the nominal reward (in modern terms, to eliminate fringe benefits or – and this seemed a more real problem to Bentham – fringe and unacknowledged burdens); to make the beneficiaries of any service bear as far as possible the cost of providing it, but not to allow fees and perquisites to employees; and to set salaries at a level that would serve as a barrier against corruption. Like the general rules, these set limits to what the wise employer would do, though they did not provide him with a blueprint for action.

The theory of resource-usage which emerged from Bentham's production-economics and his speculations about reward was not a theory of government nor a definite part of such a theory. Its apparent bias was towards the industrial and commercial enterprises in which resources were being combined on an increasingly large scale and in increasingly complex ways during Bentham's lifetime, and its author certainly had such enterprises in mind. Its obvious line of development was towards the general theory of organization and management into which (after it had absorbed some of the principles of indirect legislation) it later evolved. But its propositions could fairly readily be applied to government, because Bentham had stated them in such general terms. His advice to save time in comings and goings or to facilitate knowledge of the fact of an offence was applicable in principle to government offices no less than to factories or to the community as a whole. And it is clear that Bentham grasped the point. The rules of reward were addressed to governments along with other employers. This was true especially of the rules for salaries, which he thought were more appropriate in government than in private employment. Even before he had completed his essays, he was applying some of the principles of reward and of indirect legislation to the official establishments that he was designing for his projected Shipbuilding Board and Office of Intelligence. He paid special attention to the systems of remuneration and to the systems of records in those bodies;[54] in these respects the essays were in part a generalization of his thinking in those schemes. And in his discussion of reward he included some points which related specifically and more or less exclusively to governments, points on which he unexpectedly took a line opposed to the emerging orthodoxy of the reformers with whom he usually agreed.

He presented a case for both the sale of official posts ('venality') to candidates for employment, and the 'farming' of official services and functions to private contractors ('entrepreneurs') as an alternative to direct management by the state.[55] He proceeded cautiously in these matters, purporting to provide a balanced view by bringing to light points that were often overlooked. He argued that the private contractor would have a greater interest than the government employee in doing the work efficiently, that a contractor would be more efficient than a government in supervising his own servants and agents, and that an official who invested his own capital in purchasing a post would have a heightened interest in retaining it and must be assumed to have an 'affection' for its duties. He assumed at all points that there would be an effective system of supervision and control to prevent mere exploitation or neglect of duty, and he assumed that the purchaser of an official post would not acquire a genuine 'freehold' in it but would be liable to ejection without compensation if he misbehaved. These were substantial components of a programme for the organization of government services, though of course much less than a total programme.

Although Bentham left them incomplete, the essays of the mid 1780s extended and rounded off the initial – the purely jurisprudential – phase in his thinking about government. They spelt out many of the ideas that he had canvassed but not developed in the early major works. At the same time they provided few prospects for further development along the same lines and through the use of the same techniques of analysis.

Bentham had used them to expand his utilitarian criteria for the functions and activities of government and to provide a large body of commentary on how they should be interpreted and applied. The original 'end' of utility had spawned the four subordinate ends of subsistence, equality, abundance and security, and Bentham had considered in some detail how at least two of those – security and abundance – might best be promoted. Mingled with this was an extensive account of, and a further commentary on, the devices and courses of action available to governments in their work of social control. This took the discussion beyond the functions of governments to their concrete activities, beyond the forms of behaviour that they sought to encourage or discourage to the sorts of things that they themselves might do in order to influence behaviour; but it remained at the level of principles, of rules, and often of alternatives among which governments must choose for themselves in the light of their own judgements.

Bentham had used the essays, too, to work towards a clearer understanding of constitutional law and the legal provision that he must make for government in a complete code of laws. He had identified offices, analogous to the 'conditions' of private life, as the elements of which governments must be composed, and he had provided a standard method for creating and analysing such entities. This consisted in the provisions governing six major points: modes of appointment; modes of dismissal or loss of office; rights; duties; 'incapacities'; 'formalities' or additional obligations. These, then, were the things that constitutional law must cover in any particular government.

In order to give a complete account of constitutional law, or a complete guide to it, Bentham would have had to go on systematically to consider the proper offices, their relations and each of the six major points. It can be said that, in the next forty years, this is what he did. But in the essays of the 1780s he made only a very tentative and very uneven beginning on the task. Nevertheless, some of the things that he said were already important or provided the foundations for either new generalizations or more specific conclusions in the future. The point that he tackled most directly was 'powers'. With a knowledge of the contents of the *Constitutional Code*, we can see that he was taking here a small step towards the analysis of administrative activities in that work; but the step was a very small one and the destination was still obscure. He found a good deal more to say about rights, duties, obligations and the relations among offices, although he did not attempt to deal with any of them exhaustively or in a general way. He touched on appointment and dismissal only glancingly, or by implication.

His consideration of rights, obligations and relationships was dictated by two concerns, each of which was an aspect of his utilitarian outlook. He wanted to ensure that governments should

devote themselves to maximizing utility and seeking the four
subordinate ends that served utility; and he wanted to ensure that
they did so in the most economical, least costly (and therefore
least painful) way. In most respects, his analogy between offices
and conditions implied that different offices were similar to each
other and should have similar or common rights and obligations,
but he recognized one important distinction among them. This
was a difference in rank, between supreme and subordinate offices.
Correspondingly, he recognized that the offices of different ranks
should have some special rights and obligations appropriate to
the relationship in which they stood to each other.

In moving towards the specification of particular rights and
duties, he assumed that the task of keeping the government to the
lines he had laid down for it was very like the task of policing
the community, and that the same devices of preventive police
were applicable to the community and the government. This
meant that the most general obligation on the government and on
each office within it was to be available for policing, to make itself
available to observation and – in the event of an offence – to
punishment and correction. He prescribed two forms and sources
of observation and correction: one deriving from the community,
and extending over the whole government; and one deriving from
the supreme office and extending over the subordinate offices.
It followed that the supreme office must possess special rights –
as yet, unspecified – to regulate and control its subordinates.

The analogy between regulating the government and policing
the community is, however, imperfect or at least incomplete.
It gives too little weight to the second aspect of Bentham's utilitarian outlook, the pursuit of economy or efficiency. In this respect
the task facing the government, and especially the supreme office,
was less like preventive police than like the work of a factory
manager seeking to employ and deploy labour and other resources
as efficiently as possible. So Bentham had to extend his strategy
for the sovereign or supreme official, to make it include the
efficiency-oriented principles and practices of reward and of
production-economics. And these would have to be incorporated
in the rights and obligations, including the rights to remuneration,
attached to the several offices.

In these ways, then, Bentham's further explorations in jurisprudence produced a clearer idea of the constitutional framework

of government, and made a start on the work of filling in and bridging over the spaces in the frame. Yet it is equally true that the same explorations more or less exhausted the approach through legal analysis that he had adopted. There remained little more that he could say about powers, functions, methods of exposing crimes or of remunerating labour, at the level at which he was then working. In order to carry the argument much further in any direction, it was necessary to take up more concrete issues of policy or to consider the character of particular institutions. As a theorist of government, Bentham might have remained stranded at the point he had reached. In practice, things turned out otherwise. He soon began to devote much less of his time to questions of abstract jurisprudence or even to his cherished code and more to particular issues, and he began to pay more attention to the extra-legal forces and processes in political life that he had tentatively noticed as forms of 'influence'. The transition from the one kind of topic to the other was made easy by the fact that parts of the essays authorized or prompted it. In particular the first of the new series of works – the plan for the Panopticon – was a direct off-shoot of his work on political economy and of the notion of 'farming' that he had developed in the essay on reward. Once he was set on that course, other events continued to keep him on it until the breakdown of the Panopticon scheme forced him to re-examine his whole body of work, and to think again about how he should proceed for the remainder of his life.

5

FROM PRINCIPLES TO PRACTICE: THE *PANOPTICON* AND ITS COMPANIONS

The chronological division between the two different kinds of speculation is marked roughly by Bentham's return to England from Russia in the winter of 1787–88. The change was not immediate or absolute. He did not immediately give up his work on the principles of jurisprudence, and he took it up again from time to time in the 1790s, possibly in order to help Dumont in the preparation of the *Traités de législation*. But after 1789 he was occupied mainly in studies of policies and institutions, above all in his work on the Panopticon. The shift in the pattern of his interests was in part the consequence of what he had done in Russia, but in part the consequence of a mass of other events; both public events such as the French Revolution, and events occurring in his own life or within the boundaries of his family. It made the 1790s the period in which he advanced most rapidly towards the detailed contents of the *Constitutional Code*.

The first edition of the *Defence of Usury* had been published by the time Bentham got back to England, and his draft of the first Panopticon essay was then also complete.[1] The modest but definite success of the former work encouraged him to think of a second edition of it, and this in turn led him to raise new economic issues in his own mind.[2] He was eventually able to find time to take these up, and to be drawn into the consideration of important problems in the field of money and banking as well as into attempts to draft elementary outlines of (or introductions to) political economy. His Panopticon essay seemed likely for a time to be still-born, but in 1790 Lansdowne arranged that he should discuss it with Sir John Parnell, Chancellor of the Irish Exchequer, who undertook to recommend the scheme to the Irish Government.[3] Bentham took the opportunity to publish the work, and to write and publish two 'postscripts' to it in which he looked more closely at some of its practical details. The Irish scheme came to nothing, but Bentham turned his attention to the British Government and by September 1792 had secured what he regarded as a commitment on its part to enter into a contract which would authorize him to construct a prison according to the plan set out in his essay, and to conduct it for profit on the terms foreshadowed there. It is well known that the scheme foundered in the end, but that before Bentham broke off negotiations in 1801 he devoted an enormous amount of his time and his energies to it.[4] Much of his time was absorbed in the purely commercial aspects of the scheme, including the securing of land, the raising of money, the construction of the prefabricated building and the completion of the legal business associated with it. But Bentham, although he entered enthusiastically (and, as far as one can judge, pretty efficiently) into these practical matters, was never a man who recognized a barrier between theory and practice or who was willing to cease speculating about practice. He continued, in his working papers, to carry forward the kind of reasoning that he had employed in his postscripts to the original essay.

In the meantime, he had become caught up, fruitfully but rather mysteriously, in the enthusiasms and passions surrounding the French Revolution. He had resolved to write about, and for, the reform movement in France as early as January 1789[5] and (partly in collaboration with Samuel Romilly) he had produced a good deal of material on parliamentary procedure and other subjects by the middle of that year.[6] This material was followed by – partly organized into – a series of published and unpublished works related more or less closely to French problems. The published works were the *Essay on Political Tactics* and the *Draught of a New Plan for the Organisation of the Judicial Establishment in France*.[7] The unpublished included his biting attack on the Declaration of Rights, 'Anarchical Fallacies', some drafts of written constitutions and some related speculations about representation and other constitutional issues. The mystery concerns a cycle in his attitudes to the Revolution and to electoral arrangements, in which he seems first to have adopted and then to have retreated from a programme of radical electoral reform.[8]

After 1793, he did not write much about France or general constitutional issues, but other topics soon moved in to replace them in his thinking. Some of these were prompted by Samuel Bentham and the course of his career. Samuel had come back to England in May 1791, and he and Jeremy intended that he should be a partner in the Panopticon enterprise. The delay in getting the Panopticon established left him unemployed. As a (supposedly temporary) measure he secured appointment as an inspector of the naval dockyards, and from 1796 he was Inspector-General of Naval Works. In that post he formed (or perhaps began with) a conviction that the management of the dockyards was both corrupt and inefficient, and he set himself the task of removing the sources of corruption and of substituting efficient for inefficient methods and procedures. Many of his proposals were technical, relating to matters of design and the employment of machinery; but others concerned matters of administration or management, such as methods of remuneration (including traditional per-quisites), systems of accounting and modes of supervision.[9] The centre-piece of his administrative proposals was a new system for the management of timber, the principal raw material of the dock-yards. He called on Jeremy to act as his draftsman and adviser in preparing his proposals for submission to the Admiralty. Jeremy thought very carefully about these matters, which were closely related to problems on which he was concurrently working, and he contributed a great deal to the completed proposals.

On his own initiative, Jeremy returned briefly to the subject of religion and the Church Establishment, and turned his mind to questions relating to the poor laws and their administration. The circumstances in which he began again to look critically at the Church, and the nature of the works on it that he planned, are both obscure. The source may have been the anti-clerical measures of the French Revolution, or the attempts made on behalf of the English Protestant Dissenters in 1787–90 to have the Test Acts repealed or modified. There is a little evidence to sup-port the second hypothesis, though it is not at all conclusive. His friend James Trail had drawn his attention to the campaign against the Test Acts while he was still in Russia,[10] and he focused attention on the question of dissent (both Catholic and Protestant) in the subtitle of one of his fragmentary manuscripts, a projected 'Principles of Ecclesiastical Polity'. A second (or alternative version of the same) work was a study of 'Church Reform' or 'Church Liturgy'.[11] These form an important link between his early writings on religion and the *Church of Englandism and Its Catechism Examined* which he published in 1818. Their relevance to our theme lies in the facts that they treated 'ecclesiastical polity' as a branch of or cognate with constitutional law (thus retaining the attitude he had adopted in his 'Projet') and that they treated the Church as an institution and its clergy as public officers whose powers, duties, remuneration and efficiency should be scrutinized and controlled in the same way as those of any other public officer. But Bentham seems not to have proceeded very far with these works before 1800.

The genesis of his interest in the poor laws is clearer, and his interest in them was much longer sustained.[12] The scarcity and dearness of foodstuffs in 1795–96 had stimulated public debate on the problems of the poor and had caused many measures to be canvassed or adopted, including the famous Speenhamland decision to supplement wages in Berkshire. In February 1796 Bentham was prompted to define his own position on some of the issues. The debate was then focused on Samuel Whitbread's abortive wage-regulation Bill of 1795 and Pitt's equally abortive poor-law Bill of 1796. Bentham began by analysing Pitt's Bill (of which he had apparently been given a copy or summary by Wilberforce), identifying its main features and drafting critical notes on some of them, for example 'the small-establishment system', the 'home-allowance system', and the 'donation of land clause'.[13] He then turned away from this purely critical work, and in the next couple of months wrote three short 'Essays on the Poor Laws' in which he took up the questions of principle.[14] He resolved finally to write a more detailed and comprehensive work which would incorporate some material from the Essays and perhaps some of the criticism of the 'small-establishment' systems that he had formulated in reading Pitt's Bill.[15] In the course of drafting it, he gradually extended its scope until it became three separate pieces: 'Pauper Systems Compared', 'Pauper Management Improved', and 'Observations on the Poor Bill introduced by Mr Pitt'. He finished the 'Observations' in February 1797, and circulated copies of it but did not publish it. He published a large part of 'Pauper Management Improved' in the *Annals of Agriculture* (vols. xxx and xxxi), but left it incomplete. He drafted a large body of material for 'Pauper Systems Compared' but neither finished nor published it.

While he was in the middle of this work, in December 1796, he became acquainted with Patrick Colquhoun, the pioneer statistician and social reformer who had been a metropolitan police magistrate since 1792.[16] Colquhoun shared many of Bentham's interests and attitudes, including his interest in the poor laws. He supplied Bentham with a memorandum of some sixteen pages in which he advocated a system of 'improved and enlarged' workhouses and made many suggestions about its management.[17] He also guided Bentham's thinking in another direction, towards the subject of preventive police. Colquhoun had recently published the first two editions of his *Treatise on the Police of the Metropolis*.[18] This work (and the earlier unpublished writings on which it was based) could be summed up as a wide-ranging exercise in indirect legislation, in the sense in which Bentham defined and understood that term. One of its central features was an attempt to prevent offences against property by harassing receivers of stolen goods and by establishing a co-ordinated network of police authorities throughout the country. The attack on receivers consisted essentially in various measures designed to facilitate knowledge of the fact of an offence. It appears that Colquhoun had been trying from 1793 onwards to give legislative form to these proposals, at first in a single Bill 'for more effectively securing his Majesty's Stores against embezzlement in the Dockyards and other Public Repositories', then in a more widely-drawn Bill dealing with stolen goods, and finally in a set of complementary measures.[19] Of the latter group, one was intended to establish the police authority and to define its priorities and duties, while others were to deal with the dockyards, the special problems of pilfering and related offences on the River Thames, counterfeiting, horse-dealing, gaming and the keeping of lodging-houses.

In many of its details as well as its broad approach, Colquhoun's scheme resembled what Bentham was advocating in his still unpublished essay on 'Indirect Legislation'. When this fact became clear to the two men, Bentham agreed to try to put Colquhoun's measures into an acceptable legal form. He had recently been drafting legislation to be submitted to Parliament in connection with the Panopticon, in collaboration with the eminent lawyer Charles Butler, and he felt fully competent to undertake the work. He proceeded to draft two complete Bills, one a measure entitled the Police Revenue Bill which tackled the general problems of policing the metropolis and country districts, and the other a narrower Thames (or Marine) Police Bill establishing regulations for the handling of cargo on the Thames and creating a body of men to enforce them. The second of these eventually passed into law, after some revisions negotiated between the Home Office and Charles Abbot, Bentham's step-brother. To the Bills themselves Bentham added a mass of summarizing and explanatory material, the most important of which was a set of 'Notes on the Police Bill' that in draft form amounted to more than two hundred pages. He did this work secretly, because his disputes with Ministers and officials over the Panopticon scheme had soured his relations with the Government, and he feared that the association of his name with Colquhoun's plans would discredit them in the eyes of the Home Office.

It is not hard to see how each part of this very voluminous body of writings, from political economy to police, was derived from and was related to Bentham's writings on jurisprudence. But it differed greatly in character from most of his earlier work. While it still contained some discussion of principle, it included very much more discussion of the application of principles and several impressive attempts to provide the legal and administrative means for giving practical expression to them. Some works were concerned from the outset with the means of implementation. Among the earliest of these was the plan for the *French Judicial Establishment* a very assured piece of draftsmanship which, as J. H. Burns has remarked, displays 'the practical constructive side of Bentham at its best'.[20] His drafting of the Police Bills for Colquhoun was of the same kind. In some other cases, what began as a discussion of principles went on to cover questions of implementation. There are some examples of this process in his work on political economy, where he prescribed quite detailed arrangements for the administration of the escheat-duty and for the issue of the circulating annuities (low-denomination negotiable securities) that he was urging the Government to introduce. There are still more striking examples in his writings about pauper-management, which were probably the most daring and imaginative of all his works in the 1790s, and in his constitutional writings which proceeded rapidly from a consideration of the separation of powers to sophisticated and technical schemes of parliamentary

procedure and electoral arrangements. The gap between the
abstractions of *Of Laws in General* and the patient draftsmanship
of the *Constitutional Code* was a large one, but it was substantially bridged in 1789–90 and was almost completely bridged by
1800.

In his essay on 'Anarchical Fallacies' (which was not published
until after his death) he stated more bluntly than ever before that
law and the legal system were the only reliable sources of rights
and protectors of security. The form of his argument in the essay
was a demonstration that the several Declarations of Rights were
riddled with confusions and ambiguities because they tried to
employ natural-law rather than utilitarian moral criteria, or tried
to use both at the same time and to treat them as equivalent.
The *point* of the argument, however, was not simply to defend
utilitarianism against natural law. It was to defend positive law,
the sovereign's law, against forms of argument and consequent
claims that might undermine its authority. '*Right*, the substantive
right is the child of law: from *real* laws come real rights', he
argued.[21] Natural rights were dangerous because they were 'anti-
legal rights, the mortal enemies of law, the subverters of government and the assassins of security', and 'must ever be the rights
of anarchy – the order of chaos'.[22] The preservation of the
sovereign's law, and the preservation of the integrity of the system
that created and sustained law, were necessary elements in his
political programme.

   In his account of the legal system he now adopted formally a
point that he had advanced tentatively in his 'Projet' manuscripts.
He divided sovereignty into two parts, a superior 'sovereign constituent power' and an inferior 'sovereign efficient power', and
he located the former in the 'body of the people'.[23] He did not,
however, abandon his earlier distinction between 'governors' and
'subjects'. Instead he buttressed it with a new distinction between
the power of determining who the governors should be – in which
'it is not only possible but easy and expedient' that everyone
should have a share – and 'the power of making laws, of governing, of carrying on the business of government' which only those
with a 'particular education' could exercise.[24] The legislative
sovereign was thus demoted from its previous pre-eminence in
society, to become the 'sovereign efficient power' or supreme ele-

ment in the system of government. The distinction between the two sorts of sovereignty functioned as one of the theoretical props for his democratic programme, but he did not drop it when he became less radical after 1792 or 1793. It remained a permanent element in his thinking. In this new situation, the Legislature functioned as the agent of the people, but it enjoyed a plenitude of power with which to do so, and it maintained its superiority over the Judiciary and the Executive. Indeed, Bentham specified certain judicial powers which the Legislature should itself exercise, including powers to punish ordinary judges in the event of their misbehaviour.[25]

The supremacy of the sovereigns, both constituent and efficient, implied the subordination of other elements in the system. Bentham stressed that point in new assaults on the separation of powers (which the Declaration of Rights of 1789 had endorsed in its sixteenth article), and he provided a new treatment of subordination. He reinterpreted it as 'dependence' – legitimate dependence – and he linked it negatively with 'influence', the non-legal force that he had begun to analyse in his early drafts for *Of Laws in General* and in his working-papers for 'Projet'.

He now described influence rather obscurely as 'an effect resulting from the indirect exercise of power to the accomplishment of an object different from and collateral to that which is the object and obvious end of its institution'.[26] He was striving here to make two points: to continue to see it as a form of power analogous to but distinct from law; and to label it clearly as an illegitimate and harmful form of power. He attacked it on two grounds, firstly as an invasion of the individuality of the persons subject to it, and secondly as a perversion of the system of government. He expressed his first objection by identifying it as the action of 'will on will', and distinguishing it from persuasion by rational argument which he called 'the influence of understanding on understanding' and which he saw as legitimate.[27] The subordination of one will to another seemed to him to be an intolerable and indefensible denial of individuality. The distinction between it and the legitimate influence of understanding on understanding became a vital part of his theory, enabling him to proceed to a more comprehensive analysis of influence as he recognized more and more situations which could not be described as the operation of understanding. His second objection to influence was that it

undermined responsibility.[28] Where it existed on any considerable
scale it was incompatible with the sovereign legislator's control of
the machinery and purposes of government, and incompatible
with the constituent sovereign's control of the whole legal system.
Bentham's antidote to such threats to good government was to
seek the 'dependence of all power-holders on the people',[29] and to
reduce the dependence of any part of the people on the power-
holders. 'In so far as a man who is independent has power,' he
argued, 'he will make use of it for his own benefit; in so far as he
is dependent upon anyone he will find himself obliged to employ
it for the benefit of him on whom he depends'.[30] Thus by gaining
clients or dependants, a patron-official could bind them to himself
and make them responsive to his will and instruments of his self-
interest; but equally, if he could be shorn of resources of that
kind and made dependent on the public he could be turned into
an agent of the public interest. As a constitutional force, dependence on the public would be effective where the separation or
division of powers could not: 'the efficient cause of liberty or of
good government which is but another name for the same thing is
not the division of power among the different classes of men
entrusted with it, but the dependence direct or indirect of all of
them on the body of the people'.[31] The separation of powers was
dangerous precisely because it compromised that dependence and
created islands of independence within the constitution. Similarly
the dependence of power-holders on the people could help to
secure real rights, rights recognized in positive law, where claims
to natural rights could destroy them.

In his radical phase, Bentham relied heavily on popular election
as a means of making the rulers dependent on the people. But
even at the time of his greatest enthusiasm for electoral reform he
did not propose to rely on it exclusively or to make election universal throughout the official establishment. He continued to see
as equally necessary the precautions against the misuse of authority that he had advocated on previous occasions, including the
'publicity of state proceedings', freedom of speech, of assembly,
of writing and printing, and 'the liberty of communication for
whatever is written or printed, under which is included not only
the liberty of the post office but of every other channel of con-
veyance'.[32] And he was always prepared to concede that dependence might be 'indirect' as well as 'direct'. This meant that he

envisaged the possibility of a line of subordination and dependence, in which the sovereign efficient power would be directly dependent on the people, and would control other elements in the system on behalf of the people and in accordance with the people's wishes, but not necessarily by the use of the same weapons as ensured its own dependence. In practice, he endorsed the idea of election to the Judiciary, but simultaneously explored other methods of controlling subordinate officials. When he retreated from radicalism and began to find some objectionable features in democratic elections, he retained in his programme most of the other measures that he had intended to employ as complements to the electoral system.[33]

Bentham's studies of institutions and problems did not require him to consider the structure of government in a systematic way. In his draft constitutions he set out to do little more than match the performance of the French National Assembly, which had provided only a sketchy outline of the proposed institutions of government other than the Legislature. His other writings, though often very detailed and carefully-drafted, were mostly focused too narrowly to lead up to or imply a treatment of the structure of government as a whole. Nevertheless both kinds of works contain evidence that additional ideas about that structure were present or were taking shape in his mind.

As we have seen, he was still working with the orthodox framework of Legislature, Judiciary and Executive, and he wanted to turn it into an efficient instrument for the making and enforcement of law, to ensure within it the supremacy of the Legislature, and to make it truly national in scope. These objectives dictated that the Legislature should be the centrepiece of his programme, that the Judiciary should be the next most important branch of government, that the institutions and operations at the periphery should receive attention along with those at the centre, and that the Executive – as little more than an appendage to the system – should receive only cursory attention. But he found that he could not ignore the Executive altogether. It was forced to his attention from time to time by his fear of influence and official independence, and later by his interest in specific functions which – it turned out – could not properly be performed by the Legislature or the Judiciary. The first of these factors weighed more heavily with him. His thinking was still affected (perhaps more than he realized) by the Whigs' outlook, and he saw 'the influence of the administrative power over the legislative'[34] as the most pervasive and objectionable of the forms of influence against which the community must contend. Similarly he feared that, even if the Executive could be deprived of influence at that level, it might retain an area of independence and thus an opportunity to behave in a self-interested way. An efficient plan for making the rulers dependent on the people must therefore encompass the Executive as well as the Legislature and must specify the ways in which the Executive would be stripped of independence and rendered totally responsive to the Legislature. But Bentham was reluctant to pursue this argument very far at that time, or was perhaps confident that the solution to the problem was relatively easy. The outcome was that he produced substantial plans for legislative arrangements and processes, a highly sophisticated programme for a nation-wide judicial system, a scheme for local government which (like his French models) treated it as an extension of the central government, and a more sporadic and less comprehensive discussion of the Executive and its parts.

Most of what he had to say about the Legislature concerned either its internal operations or its relations with the electorate, and except at a few points did not impinge directly on its place in the general structure of government. The exceptions related to its institutional form, its functions in the system and its share of the powers of government.

As part of his campaign against the influence of the Executive, he wanted to avoid conferring on the latter any executive power as such, that is any power which it might claim against the Legislature or any power which it might turn into influence. He therefore tried to reserve to the Legislature all powers that had a legislative character. In particular, he allocated to it the powers of declaring war and making treaties, which had often been appropriated by the Executive but which he deemed to be a form of commanding or legislating.[35] Consistently with his hostility to checks and balances in government, he favoured a unicameral form of Legislature. He intended that its activities and procedure – prescribed at great length in his essay on 'political tactics' – would be adapted entirely to the roles of decision making for and supervision of the whole system.[36] But like Turgot, Necker (and to a smaller extent the draftsmen of the National Assembly) he did not believe that *all* political decisions could conveniently be made at the centre; he thought that there must be subordinate decision makers to fill out and complete the centre's work. This brought him to the first and major element in his conception of local government. He proposed a network of local authorities in the form of Provincial legislatures and sub-Provincial legislatures distributed uniformly throughout the country. They were to be the creatures of the central legislative body but were to be capable of relieving it of responsibility for matters of purely local concern.[37] Local government, as Bentham conceived it, was to be dependent on, to support and to resemble the Legislature, not the Executive, in the national system of government.

His ambition to provide a complete, uniform, nation-wide set of institutions was still more apparent in his treatment of the Judiciary.[38] He was here commenting explicitly on a French official draft scheme and was undoubtedly influenced by its example, but he differed sharply from it in several important points. One of these was his preference for a 'geographical' over a 'functional' principle in the arrangement of jurisdiction; another was his rejection of the collegiate principle in favour of 'single-seatedness' in the composition of courts. He proposed a hierarchy of courts[39] running parallel to the system of local and departmental government established in France by the decrees of December 1789: Parish Courts, District Immediate and District Appellate Courts, and a Metropolitan or Supreme Court of Appeal. These were an alternative to the mass of courts dealing with particular branches of the law – Courts of Trade, Family-Tribunal, Judges of Police and so on – that the official committee had recommended. Bentham breached his geographical principle only by adding to his basic structure certain 'tribunals of exception', namely courts-martial, vessels at sea, ecclesiastical courts, and representative assemblies acting to maintain order in their own proceedings; these were clearly analogous to the 'particular codes' which he recognized within the comprehensive code of law. The courts were to be 'given authority over all sorts of persons and in every sort of cause', subject to the distinction between original and appellate jurisdiction and to the authority of the tribunals of exception.[40] To man and to serve the courts, he provided not only a body of judges but also two other classes of officials, namely pursuers-general (prosecutors) and defenders-general. The three groups were to constitute distinct but parallel classes within a single judicial service.[41] The whole judicial system was assured of independence from the King and was explicitly denied any 'share in legislative power'. But just as explicitly the judges were to be endowed with the 'suspensive power' whose merits Bentham had canvassed in *Of Laws in General,* and they were to judge the validity of the acts of the subordinate legislative assemblies.[42] The courts' procedure was to be uniform throughout the entire system.

In those parts of his constitutional schemes which dealt with the Executive, Bentham's main purpose was to complete the process of stripping it of sources of influence and of powers which belonged properly to the Legislature. His principal strategy was to concentrate on the question of powers, and to stick to the line that he had foreshadowed in the *Fragment on Government,* namely to make executive power a residual, consisting of 'whatever public power is not either legislative or judicial'.[43] He acknowledged again, as he had done in the *Fragment,* that fiscal and 'dispensatorial' powers might be of special interest to the Executive, but not that they would belong exclusively to it. In another set of writings, however, he qualified his opposition to its possession of legislative power. In his Police Revenue Bill he admitted that the Crown might properly determine from time to time a number of matters relating to the composition and operations of the central police authority, and that the authority itself should be allowed to issue instructions and regulations having the force of law. He provided at this point a general defence of the practice of 'subordinate legislation', and tried to set out the circumstances and conditions that would make it legitimate. The favourable circumstances were those that would render the matter unsuitable or too time-consuming for the national Legislature to handle, including the need for frequent and small changes in the law and the need to proceed with 'the help of *patterns*' (by which he seems to have meant printed forms and examples). The conditions he wanted to impose were that the regulations should apply to 'a particular class of persons' and that 'the topics on which the exercise of the power is to bear [should be] defined and specified'.[44]

He found still less to say about the components and internal structure of the Executive, but even here he was not completely without ideas. In some of his schemes we can see emerging a pattern in which the departments or agencies of the central government would make policy and would generally supervise an operation or activity, but would delegate execution of it to some other body or bodies. His clearest description of it was in one of his early essays on the Poor Law, where he suggested that the directing element in the system of poor relief would be 'a central office of *general inspection*, to receive, abstract and publish accounts and reports'.[45] He had not yet asked himself how many of these agencies there should be, or how functions should be distributed among them. But in his 'Institute of Political Economy' he seemed to be advocating the dismemberment of the British Home Office and the dispersal of some of its functions to a separate Ministry of the Interior and a separate Ministry of Police.[46] He was also disposed to accept a monopoly of financial authority within the Executive, and to accept that in Britain it should be held by the Treasury.[47] He wanted, however, the Treasury and other departments to be parts of a co-ordinated system and therefore subject to a higher authority; he vested this provisionally in the 'Council Board' which he judged to be 'the competent and only competent authority' to settle jurisdictional disputes and other issues arising among departments and agencies.[48] At the periphery of the governmental system, he was seeking to create local agents who would form a channel of communication between government and community and who would assist in the work of preventive police. The major part of this task could be carried out by police *forces* which he and Colquhoun included in their schemes. These were to be established in two layers, one – the metropolitan – directly under the control of the central police authority, and the other indirectly responsible to it but immediately under the control of designated country magistrates.[49] (This structural distinction was both a legacy from the old distinction in the literature between 'the police of towns' and the police of country areas, and a reflection of the contemporary English opinion that the 'police of the metropolis' was the really urgent problem that must be tackled.) As a supplementary force, he had in mind the clergy, whom he viewed as 'a sort of appendage to the penal system, a branch of the police of which the object is to take measures in the view of preventing [crimes] by the prevention of the dispositions which gave them birth'.[50] He saw their function accordingly to be that of 'an officer appointed [in every parish] for the performance of certain services of a public nature', services which would include but would not be exhausted by 'moral instruction' and 'such ceremonies of a religious nature as are deemed subservient to the purpose of enforcing moral duties'.[51] He did not spell out the other services, but on another occasion he indicated that they would include the posting of the official notices about crimes, criminals and rewards which were to be circulated by the police authority.[52]

It is possible that Bentham hoped that he would never have to consider the Executive as a single structure, or to say any more about it than he had done in his draft constitutions. But the trend of some of his other arguments was making such hopes increasingly unrealistic. Despite his apparent intentions, he could not limit the functions of government in a way that would reduce the activities and establishments within or under the care of the Executive. If he wanted to treat government in a thorough fashion, this was a problem that would have to be faced.

Bentham's close interest in both political economy and social policy during the 1790s led him to consider more carefully than before the functions of government, and to arrive at a set of more complete and definite opinions on the subject. As he worked on different aspects of it he tended to change his opinions, favouring sometimes a narrowing of the legitimate scope of the government's activities and sometimes an extension of it. In the end his general stance probably remained much as it had originally been, but it was expressed more clearly and in considerably greater detail than in the 'Projet' or other early writings.

The best summary of his approach is to be found in the opening pages of his 'Institute of Political Economy', the second of the two works in which he tried to provide an elementary account of political economy and its achievements.[53] He re-affirmed there the role and responsibility of government for the community's welfare, denying that the 'uncoerced and unenlightened propensities and powers of individuals' could produce the maximum of well-being 'without the controul and guidance of the legislator', and asserting that it was 'incumbent on the legislator' to ensure that 'the most eligible course of conduct be pursued'. But he immediately added that 'it does not follow that whatever step is taken in that course should be the result of measures taken by himself... What concerns him is – that the desirable effect should take place: not that it should have his own agency for the cause.' The wise legislator would therefore rely on autonomous forces and acts – *sponte acta* – wherever he could find them, and might stimulate or commission private activities instead of undertaking them himself. Bentham forecast that most of the legislator's activity would be concerned with security, and that 'in regard to subsistence, opulence and equality his interference [would be] comparatively unnecessary'.[54] But that was an expectation, not a firm programme, and it did not prescribe a total absence of activity outside the vaguely-defined area of 'security'. He admitted, too, that the list of *sponte acta*, and the conditions of security and other relevant factors, would depend on local circumstances and would differ from country to country and from time to time.[55]

Several lines of argument that he took up in the 1790s encouraged him to rely more on *sponte acta* and to find less for governments to do. The most important of these were the product of his first substantial essays in political economy, in which he became more conscious of the economy as a set of forces achieving socially-desirable objectives or setting limits to what could be achieved. As in the work of the nineteenth-century classical political economists – 'the pessimistic science' – the setting of limits and the consequent impotence of governments was as important a part of his theory as was the beneficent operation of market forces. He stressed both the disruptive effects – the interruptions to supply – of interventions designed to help purchasers, and the difficulty or impossibility of transcending the limits to trade set by the existing volume of capital.[56] Closely-related to his political economy was an enthusiasm for 'saving measures' on the part of governments.[57] This was fed partly by a simple concern with economy and the minimization of taxation, and partly by a desire to reduce the places and patronage that might form the bases of 'influence' to be wielded by the Executive. Finally, he had a share of the eighteenth-century economists' scepticism about the efficiency of governments. Believing that all legislation must operate through the imposition of evils, he tended to find more and more reasons why governmental activities would be groundless, inefficacious, unprofitable or needless.

The movement in his thinking towards (but never arriving at) laissez-faire was most marked in the first half of the 1790s. From the middle of the decade, it was counteracted by a set of other considerations. His further inquiries into economic problems and conditions, especially money and banking, persuaded him that there were many points in the economy at which unaided or unsupervised market forces did not work sufficiently well. Similarly his thinking about security, that is the protection of the community against external enemies, malefactors and calamities, encouraged him to approve of and advocate several important sorts of activities, including a good deal of close regulation of some economic enterprises. He was still attracted by the idea that some socially-desirable functions need not be performed directly by the government itself, but could be handled better by private persons hired or authorized by the government to act on its behalf. His own Panopticon contract was in line with that trend in his thinking. But late in the decade he began to develop an enthusiasm for, a belief in the economic advantages of, collective rather than individual action. He tried to associate those advantages with collective private and not with public enterprises, but as he developed his argument more fully he found it extremely difficult to maintain that distinction.

Apart from economic policy, the principal areas where he looked forward to a considerable contraction of activities were foreign policy and religion. The main purpose of his writings on religion was to demonstrate that 'in respect of Ecclesiastical Polity...there is nothing or next to nothing for the legislator to do: and that...whatever is done will be with little or no exception tyranny or prodigality or abuse'.[58] He argued that the Church's work in preventive police constituted its only claim to a place in public policy, and that this function could be performed by a comparatively exiguous structure.[59] He hoped to see most of the existing Establishment, and especially its episcopal element, swept away. In foreign policy he favoured a more defensive stance, fewer foreign and colonial adventures and the abandonment of colonial rule and of the establishments on which colonial rule depended (although he advocated emigration, even 'within the empire', in certain circumstances).[60] He thought that these changes would facilitate reductions in military and naval expenditure: a smaller navy, consisting of 'so much only...as is necessary for defence against the piratical states', and the sub-stitution of a militia for the existing army.[61] In all these matters, concerning the Church as well as foreign policy, he was hoping to strike at influence along with needless expenditure and taxa-tion.

He was still fully committed, however, to the ideal of efficiency in the making of law, in the administration of justice and in the policing of the community. In the pursuit of efficiency in the first two of these fields, he was prepared to countenance a good deal of activity by the government in the collection of information and the publication of statistics. He offered in this connection his usual warning that 'no institution should be set on foot for the furnish-ing of any such articles without a previous indication of the benefit derivable...and a conviction that it will pay for the expense'. But he supplied a number of reasons why governments should keep records and should publish statistics of legal proceedings, of births, deaths and marriages, and of the more important sorts of contracts.[62] In the search for a more effective policing of the community, the plans on which he collaborated with Colquhoun implied a definite expansion of the activities of the central govern-ment and its agents. They provided for the appointment of police officers (although with rather limited responsibilities) in London, on the Thames and in country districts. They also provided for the collection and dissemination of information about crimes and criminals on an unprecedented scale. The police officers (to be known as Surveyors or Constables) were to be directly or indirectly under the control of the authorities in London.[63] These measures had been foreshadowed in Bentham's earlier writings on preven-tive police, but what is to be observed now is that they remained unaffected by his anxiety to identify 'saving measures' and to strike off official 'places', and unaffected by his predilection for drawing up lists of non-agenda. The policing of the community remained firmly in the category of agenda.

No less firmly set among the agenda were a group of social welfare activities embracing the maintenance of the poor, public health services, education and a rudimentary form of social insur-ance through friendly societies. Bentham's advocacy of these measures rested on a concern to protect individuals against calamities, combined with a concern to protect the community against the depredations of an uneducated and starving populace.

He always believed that any provision for the poor should be parsimonious and he was very ingenious in devizing frugal arrangements and standards for their upkeep. Nevertheless he did not waver in the belief that there should be 'establishments for the occasional maintenance and employment...of such by whom either the one or the other is unobtainable from the ordinary sources'.[64] He argued the case at length in his first and second essays on the poor laws. He maintained there that 'many must starve but for relief' but that 'none should be left to starve out-right...nor gradually'.[65] Many of those in danger of starving would be minors, but some would be adults. In return for relief, the recipients could reasonably be required to work and thus contribute to their maintenance to the extent that they were capable of doing so, and could be required to live in industry-houses and to submit to the 'mode of living' prescribed by the relieving authorities.[66] (In general, he intended that, once admitted at their own request, they should not be released again before 'working out the expense of [their] relief'.)[67] Outdoor relief should be provided only in very few and special circumstances. Beggars should 'be *taken* to the House of Industry' and should not be released before they had 'worked out' through their own labour the expenses of capturing as well as maintaining them.[68] Bentham's attitude to the labour of all the inmates of Industry Houses was that it could and should be treated as a general economic resource and employed as efficiently as possible. (In these matters, he was strongly influenced by Count Rumford's proposals and experiments, both social and mechanical.) He argued that this would be impossible if the organization and conduct of the Houses were left in the hands of Parishes or other local or voluntary bodies; that was the basis of his objection to the 'small-establishment system' that he had found entrenched in Pitt's plan. He believed that the problem must be tackled on a national scale, by the national government. He therefore proposed a stupendous system of about 250 centrally-directed and uniformly-distributed Houses, each of which would provide accommodation for about 2000 persons and would provide work for all but the feeblest of them.[69] The establishment, if not the management, of this system must involve public powers and public policy.

His arguments relating to the poor were extended at some points to cover problems of public health. In practice he did not

distinguish between those persons who could not support themselves because they were unemployed and those who were incapacitated by physical or mental illness. Provided that they were
genuinely indigent, the sick and the unemployed had an equally
good claim on the government, and the government was equally
responsible for all of them. He intended that the sick, the insane
and the permanently incapacitated might all be accommodated
within the Industry Houses, although the different classes might
be 'segregated' in parts of Houses or in separate 'appropriate
establishments' for reasons of health or in order to avoid
disturbances to the tranquillity of a House. He also favoured
public 'lying-in dispensaries' and a public medical service 'affording medical assistance to the independent poor at their own
homes, in cases which [did] not require their being removed to the
Infirmary attached to the Industry House'.[70] He thought that this
should include 'not only medical service and advice but the
medicines',[71] and he suggested that it should be provided free to
agricultural labourers 'to whom might or might not be added
such manufacturers and other handicraftsmen whose weekly pay
did not rise above a certain amount'. He even envisaged that it
might be extended on a fee-paying basis 'to the better-paid
handicraftsmen'.[72] For the community as a whole, he thought
that the government should maintain 'establishments for the
prevention or mitigation of contagious diseases', which would
include centres for inoculation and vaccination.[73]

Although he stressed the responsibility of the government to
provide help for those individuals who suffered the 'calamities' of
unemployment or ill-health and who had no means of helping
themselves, he thought it wise to encourage people to equip
themselves with the means of self-help. He was greatly attracted
by the contemporary experiments and innovations in life insurance, friendly societies and savings banks. He believed that on the
whole, and especially in the last two categories, government-run
or government-sponsored enterprises would be at least as efficient
and successful as autonomous private enterprises, and would
succeed in reaching a great many more people. He advocated at
different times various Poor Man's Banks, Friendly Society Banks
(i.e. banks for the use of friendly societies), annuity-dealing
schemes, and Frugality Banks. In the most ambitious of these he
was aiming, as Werner Stark has said, at 'a public system of social

insurance on a voluntary basis', including as one alternative form
of benefit 'contributory old-age pensions'.[74] He considered carefully the possibility of unemployment-insurance, sickness benefits
and widows' pensions, but felt that these would probably introduce too much uncertainty and scope for fraud into a nation-wide
scheme; but he concluded that the nation-wide scheme might
offer 'encouragement and assistance' to voluntary associations
(for example 'associations bound for annuities to commence at
widowhood'), perhaps by undertaking on their behalf the collection, care and management of their funds and in some cases even
by making modest contributions to their capital.[75] He wanted
particularly to encourage small savings and saving by young
people before marriage, and shaped his proposals particularly to
those ends.

In the account of 'saving measures' that Bentham prepared for
the use of Mirabeau and the National Assembly, he implied that
governments should and could eschew involvement in the field of
education, except to a very minor extent 'as concerns the providing instruction for the poor'.[76] Within a few years he was
commending some quite varied educational activities, not all of
which were directed exclusively to the poor. The most substantial
concerned the large numbers of 'minors' whom he expected to be
drawn into the Industry Houses; the majority of these would of
course be either orphans or the children of paupers, but Bentham
hoped that there would also be a number of children placed there
voluntarily, either permanently or temporarily, by their parents.[77]
Other forms of education and instruction that he deemed worthy
of public support were lectures in midwifery, the provision of
general information about public health (for example, the benefits
of vaccination), lectures in veterinary science and possibly in
other arts and sciences connected with husbandry, and the work
of the Board of Agriculture and perhaps of the Royal Institution.[78]

In his attempts to make these social provisions, Bentham was
incidentally proposing a number of incursions by the government
into the economic life of the community. He proposed more direct
forms of economic regulation or participation on a variety of
other grounds. Some were the product of an ambition to ease the
burdens of taxation by finding simple services that governments
could provide and sell at a profit, some were connected with the

drive towards security, and some were concerned with overtly economic considerations of subsistence or abundance. As he extended his knowledge of economic processes he recognized a growing list of circumstances in which individuals' knowledge and power might be increased by judicious governmental action, and even some circumstances in which their inclinations to promote output might be usefully stimulated. The last point followed from a recognition that in practice there could be a gap between private net profit and social net product.[79] In the course of the same economic studies he recognized that the working of market forces would leave gaps in the provision of desirable goods and services – especially those useful to the poorer members of society – and that it might even have harmful effects. His most radical critique of markets related to the system of money and banking, where he feared that their unregulated working would tend to produce an ever-increasing quantity of paper money, ever-rising prices and ultimately the bankruptcy of the banking system and general economic disruption and distress.[80] In the later 1790s he sometimes admitted, however, that monetary expansion might be helpful rather than harmful, if spare resources (including labour) existed in the economy.[81] That admission involved some modification of his earlier view that trade was limited by capital.

In order to make the market economy work well, he thought that the government should supply both the patents-legislation that he had earlier favoured, and '*political* power of an *appropriate* kind' in the form of legislation facilitating or regulating the formation of joint-stock companies.[82] It is not clear whether he had in mind here a general body of law governing incorporation, or charters and private Acts dealing with specific corporations. Like Adam Smith, but more warmly, he judged that the post office was a suitable enterprise for governments to run, and he wanted them to continue to run it: he commended in particular the British postal service for its 'dispatch, punctuality, cheapness in the transaction of the business, sufficiency of number and equality of distribution in regard to the stations'.[83] He proposed too that the government might establish its own agency for the disposal of its surplus stores through retail outlets, instead of selling them in large lots by auction.[84] And he suggested that governments might offer (perhaps through the post offices) many of the financial services that banks and insurance companies were already offering to the public, including the issue of paper-money.[85] These proposals were closely connected with his plans for savings banks and friendly societies, but were less exclusively shaped to the needs of the poor.

The poor were, however, intended to be the beneficiaries of another set of his recommendations which were also closely connected at some points with the savings banks and the friendly societies. The most substantial of these concerned what Bentham called 'magazining', a practice that he favoured over a very long time. It was the ancient practice of maintaining stocks of food that could be used to feed the poor in times of dearth. Bentham had little confidence in the ability of market forces to offset the natural fluctuations in harvests, and he believed that it was the government's responsibility to try to prevent the worst effects of these 'calamities'.[86] At the time of the actual dearth in 1800–01, he defended the still more radical policy of setting maximum prices for grains, representing it as 'but a temporary expedient' and a 'palliative' but arguing that it was perfectly unobjectionable in the absence of any suitable remedy provided by the market itself.[87] On a less extensive but still notable scale, he proposed that the poor should be provided with facilities for the remittance of small sums of money, with employment exchanges and an official *Employment Gazette*, and with inns and common animals for hire that would help them to move around the country in order to seek work or for other reasons.[88] He provided the rationale for these measures in his discussion of poor men's banks. 'Everything goes on smoothly in the transactions of the people in easy circumstances,' he argued; 'everything goes on badly, if at all, in the transactions of the Poor.' In particular, he thought, the rich man could easily find a banker, but only charity 'would induce the rich man's Banker to do the same office for the poor man: and charity has never yet shown itself in so burthensome a shape'. He concluded that 'if the poor man is to have a Banker' the government must find him one, and the government should accept that responsibility along with the responsibility to find employment agencies, inn-keepers and livery-stables for the use of the poor men who would otherwise lack them.[89]

Finally Bentham advocated the direct and comprehensive regulation of certain trades and activities. His concern with monetary stability led him to investigate ways in which the 'money-traffic' could be rendered innocuous. He recommended at different times that bankers and stockbrokers should be licensed, that their numbers should be restricted, that the issue of notes by bankers should be regulated and made subject to a tax, and even that governments should attempt to 'manage' the volume of paper-money (or at least its own share of the issue) in the light of conditions in the market for labour.[90] His final scheme would have been implemented through two complementary statutes, 'one on the registration of banking houses, the other on the taxation of banking issues'.[91] The former measure was intended to restrict both the number of banks and the total of their issues, and to require each of them to furnish 'security either with or without a pledge, in a certain proportion to the greatest sum of paper-money which he is entitled to keep in circulation at any one time'.[92] It included supplementary provisions about the keeping of accounts, designed to prevent evasion of the limits on note-issues. The second imposing the tax and partly by prescribing the denominations in statute was intended to provide a further deterrent, partly by which notes could be issued.

Banking would have been a highly regulated activity in Bentham's ideal economy. But his plans for it were far surpassed in thoroughness and in depth of penetration by the system of preventive police that he and Colquhoun devised in their draft Police Revenue Bill. The Bill consisted of fifty-five sections grouped in six parts.[93] It identified thirteen classes of traders who must take out licences and submit to the supervision of the Police Revenue Board's officers, including second-hand dealers in various kinds of goods, pawnbrokers and scrap-metal dealers. Each licence was to be valid for only one kind of trade or goods and at only one place of business.[94] (Itinerant dealers were to be licensed separately.) The Bill vested in the Board power to issue licences at its discretion (Part III), extensive powers of search and inspection (SS 33–35), and the power to make regulations and issue orders about a variety of matters including hours of trading, notices to be displayed by licensees and forms of book keeping (SS 25–27, 29 and 32). The powers to search and inspect included authority 'to enter into and make search in any dwelling house as well as any warehouse, shop, yard or other place' (S 33)[95] and 'in case of necessity to enter into and upon the premises and make search for [stolen] goods or valuables by force and for that purpose to break open doors, locks and packages' (S 34),[96] 'to search out and examine the contents of any pack or bundle which any and every [itinerant licensee] shall have about his or her person or otherwise in his or her possession' and 'to inspect and take or cause to be taken extracts or copies from any and every book' which the licensee was required to keep (S 35).[97] The power to prescribe 'license inscriptions' and forms of book-keeping extended to the size, shape and position of notices and the recording of the physical details of each transaction, and it included authority to issue supplementary Instructions.[98] Bentham had no economic motive in putting forward this scheme, but it amounted to an unusually intensive and complete system of control, through complementary procedures of licensing and inspection, over an established (and not negligible) part of economic life. It rightly seemed to him to be analogous to the licensing and supervision of 'ale-houses', which he also endorsed.

The kinds of tasks that Bentham was recommending to governments were so varied that it was clear that different agencies and perhaps agencies of different kinds must be employed to administer them. For example, the regulation of second-hand dealers and the provision of 'inns for poor travellers' or 'lying-in dispensaries' required quite different administrative arrangements. But while he took account of such differences, Bentham introduced two peculiar features into his proposals. He thought that most of the services (as distinct from the functions of regulation and supervision) could be provided through a single agency, the system of centrally-directed Industry Houses. He intended that the Houses should not only house, educate and employ the poor and the sick, but should also run the frugality banks, the inns, the employment exchanges, the lying-in hospitals, the midwifery and veterinary schools, the public health service and possibly the 'magazines' of stored foodstuffs. The range of these functions is the most astonishing feature of an astonishing scheme. He did not, however, propose that the system should be run as a government department or even as a public corporation. He recommended instead that it should be organized as a public utility joint-stock company to be called the National Charity Company. The company should be equipped with some public powers and some public revenues (principally a portion of the existing poor-rates) but should raise its own capital and should aim to make a profit.[99] Its constitution and some other features of its operations were to be similar to those of the East India Company, which seems to have served Bentham as a model. The character of the scheme provided him with a challenge to demonstrate that such a vast undertaking could be conducted successfully, and that it could be conducted more successfully as a 'farm' or public utility than as a government enterprise. He accepted both parts of the challenge willingly and confidently.[100]

His answer to the first part referred initially to considerations derived from production-economics, namely the advantages of the division of labour and other technical advantages available under conditions of 'ample-scale' production. He extended this line of argument to 'that particular species of labour which consists in the business of management and superintendence',[101] contending that the 'line of good management'[102] could be followed in large and multi-branch enterprises to an extent that was not possible in a single, small establishment. The superiority of the large over the small enterprise in this respect supposedly lay substantially in the factors that partisans of planning, mergers and rationalization have commonly emphasized: the ability to take a broader view and to exercise foresight; the ability to aggregate resources and thus to be more economical in their use; the ability to aggregate problems, so that things that in their isolated state were not 'sufficient to render them important' became 'considerable enough in magnitude to pay for the quantity of attention they would absorb if investigated to the bottom';[103] the ability to integrate and re-deploy resources in the light of changing circumstances and so to 'prevent that depretiation [sic] by the glutting of the market, a misfortune to which the contending efforts of unconnected individuals would be perhaps inevitably exposed'.[104] The argument merged finally into a view that must have coexisted very uneasily with Bentham's fundamental individualism. This was that collective action, especially action within an organization such as a joint-stock company, was likely to be more efficient than purely individual action.

Bentham explained the superiority of collective action largely as a product of the accompanying organizational structure, which he identified as 'steadiness'. By this he meant firstly *permanence*, the continuing network of posts and activities which enabled the organization (as he believed) to survive and retain its energy after its founders began to falter or had died; secondly its tendency to operate according to written *rules*; and thirdly its ability to *record* its own operations and experience and to use its records as a basis for continuing improvements. 'In individual management', he asserted bluntly, 'no such steadiness can be expected', because the individual manager 'never finds himself called upon so much as to consign his practice to written rules', and because 'whatever there is more particularly good in the mode of management pursued by the individual, is liable to die with the individual or even before him, in consequence of any abatement which may take place in the measure of his attention or of his intelligence'.[105] In the joint-stock enterprise, on the contrary, 'whatever there is good in the plan of management at any one time may be expected to continue: to continue without change unless any change has been discovered which would be for the better'.[106]

Bentham's adoption of this view marked a significant new stage in his thinking. In one sense at least he had become a partisan of collectivism, and of collectivism set within a markedly bureaucratic framework. He was now seeing the bureaucratic devices of organizations as potentially dynamic forces; not just as means of preventing offences, but as forces capable of making a positive contribution to efficiency, and capable of transcending the limitations to which isolated individuals were subject. This shift in his perspective opened up for him a new range of possibilities which he was to exploit (and was already exploiting) in important ways. Immediately, however, it introduced complications into his attempt to meet the second part of the challenge that confronted him, which was to show that government's administrative performance must be inferior to that of joint-stock companies.

His demonstration of the inferiority of government was along familiar lines. It pointed to 'the comparative want of personal interest, that indispensable whetstone to ingenuity and spur to interest'; the 'practice in almost every department of government to committ [sic] agency to boards'; the prevalence of patronage and sinecures, and of personal ties between superior officers and their subordinates 'who are of course their obsequious servants, and in many instances their creatures';[107] the consequently lax discipline to be found in government offices;[108] the many competing demands on a Minister's time, and the fact that the talents needed for the gaining of office were 'such as tend rather to disqualify than to qualify [a man] for...administration'; the fact that on a change in the Administration, 'the establishments of a predecessor in office are more apt to present themselves in the character of an abuse which calls for extirpation than in that of a pattern which calls for adoption and adherence';[109] and the absence of the disciplines of the market, and more particularly of the threat of bankruptcy, to which private concerns were subject.[110]

Despite the conventional character of this critique, it could not be dismissed as the mere repetition of a formula. It expressed some of Bentham's most deeply-felt convictions, convictions that he had formed (or had had reinforced) in recent years during his negotiations concerning the Panopticon with the Treasury, the Home Office, and some of the legal officers. The confusions, the unexplained delays, the false starts and the apparently wilful obstructiveness that cropped up so plentifully in those negotiations provided him with sufficient illustrations of all the points that he had made. Nevertheless his argument remained, as he was uneasily aware, vulnerable in some respects, while in others it threatened to prove too much.

It was likely to prove too much because Bentham did not in fact want to 'farm' all government services or productive enterprises, and because some of its points could be applied fairly plausibly to the National Charity Company. As we have seen, he wanted to retain or place in government hands the post office, the naval dockyards, the issue of currency-notes and some of the other ventures into banking and insurance that he advocated. And some of the arrangements which he found harmful in government were also built into the National Charity Company; for example, the use of boards in management and 'the comparative want of personal interest' that he thought characteristic of an enterprise managed by employees. The similarity between government and company could also be restated in terms of Bentham's arguments relating to the joint-stock character of the enterprise. These explicitly drew an analogy between the management of labour and 'the art of government', on the ground that both were concerned with bringing about 'the junction between interest and duty'.[111] He felt obliged to admit that the line of good management was available to government and applicable to its operations.[112] If the disadvantages of 'trust-management' could be overcome in some parts of the government, and could be triumphantly overcome in the National Charity Company, it was difficult to see why they could not be overcome throughout the government's service.

Bentham tried to meet the difficulty by arguing that those services suitable for direct management were of a relatively simple kind, and that a joint-stock company would remain subject to the threat of bankruptcy and other external forms of discipline in a way that governments would not. But he seems to have seen that these contentions did not quite meet the case, for not all the services that he wanted to leave in the government's hands were notably simple, and the economic pressures on the National Charity Company were not notably strong. He fell back on a sort of evolutionary (or dialectical) theory, a theory of progressive stages in the development of 'the state of society and the progress made by political knowledge' and consequently in the development of the institutional forms of economic activity.[113] The first stage had been one suitable to purely individual enterprise; it lasted at least until the time of the South Sea Bubble. The time at which he was writing was in a more advanced stage, 'precisely the period for the establishment of an institution' such as the Charity Company: society and knowledge were 'up to the requisite pitch' but not beyond it, and so the 'economy of Joint Stock Management [was] up to it, and the economy of Government management [was] not yet up to it'. But he could not maintain that this stage would last indefinitely; he had to concede that further progress was possible, and that in 'another century or even half a century...the discipline of Government might have made such a progress, and to such a degree outgrown its present habitual disease of relaxation' that it too might have been brought nearly to the level of the joint-stock concern.[114] In those circumstances the functions might properly be performed directly by a government.

The conclusion of this argument left the functions of government in an indeterminate state. Bentham's attempt to prescribe an inexpensive and influence-resistant form of government had failed on two separate counts. The new Smithian political economy had not succeeded in showing that the goal of abundance could be wholly left to *sponte acta*; it soon began to yield its own list of 'agenda' for government. Moreover, it had not been able to outweigh the powerful humanitarian (or egalitarian) implications of Bentham's utilitarianism, or his equally powerful desire to provide a comprehensive ring of protection against the calamities and offences that threatened security or subsistence. These too generated an ever-growing list of agenda. Bentham had sought a way out of this awkward situation by suggesting that many of the government's tasks could conveniently be farmed to private contractors. But his developmental theory of management rendered this only a temporary solution. The prospect was that the natural progress of society in the next century or half-century would bring governments 'up to the requisite pitch', and that more and more functions would legitimately pass into their hands, but at a rate that could not be predicted.

If there was an element of illusion in Bentham's belief that 'a line of good management' was already available to a joint-stock company encompassing half-a-million workers, it was nevertheless true that he himself had made remarkable progress in developing and applying a set of ideas about organization and management. These were expressed partly in his choice of points to be covered in his legislative and other schemes, and partly in the explanations that he added to them, including his notes and observations on his Bills, a lengthy essay on personnel management attached to his plan for the Judiciary of France, the more discursive parts of his essays on pauper management and on the Panopticon, and his working papers for all of these projects. His ideas drew heavily on the principles of indirect legislation, reward and production economics described in chapter 4, and to a smaller extent on his first institutional schemes, but they were much more than a repetition of his earlier points. They developed them by demonstrating how some of them must be qualified, what conditions must be met before they could be applied, and how they could be made mutually reinforcing. He provided, too, a new context for them by exploiting his perception that management was a distinct activity or 'business' in a productive enterprise, and that it could be separately described and analysed and could be equipped with its own principles and rules. Finally, Bentham supplied legislative or other forms for applying his rules and principles in a number of concrete situations, including the Panopticon, the National Charity Company, the projected police forces, the dockyards and the financial agencies that he proposed to set up to administer new taxes and the note-issue.

The link between his jurisprudence and the theory of management was provided by his assumption that managers' tasks were much the same as those of rulers. Managers, like rulers, had to accept responsibility for decision making, for the issuing of appropriate instructions, for the engagement of the motives of the subordinate personnel in the most economical and least burdensome manner possible, and for the oversight of all activities and procedures in order to ensure that their decisions and instructions were being translated into action. The main body of his theory was devoted to the discovery of principles and arrangements which might facilitate the performance of those tasks. It gave some weight to points of organization but a good deal more to communications, which turned out to play a role in the performance of each kind of task.

The foundation of all decision making was information, and most of Bentham's schemes included some arrangements for getting information to managers and other decision makers. These generally reproduced and adapted the statistical collections that he had advocated on previous occasions, and sometimes the suspensive and advising power that he had allocated to the Judiciary. Versions of these were combined in the Police Revenue Bill. That measure provided for the publication, in a regular Calendar of Delinquency and in annual reports, of the information about the working of the criminal laws that the Police Commissioners were required to collect. It also imposed a definite obligation on the Commissioners to suggest 'such a regulations as in their judgement shall appear best calculated for augmenting the efficacy [and] diminishing the severity of the penal branch of the law...and for diminishing...the expense...incident to the execution of the same'.[115] In the economic enterprises in which he first explicitly recognized the activity of management, decision making meant more specifically the selection and combination of resources and processes in the most advantageous ways, and this imposed special requirements on the form in which information should be submitted. Bentham thought that managers should make their choices through a distinctive kind of trial-and-error which he called 'comparison and selection'. As he described this in relation to the National Charity Company, it was to consist in a careful comparison of the methods and results of each Industry House in order to determine the most successful practices, and the subsequent adoption as a common rule of 'the practice of that establishment which has succeeded best'.[116] In this form it was most readily applicable to multi-unit enterprises, where its application would be assisted by what he called 'uniformity in management', which would create a common setting in which the effects of different practices could be measured. In principle, however, the device could be applied in a single-unit enterprise, wherever opportunities existed for doing the same thing in different ways and measuring their respective results.

Although trial-and-error was thus important in the making of decisions about the optimum use of resources, Bentham did not suppose that it constituted the whole process. He assumed that it would be preceded by a survey and analysis of all the aspects of the activity which was to be undertaken, and that it would be guided by the latest and most complete information about technology and by the principles of production-economics. In order to provide the Industry Houses and the Panopticon with an instalment of the first part of this information, he embarked on, or commissioned, an extensive classification of 'trades', according to the material employed (for example, wood and metal) and the nature of the process to be undertaken (the turning of wood, the casting of metal).[117] He went on to draw attention to, and in some cases to modify or tighten-up, some of the important ideas in production-economics that he had identified in the economic parts of his 'Projet', such as the economies of large-scale production, the saving of time spent in comings and goings, the saving of materials through re-using them, and the improvement of the quality of materials without making them dearer.

His critique of the 'small establishment system' implied confidence in the economies of large-scale production, and he certainly stressed those economies in parts of his argument. But he soon saw that the enlargement of scale might bring diseconomies as well as economies. The principal economies were of course those of the division of labour, and they would be secured through the sub-division of tasks and processes, the use of machinery and the employment of a wide range of manual skills: in the large establishment, he argued, 'the system of movements in any line of mechanism may be broken down and simplified to the very utmost, [and] thus supported mechanical ingenuity may give itself the most unbounded range'.[118] But on a closer examination he found that the process could not be continued indefinitely. At a certain point, he believed, supplies of suitably skilled labour would no longer be available, and expensive buildings and machinery would therefore be left idle or unemployed. The problem could be minimized by measures designed to reduce the turnover of labour and by concentrating particular processes or stages of production in particular units of a multi-unit system such as the National Charity Company. But these measures would also prove to be uneconomical before very long: heavy costs for the transport of materials and semi-finished goods between the units, he argued, would at some point offset the rise in physical productivity.[119] He thus arrived at the notion of an optimum size for an establishment, the point at which economies and diseconomies would be balanced. It seems to have provided his rationale for setting the size of Industry Houses and the Panopticons at about 2000 hands, and for his reluctance to consider changes from that size.

In order to achieve the economies of scale, to save time in movements within an establishment, and in general to make labour more efficient, he judged that it was essential to pay close attention to the lay-out and design of the building. He drew attention here to a number of considerations, which he saw as different aspects of 'convenience with regard to work':

(a) The whole *quantity* of room adequate to the whole quantity of the work competent to the establishment; and the *size* of each room adequate to the quantity of work allotted to that room.
(b) Form and dimensions of the rooms suitable to the nature of the work.
(c) *Light* sufficient for the nature of the work.
(d) Compactness – the distance [between] room and room, and thence the time consumed in passing to and fro, being as short as possible.[120]

These ideas brought him close to one side of the 'scientific management' school. He himself took them very seriously, especially in his design of the Panopticon, where he paid attention not only to the size of rooms and the availability of light but also to the design and location of staircases, doorways and internal passages and galleries.[121]

He moved on from the working environment to say some additional things about the full exploitation of resources, both human and non-human, in the interests of productivity and economy. The basic points from which he started were the avoidance of waste or idleness in any form, and 'use-multiplying': 'let care be taken not to leave in the instance of any individual whatever the smallest fragment of ability unemployed';[122] 'take care that not the smallest portion of [animal or vegetable] refuse should ever be thrown away in waste';[123] and 'it should be a standing topic of consideration for every...article whether it is not susceptible with advantage of more than one use'.[124] In applying the last point, he added, care should be taken to ensure that 'the uses be not obstructive to each other' and to avoid a situation in which 'the instrument by being applicable to so many uses' might become 'comparatively the less applicable to each'.[125] Human resources were subject to some special considerations and recommendations, which he labelled 'employment-appropriation' and 'employment-mixing'. The first meant that the tasks most suitable for the 'imperfect' or handicapped workers should be reserved in the first instance for them; Bentham was assuming here that the 'perfectly able hands' would be 'equally susceptible of any species of employment in the whole list'.[126] His second point meant that each worker should be trained and given experience in more than one kind of task, so that they might individually be given some relief from the more laborious and exacting kinds of work, and that the enterprise could respond quickly to changes in the demand for its products, to changes in the availability of raw materials or to changes in weather conditions which might restrict or permit certain kinds of activities.[127] In making these glosses on his general plea for economy, he was thinking primarily of the Industry Houses with their fixed stock of inhabitants, many of whom would be 'imperfect hands', but his argument was not wholly irrelevant to other sorts of establishments.

In his draft chapter on economics for 'Projet', Bentham had seen that the quality of resources and the cost of resources were important but normally competing considerations for management. During the 1790s he did not find much to add to what he had already said about materials and equipment, but human resources now attracted his attention in more than one way. He was conscious of differences in skills and in education, and of the need to relate them closely to the requirements of each post. He sometimes prescribed particular qualifications, as in his plans for the French Judiciary where only persons who had enjoyed extensive experience as 'men of law' were to be eligible for appointment.[128] He thought that education was a very important qualification for management: 'want of liberal education and general knowledge on the part of persons intrusted with the management of the burthensome Poor' was one of the reasons why the best managerial practices had been neglected in the parochial work-houses.[129] He hoped that the Panopticon would act as a 'school' in which a knowledge of management would be taught or at least acquired.[130] Both education and skills acquired through education were clearly scarce and therefore expensive. He sought to reconcile high qualifications with economy in the French Judiciary by proposing what he termed a 'patriotic auction' as part of the process of appointment or election. The patriotic auction would involve the sale of offices, but it would differ from any existing kind of 'venality'. It would take the form of an open, competitive auction among the qualified candidates, the proceeds of sale would go to the establishment instead of to the previous incumbent of the post, and the post would not necessarily go to the highest bidder.[131] Bentham saw this as one of his most original contributions to public economy. He proposed to supplement it with provisions for honorary officials and unpaid deputies, partly as an economy measure and partly as a means of training and testing people for future service.[132] But he had to reconcile the patriotic auction with another device that attracted him at that time, namely a 'career-service' in which new employees would enter at the bottom rank and would move through a succession of more responsible posts, normally by one step at a time. He saw the career-service as a means of making available (or of retaining) expertise acquired in the lower ranks of the service, and as a means of accumulating information about the talents of those who would be competing for the higher posts. He prescribed a strict form of it in the judicial service, where he made previous service in the same or the immediately lower rank of courts a condition of eligibility for appointment to all but the most junior posts.[133] In the Industry Houses he clearly assumed that promotion from within the service would be a – or the – normal mode of appointment to the higher posts, but he did not bind the National Charity Company in as strict a fashion as the Judiciary.[134]

Those proposals were closely connected with a larger body of speculation about the means by which managers might engage the motives of their subordinates. His thinking on that subject was of course based on his established principles of reward and punishment. The opportunity to consider the use of his principles in particular circumstances stimulated him to bring some of them closer to operational terms, but at the same time it exposed difficulties and limitations of which he had not previously been aware.

A considerable part of his new speculations consisted of efforts to find honorary rewards that could be substituted for monetary payments, and to show how and on what conditions piece-work could be used as the basis of remuneration. These proved to be theoretically interesting, but to be less successful in carrying him towards the clear-cut programme of action for which he was looking.

Some of the difficulties flowed from the general character of his argument, which required him to focus attention on individual responsibility, individual performance and individual reward. In an industrial or administrative environment, this meant that tasks should be performed by individuals, and that the tasks should involve kinds of work 'of which the quantity is capable of being accurately measured and described'.[135] He recommended in general terms that tasks should be allocated to individuals rather than to groups or gangs, but he recognized that the nature of the work to be performed might not permit such an arrangement. He then tried to find ways of providing information about individual workers within gangs, by reducing the gangs to the smallest practicable size, by switching workmen from group to group and by deliberately composing the gangs of workers who were believed to be unequal in diligence.[136] He tackled the problem of measurement in an ingenious way. His solution involved the offer to workmen of a choice between doing a task that could not be accurately measured or doing a certain amount of the work that could be measured; their preferences could, he argued, place the different tasks on a common scale of difficulty or effort. But it was clear that this was a limited solution: it could be easily applied only to manual tasks, and only to those where the expenditure of effort was the prime criterion for payment.[127]

He tried persistently to discover or invent honorary rewards that could act as incentives in different kinds of circumstances. He advocated the use of minor titles for this purpose in the organization of the police force, especially the award of the title 'Honourable' to the unpaid magistrates who were to supervize the country officers of police.[138] For the inmates of the Industry Houses he recommended a series of rewards modelled on those which were commonly employed in schools, including distinctive forms of dress and decorations, and precedence in processions or on similar public and semi-public occasions.[139] He wanted to add to these devices certain bonuses or rewards ('prizes' or 'peculiar-premiums') for outstanding work such as 'pieces of plate' for the governors and other officers of the Industry Houses who had 'distinguished themselves in their respective situations'.[140] His reasoning was that 'by paying one or a few victors you get the result of the extra-exertions of the whole multitude of competitors'.[141] He thus demonstrated that honorary rewards and peculiar-premiums were more than fictional categories or empty boxes, but not that they could replace ordinary monetary remuneration on a significant scale.

He was again flexible and ingenious in applying the piece-work principle to different kinds of situations. It could be applied in the most straightforward way to the industrial operations of the Panopticon, the Industry Houses and similar establishments, but he was anxious to find wider uses for it. One variant of it was poundage or commission on the amount of fees or revenue collected. Bentham had some reservations about this, but he recommended it for the 'escheators' or 'administrators general' whom he wanted to add to the revenue-establishment, and for the lower ranks of the police force whose functions included the collection of licence-revenues.[142] He proposed to use another version of it for the 'managing hands' of both Panopticon and Industry Houses, in the form of bonuses to or deductions from salaries or profits. The adjustments to incomes were to be a function of the death-rates within the institutions, either for the inmates as a whole or for particular classes of them; thus, the senior officers were to receive bonuses or higher salaries according to the number of children in their care who survived until adulthood, but they were to suffer deductions according to the number of women inmates who died in childbirth.[143] Bentham also envisaged that 'in process of time, as the expenses and returns of the establishment became ascertained' it would be possible to reduce or do away with the salaries in the Industry Houses and to substitute participation in profits 'upon the footing of contract or partnership'.[144] When he turned, however, to the individual applications of the principle in the Industry Houses, he found that unexpected difficulties began to emerge. One of them was that many of the inmate-workmen – in general, the aged and the least healthy – might not be capable of earning their own maintenance if they were employed on piece-work. For them he proposed the principle of 'earn-first' or 'working before eating'. This required the setting of norms; he was confident that it could be done, provided that his method for establishing the equivalence of different tasks were used.[145] But on reflection he perceived that, even in relation to the more able workmen, piece-work could not be used indiscriminately. He saw it as potentially dangerous to health, especially to the health of the younger workers, and as liable to encourage all workers to increase their output by allowing the quality of their work to fall. The deterioration in quality was most likely to occur, he noted, 'where badness of quality may be masked – ex. gr. in those parts of a house or ship which are covered up – inside brickwork, caulking etc.'[146] He finally recommended the practice to the managers of the Industry Houses in qualified terms, deeming it useful only 'where increase of quantity can be encouraged without prejudice to quality and without loss by waste, and...without prejudice to health'.[147]

Despite his preference for piece-work and honorary reward, he was always reconciled to the fact that many public posts and some private ones must be salaried. Since he had little faith in salaries as incentives, he was pushed towards finding mechanisms of discipline and punishment that would replace the positive incentives of reward in those employments in which salaries predominated. His treatment of these problems was less interesting in theoretical terms than his work on reward, but it provided some relatively sophisticated examples of the application of penal law to administrative and managerial situations, especially in his plan for the French Judiciary and in the Police Revenue Bill.

For a disciplinary system based on the threat of punishment, two things were essential: the identification of offences and the provision and administration of penalties. One way of supplying those things was to rely on the ordinary law of the land and its procedures of enforcement. Bentham intended to adopt that approach in his draft French constitution, where he wanted to make 'every man in authority but the King responsible in a judicial way' for all acts which would be offences 'on the part of a private person', unless those acts were specifically authorized by 'the powers attached to the respective offices'.[148] But, in his more detailed schemes, he drafted his own law for the purpose. He created offences by carefully defining powers and setting limits to their exercise, and by stating clearly the duties attached to each post: failure to perform the duties, and actions not authorized by the powers, were the offences which rendered the official or employee liable to punishment. He then conferred on some specific authority the power to impose penalties, and he sometimes allocated particular penalties to particular sorts of offences.

He gave an unusually clear statement of powers and duties in his plan for the French judicial system. The powers were set out in the first place in his treatment of jurisdiction, where he distinguished between 'the tribunals of exception' and the ordinary courts, divided the latter into immediate and appellate courts, and stated the kinds of causes which each might hear. He added, for each judge, certain powers of appointment, and a power of 'command over all persons without distinction, within the bounds of his territory, the king only, and judges of equal or superior rank, excepted', in so far as this was necessary 'for the enforcement of his decrees judicially given'.[149] The exercise of these powers was subject to a corresponding set of obligations and duties: in general, to observe the law and to administer it without fear or favour; and, more particularly, to publicize or keep secret the proceedings before the courts as the law demanded, to avoid undue delay or precipitation or the hearing of causes out of turn, to prevent unnecessary expense, to attend regularly the court at the prescribed times, or alternatively (in the event of an unavoidable or authorized absence) to supply a deputy, and not to engage in any other profession or occupation. Most of these obligations were also to apply to the prosecutors and public defenders attached to the courts.[150]

In the Police Revenue Bill he succeeded again in creating a mass of offences for which officials might be punished, but he proceeded in a slightly different way. His definition of duties was somewhat looser, although some points were quite specific and he intended that others should be made so by regulation, order or instructions from the Home Office or the Treasury.[151] Among the most specific were those relating to the handling of money which provided, for example, that all sums collected by the Country Surveyors should be remitted 'weekly through the Post' unless and until the Commissioners directed otherwise, and authorized the magistrates to require the Surveyors to account for all moneys passing through their hands.[152] His more remarkable achievement in the Bill was to set precise boundaries to the exercise of the powers conferred on the Commissioners' servants, especially the powers of search. In general, the entry into premises was permitted only after the issue of a search warrant, and in most cases only during the daytime. And Bentham made it a condition of the issue of the warrant that the officer applying for it should not only swear before a Justice that he had reasonable grounds for suspecting the presence of unlawful goods, but should also satisfy the Justice that his suspicion was reasonable. Night-time searches and the forcing of entry were permitted only if they were specifically authorized in the warrant. The dividing-line between legitimate act and offence on the part of the officer conducting a search was thus clearly marked.[153]

The penalties that he assigned most commonly to offending officials or employees were reprimand, suspension, dismissal and fines. Occasionally, however, he prescribed imprisonment or some special financial penalties. The most serious offences that might be committed by members of the judicial service were deemed to merit imprisonment.[154] A police officer who was guilty of misappropriating funds might be subjected to distraint, imprisonment or both.[155] For each day that an officer of a court was absent from duty without authority, a deduction was to be made from his pay.[156] The administration of the penalties in the judicial service was made the responsibility of the courts themselves; their hierarchical arrangement rendered it easy for each layer to supervise and to deal with complaints about the one below it. In the police force, most of the penalties were similarly to be determined and applied internally. The Police Commissioners were granted, for this purpose, a general power to 'suspend or remove' their own employees.[157] Bentham noted that, in strictly legal terms, it was perhaps unnecessary to set out this power in the Bill, but he remarked that 'a power of this sort in black and white may have its use with a view to the making of a proper impression on the minds of the several subordinates'.[158] For the Country Surveyors, the Bill provided a two-tier disciplinary process: their immediate superior, the Magistrate, might suspend them; but the final penalty was to be determined by the Board, which might decide on reinstatement, dismissal or – on the petition of the offending Surveyor – fine and reinstatement.[159]

Between the offence and the punishment was the activity of detection, that is the establishment of the fact of an offence and the identity of the offender. Bentham devoted a great deal of effort to considering the ways in which that activity might best be carried on, and how it might benefit from the principles of indirect legislation. But he did not treat it as a self-sufficient or independent activity. It was one aspect of – one purpose to be served by – information and communications within organizations and establishments. He tried to prescribe a single, flexible set of measures that would simultaneously provide for the transmission of instructions and the collection and distribution of information needed for decision making and for the detection of offences and offenders. He thought in terms of a set of measures rather than a single device because he recognized that the problem had several different aspects, coinciding with the different sorts of environment in which it might arise.

The simplest environment was a single establishment located in a particular spot. This was the environment for which the Panopticon was designed; that is, the Panopticon-principle, as distinct from the Panopticon-penitentiary in which Bentham first proposed to apply it. The principle, he maintained, was 'applicable to any sort of establishment in which persons of any description are to be kept under inspection: and in particular to Penitentiary Houses, Prisons, Houses of Industry, Work-Houses, Poor Houses, Manufactories, Mad Houses, Lazarettos, Hospitals and Schools'.[160] It solved many of the problems of communication by reducing them to direct observation on the one hand, and accessibility to verbal instruction on the other: the design of the building was adapted to facilitate both these processes. So, in the penitentiary, the central tower or lodge was to become more than an observation-point; it was to be 'the heart which gives life and motion to [the] artificial body: hence issue all *orders*: here center [Bentham's spelling] all *reports*'.[161] To make communications more certain in the penitentiary, he proposed that the building should be fitted with 'conversation-tubes' – thin metal pipes – running from the inspection-tower to the galleries in which the prisoners were to work and be housed.[162] Even in this limited environment, however, the architectural arrangements could not meet all the needs for communications or information. They could not fully meet, for a start, the needs of the managers of the enterprise, or the proprietors if they were distinct from the managers, for employee-managers must be supervised, and both managers and proprietors required information (about output, costs and markets) in a more abstract form than direct observation would yield. Similarly, architectural design could not fully meet the needs of the public, who had an interest in ensuring that the prisoners were not unduly oppressed and that the standards of diet and health prescribed for the establishment were fully observed. The principle was of still less use in more diffuse organizations such as that of the police, or more elaborate ones such as the National Charity Company.

To supplement the Panopticon-principle, Bentham proposed firstly to use various kinds of publicity and inspection. The responsibility to prepare and publish reports or to allow open access to certain documents was a common feature in most of his schemes. These arrangements were intended partly to facilitate internal control and decision making (especially in the Judiciary) and partly to promote public oversight and control. The penitentiary-contractor, for example, was to be required to maintain and publish records and accounts covering 'the whole process and detail of his management, the whole history of the prison'.[163] Bentham also tried to devise forms of inspection, utilizing members of the public (especially in the penitentiary), the clergy and the magistrates acting as 'visitors *ex officio*', the judiciary, and specially-appointed employees. The most straightforward example was in the Thames Police Bill where the Justices were to be authorized to appoint a special class of Surveyors whose principal functions would be 'inspecting and directing the other Constables'.[164] At other points he tried to arrange for the work of inspection to be carried out not by a separate set of inspectors but by the ordinary employees who would watch each other in the normal course of their duties. In the National Charity Company and in the general police service, the subordinates were to act as a check on their superiors. In the latter scheme he tried to achieve this by inserting in the Police Revenue Bill a clause stating that licences issued by a magistrate would not be valid unless they bore the Surveyor's receipt: this, he maintained '[would] give occasion to the officer (who [would] be responsible to the Board for the character and conduct of the party applying for a licence) to interfere, and, where the case [appeared] to call for refusal of the licence, to make representations to the Justices', and it would ultimately 'give the Board, through the channel of...their officer, a sort of virtual control, though not displayed as such, over the discretion committed to the local Magistrates'.[165] In the Industry Houses he sought to achieve the same object by a strange mixture of collective and individual responsibility, which required the governor of each house to inform all the officers of his acts and decisions, and required any officer to record his dissent if he wished to escape being held responsible for any of those acts and decisions.[166]

The final phase of Bentham's attack on the problem of communications was to consider the form of the reports, accounts and records for which he was asking. He was concerned above all with the very complex managerial environment of the National Charity Company, but he was determined to devise an approach which would satisfy all the kinds of demands that he was making on accounts and other documents. His inquiries thus covered book-keeping or accountancy in the conventional sense, but he treated that as a special case rather than the core of the problem. He began working with others' ideas on the subject, but he soon developed them in novel ways and in unprecedented detail.

His fundamental point was that in book-keeping 'the heads' should be 'governed by the objects or ends which it has in view', and that for the purposes of management these must be much broader than the 'pecuniary economy usually regarded as the sole object of book-keeping'. They must include not only financial transactions but also all other aspects and activities of the enterprise which might be relevant to management; and even within the field of financial transactions or pecuniary economy they must extend beyond the traditional concerns (overall profit and loss, and the detection of dishonesty) to more detailed matters such as 'the rate of expense...on each of the articles consumed or used; and...the rate of expense, on each of the articles produced'. They must provide 'neither more nor less than the history of the system of management in all its points'.[167] They must also, in order to facilitate 'comparison and selection', be capable of yielding data in the form of what Bentham called 'tabular-statement' or statistical tables.[168] He was advocating and demanding, in short, a set of management statistics, not just financial records or accounting in the conventional sense.

He nevertheless looked briefly at orthodox accounting principles and methods, in order to see how well these met his criteria. For information about the orthodox theory, he seems to have relied mainly on the article on book-keeping in the Third Edition of the *Encyclopaedia Britannica*.[169] This was a straightforward exposition of the eighteenth-century view of double-entry accounting. It set out definitions, rules and examples that had already appeared in a popular text-book entitled *An Introduction to Merchandise* (by Robert Hamilton), and it described and recommended the principal books used in the double-entry system. Bentham found the terminology and procedures of this system – notably the use of the misleadingly-named 'waste-book' – to be confusing, irrational and beside the point. He set down hostile comments on much of the contents of the article.[170] But he found in it one item of greater interest. This was a list of the 'subsidiary books used by merchants', namely cashbook, book of charges of merchandize, book of house expenses, invoice-book, sales-book, bill-book, receipt-book, letter-book, pocket-book and memorandum-book. He made his own list of these books, summarized their subject-matters, and put marks beside the cashbook, the book of charges, the bill-book and the letter-book.[171] These could come closer than the conventional journals and ledgers to providing 'the history of the system of management in all its points', for they were all records of individual occurrences arranged in a fundamentally chronological pattern, and some of them drew attention to the 'real' as well as to the 'pecuniary' aspect of the occurrences. Perhaps the most promising of them was the book of charges, which covered 'particular charges on goods and voyages; such as carriage, custom, freight, cranage, wharfage, etc.: as also other expenses that affect trade in general; such as, warehouse rent, shop-rent, accountant's wages, postage of letters and the like'.[172] This book, together with the others that he marked, seems to have

provided him with a starting-point for his own further speculations.

Those speculations were further stimulated and shaped by the
fact that, in the same period, in his draft of the Police Revenue
Bill, he was thinking about the design of a set of books for a
different but comparable purpose. The Police Bill's books were
required for the realization of Colquhoun's intention to oblige
licensed dealers to record their transactions in a form that would
facilitate inspection. In adapting this familiar device of preventive
police to the trade in second-hand goods, Colquhoun proposed
from the outset that every significant transaction should be
recorded, and that the record should include a full description of
the article purchased, and the name and address of the other
party to the transaction.[173] When Bentham came to prepare his
draft of the Bill he had an opportunity to consider at length what
information would be needed and how it might best be supplied
by the dealers. He proceeded to answer those questions in characteristic fashion by analysing the transaction and its attendant circumstances into their component parts, and by directing that
these be severally recorded under appropriate headings. They
included the vendor's full name and address, his apparent age,
whether he was known to the dealer or not, whether he was
accompanied by any person at the time of the transaction,
whether he claimed to be a householder or a lodger, a full description of the goods purchased, the vendor's account of how he had
acquired them, and the price paid for them. Bentham added,
again characteristically, that several of the headings would 'admit
of *ramifications* which [would] require Instructions from the Board
to accompany the Books'.[174] The particular headings in this list
were not of much significance outside preventive police, but the
exercise of deriving them served as a pilot study and a model for
the development of a more elaborate set of books or records that
could be used within an enterprise or institution.

He decided that the basis of his system must be the recording of
information in great detail in 'elementary books' which must not
be primarily financial records, but which might be either 'chronological' or 'methodical'.[175] By a 'methodical' book he meant one
which recorded transactions and events according to 'the purpose
it [was] designed to serve'.[176] The information recorded in the
elementary books could then be transferred, he believed, to

'aggregate' books constructed on the same plan and covering a separate establishment or the whole enterprise. The exact nature of the information to be collected (and the list of books to be maintained) would depend on the character of the institution and its activities. But he was clear that in a productive enterprise there must be a record of (and usually separate books for) sales, purchases, output, durable assets, consumption of materials and equipment, stocks, cash and credit transactions, productivity and profit.

He proceeded first to try to identify the kinds and relevant aspects of the transactions and events that would occur in the economy of the Industry Houses, and to propose a class of books for each significant aspect.[177] He distinguished at one level the broad subject-matters or components of the Industry Houses' activities – the population or inmates, the non-human resources, the productive activities, the credit transactions, the cash transactions and the correspondence. At another level he distinguished the sub-divisions within each of these subject-matters, for example, the principal kinds of physical resources, and the different processes to which they might be subject. He then tried to make the whole set consistent, to distinguish between elementary and aggregate books, and to indicate the relationships that should exist between particular books, especially the population and stock books on the one hand and the 'progress books' covering physical production on the other. His most complete list ran to more than 60 items.[178] As he was completing his scheme, he was encouraged to learn that Arthur Young had adopted a similar approach in a plan that he was recommending to farmers. Young sought to distinguish and to cost separately the different activities of the farm, to provide separate accounts for each of them, to highlight their comparative profitability, and to build up estimates of cost by collecting detailed and accurate data about activities and the use of resources, including 'the work of the teams and men every day in the year, specifying the field or business they are employed in'.[179] This was close enough to Bentham's proposals to make him confident that he was thinking realistically, or that at least he had a chance of getting a sympathetic response to his views once they were published.[180]

In the form in which his proposals were published (originally by Young, in his *Annals of Agriculture*), they provided a rather simpler or more summary scheme for the National Charity Company than he had envisaged in his working papers. The books were gathered there into five sets: '1. Population-books, 2. Stock-books, 3. Health-books, 4. Behaviour-books, and 5. Correspondence-books.'[181] The health-books and behaviour-books were included because of the special responsibilities of the concern to and for the paupers whom the National Charity Company was undertaking to house and employ. Most of its commercial and productive activities were to be recorded in the population- and stock-books. The elementary chronological population-books were to record a mass of information about each inmate including the nature of his employment each day, the 'utensils' with which he worked, his earnings and his output. The elementary stock-books were to record in similar detail the history of physical materials or assets, including the mode in which they were acquired, the ways in which they were used or absorbed, and their disposal. There were in addition to be closely-related 'methodical' books which would focus on the ways in which resources were used and the course of productive activity and of work performed. And all of course were to lead up to 'aggregate books' which would summarize and compare results for the benefit of the central management.

Bentham applied this approach for a second time in the set of Instructions that he and his brother drew up for the new office of Timber Master, which was a key element in their plans for the reform of the naval dockyards.[182] One of the Timber Master's functions was to manage the conversion of timber economically; another (and in Bentham's eyes equally important) function was to prevent the waste, theft and misuse of sawn and unsawn timber. His Instructions required him to measure carefully every cargo of timber that arrived in the yard, and to keep track of its movements thereafter, and to keep a daily account of the work of his subordinates.[183] To enable him to carry out these tasks, he was provided with a set of 23 printed forms which covered the various aspects of the activities under his control: the receipt of timber into the yard; its issue by the Storekeeper of the yard; its conversion into specified shapes; its return to store; the existing level of stocks; its final use; the use of other implements and materials by the Storekeeper and his servants; and the work done by (and wages due to) the sawyers and other workmen. These forms were in effect the 'elementary books'. They were to be sent when completed (usually daily) to the Navy Board, where the clerks were to compile aggregate books in the form of 'a Register of the receipt and expenditure of each denomination of timber...in the same printed form as those ordered for the dockyards'.[184] The last paragraph of the Timber Master's Instructions reminded him 'that at the end of every year, the total expense incurred in his Department, together with the total quantity of work done by those employed in it...will be compared with the corresponding articles of expense incurred and effect produced in each of the other of His Majesty's dockyards'; and that 'the making of such a comparison, with due allowance for...local circumstances, cannot fail of throwing light on his merit or demerit'.[185] In other words, the records accumulated by the Timber Master were to lead on to tabular-statement and, ultimately, to comparison and selection.

These two schemes shared, then, the distinctive features of Bentham's programme for book-keeping: the shaping of information into a form that facilitated both decision making and control; the recording of all operations and transactions affecting any of the resources employed within the enterprise, of which money was but one; and a switching of attention from the concern's transactions with outsiders to its internal operations. And, in these schemes, Bentham demonstrated that he had proceeded far beyond the statement of principles, and was capable of translating the principles into operational systems adapted to the needs of different institutions.

His success in carrying his argument to that point was vital to Bentham's schemes, especially in relation to the complex and geographically dispersed National Charity Company. His confidence in the ability of the company to operate profitably depended on the existence of adequate book-keeping, which meant *his* system of book-keeping: 'In a system of poor-houses of the proposed extent and magnitude, good book-keeping is the hinge on which good management will turn... *Without* this advantage everything would be too much; *with* it, nothing would be too much. *Without* it, any single one of the collateral benefits hereinafter proposed, might be deemed visionary; *with* it, all of them together would be found practicable, easy and secure.'[186] But the significance of his system of book-keeping was wider than the single institution. It showed how records and accounts could be used as an analogue

to the Panopticon (or inspective-architecture) principle in complex organizations, and as a complement to it in all organizations.
It amounted to a new approach to industrial and commercial
accounting, and the final instalment of his solution to the problem
of communications in any enterprise or institution.

In comparison with the sophistication and elaboration of his
views on book-keeping, his treatment of organization was fragmentary and incomplete, and many of his points were not clearly
separated in his own mind from other topics such as punishment
and reward. Some of them were nevertheless important.

He still thought of an organization or establishment as consisting of a set of offices or posts, each having its own powers and
responsibilities attached to it, each ideally occupied by a single
person who would be individually responsible for the performance
of its duties and individually subject to penalties if its duties were
ill-performed. He did not develop an explicit or general notion of
hierarchy outside the Judiciary (where it was implied by the
process of appeal), but he assumed some version of it wherever he
countenanced the idea of a career-service, and in most of his
schemes he paid careful attention to the relations of authority
between adjacent posts.

His treatment of the individual offices was an amplification of
his earlier account based on the legal notion of a condition.
He included most of it in a prospectus (drafted for Morellet in
1789) of what he intended to say about presiding officers in his
Essay on Political Tactics: 'their functions – numbers – subordination to the Assembly – dependence on the Assembly – the powers
they ought to have – by whom they should be appointed – who
they should be – and how chosen'.[187] This list served him, with
due alteration of details, as the basis of a standard set of points
that must be determined for all offices. He soon added to it a few
more points, namely pay, attendance and the mode of dismissal or
other termination of employment, and then adhered to it pretty
closely in his other schemes.

In many of those schemes, he remained strongly and out-
spokenly committed to 'single-seatedness' or individual responsibility, and against boards or collegiate management, but in some
of them he made provision for boards at one or another level of
authority. Notable examples of this retreat from his principles
included the directors of the National Charity Company, and the

two sets of Police Commissioners. The Police Revenue Bill is particularly interesting in this respect because in it Bentham was careful to ensure that in each country district the most senior official should be a single magistrate, but he vested authority for the whole system in a board. He did not clearly explain why he chose joint rather than individual responsibility on these occasions. In his 'Elucidations Relative to the Thames Police Bill', he noted the case for individual responsibility at the top, but simply remarked that 'on other accounts [it] would be inadvizable and impracticable'.[188] He came closer to an explanation in relation to the National Charity Company, where he argued that its 'plurality of hands' would contribute to its 'permanence' and its 'security', and might help it to 'rid itself of the incumbrance of plurality in its local and subordinate departments'.[189] But these statements read like rationalizations rather than accounts of his real reasons. Perhaps the best explanation is that in these cases he was to some extent governed by the wishes and expectations of others; in the Charity Company, by the prejudices of potential shareholders who were accustomed to see joint-stock concerns managed by boards of directors; in the police schemes, by the wishes of Colquhoun and possibly of the merchants who were interested in securing a police force for the Thames and its docks. His own explanations make it clear that in theory as well as in practice he was treating individual responsibility as the norm, from which deviations might be permitted but had to be explained and justified in each case.

His inclusion of 'subordination', appointment and dismissal among the aspects of each post already implied relations among the several offices in any establishment. At several points he found it necessary to say more about those relations and thus to work towards a pattern for an ideal or typical organizational structure. He saw that individual responsibility might conceivably function as a weapon for evading responsibility ('buck-passing'), and he developed his own counter to it. This was to make each official responsible not only for his own conduct but also for that of his subordinates, especially where they were chosen and appointed by the officer himself. One officer who was in that position was the Timber Master, and he was solemnly warned that 'the blame of any bad management (though it may appear to arise from [his subordinates'] neglect or unskilfulness) will always fall heavily

upon him; more especially if he should have omitted any opportunity of bringing to light [their] misconduct'.[190] In this way the
responsibility and the authority of each office were diffused downwards through other offices, binding them together and providing
some elements of a framework into which they all fitted.

He provided other elements of a framework as he strove to
eliminate, in particular institutions, all gaps, inconsistencies or
discontinuities in the transmission of authority and the pattern of
subordination. The police structure that he sought to create was
a good example of his skill in achieving his objective: responsibility and authority flowed smoothly downwards from the Home
Office (or in some matters the Treasury) to the Commissioners,
and from them in two branches: in the metropolis to their own
employees, and in the country to the police magistrates and
ultimately to the Surveyors employed by the magistrates. Although
the system was asymmetrical, it preserved the authority of those at
the top. He made a still more interesting attack on discontinuities
and inconsistencies in the Timber Master's Instructions. The
Timber Master's post was a potential source of difficulty because
it had something of the character of a 'staff' office standing
outside the main 'line' of authority, and would therefore partici-
pate in transactions with other offices to which it was not
clearly either subordinate or superior. These transactions involved
the supply of men or other resources to the Timber Master, the
attendance of other officers with the Master to supervise the
measuring of newly-delivered loads of timber, and the supply by
the Master of sawn timber in suitable shapes and sizes. Bentham's
technique was to specify the respective rights and responsibilities
in each case, and to require in general that requests or notifications
from one officer to another should be made in writing and that
they should be faithfully attended to. In the event of disputes
about the quality of sawn pieces, he established procedures for
settling the matter in both urgent and less urgent cases.[191]

There were, finally, two other elements in Bentham's theories
which tended to bind the individual offices together and to provide
an organizational framework. These were the two closely-related
principles of uniformity in management and unity of authority.
The role of uniformity in management in facilitating comparison
and selection and in applying its results has already been mentioned. It was also one of the things that gave to the organization

the 'steadiness' on which the superiority of collective enterprise was to depend. It depended, in its turn, on unity of authority, which would provide a focus and an activating point for all offices and activities, would 'sit in judgement over the management of any one' and would ensure 'regularity' in each of them and 'uniformity in the whole assemblage of them taken together'.[192]

Bentham developed many of his ideas about organization and management as solutions to particular problems in particular institutions. But once he had devised them, they were available to be used again and he himself rarely saw them as having only a local application. He freely translated them from one institution to another; he often defended them in general terms, as he sought to follow his own precepts by supplying 'reasons' for the legislative and other provisions in his plans. Finally he gathered many of them together, with some other points applying more exclusively to pauper management, into principles (sometimes rules) of management for Industry Houses. He made various lists of these, which differed slightly in content and terminology. With the exception of those items (such as 'life-assurance') which were directed only to pauper management, the most regularly-appearing principles or rules were:

Inspective-architecture
Transparent-management or publicity
Duty-and-interest-junction
Unity of authority
Piece-work
Peculiar-premium or prize-giving
Honorary-reward
Separate-work
Ample-scale
Labour-division
Employment-mixing or sundry-trade
Habit-respecting
Refuse-employing or save-all
Use-multiplying or many-use
Uniform-management
Local-consideration-consulting
Tabular-statement
Comparison and selection.[193]

Most of these have been discussed individually in the text above. But by gathering them together and treating them as, collectively, the 'principles of management' or 'the principles of pauper economy', Bentham was representing them as both comprehensive and mutually-supporting. They summed up, moreover, the 'line of good management' which he had acknowledged to be applicable to government as well as to joint-stock enterprise. Together with their attendant descriptions and rationales, they thus constituted a general theory of organization and management which was something more than the sum of its parts.

Bentham embarked on his studies of particular institutions and policies with a fairly clear but limited idea of the structure of government, a well-formed attitude to its functions, and a mass of principles, criteria and devices for making any establishment or public trust work effectively. He emerged from those studies with a rather more complicated view of a government's structure and its functions, and a more sophisticated view of the nature and working of public trusts and other establishments.

His original view of the structure and operations of government was focused on law-making and law-enforcement, and it was his ambition to devise an economical style of government. This approach seemed to be reinforced by the political radicalism that he espoused in the 1790s, for his radical objectives would be served by 'saving measures' which reduced places and patronage, and their fulfilment required the strict subordination of the Executive to the Legislature. But he soon found it necessary to expand the simple structure with which he had begun, and to fill out his account of its parts and their relationships.

At an early stage he acknowledged the need to add a layer of local government to the structure, in order to complete its coverage of the whole nation. He was induced to add other, mainly administrative, elements to it as he thought more carefully about the functions and activities of government. Political economy had seemed likely for a time to confine these within narrow limits, but that expectation was soon exposed as an illusion. His demands on government implied a wide range of functions, most of which required *administrative* activity beyond what could be supplied by the Legislature and the Judiciary, and therefore required administrative bodies to perform the necessary tasks.

In his plans for the Legislature and the Judiciary, he very skilfully translated his principles of jurisprudence into blueprints for concrete institutions. In one of his essays in those fields – his programme for the re-organization of the French Judiciary – the arrangements that he proposed for the recruitment, pay, deployment and discipline of the full-time employees were sufficiently comprehensive and precise to serve as a model for any official establishment or Civil Service. And here and elsewhere his civil-law notion of a condition and his principles of indirect legislation, punishment and reward were incorporated at many points and provided the basis for much of his reasoning. The same notions and principles were available for, and were employed in, his designs for administrative institutions. Because of the nature of the tasks that these institutions were to perform, and because he was by this time conscious of the dangers of 'influence' and the need for 'responsibility' or 'dependence', some of his plans had to be very fully worked-out. On these occasions he exhibited a mastery of detail in defining particular parts of the establishment, and a grasp of structure and inter-relationships in building the separate parts into complete institutions and systems. The plans for the National Charity Company and the scheme based on the Board of Police were especially impressive for their scope and their attention to detail.

As he worked on the details he was prompted to speculate further about many of the principles and much of the reasoning that he was trying to apply. The result of his speculations was that he expanded his ideas about indirect legislation, reward and production economics into the theory of organization and management which they had begun to resemble and to foreshadow in the 1780s. In formulating this theory he recognized management as a distinct activity and as a common element in diverse administrative situations. The contents of the theory did not include much that was wholly new, but there was much new and close reasoning added to some of the familiar points. One of the most striking and valuable parts of the new reasoning was concerned with what Bentham called book-keeping but which is more properly to be seen as a programme for records and communications within a complex administrative system. This programme substantially increased the scope and power of his approach to the control of subordinates and of the other resources on which managers and decision makers might draw. A second set of new conclusions followed from his further examination of the economies of large-scale production. This led him in an unexpected direction, to an enthusiasm for collective action and permanent institutions, and a corresponding scepticism about the effectiveness, in the long run, of purely individual action.

The theory of management, including its collectivist implications, was applicable to institutions and enterprises in general, not specifically to government. Bentham sought to limit the expansion of government, and thus to make it approximate to the economical style that he favoured, by transferring some of its functions to contractors. This policy was consistent with the principle of 'venality' that he had advocated in his essay on reward, and he found further support for it in a theory of social progress which located contemporary society in a stage insufficiently advanced to permit effective public administration. But his account of social development allowed him to set up no more than temporary barriers to the growth of government, for it left room for a steady improvement in the efficiency of public officials and public institutions. Nevertheless the barriers seemed sufficiently firm and permanent to relieve him of any immediate obligation to treat the executive branch of government on the same scale as the legislative and judicial branches which he regarded as closer to the heart of government.

Thus Bentham's major achievement in the Panopticon essays and his other particular studies was to bring almost to completion the work of identifying the principal requirements of a bureaucratic institution, and of showing how they might be met. But the institutions in which he developed and applied this bureaucratic approach were all discrete bodies, which were intended to handle some particular branch of government or to perform some specific task or tasks. He had not yet tried or decided to construct a single bureaucratic system that would incorporate all the activities and all the branches. His arguments, up to the point to which he had carried them, had not provided him with a compelling motive to present an integrated account of the whole structure of government or to apply systematically to all of its parts the theory which he had developed for some of them. He was eventually to do so, but the inquiries in which he next engaged led him initially away from that point and it took him nearly twenty years to find his way back to it.

6

FROM THE *PANOPTICON* TO THE *CONSTITUTIONAL CODE*

The Panopticon project came to an end in March 1801, when the Treasury recorded their decision to substitute for Bentham's scheme a smaller one and one unacceptable to Bentham. It took Bentham more than a year to recognize that he could not, by persuasion or the pressure of public opinion, induce the Government to reverse that decision. He devoted most of 1802 to agitation among his friends and to the drafting of a long critique of the Government's policies and conduct, provisionally entitled 'A Picture of the Treasury, with a Sketch of the Secretary of State's Office...' By the end, however, that had ceased to be a means of bringing about a change of mind and had become merely an instrument for punishing the Government. In 1803 Bentham recognized, though with many backward glances, that the episode was over and he began to turn his mind to other subjects. While he continued to see his tracts on the Panopticon as among the most valuable and most characteristic of his works, it did not again occupy a central place in his thoughts except for short periods in 1807–8 and 1811–13 when he was involved in negotiations with the Government concerning the financial and legal problems left unsettled in 1801.[1] From 1802 onwards his activities and writings display what appear to be rapid changes and a wide range of interests and subject-matters until he began to concentrate mainly (but not exclusively) on the *Constitutional Code* in 1822.

The bare record of his life and achievements between 1802 and 1822 suggests that this was a blank period in his progress towards a comprehensive theory of government. At the beginning of the period he seemed to retreat, physically and psychologically, into his famous 'hermitage', and intellectually into the study of technical legal subjects such as evidence, the system of judicial appeal, court procedure and the jury system. When, after about 1808, he emerged intellectually and politically, it was by taking up a set of subjects that seemed to have no direct connection with the Executive. In so far as these had any central focus it was in Parliament and the electoral system, while many were much more remote from the day-to-day activities of governmental administration, including language and logic, religion, education, individual psychology and the principles of codification. It is not easy to see in the unadorned record either the means or the motives for assembling his ideas of responsibility and management, or for bringing them to bear on the non-parliamentary institutions of government.

The appearances are, however, misleading. Bentham's physical withdrawal was less complete than he sometimes represented it, and his psychological retreat was still less so. He maintained throughout these years many links with the world outside his study, and he continued to use them successfully as means of information and sometimes in efforts to influence events. Moreover, despite the undeniable differences in subject-matter and overt political stance in his works written before and after 1808, it is possible to see nearly all that he wrote between 1802 and 1822 as parts of a single intellectual enterprise, the development of a campaign against 'misrule' in all its forms.

Bentham's image of himself as a hermit had some elements of truth in it, but some elements of make-believe and possibly some elements of calculated misrepresentation.[2] His mode of life was designed to enable him to regulate his contacts with the outside world, not to cut them off entirely. As a member of the prosperous middle classes, he was able to employ secretaries and servants, and to use them to screen him from the physical burdens of daily living. But he also used the secretaries whom he employed at different times – J. H. Koe, Walter Coulson, John Colls, Richard Doane, Arthur Moore – as channels of communication with outsiders. And while he was both discriminating and calculating in his personal relationships and in admitting people to his house, in practice he had many visitors and formed some long-lasting relationships. Many of his best-known and most significant friendships dated from the period of his hermitage. Mill, Brougham, Place, Ricardo, Joseph Hume and Bowring are the most obvious names; others included John Whishaw, James Abercromby, Sarah

Austin, Edward Blaquiere, Aaron Burr, W. E. Lawrence, the Hills of Hazelwood, John Neal, William Thompson of Cork, Robert Torrens, Frances Wright and the American diplomats Richard Rush and John Adams Smith. He was always intensely curious about the doings of governments and of other public figures, and he went to considerable trouble to satisfy his curiosity. He assiduously read newspapers and official reports, and marked passages which his secretaries copied. He secured additional information from his friends and other contacts. Of particular importance here were the journalists whom he cultivated: the Hunts of the *Examiner*, James Perry and John Black of the *Morning Chronicle*, and Torrens and Coulson (his former secretary) of the *Traveller* and the *Globe*. On the whole he was as well-informed about the daily course of politics and administration, and about the deeper trends, as anybody who was not himself a politician or an official. Occasionally, in later years, he exploited his contacts with the journalists to 'place' items that he wanted published.

The diversity of his writings in the period concealed an inner logic in his progression from one topic to another. His writings on parliamentary reform were neither distinct from all the rest, nor self-sufficient. They were in some respects an outgrowth of the legal studies that preceded them, and there were close connections between them and his studies of religion, language and other subjects. They tackled the problem of misrule at one vital point but he had become aware that misrule had many other aspects and buttresses, and he was trying to locate and to deal with all of them. As he took them up one by one, he was working towards the idea that there was a single system of misrule against which he was contending, and towards the view that he needed a correspondingly comprehensive programme to combat it. The programme had therefore to cover the Judiciary and the Executive as well as Parliament. By 1822 he had developed some ideas on the Executive which he could add to his earlier and more complete scheme for the Judiciary. And what he had written on other topics, including the Judiciary, made it inevitable that his treatment of the Executive should be based on responsibility and management rather than on electoral processes.

The principal themes of his writings in the nineteenth century were foreshadowed in the work he drafted in 1802 as a commentary on his experiences during the previous decade, the 'Picture

of the Treasury...' In that work he represented himself as to
some extent the victim of official incapacity or 'inaptitude', but
still more as the victim of 'influence', the extra-legal force that
he had begun seriously to denounce and to analyse in his radical
writings about ten years earlier: in this case, the influence
possessed and used by members of the Spencer and Grosvenor
families and (as he supposed) by the Royal family. With influence
he coupled, as its instruments, two other things that also figured
in the Whigs' ideology, namely despotism and the dispensing
power.[3] The dispensing power meant the power of the Executive
to override and ignore Parliament, as the Stuarts had done in the
seventeenth century. Bentham had long been accustomed to refer
to despotism and to contrast it with free government, but he now
described it more precisely as power without responsibility.

In casting his complaints about the Government's conduct in
these terms, Bentham was doubtless trying to win the sympathy
of the Whigs,[4] but he was also expressing his own long-established
values and orientations. His complaints were that the vital
decisions about the Panopticon had been taken by members of the
Government, that the latter had paid no attention to the wishes
of Parliament, and that no means existed for subjecting them to
Parliament's discipline. The Duke of Portland, he maintained,
had resolved to prevent 'Parliament from putting convicts where
Parliament chose to have them put', to 'put them into places of
his own choice, where Parliament chose *not* to have them put',
and to prevent the judges from acting 'in execution of [their]
duty...as prescribed to them by Parliament'.[5] And the Duke was
able to achieve all of his objects. Bentham interpreted his success
as totally incompatible with, and as undermining, the supremacy
of the Legislature and the legal system. 'If there be one "*law of
the Kingdom*" more "fundamental" than another,' he asked
rhetorically, 'is it not that which establishes the supremacy of
Parliament? And has not the Duke of Portland in words as well
as in deeds set his own individual will above the supremacy of
Parliament? If there be a "*liberty*" worth preserving is it not the
liberty of not being bound in repugnancy to the law of Parliament
by a spurious law made by the single authority of a servant of the
Crown?'[6] But Portland's defiance of Parliament had a significance
beyond the particular case in which Bentham's personal interests
were involved. It was, he argued, subversive of the whole Con-

stitution, because of its 'character of a precedent – from its tendency in that character to give birth to other similar acts, to like usurpations of power' until finally 'the authority of Parliament' would be quite destroyed.[7]

In attacking influence, despotism and the dispensing power Bentham was thus defending the integrity and efficiency of a legal system emanating from a legislative sovereign. These were the ideals to which he had been committed from the beginning of his work on law and government; and they were the ideals to which he remained committed in the years after 1802. He sought to defend them first in the series of essays on legal topics which occupied him between about 1803 and 1809. His concentration on technical legal questions in this period of his life was not a withdrawal from the field of politics and government but was only a change in tactics and immediate targets. It sprang from his understanding of the political functions of law; it led back to questions of politics and government by more than one route.

The earliest of these studies – the first, that is, to be started – was his work on Evidence. This seems to have been his principal concern from 1803 to 1806. In the middle of the latter year, for example, he assured Samuel (who was then on his second long visit to Russia) that 'I for my part do not like writing anything except evidence.'[8] But in the same year his attention was caught by a proposal to reform the Scottish law of procedure, and in the next two years he spent much of his time writing about 'Scotch Reform' and about the 'Court of Lords' Delegates' that he wanted to graft upon the House of Lords. These two projects were closely related in his own mind, and he seems to have switched some material from one to the other while he was drafting them. One link between them was that the official proposals for Scotch reform included a new Court of Appeal which would lie between the Scottish courts and the House of Lords, and Bentham was hostile to that idea. He published some material on both subjects in 1808, but the works that he planned and largely drafted were substantially richer and more elaborate than the published versions. The little *Summary View of a Plan of a Judicatory under the name of the Court of Lords' Delegates* gave a particularly inadequate picture of the real scope and nature of what he intended to write on the system of appeal.[9]

At about the time when – for political rather than intellectual reasons – he gave up further work on those subjects, he took up two others related to the courts and the judiciary. The slighter of the two was an essay entitled 'Law versus Arbitrary Power'. This was a commentary on a passage in William Paley's *Principles of Moral and Political Philosophy*, in which Paley had offered a utilitarian defence of the English practices of prescribing death as the penalty for a multitude of offences but of frequently substituting lesser penalties after conviction.[10] Bentham's second and more substantial work was a proposed code for ensuring the liberty of the press, together with an essay on the press. The Press Code was designed for the use of the Government of Venezuela and Bentham intended that it should be taken there by Francisco de Miranda. The essay may have been designed as a rationale or commentary to accompany the Code, although it was probably prompted by recent English events. In this context Bentham proceeded to examine the law of libel, which for him meant in practice the law concerning the defamation of politicians and officials.[11] His examination led him finally to the nature of the juries employed in the libel trials, which he found to be not 'common' but 'special' juries, selected by the judges' officers. He condemned both the principles and the practice in his fierce little pamphlet, *The Elements of Packing*.[12]

In all of these works Bentham's objectives were constitutional and much of his argument was on constitutional themes. He was striving to eliminate from the administration of the law those features which he believed functioned as weapons or armour for the Executive, to add to it certain forms of protection for citizens and Parliament against the Executive, and to equip the Judiciary to perform its constitutional role while depriving it of any opportunity to go beyond that role. Its proper constitutional role was, of course, to remain aloof from the Executive and to act as an obedient and efficient servant of the Legislature and as guardian and enforcer of the rights and obligations established by law. On the question of obedience, his views were virtually identical with those that he had advanced in the *Fragment on Government* and *Of Laws in General*. In 'the most perfect and most easily conceivable state of things', he asserted,

the rule of action is, in all its branches, the expressly declared will of the person or persons possessing the supreme power or at any rate the legislative br unch of the supreme power in the state.

This declared will, how perfectly or how imperfectly soever conducive to the well fare [sic] of the community taken in the aggregate must to all practical purposes, so long as that obedience is manifested in which the supreme power is consituted, be taken for the standard of rectitude.

This rule of action being thus declared – this standard of rectitude fixt, the function of the supreme judicial power or supreme judicature consists in the issuing of such particular orders or commands as are necessary to the causing the conduct of the several members of the community, in the character of subjects, to be kept on all occasions as near as is possible to a state of perfect conformity to the standard of rectitude.[13]

The need for efficiency raised different sorts of questions. The essential point here was that the decision of the judge consisted of two elements or 'propositions': 'viz. a proposition concerning the state of the *law*, and a proposition concerning the state of certain matters of *fact* – of matters of fact which belong to the case, and to which the law that belongs to the case is considered as applying itself'.[14] If the judge were to function effectively on behalf of the sovereign-legislator he needed to have access not only to a determinate body of law, but also to the means of judging matters of fact with perfect accuracy.

The actual performance of the Judiciary, he maintained, fell a long way short of those standards. It was condemned to inefficiency by an archaic procedure and obscurantist rules of evidence. And its behaviour was very different from the strict conformity to the will of the Legislature that he was prescribing. It enjoyed and exercised large discretions, for example in the matter of sentencing policy to which Paley had drawn attention. It was also guilty of many faults resembling or identical with those that he had criticized in the Executive in his 'Picture of the Treasury...': 'insubordination', 'usurpation of legislative authority', 'non-conformity of the judge's decision to the will, declared or conjectural...of the sovereign power in the state', 'nullification to legislation', 'a dispensing power exercised by the King's Judges' in defiance of the principles of the Revolution and finally and comprehensively 'a habitual and undisguised contempt manifested by judges and other subordinate functionaries as towards the authority of Parliament'.[15] Still worse, it was often joined in alliance with the Executive – the Crown – to enable it to defy Parliament, to avoid public scrutiny and in general to promote sinister interest. This was, for example, the case in relation to the 'packing' of special juries and the administration of libel law. His consciousness of this alliance led him ultimately to a new understanding – not incompatible with his first formulations of it, but more thorough – of the system of influence. He found first that the co-operation between Judiciary and Crown was facilitated and encouraged by a group of non-official persons, the lawyers, those 'irreconcilable enemies of the people' whose 'interest and influence' led them to adopt that role.[16] And then he began to see Crown, judges and lawyers as participants in still wider groups engaged in promoting and benefiting from the perversion of the legal system. Sometimes he characterized them as the 'men in power' whose 'first object and only immediate object was to keep the people in quiet that [they] themselves [might] enjoy their good things at their ease.'[17] At other times they appeared as a more amorphous 'tendency among members of the higher orders, even of opposite parties, to join in supporting one another against justice', or even a 'conspiracy quietly going on – a quiet and safe conspiracy which [required] neither consultation nor concert – the conspiracy among the high and opulent to support one another against the low and the indigent'.[18]

When Bentham wrote the last of this series of legal works, *The Elements of Packing*, he was convinced that no remedy for the 'contempt of Parliament' would be adequate unless it included electoral reform. But he never supposed that reforms aimed directly at the legal system would be irrelevant, and in earlier years he seems to have supposed that they might well be introduced and made effective prior to changes in methods of election. His works on these subjects invariably included more or less detailed, and in some cases very detailed, proposals for dealing with the problems that he had pinpointed.

His writings on evidence and procedure were voluminous and highly technical, but his general approach can be summed up quite briefly. It was to transform the courts into effective guardians of rights, by orienting procedure and the rules of evidence primarily to the needs of the judge and not to the interests of plaintiffs, prosecutors or defendants. (Litigants needed and were entitled to free access to the courts, and to protection against delay and other forms of vexation; but they were not entitled to withhold evidence in their possession.) Rights could be fully protected, he believed, only if all offences were detected and punished, sinister interest would be served if offenders escaped punishment through judicial ignorance or through technicalities which permitted the exclusion of relevant evidence, or if bogus offences were admitted for the same reasons.[19] The need for the judge to have access to the relevant evidence, to have it in a complete and correct form, was paramount. He expressed his demand for completeness in terms of two complementary ideas, the 'forthcomingness' and the 'non-exclusion' of all evidence that had a bearing on the question before the judge.[20] His search for correctness led him to reject as misleading many forms of written evidence, and to place great value on 'oral interrogation' as a means of eliciting the truth.[21] But he also wanted to extend the range of certain forms of written evidence available to the judge. He called these 'pre-appointed' evidence. They would consist of more complete and trustworthy records of various kinds of official and private transactions that would be likely to have a bearing on litigants' rights and obligations.[22]

Bentham believed that the adoption of his approach to evidence and procedure would contribute to curbing the independence and insubordination of the Judiciary. But for this purpose he proposed to rely also on two other measures. One, which was his answer to Paley, was to seek the precision in the law which he had always demanded, to leave no vagueness in the penalties provided, no loopholes for the determination of lesser penalties or the issue of pardons in extenuating circumstances which might endow judge or official with a 'dispensing power'.[23] The second was a new pattern of judicial organization which he described and defended at length in his related works on *Court of Lords' Delegates* and *Scotch Reform*.

When he was demanding the obedience of judges to the will of Parliament, Bentham observed that two problems or levels were involved. After declaring, in a passage quoted above, that the 'supreme judicial power' must follow Parliament's directions, he went on:

But like as by the supreme judicial power the will of the supreme legislative power naturally is and ought to be regarded as the standard of rectitude; so is and ought to be the will of the supreme judicial power regarded by the subordinate judicatures.

The supreme legislative power being supposed to be happily and rightly lodged, that system of judicature will be the most perfect in which the conduct of the supreme judicial power being most exactly and constantly conformable to the declared will of the supreme legislative, the conduct of the subordinate judicatures is most exactly and constantly conformable to the will of the supreme judicature.[24]

There were, accordingly, two relationships to be attended to, that between Parliament and the highest court, and that between the highest and the inferior courts. In each relationship he sought the 'substituting of a responsible for an irresponsible judicatory',[25] but because of the character of the respective parties he did so in different ways.

At the top, he argued that it was desirable to preserve the status of the House of Lords as the ultimate source of judicial authority, for 'supreme judicial power [could] not with propriety or even safety be lodged in any other hands than in one or other of the three branches of the legislature'.[26] Since the Peers had 'conquered' appellate jurisdiction the best course seemed to be to preserve and exploit that conquest rather than to look for another way of binding the Judiciary to the Legislature and of isolating it from the Executive.[27] But he judged that the House of Lords itself was incapable of exercising the jurisdiction efficiently. He therefore proposed that it should delegate the function to a group of four 'Lords' Delegates', but that it should preserve its authority and the Delegates' responsibility by electing them and requiring them to submit themselves for re-election at the end of a fixed, short term of office.

He proposed to enforce responsibility at lower levels by making the Delegates something more than and different from a court of final appeal. Although he had been willing to rely on appeals as a method of judicial discipline when he drafted *French Judicial Establishment*, he was now rather hostile to them on the ground that they were a fertile source of delay and vexation. He therefore assigned to the Lords' Delegates the positive 'function of exercising a superintending authority over the several courts of justice their subordinates'.[28] This meant that the Delegates should not wait for the vagaries of appeal to bring to their notice examples of misdecision or other judicial shortcomings, and that they should not rely on the gradual adoption of principles enunciated in their judgements in order to produce conformity with their opinions. They were to engage instead in a form of judicial management, actively seeking information about good and bad judicial performance and taking definite steps – issuing definite instructions – to correct what was unsatisfactory. In performing these managerial tasks, the Lords' Delegates were to use the devices of management which he had developed and applied in his studies of the poor law and police: the clear definition of powers and responsibilities and the monitoring of official behaviour by inspection, records and statistics.[29] The system of responsibility was to be completed by the extension of monitoring to the Delegates themselves, for they were to be obliged to submit to Parliament regular statistical and other reports on which their performance – their claims to re-election – could be assessed.

Bentham was confident that if all these reforms were carried out the Judiciary would for the first time be fully integrated into the structure focused on and deriving from the sovereign-legislator, and that it would become capable of distinguishing real from fanciful invasions of legally-created rights. His hopes that they could be effected in advance of electoral reform seem to have survived until about the middle of 1808. They were strongest during the life of the Grenville Government in 1806–07, when Dumont (who still enjoyed access to Lord Henry Petty, Grenville's Chancellor of the Exchequer) encouraged him to believe that it might take up his schemes.[30] The precipitate expulsion of Grenville and his colleagues in March 1807 cancelled that prospect. Nevertheless he thought it worthwhile in 1808 to publish the two hastily-devised short versions of *Scotch Reform* and *Court of Lords' Delegates*, and in the same year he contemplated a direct approach to the House of Commons by petition.[31] These were presumably attempts to bring pressure on the new Portland Government, which could only be apathetic or hostile to his ideas. He did not, however, proceed with his petition, and at some point in the next year he again became convinced that nothing short of radical electoral reform could ever be successful. He then embarked on the political course to which he stuck for the remainder of his life and which became characteristic of Benthamism as a political movement.

The nature of and the reasons for his change of front have been widely discussed by historians.[32] Particular attention has been paid to the role of James Mill with whom he had recently become acquainted. His early exchanges with Mill in 1808–9 are not well-documented, and any assessment of Mill's influence on him must rest heavily on circumstantial evidence. I do not want to take a

definite position on the issue. But I suggest that if Mill converted
Bentham back to democracy, he must have found a ready convert.
In the light of the views Bentham had been expressing in his work
on the courts, the change in course brought about by the conversion was a relatively small one. It was, like the original decision
to concentrate on legal issues after 1802, a change in tactics not in
fundamental political judgements. In some respects it was
directly anticipated by some of his arguments relating to the
courts. It was also invited by certain political events and circumstances in the years 1807–09 which affected him more or less
closely or to which he was particularly sensitive.

His anticipation of democratic ideas had appeared in those
parts of his work on *The Court of Lords' Delegates* in which he
set out the relationship between the Delegates and the Peers.
This material was not extensive but it included both democratic
political devices and arguments with a democratic tendency.
The arrangements for the election of Delegates were a radical
electoral programme in miniature. They prescribed annual elections, voting by secret ballot and the careful division of the Peers
into homogeneous constituencies.[33] And they were not lightly
chosen. Bentham defended them in terms of what he described as
'a principle [having] the character of a fundamental principle:
viz. that the mind and conduct of a body delegated may be as
exact a representation as possible of the mind of the body dele-
gating'.[34] In more detail, he defended the secret ballot as a device
for ensuring that the electors would be left as 'free as possible, as
against all influences of *will* over *will*';[35] that is, against the kind
of influence which was sinister and served sinister interest and
misrule. He was stating the points in so general a form that they
could just as easily be applied to the relationship between the
community and Parliament as to the relationship between Parliament and some of its servants. It is not easy to suppose that
Bentham was unaware of this other application of them. He seems
already, in this discussion, to be writing as a convinced electoral
reformer, although perhaps one who felt that it would be tactful
to postpone debate on the full implications of his position.

One of the circumstances which encouraged him to be less
patient and less discreet after 1808 was the absence of any public
response to the publication of *The Court of Lords' Delegates* and
Scotch Reform. A second was the wider significance of the fall of

the Grenville Government and of the circumstances in which it fell. In addition to his hopes that it would sponsor his proposals for judicial reform, Bentham had been able to view the coalition Ministry as, in a general sense, 'our Ministry'.[36] The return to power of Portland and his colleagues amounted to the reinstatement of his own oppressors and of the unrelenting enemies of reform. Almost as threatening, from his point of view, was the King's role in dismissing Grenville; it provided new and cogent evidence of the power of the Crown to dominate the Legislature. For a short time he hoped that the House of Commons would assert itself and demand the restoration of Grenville, but he was soon forced to recognize that this would not happen.[37] His disillusionment with the unreformed House of Commons was then complete, although he never stopped suggesting things that it ought to do.

His disenchantment with all the branches of government was confirmed in the same period by a mass of new evidence, produced by official inquiries, of scandals, illegality and mismanagement on the part of officials and Ministers. The most spectacular of these inquiries concerned the alleged sale of Army commissions by the Duke of York's mistress, but the most fruitful of them from Bentham's point of view were those conducted by the Select Committee on Public Expenditure which was set up in 1807.

The Select Committee produced three reports by the middle of 1808, and it added a supplement and a fourth report in the following year.[38] It brought to light some cases of flagrantly dishonest or illegal behaviour and (what was more important from Bentham's point of view) it documented on a massive scale many aspects of the existing financial system and it applied to them a set of utilitarian criteria. The bulkiest and most revealing of these early reports was the Third, on Pensions, Sinecures and Reversions, which the Committee produced in response to a direct Instruction by the House of Commons (7 July 1807) to investigate the subject.[39] The Fourth, on the Commissioners for Dutch and other Prizes, was also revealing and seems to have made an impression on Bentham.[40] The Committee demonstrated that large sums of public money were annually absorbed in an extraordinarily diverse and tangled set of pensions, sinecures, offices executed by deputy and other privileges of doubtful origin, that the existing means for regulating or even reporting these (such as the Civil List Act of 1782) were limited and haphazard in their operation, that there still existed some offices which might be sold by various persons and that public officers such as the Commissioners for Prizes were able to make *profits* out of their offices far in excess of their formal or nominal remuneration. The Committee condemned many of these practices and made recommendations that often resembled Bentham's: the simplification of procedures, the clarification of lines of authority, the recognition of power and status as elements in official's rewards, and acceptance of the principles that 'offices ought to be regarded as created solely for public utility' and that 'the Public ought unquestionably to be served as cheaply as is consistent with being served with integrity and ability'.[41]

The inquiries of the Select Committee and its successors (which included a further Select Committee on Sinecures, and Crown-appointed Commissioners inquiring into saleable offices in the courts of law) dragged on for some years, and their immediate impact on administrative practice was not very great.[42] Bentham, too, found some their views unwelcome, especially their attacks on the sale of offices.[43] But they had provided detailed and voluminous evidence that the Executive did, as he maintained, dispose of large sums of money and other rewards which might be used to cultivate influence. They also provided, in their use of utilitarian and efficiency-oriented criteria, some grounds for believing that the public was becoming more receptive in this area at least to the kinds of argument that he habitually employed. So he could find both encouragement and ammunition in their reports.[44]

He found still further evidence of inefficiency and official independence, although very little encouragement, in his exchanges between June 1807 and May 1809 with the Commissioners for Auditing the Public Accounts and their subordinates. The origin of these exchanges was the Auditors' belated attempt to make him account for the £2,000 which had been advanced to him in 1794 so that he could make preliminary arrangements for the construction of the Panopticon. He found the officials' behaviour so objectionable that he turned his side of the correspondence into a critique of the Auditors' procedures.[45] He fastened on three points of general significance, arguing that they adopted a thoroughly unsatisfactory approach to *evidence* by over-rating written at the expense of oral evidence (a vital matter, he believed, in a body that combined administrative and judicial functions), that their structure and arrangements ignored the principle of individual responsibility, and that there was no disposition or pressure to correct those or other deficiencies. In sum, the Auditors shared with other parts of the Executive a freedom from legal control that permitted them to serve or exercise arbitrary power. His case against the existing system was completed by the prosecutions of authors and publishers that prompted him to detach *The Elements of Packing* from his general study of the press.[46] They showed the Executive and the Judiciary acting together in what he was convinced was a conspiracy against the freedom of both press and public.

As he accumulated and studied this body of evidence concerning misrule, he began to develop again a more general, a less technical and more overtly political, approach to it. This appeared in an embryonic form in two rough summaries of contemporary political conditions that he drew up, the first a list of the community's 'sacrifices' that he composed in August 1807, the second a similar list of 'grievances' dated July 1809.[47] These covered some of the familiar weaknesses in the law or legal machinery about which he had been complaining for so long, such as 'the rule of custom left in the form of unwritten or conjectural law', 'the statute law in a state of chaos without parts capable of being referred to', and 'virtual outlawry of the bulk of the people' through the expense of litigation. But he associated these shortcomings in the law with sinister influence and officials' independence, and focused attention on the instruments and processes through which influence operated and independence was maintained and on their results. He mentioned here 'the King's personal interest in respect of the appointment of Clergymen to sinecure places and pensions', the benefits granted to 'Lord Eldon to pay him for his obsequiousness as an instrument in making up a party to support the King against the Grenville Government', 'money raised in the shape of fees without the cognizance of Parliament', and a trio of points that more or less summed up his understanding of the existing system of government:

1. Contempt of the Legislative by judges and other judicial officers
2. do. by members of the Administrative departments.
3. Corruption of the Legislative by the Executive.

Finally, he introduced into the 'grievances' a more radical or more populist line of thinking, in a condemnation of 'preferences given by the Laws to the superior to the prejudice of the middle and the inferior' classes in the community. This was a clear reference to and a revival of his idea of the conspiracy dominating English political life. Together with the above three points it ensured that he could not see parliamentary reform as an end in itself or as purely a matter of electoral machinery. His object must be to right the relationships among the several branches of government and the community that they were supposed to serve, and his means must include the destruction of the conspiracy and of all the resources on which it depended, namely corruption and influence in their manifold forms.

The existence of the conspiracy did not, however, make parliamentary reform any less necessary and he decided to concentrate on it as a first step. His decision to do so coincided roughly with his composition of the statement of public grievances, and probably preceded it by a few weeks.[48] Once he had taken it, he applied himself to the task of carrying it out with characteristic energy but with an equally characteristic dispersion of effort. By 1811 he had partly drafted a cluster of five or six works in which he set out his proposals for reform and in which he incorporated and carried further the kind of argument that he had recently employed in his work on the courts.

The centre-piece of the cluster was a major work entitled 'Parliamentary Reform'. Bentham never published it or got it into a publishable form, but he drafted many pages for it in 1809 and 1810, and he drew up a more or less orderly scheme into which they might be fitted. The scheme provided for three parts or 'books' entitled respectively: 'I, Necessity; II, Influence; III, Plan.'[49] In later years it served him as a reservoir from which he drew materials for his other and better-known writings on the same theme. It was flanked by a separate essay on sinecures, a critical study of the Admiralty Prizes Acts of 1805 and 1809, possibly a separate essay on influence, a version of the material which he later published as his *Defence of Economy* against Burke and against George Rose, and a re-working of some of his drafts on the theory of reward or remuneration.[50] The presence of his work on reward in the cluster was a mainly fortuitous product of the fact that Dumont was preparing his edition of the

Théorie des peines et des récompenses at that time, and was consulting Bentham about the manuscripts and their proper arrangement.[51] But once the material caught his attention it re-entered his own thinking. It may have stimulated him to write his attacks on Burke and Rose, and it certainly played a part in his argument in those pamphlets, in the study of the Prizes Acts and in the essay on sinecures.

One function of these works was to describe the kinds of reform that Bentham was now demanding: annual Parliaments, the secret ballot, a franchise based on a taxpayer qualification and a number of the 'saving measures' or 'economical reforms' that he had favoured in his first radical phase. Their second function was to enable him to develop the case in favour of those measures and the theory underlying it.[52] The theory that he presented continued to be a set of variations on Whig themes, but it was now enriched by the ideas that he had developed when he was reflecting about the political functions of the Judiciary. His variations were consequently more elaborate, original and vigorously-stated than ever before.

He built his theory around the familiar notions of influence and corruption and the slightly less familiar notion of obsequiousness.[53] Obsequiousness was practically equivalent to obedience; it meant any positive response to power or influence. Neither it nor influence was necessarily an evil force. Influence was, in itself, no more than 'power working by comparatively gentle or inconspicuous means';[54] that is, consistently with his earlier view of it, it was power operating outside the legal system and without legal sanctions. Moreover, any political system needed obsequiousness in order to make it work: a government's business could not be carried on 'any farther than as towards the will of each superordinate functionary an habitual obsequiousness – so far as concerns the acts lawfully to be done in execution of that business – is manifested by each subordinate'.[55] Obsequiousness became bad only when it was the response to sinister influence, the illegitimate kind of influence that led to despotism and misrule. Corruption, however, was inherently bad. It consisted of all the means, whatever they might be, that could build or maintain sinister influence.

Bentham was thus still using Whig terminology but he was giving it – especially corruption – a different content because he was drawing the line between sinister and legitimate influence in a different way and at a different point. Sinister influence was not identical with or exclusively the influence of the Crown; it might be possessed and used by any member of the community. It drew its sinister character not from the personality of the possessor or wielder of influence but from the nature of the inter-action between influencer and respondent. He continued to base his distinction between the sinister and the benign on his old contrast between the action of will on will and the action of understanding on understanding. In his moral system, the appeal to rational argument was a proper and acceptable means of acting outside the legal system; but the diversion of overpowering of one will by another, except with the aid of legal sanctions, was improper and sinister.[56]

In making his distinctions on these grounds, Bentham was not abandoning or weakening his grip on the idea that the Crown was the chief *beneficiary* of the system of sinister influence. He remained as firmly wedded to that idea as he had been when he was in Shelburne's entourage or in the period of his acute dis-appointment immediately after the failure of the Panopticon project. What was distinctive about his approach, and what separated him decisively from the Whigs on that matter, was his belief that private influence must co-operate with – be joined in a conspiracy with – the Crown's influence to the ultimate advan-tage of the King. Surveying all the wielders of influence in the community, he concluded that the King had made them *all* 'conspirators with himself in these sacrifices of public to private interest...[and in] an all-pervading and constantly pursued system of breach of trust and misrule'.[57] He did not believe that non-intellectual forms of influence, those that relied on anything other than rational persuasion, could ever outweigh or operate against the Crown's influence, or could ever be a benign force in society.

This belief could be seen as an application of a more general point on which he was accustomed to disagree with the Whigs: his scepticism about the efficacy of any balancing of powers in government or any balancing of forces in society. But behind that, and reflected in his treatment of influence, lay a more funda-mental disagreement about what was the legitimate form of society. He totally rejected the Whigs' ideals of order, balance and the cultivation of social bonds. His own ideal was still that which he had set out thirty-five years earlier in the *Fragment on Government*: it was a society consisting of a mass of individuals, each of whom would be unimpeded by social bonds, who would be acting rationally in pursuit of his own interests as judged by himself, and who could properly be restrained or hampered only by a sovereign acting through law on behalf of the general happiness. His experiences in the intervening thirty-five years had taught him clearly enough that contemporary society did not have that individualist and voluntarist character, and that concentrations of non-legal power (or influence) existed widely within it. But he was still quite unreconciled to their existence, and quite unwilling to follow the Whigs in giving them a positive function in maintaining the cohesion or the liberties of the community. Most of his work up to this time had been directed to the shortcomings of government as an agent of the general happiness; the concentration of his attention on influence from 1809 onwards marked an attempt to apply his ideal critically to society itself, and to inquire whether it could not be re-shaped along individualist and voluntarist lines. The concept of influence came to play much the same role in his thought as property plays in many theories of socialism; that is, it functioned as the principal target of and obstacle to reform, the source to which all grievances, dissatisfactions, differences in power and injustices could be traced, and a principal tool for analysing and depicting social and political relationships.

His rejection of the Whigs' philosophy found expression in the ferocity of his critique of Edmund Burke's famous speech on economical reform, and in a mass of abuse that he directed at their other spokesmen and their panaceas: Burke's economical reform was a sham designed 'to preserve for use the principles of waste and corruption in the event of his finding himself in possession of the matter and the means';[58] 'Dunning's system of mitigated or reduced corruption' left the real problems untouched;[59] the separation of powers tended to reduce not increase the necessary degree of dependence of functionaries on the public;[60] 'bands' (that is, political parties) and official Oppositions were illusory forms of protection, because 'dependence on a party though in opposition is dependence on the King', and 'changes in administration prevent not despotism, only cause it to change hands'.[61] The course that he proposed for himself was different from theirs. It was to try to track down the private concentrations of power, the ability of one will to over-ride another by other than legal or rational means, and then to find ways of destroying them.

He directed himself to this task especially in the twelve chapters (chs. 7–18) that he devoted to the theme of corruption in 'Parliamentary Reform – Influence'. He followed the processes of corruption through to its effects on officials, members of Parliament and electors, as well as the state in general. He had already gone a long way towards tracking down the offenders when he was naming the various groups who contributed to the maladministration of justice. His more deliberate approach in the years 1809–11 yielded some more members of the conspiracy and a fuller understanding of the methods that they employed.

The vague category of the 'high and opulent' was now shown to include specifically the local magnates or gentry who wielded the influence of property in their localities, and the clergy of the Established Church. He denounced the influence of property in elections as 'more adverse to the purity of election' than bribery.[62] He was still more outspoken in his criticism of the Church: it was, he wrote, a cradle of 'sinister interest and interest-begotten prejudice', 'a seat and source of corruption and sinister dependence, hostile to good government'.[63]

Bentham's catalogue of the means of corruption covered the many forms of bribery and patronage that had been brought to his attention by the recent official inquiries or in other ways:[64] the Executive's stock of profitable offices, honours, pensions, preferential contracts, sinecures and moneys outside the control of Parliament, which he believed to be disposable almost at will through warfare and the acquisition of colonies and dependencies; and analogous rewards held in private hands and constituting much of the 'influence of property'. The more novel and original items in his catalogue were social and psychological sources of influence and domination, such as beliefs, emotions and relationships which might produce a 'state of habitual dependence'.[65] They included religious faith, gratitude, fear and loyalty, and forces which interfered with the free play of intellect or respect for truth, notably the 'enslavement of the Press' against which he had been protesting in the *Elements of Packing*, and the operation of laws imposing religious tests and thus promoting 'insincerity'. These last two forces, he believed, tended to corrupt the

morals and the understanding of the members of the community
and made it easier for the King and his toadies to mislead and
confuse their potential victims and to tempt their potential
collaborators.[66] As he summed up the matter a little later, he now
believed that the conspiracy flourished by preventing 'the subject
many from entertaining a true conception of their own interest:
giving all possible currency to fallacies directed to that object:
doing what can be done towards the suppression of discourses
tending to the exposure of those fallacies'.[67]

In terms of his advocacy of electoral reform, the direct and
obvious successors to 'Parliamentary Reform' and its companions
were about a dozen works generally shorter and narrower in
scope than the original study and mostly abandoned before they
were nearly ready for publication. They included the published
Plan of Parliamentary Reform (in some editions entitled *Catechism of Parliamentary Reform*), *Bentham's Radical Reform Bill*,
and *Radicalism Not Dangerous*; the draft Resolutions that he
drew up for Burdett in 1818; and the unpublished 'Essay on the
British Constitution' (1815),[68] 'Political Deontology' (1816–17),[69]
'Constitutional Catechism' (1816–17),[70] 'Government as viewed
at 27 and at 70' (1817),[71] 'Picture of Misrule, or things as they
are and as they ought not to be' (1818),[72] 'Letters to Lord
Erskine' (1818–19),[73] 'Parliamentary Reform Dialogue' (1818–
19)[74] and 'General Political Catechism, in which Government as
it is is contrasted with Government as it ought to be' (1820–
1821).[75]

In these works he repeated and applied the concepts and the
analysis around which he had built his argument in 1809–11, and
in certain respects he went beyond the programme of 'Parliamentary Reform'. The notions of 'sinister influence', 'misrule'
and dependence continued to supply the basis of his case for
reform. It remained his position that the control of offices,
honours and privileges by the Crown ensured that 'the representatives of the people' would be liable 'to be seduced from their
duty, and induced to sacrifice the universal interest of the people
their constituents to the particular interests or supposed interests
of the Crown, its servants and their adherents', that the attempts
made since 1780 to reduce sinister influence had all been frustrated by the growth of the Standing Army and of 'distant
dependencies', a growth which was irreversible; and that 'no

adequate diminution of the influence of the Crown [could] now be effected' except by stepping outside the system and ensuring that 'the administrators of public affairs' should be 'chosen and removable by those whose affairs are being administered'.[76] But as Halévy and others have pointed out, he now set more rigorous conditions for achieving that objective, discarding the 'taxpayer suffrage' with which he had been satisfied in 1809–10, and adopting the 'virtually universal suffrage' of his *Plan* and Burdett's Resolutions. In some of these works, too (notably 'Political Deontology' and the 'General Political Catechism'), he tried to give a more comprehensive account of government than in 'Parliamentary Reform' or the *Defence of Economy*, covering its ends, forms, powers, means and the obstacles it faced.

We shall have occasion to discuss some of that material in a later paragraph. But in relation to the development of Bentham's political *analysis*, those works were less interesting and fruitful than a series of other, more or less contemporaneous writings which were not explicitly about electoral reform but which were closely related to it in Bentham's thinking. They dealt with religion, education, language, logic, psychology, colonial policy and codification. They usually had more than one purpose, but one of these was in each case to reinforce his attack on influence or to add some refinement to his earlier argument about it.

Of these works, the most substantial and the one in which influence figured most prominently was *Church of Englandism and its Catechism Examined*, published in 1818. This was perhaps the most chaotically-arranged of all Bentham's publications. The 'body of the work' was, as its title implied, a quite detailed critique of the Catechism, but it was surrounded by prefaces and appendices, some of which were separately paginated and most of which dealt with contemporary political issues or the Church's organization.[77] (These curiosities are partly to be explained by the familiar circumstance that Bentham had been working on the subject since 1812 but mainly on a different plan, or two different plans, from that which he ultimately adopted.)[78] As he confided to José Mora some years later, part of it was 'purely political' and the doctrinal remainder was 'for the sake of the political'.[79] He also suggested, with some truth, that it was an essay on the constitution, in the form of a portrait of the 'spiritual nature' of the constitution which would complement the sketch of its 'temporal nature' that he was providing in his Introduction to the *Plan of Parliamentary Reform*.[80]

The occasion of its publication, and a topic frequently referred to in its pages, was the struggle between the Established Church's National Society and the British and Foreign School Society for control of the schools. Bentham took his stand against what he called 'the exclusionary system' of the National Society; that is, its insistence that the Catechism must be an essential part of teaching in the schools, and that those unwilling (or not allowed by their parents) to be taught it could not be admitted. He represented their policy as a denial to the Dissenters of the benefits to be derived from 'the capital and new-invented instrument of virtue and happiness', the Lancaster-Bell system of monitorial instruction.[81] It is clear from what he wrote in his pamphlet on education (*Chrestomathia*) and elsewhere that he was a fervent believer in the monitorial system and wanted to make it more generally available. But more was at stake for him than that. He was asking how well the Church served, or how far it failed to serve, the legal system and the maximization of utility, and his answer was that it promoted sinister influence and misrule. His real concern was the Church's place in the system of influence, and the accession of influence that an educational monopoly would ensure to it. His critique of Church and Catechism was a case-study of influence in action, providing evidence for his earlier denunciation of the clergy by showing firstly how the Church was fitted into the general, Crown-supporting network of influence and secondly what was its special contribution to the network.

The first theme provided him with an opportunity to demonstrate again and to document more carefully the use of patronage for political purposes. He found the fulcrum to be the simple fact of the Establishment: 'the main root of all abuse in the field of religion and Government [was] an Established Church'.[82] The Establishment bound the Church and its clergy to the Executive and not the Legislature, gave the Executive the effective rights of patronage, and thus placed in its hands the matter of reward as well as certain legal sanctions and ensured the compliance of the clergy. He argued that the clergy complied with the Executive's wishes – made their contribution to the network of influence – in two main ways. The first was to act in secular affairs, in the

House of Lords, or the local justices' bench, in making representations to officials or in granting character references, as their
political masters desired and with cynical disregard for legally-
established rights and obligations.[83] The Church's second and
more distinctive contribution was to assume a major part of the
task of corrupting the morals and understanding of the community, through its doctrines, its preaching, and its control of
education.

He believed that this corruption was achieved through a foist-
ing of false and irrational opinions on a defenceless community
by a legally-privileged Church that also had a privileged position
in the educational process. His critique of the Catechism was
designed precisely to show that the Church's doctrine, and this
particular sample of it, were riddled with deceptions, errors and
illogicalities. It was, by his reckoning, a 'mixture of error and
insincerity' which could not command rational assent.[84] In the
absence of rational assent, he maintained, it must be disseminated
in two typical ways: either by persuading people to accept it
willingly, through confusion or habitual acquiescence in the
dictates of authority; or by obliging them to adhere to it un-
willingly and insincerely, as he had adhered to the Thirty-nine
Articles when he was an undergraduate at Oxford. In either case,
he argued, the effect would be corrupting. The unwilling or
merely nominal adherent would be led on from 'momentary
mendacity to...perpetual insincerity'.[85] The willing adherent
would have to undergo 'a prostration of the understanding and
will'.[86] Each condition would be incompatible with the 'rational
obedience' and the free exercise of understanding and will that
were the marks of a soundly functioning society;[87] each condition
would provide the circumstances in which habitual dependence
and thus sinister influence could flourish unchecked.

Church of Englandism added content to the theory of influence
by translating some of the generalizations of 'Parliamentary
Reform' into concrete terms. It did not, however, round out the
theory or tidy up certain loose ends of which Bentham was more
or less conscious. One of these concerned the identification of the
influence of will on will as *sinister* influence. While Bentham
clearly had good grounds for seeing this form of interaction as
falling short of his rationalist ideal, it did not follow that the
prevailing will must always work in a sinister direction; that is,

contrary to the public interest. It was at least conceivable that the
wielders of influence might be concerned for the greatest happiness and might deploy their influence to promote it, or that their
inclinations to exploit their power might be moderated by a
desire for respect or by some other of the social motives. Bentham's
insistence that this would not happen was not obviously or
necessarily correct. A second loose end was the product of a ten-
sion between his nominalism and a mode of thinking and writing
that he had adopted in dealing with influence and the Church.
He had begun to employ the notion of a 'system' in a way which
implied that it was clearly distinguishable from its members, and
had an existence and an impact – including an impact on them –
that were separable from theirs. A striking example of this use of
the notion occurred in *Church of Englandism*, where he described
the individuals whom he was criticizing as 'but the children of
the system – bred under the system', and where he argued that
'had the existing individuals never had existence, under that
system others exactly like them, differing in nothing but name,
would have occupied their places'.[88] Later, in the 'General
Political Catechism', he was still distinguishing between the individual actor and the system in order to make the point that
permanent forces were at work to produce corruption.[89] He was
attributing existence (if not reality) to systems in a way that
challenged his nominalist assumption that it was impossible to
give 'any intelligible representation' to them except in terms of
individuals. A third loose end was that he had provided little
information about the ways in which intellectual corruption was
achieved.

His answer to the first problem was the more rigid notion of
his hedonist psychological theory that he set out in his commentary on his *Table of the Springs of Action*. He repeated there,
among the several 'applications' and implications that constituted
the real point of the work, his charge that the 'ruling few' were
engaged in a continuous but informal conspiracy against the subject many: 'Cooperating without need of concert with the rest of
the opulent of all classes they will so order matters as to have,
without the notice and odium, the benefit of a *licence* for inflicting on the subject and unaffluent many all the miseries out of
which they can contrive to extract profit for themselves.'[90] But,
before drawing that conclusion, Bentham modified his original

theory in a significant way. He relegated the social motives to a secondary position and gave the theory a more egoistic cast by insisting on 'the predominance of self-regarding over social interest'. On this basis he was able to argue that the ruling few must make it their 'constant object to sacrifice to their own interests that of the subject many'; they would not be restrained by any sense of the public interest where this came into conflict with self-interest.[91]

He approached the other two problems through a discussion of the use and abuse of language. The misuse of language, he argued, could be made into an element in 'the system of deception' by 'rendering the subject – whatever it be, law, religion, anything... as incomprehensible or (what is the perfection of incomprehensibility) as uncognisable as possible to all whom you have to deal with, and that to their own conviction and satisfaction'.[92] He described the process more precisely in the set of papers on language and logic on which he was currently working, and which were designed to set out at greater length and in operational terms the ideas about classification, clarity in expression and the use of fictions that he had espoused in his early pronouncements on methodology. He singled out his familiar enemies the lawyers and the clergy as the principal agents and immediate beneficiaries of linguistic corruption, and the cultivation of ambiguity and the mischievous use of fictions as their principal means. He cited as a typical example of ambiguity the word 'church' itself: its meanings embraced the assembled worshippers, the place where they worshipped, and those who led the worship; and the sanctity attached to the worship was thus extended to the worshippers and their leaders – 'holy functions made holy places, holy places and functions made holy persons' and a 'mixture of respect and terror came to extend itself to, upon, and to the benefit of, the class of persons in whose hands was reposed the management of whatsoever was done in those holy places'.[93] Mischievous fictions were typified by those that he had been attacking in the language and procedures of the lawyers for so many years. They were mischievous because they lacked the two features which could make a fiction legitimate, namely that it should be a necessity of language (a condition of our communication with each other) and that it could be re-expressed in terms of – could be reduced to – real entities.[94] The distinction between legitimate and illegitimate fictions provided him at the same time with a rationale for his references to 'systems' in *Church of Englandism*; as long as he believed (however unjustifiably) that he could re-express his statements about them in terms of the real entities, their individual members, he could feel entitled to use them.

As the decade advanced, Bentham began to make freer and more frequent references to influence and its associated concepts in his commentaries on policies and events. This practice led him in the end to add the final touches to his theory and to complete its translation into a general account of the distribution of power in society.

He took his first steps in this tidying-up process in his writings on colonies and colonial problems in the years 1818–20. Among the sources and props of influence, he had always counted the possession of colonies. In 1818 he began to show an interest in developing that side of his argument more fully.[95] His first approach to it was the drafting of a Preface for a new edition of *Emancipate your Colonies*, the pamphlet which he had addressed to the National Convention of France. Nothing came of that. But two years later, the progress of the Latin American revolutions and the revival of the Constitution of 1812 in Spain encouraged him to try again. He drafted (after his usual changes in plan and a change in title) the pamphlet 'Rid Yourselves of Ultramaria', addressed to the peoples of Spain in the form of forty-two letters and an introduction.[96] Its purpose was to persuade the Spaniards that they, as well as the peoples of Latin America, would be better off if the colonies were independent.

He tried to cast his conclusions in terms of his habitual distinction between the ruling few and the subject many. His advice was of course addressed to the latter and its substance was that the retention of colonies would bring them 'no profit', personal losses, and (more serious still) public losses. He produced many arguments, including economic arguments, to demonstrate the certainty of damage to the public interest; but at the centre of his case were the 'constitutional evils' which followed from dominion, 'the mischief that would be done by it to the Constitution: by means of corruptive influence'.[97] The reverse of this would be the gains to 'the particular and sinister interest of the ruling few by whom both countries [colony and Spain] are governed'.[98] He enumerated these gains in some detail and in a fairly systematic form: 'profit in the shape of money...profit in the shape of power through the medium of services other than pecuniary... profit in the shape of incidental vengeance';[99] 'profit in the shape of factitious dignity';[100] power in the form of 'the faculty of introducing relative appropriate inaptitude into official situations', of 'impunity for misdeeds of all sorts, for misrule in all shapes' (one of the 'two ingredients by the union of which complete despotism is composed'), of 'personal ease in official situations' and of 'public esteem, reputation, fame and so forth'.[101] But as he proceeded with his argument, he found his simple contrast between the ruling and the subject elements in society inadequate for his purposes. He exposed its inadequacy by asking where support for and opposition to an active colonial policy might come from. He felt compelled to admit that even among the 'subject many' there might be some 'who in possession or in expectancy [looked to some] share in the government' of the colonies, and who would accordingly favour a continuance of dominion.[102] This prompted him to reconsider the personnel and the distinguishing characteristics of the sinister conspiracy, 'the ruling and otherwise influential few' who 'stand permanently in opposition to, or are those particularly liable to stand in opposition to, the universal interest'. He listed seventeen classes of such persons, ranging over the Royal family and its personal servants, members of the Cortes, judicial and administrative officials, members of the army and navy, the clergy, and several groups right outside the formal structure of government including landowners, wholesale manufacturers and political writers and publicists.[103] This brought together the various kinds of participants in the conspiracy that he had recognized separately in *Scotch Reform*, 'Parliamentary Reform', *Church of Englandism* and elsewhere, and added some new classes, namely manufacturers and political writers. The last point showed Bentham exploring in a new way the logic of his position; if the possession of power in the form of influence was the monopoly of the ruling few, the latter group had to take in everyone who had access to influence in any form.

He completed the process of restatement and generalization in yet another work, an essay which he intended to include in his *Codification Proposal*, but which he eventually suppressed except as a fragmentary footnote.[104] In that essay he referred to and analysed the 'ruling, influential and otherwise privileged few' as an 'aristocracy'; not in the sense of titled nobility, but in a more general sense close to that now assigned to 'elite'. He provided a classification of the aristocracy that was similar to, but was more elaborate and more systematic than, the list in 'Rid Yourselves of Ultramaria'. He divided it first into eight branches:

1. The Legislative Aristocracy
2. The Executive, Administrative or Official Aristocracy
3. The Titled Aristocracy
4. The Landed Aristocracy
5. The Moneyed Aristocracy
6. Ancestor-boasting Aristocracy
7. Talent-displaying Aristocracy
8. The Spiritual Aristocracy.[105]

Then in his usual fashion he proceeded to sub-divide most of these main branches, finding six or seven sub-branches in the Executive branch, four in the Talent-displaying, three in the Moneyed and so on to a total of about twenty, some of which he was tempted to sub-divide again.[106] The distinctive feature of each branch and sub-branch was explicitly the possession of some actual or potential advantages in terms of power, influence or privilege: for example, 'Aristocracy constituted by official power belonging to the Executive branch', 'Aristocracy constituted by factitious dignity', 'Aristocracy constituted by present opulence' and 'Aristocracy constituted by the influence of talent applied to the political field of government', or, more generally, 'a particularly large proportion of the general mass of the objects of general desire in any shape'.[107] Strictly speaking, it was a classification not of persons but of their political characteristics, for any given person might possess several of these claims to aristocracy. It was, in conception at least, an exhaustive account of the exercise of power in society, for outside the boundaries of the aristocracy were only the subject many who by definition possessed and exercised none. It was also – and this was its main point for Bentham – a classification of the politically *active* members of society, for he believed that each segment of the Aristocracy had or was liable to have 'a distinct and particular interest'[108] which it would actively seek to protect and promote at the expense of the 'universal interest'. Throughout the essay, his analysis proceeded in terms of these 'classes and sub-classes into which in any

country the aristocracy of the country is divided'.[109] This meant
that the political actors in the community were not a multitude
of separate individuals but were a plurality of groups whose
members acted together in pursuit of some particular interest
which they shared. Bentham's hostility to the Executive, the
lawyers, the clergy and others had brought him finally to discard
his individualism for a form of pluralism. But his pluralism was
still limited in two respects. He had not abandoned his idea of a
comprehensive conspiracy or sinister confederacy in which all
members of the Aristocracy participated: each branch could
promote its 'wider interest' by allying itself with 'the most
preponderant of all sinister interests the Monarchical'.[110] And his
description of groups and group-activities remained an account
of politics 'as it is', and not as it ought to be or must be. He continued to regard the operation of group-interests as sinister and
as illegitimate, and he continued to believe that the function of a
democratic constitution was to contribute to the taming or expulsion of such interests and not to give them scope for uninterrupted
activity and influence.

The evolution of Bentham's ideas about influence, corruption
and misrule, and the crystallization of many of them in his novel
notion of Aristocracy, were decisive for his thinking about policy.
They confirmed that his programme could not consist only of
electoral reform, and they established clear guidelines for its
other components. The democratization of the parliamentary
system had, as I have just suggested, a vital part to play in the
campaign against misrule, but it could not make its contribution
without help. The resources of sinister influence were so many
and so varied, and could be deployed in such mutually-supportive
ways, that electoral reform would be ineffective unless it were
accompanied by other measures. These must include the disciplining of the Judiciary, 'the euthanasia' of the Establishment in
religious life,[111] the freeing of the press, the purging of language
to eliminate all mischievous fictions and opportunities for ambiguity, the breaking of the Church's grip on education, saving
measures aimed at the pruning of official salaries and other
expenses, and (where official establishments must survive) the
regulation of patronage and of any matter of reward that remained in official hands. Economy and influence, for example,
were 'conjoint points':[112] 'in the members of the official Establish-

ment, privates as well as officers included, [the King beheld] so many special and immediate instruments of his pleasure';[113] and the Aristocracy (in all its branches) had an interest in maintaining numerous and expensive 'sources from which and channels through which [money] is drawn from the people' in the form of needless and useless offices, sinecures and modes of appointment which involved no objective tests of 'intellectual aptitude and active talent'.[114] It followed that 'the nature and quantum of the remuneration proper to be attached to official situations [and] official service' must be among the topics covered in an 'all-comprehensive code'.[115]

Several of these points were either aimed directly at government or had clear implications for its functions or its organization. They provided new and powerful grounds for thinking about questions of organization and efficiency, because they sanctioned the installation of 'sinister interest' as the third and most important of the 'obstacles to good government' that Bentham habitually recognized, alongside 'deficiency in appropriate active talents' and 'deficiency in appropriate intelligence'.[116] While he was developing his ideas about influence and aristocracy he gave these questions less attention, on the whole, than he gave to the details of his electoral schemes, partly because they were more diverse and diffuse and represented a greater challenge to his ingenuity. But even in that period he did not allow them to drop out of sight for very long. In relation to the Judiciary, as we have noted, he responded to the challenge in a wholehearted and sophisticated way. His plans for the Church and – at the level of the school – for education were also quite detailed and carefully constructed.[117] And in his 'Defences of Economy' and in some other places he addressed himself to questions of remuneration and occasionally to other aspects of organization in ways that reaffirmed his accumulated ideas on those subjects and sometimes added a little to them.

From occasional statements and allusions (some of which have been quoted already) it is clear that he still saw government as necessarily substantial and complex in both its judicial and executive branches. His plans for the Judiciary implied, though they did not describe, a mass of inferior courts below the Court of Lords' Delegates. His account of the 'executive, administrative and official aristocracy' similarly implied an array

of distinct offices in which the influence-wielding officials would
be located:

The General Superintending branch
The Financial branch or Money-disposing branch
The Home-Affairs branch
The Military Land Service branch
The Military Sea Service branch
The Foreign Relations branch
The Distant-dependency Governing branch.[118]

In each branch there were liable to be, as we have just seen,
'privates as well as officers', or in more general terms a variety of
officers placed 'superordinate, co-ordinate or subordinate' to
each other.[119] The implicit commitment to hierarchy was reinforced in other remarks and references; in each office there
would normally be 'a chief manager or managers',[120] just as in
the Judiciary there must be a 'head judge' (the Lord Chancellor),
a 'chief' under whose 'eye and authority and protection' the
other judges must 'conduct their operations'.[121] Apart from the
Judiciary, he offered no substantial discussion of what any of
these branches and offices would be doing. Some of his remarks
about the Church, like his little pamphlet of 1821 on Spanish
economic affairs, imply that he was moving again in a free trade
direction in economic policy.[122] On the other hand, his demand
for pre-appointed evidence required a certain governmental
apparatus to perform this 'registrative' function. He hoped to
make that apparatus spare and economical by devolving much of
the work onto lawyers and other 'professional agents, managers
and advisers', but there would remain a need for a 'fixed, central
[office]' to receive and hold the records and make them available
when required for judicial purposes.[123]

In his 'Defence of Economy', Bentham had identified his
administrative objectives for 'the whole of the official establishment' as 'two intimately connected practical operations, viz. minimizing official pay and maximizing official aptitude'.[124] Despite
the renewal of his interest in and enthusiasm for electoral processes, he never suggested that these objectives should be sought
through the popular election of all officials. Except in isolated
cases, his standard model for non-legislative 'functionaries' seems
to have been that which he adopted in the Judiciary, namely a
direct dependence on the Legislature at the top, and some form

of internal nomination and supervision of the subordinate officials.

The one non-legislative area where he favoured the general election of functionaries was the Church. He proposed here to weaken the hierarchy almost to the point of extinction, and to have the local clergy (or, alternatively, lay-preachers) chosen by, paid by and responsible to the local congregations, as in Dissenting communities.[125] This choice was potentially of administrative significance. It was presented, in part at least, as an answer to administrative failings which he had denounced in his critique of the Church under three main headings, 'Vices having relation to service' (that is, efficiency in performing its functions), 'Vices having relation to pay', and 'Vices having relation to discipline.'[126] Moreover, his preference for congregational control was explicitly grounded on managerial criteria: 'In the English Established Church may be seen the *forms* of discipline without the substance: in the Scottish *form* and *substance* both: in the Non-Established Churches, no form, but nevertheless the *substance*, and this but the better for being *without* the forms.'[127] But these were not general arguments about organization and management; they were more limited arguments about meeting the specific needs of the Church, or more correctly the needs of the several congregations. Bentham had no sense of the Church as a community, spiritual or of any other kind, and consequently he had no sense of a common life, a set of beliefs, uniform practices or interparish intercourse to be maintained. As he understood the services of a parson or lay-preacher, they were mainly of local interest, and were of a kind that could be supervised and judged directly by the local parishioners. The simplest and most effective form of direct supervision was election.

It was conceivable that some governmental services might have the same character and be liable to be treated in the same way. He assumed, however, that the typical office would be providing a service to the public at large and would need to be located at or managed from some central point. He did not think that the ordinary citizens could judge effectively the respective qualifications of the candidates for appointment to all these offices or the quality of the officials' performance in office, though he did not want to discourage them from expressing opinions about performance. The difficulty he saw was that these judgements would require a level of knowledge and attention which most people could not supply because they would be distracted by 'their continued occupations, including [making the] provision necessary for subsistence'.[128] It was enough to ask of them that they should exercise their judgement once a year in electing their 'delegates' to Parliament; anything more would be unreasonable. This line of argument obliged him, as in the 1790s, to rely heavily on the power of the electoral system to reach down into the lower reaches of the administrative structure. By this time, considerable information about the functioning of democratic institutions in the United States of America was available to him. His interpretation of American experience was that it demonstrated that elections were effective in enforcing responsibility, and demonstrated that they were more or less equally effective irrespective of whether particular non-legislative officials were 'immediately' or 'unimmediately' responsible to the people.[129]

There is sufficient evidence that he regarded the principles and devices of management as the appropriate way of enforcing 'unimmediate' responsibility, and that they were still a living if relatively quiescent part of his thought. He unhesitatingly fell back on them on the few occasions when he was faced with a situation of unimmediate responsibility, as in his essay on the Prizes Acts or in his plans for the management of the Judiciary. A number of the principles appeared, unexpectedly and in a slightly disguised form, in his *Chrestomathia* among the principles of school management: for example, the 'master's time-saving principle', the 'regular visitation principle', the 'punishment-minimizing principle' and the 'progress-registration principle'.[130] And in his theory of preappointed evidence he provided a new rationale for book-keeping and statistics, linking these activities with the fundamental notions of forthcomingness and non-exclusion on which he based his approach to evidence. His consideration of official evidence in the *Introductory View of the Rationale of Evidence* began to resemble a new, management-oriented essay on book-keeping in a governmental setting, in which problems of managerial control tended to overshadow the Judiciary's needs.[131]

These appeals to and applications of his theory of management did not carry it far beyond the point to which he had brought it in the 1790s. But they were important in other ways. They demonstrated his continuing mastery of the techniques that he was advocating. This was true especially of the detailed provisions in the *Court of Lords' Delegates* for the 'periodical collection of judicial accounts' whose 'express object and use' was to reveal how far 'the ends of justice' had been achieved 'at each point of *time*, in what respects and to what degree, in each division of place within the authority of the Court...[and] in respect of each several point'.[132] These provisions, and the commentary that Bentham added to them, were sophisticated pieces of work, which bear comparison with his achievements in his writings on the Poor Law and the Police Bills.[133] At the same time they demonstrated the flexibility of his techniques, his ability to apply them to a variety of problems and institutional settings, including the problems and institutions of government, and his consciousness of their flexibility. In the 1790s, we saw, he believed that the line of good management was potentially but was not immediately available to government. A decade later he was arguing that at least the book-keeping component of it was already both available and necessary. The 'perpetual and unremitted exercise' of the statistic function was, he contended, 'necessary to good government' not only 'in the department in question, viz. the judicial', but also 'in relation to every department'. In developing the argument he gave it an even more general form. 'Under every form of government', he assumed, there must be 'ruling hands', and they would need 'a correct, compleat and constant knowledge of the transactions of every subordinate department'. That knowledge was necessary for the prosperity of the state. In that respect the needs of the state were comparable with those of 'a householder' or, 'a manufacturer', and the techniques that were suitable for the one were, when adapted, equally available to and suitable for the other.[134] A few years later he repeated the argument in slightly different terms: the 'chief managers' of government offices would require information about the 'merit and demerit' of the system of management in each office and the 'merit and demerit of the several persons employed in the execution of it'.[135]

Within the broad field of management, the topics on which he tried hardest to develop new ideas were remuneration and recruitment. His consciousness of the ravages of influence made him particularly anxious to devise influence-resistant schemes for both processes. He was led in this way to modify his attitude to honorary reward. This had appeared in most of his lists of management-principles, and in practice he had applied it in the form of titles of honour in the higher ranks of the police administration. It was the practical application rather than the principle itself that he now turned against. His strengthened understanding and suspicion of influence persuaded him that official honours – 'factitious dignities' as he now called them – were a source of mischief and part of the matter of corruption.[136] He concluded that this form of honorary reward should be driven out of political and administrative life and should never be used as an alternative to salaries. But he was prepared to consider other alternatives. He tried to identify offices where it would be reasonable to place the burden of maintaining them on those persons who used their services; but the old stumbling-block, his hostility to law fees, convinced him again that this was not a very productive approach.[137] In the same place, he considered the use of special fees and allowances as incentives, but he was similarly discouraged by the likelihood of abuses. Without finally discarding these devices as unworkable, he chose as his main approach to official remuneration his principle of 'patriotic auction' or 'pecuniary competition'. One of his aims in his 'Defence of Economy against Burke' was to defend the principle of auction against Burke's sneers, and to improve its image by renaming it the principle of competition.[138] From 1810 onwards it became a standard item in his prescriptions for methods of pay and recruitment, as a 'means for reducing to the minimum the quantity of emolument attached to public offices'.[139]

A little later (from about 1813) he began thinking about another device which also became a standard item in his prescriptions, namely competitive examinations as tests of fitness for appointment to official posts. This reflected especially the positive side of his interest in recruitment, his search for 'appropriate intelligence' and 'appropriate active talent' in officials. The question that he posed for himself was how these qualities might best be discerned or established in candidates for posts. This was, for him, an exercise in the general field of *evidence*, not of judgement or insight, and he found it necessary to inquire what kinds of evidence might be most relevant and how they might best be made available. He had been toying with these questions intermittently since he drew up his still-born plan for a Board of Shipbuilding. They were given new urgency for him by the hostility that Samuel encountered in the Navy Board and Admiralty as a specialist among rule-of-thumb administrators.

He seems to have provided definite answers to his questions for the first time when he was writing about the Church, shortly after Samuel's enforced but honourable retirement from the Navy. By that time he had become aware of, and was favourably impressed by, the changes introduced into the systems of examination at Cambridge since 1747 and at Oxford since the new Examinations Statute of 1800. He became caught up in the contemporary movement for open competitive examinations.[140] He convinced himself that 'for proof of aptitude generally speaking, public examination [is the] sole adequate security'.[141] As time went on that conviction strengthened, so that examinations became a sufficient as well as a necessary condition for the selection of talented candidates:

for securing, in every official situation that presents a demand for it, any such thing as a sufficiency of appropriate talent, there needs but this instrument – examination so it be publickly applied, according to the nature of the official situation, and the sort of service attached to it, and the corresponding nature of the branches of art and science, the possession of which is necessary or subservient to the due performance [of its duties].[142]

This was one of the few wholly new elements in his administrative thinking between 1802 and 1822.

The impulse to call on this body of thinking in relation to the state as a whole – to initiate this part of his campaign against sinister influence and misrule – seems to have developed at about the time when he was completing his analysis of the ruling and influential few as an 'aristocracy' of many layers. He appears to have taken his first concrete steps along this path in November 1818, when he began his draft of an essay which he entitled 'Principles of Official Economy, as applied to Public Expenditure'.[143] A large part of what he wrote was addressed to official economy in a narrow sense, but the essay was conceived in broader terms. It included a rudimentary attempt to re-interpret economy as 'good management', to identify the resources and the alternative courses of action available to governments – services and things, use or exchange, moveables and immovables, offices (posts) of various kinds, and so on – an attempt to organize the subsequent discussion around these concepts, and approving references to examinations and the sale of offices on Government account. It may have been associated with, or have sprung from, some notes that he had jotted down a few months earlier under the heading 'Government – Politics – the science', listing nineteen concepts that he was proposing to expound.[144] But he seems to have dropped the project before he had got beyond the negative material on economy, and although he may have tried to take it up again in 1820[145] it must be included in the long list of his abortive works.

In April and May 1821 he returned to some of the same themes in a different kind of work. By that time his hopes were high that he would receive a genuine, firm invitation to prepare a general Code, probably from Spain but possibly from Portugal or Naples.[146] He set out to write 'First Lines of a proposed code of law for any nation, compleat and rationalized.'[147] This was intended to be not the start of the Code itself, but an introduction to and explanation of it. It was similar in scope to the *General View* of the 1780s, offering an account of the divisions of the law, the ends which government and law should serve, and notes on the several branches of law including civil, penal, constitutional and financial. But it was distinctly more radical in tone than the *General View*, for Bentham used it as another vehicle for attacking the monarchy and its influence, and for advocating electoral reform. Apart from the matter relating to elections, the sections on constitutional law were thin; they did not include, although they envisaged, a serious treatment of the subordinate offices or their powers.[148] Bentham went into more detail in the chapter or section relating to financial law. He was concerned there with the principles to be employed, and took these to be 'good management' and 'economy'. This enabled him to repeat what he had recently been saying in 'Principles of Economy', but not to go much beyond that point.[149]

He began at last to go beyond it early in 1822 (probably in February) when he started to draft a work which was conceived along the same lines as the 'Principles' but was intended to be larger and more complex. The apparent title of this study was 'Thoughts on Official Economy' or 'Thoughts on Pecuniary Economy as applied to Office'.[150] Its drafts were later (for reasons explained in the next chapter) widely dispersed among Bentham's papers, and it is not easy to locate them all or to discover the structure into which they were intended to fit. The view I have formed is that Bentham proposed to have (after his usual introductory, prefatory and/or expository matter) two main divisions,

namely 'I Aptitude Maximized' and 'II Expense Minimized.'[151]
As compared with the 'Principles', he intended to put more
emphasis on the relatively positive 'Aptitude Maximized' and
–in the expository matter – to spend more time in relating his
detailed discussion to his ideas about responsibility, the nature of
government and other issues that he had traversed in 'First
Line'. In 'Aptitude Maximized', he proposed to concentrate on
the 'securities' for each of the three branches of aptitude or talent
–intellectual, moral and active – and to deal with 'false securities'
in an Appendix. The securities were mostly variants of, or closely
related to, his usual principles of indirect legislation: the identification of rulers' with subjects' interests, minimizing the power
and other resources at the ruler's disposal, maximizing legal
responsibility, and maximizing publicity and information. 'Expense Minimized' was to be an account of 'unapt modes' of
expenditure; that is, an expansion of the 'saving measures' that he
had been recommending in 'First Lines', 'Principles of Economy'
and in other places stretching back to the material that he had
drafted for Mirabeau's edification in about 1790.

In many respects 'Thoughts on Economy' belonged to the
sequence of works about parliamentary reform. It was an attack
on misrule or the neglect of the one proper end of government,
the greatest happiness of the greatest number. It represented
economy – the substitution of economy for waste – as a means of
striking at the corruption and influence which sustained misrule.
Many of its pages were devoted to a discussion of the composition
and the choice of Parliament and of the electorate, for these were
among the 'offices' and the 'functionaries' that Bentham was considering, and he regarded them as perhaps the most important of
all offices. One of his principal themes was again that among the
institutions of government the Legislature must be supreme, but
that the Legislature itself must be subordinate to the community
as a whole and not to any one part of it. He presented and discussed many of his 'securities for aptitude' primarily in relation
to the Legislature, and as means of binding it to the interests of
the community.

On this occasion, however, he carried the discussion a good deal
further into the Executive than he was accustomed to do. While
some of his securities were more immediately applicable or relevant to the 'supreme operative functionaries' in Parliament, he

presented most of them as applicable ultimately to all functionaries, and some of them were particularly relevant to the permanent officials. In dealing with the last group, he began to look
more closely into the conditions on which the securities could be
applied effectively, and this led him finally into trying to specify
the institutions and arrangements required to make them work.
He began similarly to investigate the conditions on which the
dependence of the Executive on the Legislature could be secured,
and although he tackled this problem in an analytical rather than
an institutional way he was made more conscious of the Executive
as a structure that must somehow be accommodated within the
larger structure of government and law.

In seeking to apply his principles, he made use of several of the
doctrines and devices that he had recently been employing. Legal
responsibility, he asserted, amounted to liability to dislocability
and punibility.[152] Factitious dignity was a source of corruption
and could not be a legitimate element in reward.[153] The religious
sanction (like bicameralism) was a false security, an instrument of
influence and misrule, not an aid to moral aptitude.[154] Competitive examinations were the only reliable means of testing and thus
securing intellectual aptitude.[155] Pecuniary competition for official
posts (outside Parliament) was the best way to secure active talent
and to reduce expenditure on pay to a tolerable level.

It was in relation to the last two points that he came closest to
specifying arrangements. He was not trying there to draft a constitution or to express matters in legal form, but he did ask himself
quite seriously how it would be possible to adopt those practices
and especially to adopt both together. He answered in terms of a
possible sequence of events: the identification and advertising of
posts, and the invitation of tenders for them; the interviewing
and (if appropriate) *viva voce* examination of suitable candidates;
the opportunity for an auction (presumably revised tenders); the
final decision.[156] For occasions where a formal examination was
required in order to sift candidates, he was less able to go into
detail, but he recognized that an examination implied the existence of a definite set of examiners and definite subjects of
examination and that these needed to be selected together, with
reference to 'the characteristic nature of the Office in each
case'.[157] He also believed that a genuinely competitive examination required the 'examination of all of them [the candidates] in

one and the same place'.[158] He went again into questions relating to actual practices in considering firstly expedients for promoting active aptitude, and secondly the security for moral aptitude that consisted in reducing the quantity of money at the disposal of functionaries. In the first case he advocated the general substitution of daily rates for salaries wherever practicable (and the concomitant abolition of sick pay and 'pensions of retreat' or retirement pensions),[159] and in the second case a set of rules for the handling of public money.[160]

Bentham's other line of approach to the Executive was through a brief consideration of the character and operation of the system as a whole and its responsiveness to the electorate's will. In its initial stages this contained little that was new except in terminology. It was a sketch of the powers or branches of government of the kind that he had been making since the *Fragment on Government*. In this sketch, however, he adopted the grouping of powers which afterwards became characteristic, namely one treating the Administrative and Judicial branches as parts of a wider Executive, and linking the Executive and Legislative together as parts of the Operative which thus included all the conventional powers of government and excluded in his system only the Constitutive.[161] The argument became more interesting and novel as he tried to analyse and define some of the concepts that he wanted to use in discussing the powers and in establishing the supremacy of the Legislative within the Operative.[162]

He provided the foundation for his subsequent argument in a definition and characterization of 'office', which owed a good deal to his civil-law notion of 'condition' but permitted a development of it in some important directions. He wrote:

The word *Office* is employed to signify sometimes a single function, sometimes the aggregate of any number of functions whatever, a sort of *fictitious entity* with which the individual is considered as invested, and to which a function or an aggregate of functions is considered as attached. By him who is considered as invested with such office a correspondent *situation* – place – is said to be filled.[163]

In that way he confirmed (or reminded himself) that it would be proper to treat government as a whole and the Executive (Administrative) in particular as a bundle of offices, powers and functions which could be discussed in a general and impersonal way. (Indeed his concept of office was so general that it became nearly equivalent to 'role'; that was why he was able to refer to members of Parliament and electors as 'functionaries'; they were people performing political or constitutional roles.) And as he further elucidated the notion of office, and the powers attached to an office, it became clear that he was talking about not a simple bundle or aggregate but an organized network in which the parts could not be fruitfully considered apart from the whole, and which could not be provided for satisfactorily in terms of a few simple legal rules.

He indicated the essential element in the network when he said that one of the components of 'the nature of the Office' was 'the rank or the degree which it occupies in the scale of subordination'.[164] There was, then, a hierarchical structure of subordination and superordination in which each office had its place and from which it derived part of its nature and its effective power. So he was able to say that one of 'the dimensions of power' of an official was the 'altitude of the place of [his] office in the scale of subordination',[165] and that one of the main methods of reducing the power attached to an office was to make it subordinate to another office.[166] All of this implied that in order to understand or to prescribe for a set of offices one must treat the scale of subordination as a – perhaps the – central point of reference.

That fact in itself ensured that regulation would have to be a relatively complex affair. Although superordination and subordination could be described in quite simple terms they could not be established or maintained casually. As Bentham described them they became very similar to the relationship between sovereign and subject. They were constituted by obedience, or the readiness of one person 'to submit his will' to that of another;[167] the superordinate might be one person or a group; and superordination might be shared or partial with respect to either time or subject-matter. Subordination would need to be enforced by the provision of penalties of one kind or another, that is by dislocability or by punibility in other forms and degrees, in the event of disobedience on the subordinate's part; for example 'on the ground of an alleged improper exercise or non-exercise of the subordinate's power in this or that particular instance'.[168] And there was the rub. Just as the sovereign's will had to be expressed and enforced through an elaborate structure of law and the means of its enforcement, so each superordinate would have to operate through some definite if less elaborate procedure. Bentham did not make that point in so many words, but it is significant that he already assumed the existence of a 'Code belonging to the Office' which could be produced and referred to when candidates for posts were being interviewed.[169]

Considerations relating to the taming of power pointed in the same direction. The second main approach to this problem was the narrowing of the *field* (that is, scope) of power, in which Bentham recognized three principal divisions or aspects, the geographical or topographical, the temporal and the logical. The first two presented no particular problems but the third (which included the persons, things, acts and modes of action over which power would extend in each case) presented very formidable ones. Bentham simply denied that in any one office or even in all offices taken together would it be possible to manage this as a self-contained operation. 'Any restriction applied to [the logical field] supposes [an] antecedent all-comprehensive survey of the field of legislation, with partitions made of it from different sources, as many as the pursuit of the universal end requires: in effect an all-comprehensive Code already *in terminis*.'[170] He added that attempts were sometimes made to set out restrictions to 'the logical field of power' but that they were undertaken 'as if without apprehension of the difficulty'. The practical conclusion must be that a complete Constitutional Code, in which all powers were fully defined, would be possible only as part of an all-comprehensive Code; and that, in the absence of the all-comprehensive Code, the task of controlling power must fall on the other fields and on the pattern of subordination.

These were important general conclusions about the shape which a general regulation of the Executive must take. Bentham's concrete achievements in 'Thoughts on Economy' did not match up to those requirements and in particular did not reach the degree of integration or cover the range of issues towards which he was pointing. The organization of his argument in terms of 'securities' and economies did not, in the end, permit him to deal systematically with the Executive or any other of his branches of government; the securities that he chose for discussion, and his continuing fascination with Parliament and its corruption, did not provide the opportunity to bring to bear all the principles and devices that were already at his disposal. Records and statistics, for example, he ignored almost completely except in the special form of records of Parliamentary proceedings. The work nevertheless played a part in the process – was a link in the chain – by which Bentham brought together the materials that he had developed in a variety of contexts and from a variety of sources, and showed how they could be fitted together to serve the goal that had come to dominate his thinking in this period – the extirpation of influence and misrule.

Bentham was working intermittently on 'Thoughts on Official Economy' throughout most of the first half of 1822. He seems to have paused and taken stock of the situation at the end of May or the beginning of June of that year, and to have started revising his early drafts in the latter month. But shortly afterwards he ceased to regard it as an independent work, and it was displaced by or became absorbed within the *Constitutional Code*. The time has now come to look at what is known of the circumstances in which Bentham conceived that larger and greater work, and of the way in which he constructed it. That will form the subject-matter of the next chapter.

7

THE *CONSTITUTIONAL CODE* AND BENTHAM'S THEORY OF GOVERNMENT

The source of Bentham's decision to begin drafting the *Constitutional Code* lay in the set of circumstances that prompted him to write 'First Lines', the *Codification Proposal* and 'Rid Yourselves of Ultramaria'. The political changes and the prospects of change in Spain, Portugal, Latin America, Norway and the Mediterranean encouraged him to believe that he would soon receive a commission to draft an all-comprehensive code or a substantial component of one. His hopes were at first centred on Spain. The revival of constitutional government in that country in 1820, and his first contacts with members of the constitutional regime and with liberal publicists (notably Mora), led him confidently to expect an official invitation to compose either a complete code or a penal code.[1] When the Spaniards disappointed him, first by asking him only to work on his Paper Money proposal and then by succumbing to counter-revolution, he turned his attention to Portugal, from whose Cortes he did receive a commission in April 1822.[2] He began working on the *Constitutional Code* at about that time.[3]

Although the *Constitutional Code* was the only part of his practical work on codification that was published, he never thought of it as a self-contained project and he never intended to delay starting on the other parts of the all-comprehensive code until this was completed. On the contrary, while he was working on constitutional law he started to draft some of the other parts and made fairly rapid progress with them, especially the Penal and Procedure codes. In October 1823 he was even tempted to concentrate his own efforts on the others, leaving the *Constitutional Code* in 'other hands to be provisionally put in order and published'.[4] In the event, however, he rejected that course and did continue to accord priority to the constitutional branch of the law.

The reasons why he gave it priority are not well-documented and may have been partly accidental or the product of a series of separate decisions and circumstances. It does not seem to have been his original intention to begin with this branch of the law or to finish it first. As long as his attention was focused on Spain, a constitutional code seemed the least urgent of the codifier's tasks, because the Spaniards already had a constitution which, although it required substantial amendment, would serve them tolerably well. It possessed, in Bentham's eyes, the great merit that it formally recognized (or so he thought) the greatest happiness of the greatest number as 'the only proper end of government'.[5] In some material that he drafted for his *Codification Proposal* but discarded before publication, he indicated that he hoped to draw up a constitutional code of his own if he got the chance and that in the meantime he was willing to draft constitutions for particular countries in accordance with their instructions.[6] But neither there nor in the published *Proposal* did he give constitutional law priority over the other branches, and in his letter to the Portuguese he implied that it would be the last rather than the first to be tackled.[7] The Portuguese left the matter open when they accepted the offer of his services.

Circumstances had, however, been directing his mind increasingly to constitutional issues in the period immediately before he received the commission from Portugal. As we saw in the last chapter, in his work for 'Rid Yourselves of Ultramaria', its precursor and the *Codification Proposal*, he had accumulated a lot of material relating to such issues. He had already been thinking about how the Spanish Constitution might be adapted and improved to meet the needs of Portugal.[8] From February 1822 he was jotting down thoughts and maxims about constitutional law in his 'memorandum book',[9] and was working on 'Thoughts on Official Economy'. It is possible that he drifted into drafting parts of a constitutional code because that was an easy extension of what he was already writing and thinking about.

Once he had started, other forces and influences combined to keep him working on it both before and after the retreat from liberalism in Portugal. In the second half of 1822 his enthusiasm was sustained not only by his Portuguese negotiations but also by the development of his acquaintance with Hassuna D'Ghies, a native of Tripoli in North Africa.[10] D'Ghies (who had been granted a sort of diplomatic status by the Pasha of Tripoli) persuaded Bentham that a democratic reform or revolution was possible there, and they worked together on means of bringing it about. The most concrete result of these efforts was the short essay published in Bowring's edition of Bentham's *Works* as 'Securities against Misrule'.[11] Bentham regarded it at the time as a distraction from the real work of codification, but it seems to have encouraged him both to continue directing his mind to constitutional questions and to compress some of his ideas into a manageable length and form.[12] In 1823 D'Ghies left England and his projects gradually came to matter less to Bentham. But a new stimulus was already being supplied by the Greek insurrection against Turkish rule.

Bentham had been interested in Greece since at least August 1821,[13] but its affairs had been overshadowed for him by his Spanish, Portuguese and Tripolitanian prospects. It began to command more of his attention from February 1823. In that month he was formally asked to help the Greeks' cause by Andreas Louriottis, the first of the Greek deputies to reach England.[14] (Bowring, and therefore possibly Bentham, had been aware of the existence of Louriottis since the previous August, when the exiled bishop Ignatios had written on his behalf.)[15] Bentham responded by writing two extensive pieces of advice for the Greeks about constitutional law, one a direct commentary on the constitution that had been drawn up at Epidaurus in 1822 and the other an essay on 'Principles of Legislation as to Constitutional Law'.[16] He was soon drawn more and more into Greek affairs, partly encouraging and partly being drawn on by John Bowring and Edward Blaquiere. These two men had become his friends and disciples by acting as his go-betweens in Spain and Portugal, and they helped to establish and manage the London Greek Committee when it was set up in 1823.[17] Blaquiere took Bentham's 'Observations on the Greek Constitution' in his baggage on his first expedition to Greece in March 1823.[18] Before long, Bentham was viewing the *Constitutional Code* itself as a blueprint for the use of the Greeks, and he despatched the first substantial instalments of it with Leicester Stanhope who followed Blaquiere to Greece on behalf of the London Committee in

October 1823.[19] While the outcome of the revolution remained unsettled, and as Bowring and others of Bentham's friends became more committed to and dependent on the Greeks' cause through their participation in the flotation of loans for the Provisional Government, Bentham continued to believe that Greece would ultimately adopt his constitutional ideas. The Greek revolution and the involvement of Bentham, Bowring and their associates in it were the most important reasons why the work on the *Constitutional Code* advanced ahead of that on the other codes. After the battle of Navarino in 1827 and the final ejection of the Turks from Greece, the work was so far advanced that it would have been irrational to try to bring the other codes to the same state before finishing this one.

The process of composing the work was unusually complex and long drawn-out, even by Bentham's standards. In the early months he was concerned less with the text of his code than with introductory chapters, for which he drew heavily on materials designed originally for other works including 'First Lines', 'Rid Yourselves' and 'Thoughts on Official Economy'. (He subsequently dropped most of this material from the instalment of the work that he published in 1830, but Richard Doane rescued a good deal of it and put it into the introductory 'Book I' that he constructed and added to the *Code* when it was printed in full in Bowring's edition of the *Works*.)[20] After he turned to the drafting of the code itself, late in 1822 or early in 1823, he subjected it to counteracting processes of expansion and contraction that repeatedly delayed its completion.

In the beginning, he seems to have envisaged a document arranged in three or four parallel parts, each consisting of about a dozen chapters. The basic text was to be in the Enactive part, but this was to be flanked by separate Expositive and Rationale (or Reason-Giving) parts and (for a time at least) by an Instructional part. The principal branches of government were each to be covered in one or two chapters, for example one for the Executive, and one for the 'Judiciary Collectively' and a second for the 'Justice Minister'.[21] The division into parts was consistent with his long-held views about the desirability of 'giving reasons' for legislative provisions, and with his long-standing practice of adding rationales and notes to his own drafts. He tried hard to work to that plan, producing substantial quantities of material

for the Expositive and the Rationale and some for the Instructional. In February 1824 it still represented his design for the
work.[22] But by that time he had gone ahead more rapidly with
the Enactive chapters, and he soon found the composition of a
multi-part draft too onerous to complete. He remained convinced
that in an 'authoritative' or official work the inclusion of Expositive and Rationale would still be appropriate, but he concluded
that in his own 'unauthoritative' draft it would be better to
provide a unified text in which expositive, ratiocinative and
instructional materials would appear as 'articles' scattered among
the enactive provisions.[23] In the meantime, the originally modest
plan for the chapters and their contents had given way to more
elaborate ones, and the process of elaboration continued long after
1824. These things were a product of the way in which Bentham
conceived and developed the Code. It was essentially a work of
synthesis in which he brought together the ideas whose genesis
and growth have been described in previous chapters. But he did
not introduce them all at once, or decide at the beginning to
include them in the forms in which they ultimately appeared.
As he proceeded with his drafting he found that he needed to say
more, to call on more of his intellectual resources and in the end
to engage in re-thinking in order to reconcile points that he had
not previously considered in relation to each other, or in order to
exploit newly-perceived implications and similarities. As he responded to these needs he found it expedient to accommodate the
extra material by adding to the number of chapters and extending
their scope.

The version that he sent to Greece in 1823–24 consisted of
twenty-three (Enactive) chapters, including eleven devoted to the
Judiciary and three to the Executive.[24] When the last of the
twenty-three went off to Stanhope he had already decided to add
three more,[25] and he gradually increased the total to thirty-one.
The Judiciary acquired two and the Executive one of the new
chapters. Within chapters he added new sections and he expanded, revised, 'superseded' and adapted the argument at
numerous points in order to improve the exposition or to change
the mode of presentation. The version of the Code supplied to
Stanhope again provides a convenient bench-mark for illustration.
Its chapters on the 'Legislative', 'Ministers Collectively' and the
'Justice Minister' contained respectively seventeen, fourteen and

sixteen sections; in the published version, these became thirty-one, twenty-six and thirty-five. Moreover some of the sections (especially in the chapter 'Ministers Severally'), had already gone through a process of re-drafting in which a 'wave' of drafts composed in March 1823 was superseded by a September wave. Most of the September drafts were subsequently added to or completely re-written in later years.

As the work progressed, it was affected by yet other complicating factors, comparable to its early relationship with 'Thoughts on Official Economy' and its other predecessors. One set of these complications flowed from the fact that Bentham was working simultaneously on the several parts of the Pannomium. He was often uncertain whether particular pages of his text would be better placed in the Constitutional or the Penal or the Procedure code, and he sometimes shifted them to and fro. The material on the Judiciary was particularly subject to changes of this sort, because it raised important questions about the boundaries between the Constitutional and the Procedure codes.[26] He regarded questions of evidence and procedure as in some degree of constitutional significance and as vital to the functioning of the Judiciary, but he always intended to cover them in detail in a separate code. He had to decide which procedural points must nevertheless be included or referred to in the *Constitutional Code* for the sake of clarity, and he had to settle parts of the Procedure Code on which some provisions relating to the Judiciary must depend, before he could finally decide how to distribute the text that he had prepared on specific points and how to complete his chapter. A similar process can be discerned arising within the *Constitutional Code* itself. It was a highly-integrated piece of work: what Bentham said at one point in it had implications for what he might say or must say at other points. Every addition, omission or amendment therefore called for compensating changes elsewhere in the draft, in order to avoid repetition, to provide a necessary safeguard against a newly-introduced power or to fit in a new cross-reference. Finally, as it neared completion it became entangled with still further projects that caught Bentham's attention, such as the Law Amendment proposals that he vainly expected Brougham to promote.[27] These also stimulated him to produce drafts that he might, in the end, allocate to one work or the other.

The outcome of all these points about drafting is that the Mss. in which Bentham worked out his ideas in detail were a complex set, whose components are not easy to find, identify or interpret. They included some which were intended for the Code from the beginning, some which were drafted with other works in mind, and some which were intended for it but were re-directed or 'superseded' along the way. Some of those which would have been most enlightening, such as large parts of the intended Rationale for the Executive, have disappeared or become dispersed. But the complexity of the materials brings some advantages as well as disadvantages, for there exist partial substitutes for the lost or mislaid materials. These are to be found in the interim statements that Bentham published or sent to Greece and elsewhere, or in 'Thoughts on Official Economy' and the other precursors of the Code. So on many points it is possible to reconstruct his reasoning or at least to point to occasions or considerations that prompted important decisions affecting the Code's contents.

Bentham's construction of the Code was guided and dominated by the propositions about the contents, nature, aims and methods of constitutional law that he had worked over in his recent writings.[28] He began from the assumptions that he must retain the distinction between rulers and ruled, and that his task was to provide a body of law – similar in all important respects but its subject-matter to private law – which would establish and regulate all the constitutional powers, rights, obligations and roles of both rulers and subjects, and which would direct their activities to promoting the greatest happiness or universal interest. The powers and rights would be distributed according to a pattern that differed little from his original draft constitution for France, but that incorporated the new terminology he had devised in 'Thoughts on Official Economy'. The rulers would constitute the Operative, and would be divided into a Legislative (or Supreme Operative) and an Executive consisting of a Judiciary and an Administrative department. The Legislative would be unicameral, and it would be supplemented by a system of provincial Sub-Legislatures. The subjects of this Operative would find a place – a key place – in the Code as the Constitutive. There would, however, be no place for the Church, except as a private association; 'the euthanasia of the Establishment' would be effected within the constitution. The principal obstacle that constitutional law would have to overcome in promoting the universal interest would be self-preference; this was common to both subjects and rulers but was more dangerous in the rulers because they necessarily possessed constitutional power and they consequently had access to the instruments of corruptive influence, including delusion, the distribution of factitious dignity and other forms of patronage.

His 'course for surmounting' the force of self-preference was, in the most general terms, to treat the rulers as trustees for their subjects and to find ways of bringing each trustee's individual interest into accordance with universal interest, or 'into accordance with *duty* as the phrase is'.[29] His favoured techniques for effecting this union of interest and duty were to enhance the authority of the Constitutive department over the Operative departments of government, by means of an electoral system of the kind that he had been advocating throughout the previous decade, and by giving the public and the press official recognition as members of a Public Opinion Tribunal which might observe, record and publicize official shortcomings or official misbehaviour.[30] Electoral politics would, he believed, enable the self-interested subjects to neutralize each other and would then permit the universal interest to emerge; and the electoral system would at the same time clearly establish the rulers' status as that of trustees for the subjects, and would enable the latter to exercise the powers and rights that normally belong to principals in a trust.[31] The 'dislocability' (liability to dismissal) of the members of the Supreme Operative by the Constitutive – that is, in more conventional language, the election of the members of the Legislature for short fixed terms – was therefore the basic and indispensable element of the whole Code. The work of the Public Opinion Tribunal was important, for example as a means of determining when a functionary (including a member of the Legislature) should be subjected to the force of the moral sanction or – in more serious cases – dislocated, but it was supplementary to the electoral process. The heart of the Code was a recipe for electoral reform that clearly located the work as the last and the most complete and sophisticated of Bentham's writings on radical politics.

On this occasion, however, he acknowledged from an early stage that his arguments about influence and about the nature and needs of government had carried him beyond electoral reform and publicity and had exposed their insufficiency as a means of establishing the authority of subjects over rulers. He was now fully conscious that the Judiciary and the Administrative (Executive) must be stratified, complex and technically sophisticated, that the task of stripping them of all sources of influence was not a simple one, and that the further task of making them responsive to the Constitutive must also be tackled. The functionaries in these non-legislative branches of government were trustees like the legislators, and their interests must also be brought 'into accordance with *duty*', their aptitude must be maximized and the expenses of employing them minimized: they too, must be made responsible and dependent. So his 'ruling' or 'leading' principles demanded the *omni*supremacy of the Constitutive, a 'universal responsibility compensational and punitional' without distinction of branch or office, the dependence of 'the Executive [including the Judiciary] in all branches and individuals on Legislative thence on Constitutive', and the 'distinct delineation of the functions' of all departments and sub-departments.[32] His treatment of the non-legislative parts of government in his Code was at no point an afterthought or appendix, nor were they the subject of a mere supplementary sketch as they often were in official constitutions and as they had been in his own earliest exercises in constitutional codification. The close regulation of them was an indispensable if subordinate part of his system.

His reasoning in 'Thoughts on Official Economy' had provided him with two sorts of material out of which to build institutions, namely offices with their attendant powers and functions, and relationships of dependence and subordination. In order to carry that reasoning further, he had to perfect as far as possible his method of constituting an office in terms of its legal characteristics, to decide what kinds of offices (and if possible how many of them) there should be, to arrange them in order and settle their relationships, and to provide the matter under the various headings in relation to each sort of office. That was, accordingly, how he proceeded in relation to both the Judiciary and the Executive, but of course he worked more or less simultaneously on the four operations rather than treating them as distinct and successive stages of his task.

When he started he hoped to find a single form of analysis – a single list of headings – that would 'serve for all' offices.

His starting point here was the set of headings that he had supplied or used on previous occasions from the 1790s onwards: functions, relationships with other offices or authorities, location (appointment), dislocation (dismissal), term of service, attendance and pay. He was able to add a few more items that reflected some of his criteria for official situations, namely deputation (the supply of substitutes during the absence of officials from duty), checks (later re-named securities) and inaugural declaration (his secular and utilitarian version of an oath of office).[33] The first of these was a product of his campaign to secure the 'uninterruptedness of official attendance and service'. The other two expressed his attempts to give 'security to the people against misuse of the several powers conferred in the Code', the one by legal and 'political' sanctions, the other by moral sanctions.[34] He found that all of these headings were useful, but they did not quite add up to the single analytical scheme that he was looking for. They were applicable to nearly all offices and officials, ranging from members of Parliament to junior clerks and messengers. But they were too elaborate for some offices, and were too general to cover all the aspects and activities of many others. In practice, they provided a sort of core which might need to be adapted in some cases (for example by the division of a standard heading into two or three separate items), and which might need to be supplemented by a good many more items that were relevant to the functions and circumstances of a particular office.

When Bentham tried to settle the numbers and kinds of offices, he found it much easier to do so in the Judiciary than in the Executive (the Administrative department of government, in his terminology). For the Judiciary, he was able to draw on both his study of the French Judicial Establishment and his plans for Scotch Reform and the Court of Lords' Delegates; for his Administrative department, he had only a relatively small number of scattered thoughts, most of them relating either to the names of Ministries or to very special functions and organizations. But before going far into the structure of either branch, he was able to settle one issue which affected them both more or less equally. This concerned the composition of the top level of the branch, and the flow of authority to it from the Legislative. His decisions on the matter were determined by the way in which he intended to order and integrate his whole constitutional structure.

His aim here was of course to establish 'universal dependence' on the Constitutive. He proposed to achieve this by means of the 'scale of subordination' which he had recognized in 'Thoughts on Official Economy', but which he now increasingly described as a 'chain of service' or a 'chain of political subordination'.[35] The major branches of government were arranged in such a chain, as were the offices within a particular branch;[36] in the Administrative Department, for example, all the functionaries would be arranged 'in so many different grades forming a chain of indefinite length composed of as many links as there are grades'.[37] The significance of the chain was that each link (branch or office) acted on and was acted on by the immediately adjacent links, so that the line of dependence ran, as was noted above, from the Executive to Legislature and only then to the Constitutive. This meant that the dependence of Administrative and Judicial functionaries on the Constitutive was to be, in Bentham's terminology, unimmediate, and there had to be in each branch a link through which the authority of the Legislature could be transmitted to the rest of the branch.

In his writings on the Judiciary in 1806–07, the link in that branch had been provided by the Court of Lords' Delegates. But that body had found its rationale in the existence of the House of Lords, which he now proposed to discard. In the 1820s, too, he wanted to establish 'single-seatedness' or individual responsibility at every point in his establishment. He therefore substituted for the four Delegates a single official, a Justice Minister who would be required to perform the tasks of judicial management that he had earlier allocated to the Delegates, and who would be appointed by and responsible to the Legislature. It was important, however, that this official should be outside and totally independent of the Administrative department (the Executive). The latter department required a separate (and preferably single-seated) link of its own with the Legislature. Bentham provided its link in the form of a Prime Minister who should be responsible to the Legislature but who should have something like presidential authority over the other Ministers in his department. The result was that he created two more or less parallel hierarchies below the Legislature, the one culminating in the Justice Minister and the other in the Prime Minister. These two officials would be co-ordinates in his scheme, not subordinate and super-ordinate as the title of the Prime Minister might suggest.

The remaining offices in each department had to be determined by the nature of the tasks to be performed. The structure that he prescribed for the Judiciary followed fairly closely the model that he had devised for the French Judicial Establishment. It was based, like the latter, on a primarily geographical distribution of courts modified by a small number of 'judicatories of exception'. It was to be manned, too, by a judicial service divided into the three distinct strands of judges, prosecutors and defenders. The courts were to be single-seated and the lowest rank of judges – the Judges Immediate – were to be competent to deal with all issues that fell within the scope of the system. There was not to be a jury system on the English model, but there was to be a Quasi-Jury who were to act as assessors and as an appeal-licensing tribunal in certain circumstances. There was a somewhat grudging provision for 'professional lawyers' to supplement the work of official prosecutors and defenders, and a much more enthusiastic provision for judge-deputes to act as substitutes for the principal judges. Outside the ranks of judges and advocates there were to be several kinds of officials: Registrars, Mandate-bearers, Prehensors (arresting officers, acting on the directions of a court), Door-Keepers, Guards (at a court), Jailors, Quasi-lictors (administering corporal or capital punishment), and Vendue-Masters (selling property at the direction of a court). Strictly speaking these were functions or roles, more than one of which might on occasion be allocated to a single official. They were of course very similar to the 'judges' assistants' whom Bentham had originally identified in *Of Laws in General*. There was also to be provision for 'Judicial Inspectors', but these were to be spectators or members of the Public Opinion Tribunal allocated an official and regulated role, rather like the sight-seers whom he had wanted to visit and inspect the Panopticon.

His previous fragmentary thinking about the Administrative (Executive) had left him with an expectation that there would be five or six Ministers subordinate to the Prime Minister, of whom only two (Finance and Internal or Home Affairs) would be concerned with other than defence and foreign affairs. But when he began to explore his own ideas about the functions and activities of government it turned out that these were only slightly less generous – and in some directions perhaps a little more generous – than they had been in the 1790s, and that they required a correspondingly large and complex official establishment to accommodate them all. His views on some questions had changed since 1800. His earlier depreciation of individual activity as compared with rational, collective planning no longer appeared in his drafts. He seems also to have dropped the idea that governments should or could stimulate a flagging economy, although his statements on economic policy were too general to be perfectly clear on that point. But he found a great deal for governments to do in other familiar areas of policy.[38] Many of them were concerned with the prevention of delinquency and calamity, such as the maintenance of police forces, the 'magazining' of foodstuffs, and the regulation or supervision of building, of construction, of dangerous or unhealthy mining and manufacturing operations, of the preparation and sale of drugs, of drainage works, and of arrangements for isolation and quarantine. Others were concerned with communications (post offices, inns for poor travellers, roads, bridges and canals), with poor relief, with the provision of economic statistics and the administration of patents legislation, and with the care of government property. Items that were less familiar or had a shorter pedigree in his thinking were the supervision of education and the arrangement and conduct of elections, the printing and publication of legislation and the maintenance of a legislation-information service.

The electoral and legislation-aiding functions were a simple development of ideas that he had always held, although he had not always associated them clearly with the Executive. The educational functions were the product of several different lines of thought, some of which were relatively new. This was a topic about which he had been ambivalent and uncertain in the 1780s and 1790s when his only clear commitment had been to pauper education. His examination of educational issues in *Church of Englandism* and *Chrestomathia* reflected and confirmed a new and more urgent interest in the whole subject, above all because of its connection with sinister influence. One measure of his interest was the fact that from shortly after the publication of *Chrestomathia* in 1815 until shortly before he began drafting the *Constitutional Code* he was negotiating with Francis Place and others to launch a school conducted on Chrestomathic principles.[39]

But, in addition to his approval of such private ventures, he had come to see education as a matter for public policy, if not necessarily as a service to be supplied in governmental establishments.

One of his aims here – part of his campaign against the Church and its influence – was to provide means of discovering and exposing cases where reward and punishment were used 'to engage any persons to make professions of particular opinions as to any subject, more particularly as to politics, morals or religion'.[40] A second and very different set of considerations followed from his interest in 'intellectual aptitude' and formal examinations in the filling of official posts. He feared that enough good candidates for Ministerial and other posts would not be coming forward in any country unless it were rescued from the state of educational decay in which England was then stranded. A third matter of concern to him was medical education and the testing of the qualifications of aspirant medical practitioners.

These ideas guided him towards approving the holding of public examinations and the public supervision rather than the public management of educational establishments. He hesitated a little on the question of public management in relation to the training of candidates for official appointments. He knew that one semi-official school had been set up for just such a purpose, the East India Company's training college at Haileybury. He was interested in the Haileybury experiment, but was generally hostile to it. He seems to have objected to its system of examinations which he judged to be insufficiently public.[41] His dislike of it was fostered in his contacts with the journalist (and critic of the East India Company) J. S. Buckingham who had access to information about the school's shortcomings and its notorious difficulties.[42] But Bentham believed that alternatives were available. He had become a disciple of (or persuaded himself that he had found disciples in) the Hills of Hazelwood School, and he concluded that it would be more useful to encourage Hazelwood and similar establishments than to create new Haileyburys.[43] His educational and his administrative demands could therefore be satisfied in proposals to encourage private schools to prepare candidates for the Government's entry examinations (subsidizing them to do so if necessary), and to encourage candidates for the examinations to patronize such schools.[44] He envisaged this as a model for national education as well as a solution to the problem of official recruitment.

In his first full sketch of the Administrative in 1823, he found it necessary to group all the functions and activities under eleven Ministers and sub-departments: Election, Legislation, Interior Communication, Preventive Service, Indigence Relief, Education, Domain, Finance, Foreign Relations, Army and Navy.[45] As he thought more about them, he added to and refined the functions. In relation to several Ministers – for example, Interior Communication and Indigence Relief – he made it clear that their functions and powers extended to *private* as well as to public establishments.[46] In his later consideration of the Education Minister he struggled with the problem of reconciling his measures against religion and against the teaching of 'falsehood' with what he believed to be his commitment to freedom of speech and belief.[47] He quickly extended the Finance Minister's functions from the oversight of and accounting for the Government's own financial transactions to the control of the 'metallic-money Mint' and the 'paper-money Mint' and ultimately of the volume of money.[48] He also made a number of adjustments to take account of the conflicting or convergent interests of different Ministers in a given subject-matter or resource.

He was able to accommodate most of these changes in the structure of the eleven Ministries. But some of them could not be fitted into it, and he eventually added two more Ministers, a Health Minister in 1824 and a Trade Minister in 1826.[49] His creation of the Minister and Sub-Department of Health was an attempt to rationalize the distribution of functions by drawing off from the Education and Preventive Service Ministers those – ranging from problems of medical education and combinations among medical practitioners to health hazards in or arising from mines and factories and problems of water-supply and draining – that bore more directly on the health of the community. The Minister for Trade took over some functions, such as the administration of patents-legislation and the regulation of misleading advertising, that were not previously covered satisfactorily. The Trade Minister also provided a complement or counterweight to the economic-policy activities of the Finance Minister, for his functions included the oversight of the latter's taxing and money-regulation policies.

When Bentham turned his attention to the sub-Ministerial structure of the Administrative, he found that he had relatively little to say about most parts of it. He could not forecast how many offices or kinds of offices each Sub-Department would need, and he left the determination of these points to the Legislature. He was satisfied to specify a few offices that he thought would be vital to some or all Departments, and to add a few general points as a guide to the Legislature when it was making its dispositions.

He came closest to depicting a definite structure in his discussion of the Defensive Force. This subject became one of the major growth-points in the Code. He wanted to propose here a new set of arrangements for both the Army and the Navy. His treatment of the new arrangements began as a sub-section of the section of chapter XI ('Ministers Severally') that dealt with the Army Minister. By the middle of 1824 he found it necessary to create a completely new chapter of ten sections to accommodate the growing mass of material.[50] But this, too, did not prove adequate and he continued to add new sections until the total reached nineteen. While the work was in progress he consulted freely his friends with military or naval experience – Stanhope, James Young, Perronet Thompson, his brother Samuel – as well as others who had views or information about these matters such as the American John Neal.[51] His basic purposes were to define carefully the relationship between the Militia ('Radicals') and the Regular ('Stipendiary') forces, to make the former large in relation to the latter, and to implement his proposals relating to Prizes and Prize-Money. A secondary aim was to reduce the number of ranks among the officers. (Here and elsewhere in this chapter, the example of the 'Anglo-American United States' seems to have been important to him.) He was able to work out his ideas about Prizes, the Stipendiaries and the Radicals, but in the end he had to put his recommendations on ranks and grading in comparative terms, and to leave the matter to the Legislature's judgement.

In the civilian departments, the points that concerned him most were to ensure that for each directive situation there would be a Registrar to record his principal's proceedings, and (as in the Defensive Force) to reduce the number of intermediate grades (that is, links in the chain of subordination) between the Minister and the operative functionary. His model Sub-Department in this respect was that belonging to the Legislation Minister, for it need employ no more than a Registrar and Writing Clerks and they could all be located in one spot. But he saw that this could not be a universal pattern, for he recognized that differentiation of power and hence of grade must arise whenever one official had to give orders to another or to report to another. This situation must arise frequently in a system based on orders and obedience; partly because the tasks to be performed would be complex, and partly because of 'mere distance' between the central office and the places where its orders must be acted on. One or both of these circumstances must be present, he noted, in the Sub-Departments of Foreign Relations, the Army, the Navy, Interior Communication, and Domain. So the number of grades had to be determined separately in each department, in the light of the particular and possibly changing circumstances of each of them, and it was potentially quite large. Those points forced themselves on him increasingly over time, so that in 1826 he had to provide a separate section (ch. IX, s. 5, 'Subordination-grades') in which to set them out systematically.[52] He tried, however, to weaken their force by insisting that differences in grade did not and must not imply differences in pay, and by concentrating on particular situations in which the need for direction and reporting might arise, rather than on continuing relationships of command and obedience. He was thus able, in this discussion, to avoid referring to a distinct and permanent hierarchical line of responsibility below the rank of Minister. He lacked at this point a clear notion of 'span-of-control' which would have given him a more or less determinate standard for distinguishing grades, and he was prepared to lay aside the principle of unity of authority in order to counteract the tendency to multiply their number.

The offices that Bentham proposed to create included not only those in the Administrative and the Judiciary but also the novel posts (at least in English experience) of Local Headman and Local Registrar. Their function in his scheme was to complete the network of control over the community and to leave no gaps in the means for 'giving effect to the will of government in all its several main branches'.[53] We have seen how in earlier years he had contemplated using the clergy as a body of local officials to complete the nationwide web of executive action. The euthanasia of the Establishment deprived him of that resource. At the same time, his re-structuring of the Judiciary eliminated the local

Justices of the Peace and left areas smaller than a sub-district (the jurisdiction of an Immediate Judge) without any direct representative of the central government. Yet there remained, he believed, many problems – ranging from the suppression of riots to the settlement of domestic and industrial disputes – that could only be handled on a local basis and in a more limited area. The post of Headman of a bis-subdistrict was his device for filling the breach that his other proposals had created. It followed that there must be a Local Registrar for every Local Headman, in accordance with the principle that 'each directive situation' required such a complementary official.

The last of Bentham's four tasks – the filling in of the details for all the offices performing executive functions – was in principle a simple one. It amounted to pursuing the objectives that were common to all parts of the Code, and applying the principles of good management and the devices of control that he was employing elsewhere and that he had been developing and experimenting with over many years. His principal objective was to maximize aptitude and minimize expense in a condition of unimmediate responsibility. Responsibility implied, here as elsewhere, punibility and (or including) dislocability. The occasions for punibility could be defined in one direction by notions of good management or efficiency (the limits of *appropriate* aptitude). Punibility was to be maintained by the deterrents of indirect legislation, such as the 'distinct delineation' of all powers and functions, 'single-seatedness', the minimization of powers, and the maximization of information or evidence through the system of communications that would simultaneously facilitate good management. Aptitude was to be encouraged and expense was to be discouraged through the incentives of reward, including the detailed and dove-tailed arrangements for locability and remuneration that he had devised in 'Thoughts on Official Economy'. All of this seemed straight-forward enough. But in practice it ran into the same difficulties as the rest of Bentham's work on the Code. His original conceptions were too modest, and his thinking on some issues was less complete than he supposed. He found at many points that he had more to say than he had expected, that he sometimes had to choose between or to reconcile competing goals whose opposition he did not at first perceive, and that his hesitations and delays presented him with opportunities to draw more extensively on his accumulated ideas. His treatment of the offices slowly expanded and subtly changed its shape.

Before he had gone very far with either the Judiciary or the Administrative, he found that he needed to pause and to develop his theory of administrative activity. The necessity presented itself to him as a matter of language rather than theory. It arose out of his desire to 'delineate' clearly all powers and functions. For that purpose he required, he believed, a suitable vocabulary: 'Language [is] the instrument by which a work of this sort must be performed: dependent on the aptitude of this instrument will be the aptitude of the work. Hence the necessity of the endeavour to give to this instrument whatever it is found to want in aptitude.'[54] An 'apt' vocabulary was of course one that would be simple, 'transparent' and 'univocal', and free of delusive or fallacious implications. It was also one that dealt in 'collective denominations instead of details'.[55] The last of these points was a demand for economy and uniformity in expression: that is, for a set of general terms that could be defined once and could then be used repeatedly in different parts of the Code. It was closely connected with his attempt to identify a standard set of components for any office or legal condition, and it was the aspect of his drafting about which he himself was most forthcoming. As he explained, he proceeded first by allocating appropriate functions to particular offices, then by abstracting from them and classifying the common elements which he could discern in them, and finally by devising a 'univocal appellation for each function'.[56] Steps in this process can be discerned in certain 'functions tables' or lists of 'functions collected from different functionaries' dated from 1823 onwards. In finding names for the different functions in this fashion, he was in fact locating and distinguishing the several activities which were comprehended by the general notions of administration and adjudication.

His analysis was already in a mature form by September 1823.[57] He then divided administrative functions into the classes of those involving actions relating to persons, those involving actions relating to things, and those involving actions relating to ordinances, occurrences or arrangements. He covered most of the kinds of activities that ultimately appeared in the chapter on 'Ministers Collectively', including the locative and dislocative functions, the directive, the procurative, the statistic and the melioration-suggestive. The inclusion of the last of these was part of an attempt that he was making to extend from the Judiciary to all officials the right and the responsibility to propose amendments to the law when they became aware of obscurities, omissions or anomalies. The same list of functions served him (as he had hoped) as the basis for his account of adjudication.

He did not, however, find it possible to complete his analysis quickly in either branch. His difficulties in the Judiciary stemmed from the fact that his basic list did properly relate to administration not adjudication, and that in order to deal adequately with the latter he had to tackle it directly. He did so on a number of occasions between 1823 and 1831,[58] and set things in perspective by differentiating – apparently in 1827 – between the 'non-distinctive' and the 'distinctive' judicial functions.[59] The delay in settling the administrative functions was caused by a different sort of circumstance, namely that his ideas of the scope of the Administrative's activity were still developing after 1823, and his account of its elements had to change in order to accommodate his later views.

The underlying factor in this process was the gradual expansion and spelling-out of the activities of government as a whole that he was effecting while he was composing the Code. As he gave government more responsibility for such things as monetary policy and the arrangements and structures (both public and private) affecting the health, the wealth, the welfare and the intellectual and moral state of the community, he was extending the range of its contact with members of the community and was making it more dependent on the gathering and the dissemination of information. He was increasing the number of people with whom it might come into contact – who might have something to seek from it, or from whom it might want to secure information (evidence) or something else – and he was making the corresponding activities a larger part of the total activity of government. Accordingly one of the ways in which he acknowledged these changes was to add the inspective and the information-elicitive and the informative functions to his basic list of 'functions in all'.[60]

The same changes were reflected a second time in the scope and content of the chapter on 'Ministers Collectively'. His initial approach to this chapter was determined by his list of headings designed to 'serve for all' offices. But when he began to draft it systematically in 1823–4, he decided to provide separate sections, and therefore discussion in some detail, not only for these matters but also for some of the functions. The functions that he first selected for that special treatment were the statistic and melioration-suggestive, and a group relating to operations on physical things – procuration (later replaced by requisition), reparation and elimination.[61] The subsequent history of the chapter shows a shift in emphasis from problems of obtaining and using resources to problems of conduct, and from the internal operation of the organization to its impact on and interaction with the social environment. Reparation and elimination were no longer allowed separate sections, but that privilege was granted to the new functions, the inspective, the information-elicitive and the informative.[62] And a number of new sections were added: architectural arrangements, and a set of five closely-related sections on 'securities' against various forms of misconduct, which replaced a section on 'Ministers' Checks' and a projected section on 'Remedy against oppression by superordinates or co-ordinates'.

The revised treatment of checks and securities was similar to some of the argument in the chapter on the 'Judiciary Collectively,' but it had its origin in the Administrative where it represented the convergence of two lines of reasoning, the more outward-looking view of the organization that Bentham was tending to adopt, and the re-thinking of his views about the ways in which the principles of reward and of individual responsibility should be applied. The second of these flowed through a number of the sections of 'Ministers Collectively' before it had its impact on the arrangements for securities.

Bentham first discussed remuneration within the Administrative in a projected (but later discarded) section on 'Ministers' Pay' in 1823.[63] He took there an uncompromizing line, offering Ministers a flat rate of pay per diem, and not admitting supplements or non-monetary rewards. This was consistent with the hostility to factitious dignity and to extra pay for extra effort that he had expressed in his recent writings, including the abortive introductory chapters that he had drafted for the Code in 1822 as well as in 'Thoughts on Official Economy'. Nevertheless he gradually shifted his ground on both points. He soon found reasons to countenance extra pay for extra despatch provided that certain safeguards were introduced, including an Extra Despatch Book in which special services would be recorded as they were performed.[64] In a more thoroughgoing reconsideration and generalization of his argument in 1824, he introduced into it a résumé of many of his objections to factitious dignity (including its links with influence and corruption) but at the same time he began to provide for forms of honorary reward that he hoped would be harmless.[65] The outcome was a system of specific declarations of public gratitude, recorded in a Public Merit Register but only on the order of a Judge and at the conclusion of a judicial hearing (more than a little like a Vatican process for canonization) in which the application would be opposed by a Government Advocate.[66] The course of his reasoning on this subject is a good example of the way in which his apparently simple principles generated complications as he tried to apply them, and as he tried to preserve their essential character while modifying them in operation. His desire for economy was competing until the end with his fear that ordinary honours and dignities would buttress sinister influence.

The same sort of competition between his principles of economy and some of his other objectives was present in his thinking about individual responsibility. The core of the problem was that full and clear responsibility seemed to imply the possession of discretions and of powers of appointment and dismissal that Bentham was, for reasons of economy, reluctant to confer on his functionaries. It occurred in a relatively simple and soluble form in relation to appointment: individual responsibility and the chain of responsibility would be most perfect if each superordinate were able to choose freely his subordinates and if he were thus rendered incapable of complaining that they had been imposed on him; but to allow a completely free choice would be to disregard the merits of pecuniary competition and public examinations to which Bentham was now equally committed. He found a solution by treating the results of examinations and of bidding as information that would be useful to the appointing official but that would not bind him or limit his descretion, and as information that might be used *against* the appointing authority at some later time.[67] He did not find it so easy to deal with the relationship between responsibility and the power of dismissal.

At the start this form of the problem appeared less and not

more difficult than the earlier one. The imposition of full responsibility again required perfect discretion on the part of super-
ordinates, and there were no inhibitions corresponding to examinations or pecuniary competition. But Bentham immediately
saw that perfect discretion would amount to possession of a large
amount of power over subordinates, and in a sense to influence.
So, while providing for dislocation in the ranks below the Minister
'by any officer superordinate to the subordinate in question',[68] he
began simultaneously to hedge this about with qualifications.
He made dislocation depend upon 'authority from the appropriate judge',[69] provided suspension and transfer as interim or
alternative ways in which a superordinate might express his dis-
pleasure (and thus escape responsibility for a subordinate's 'inaptitude') and he gave the subordinate in this as in other matters
a right of appeal to the Minister.[70] In order to accommodate
these points, he devised the new section (July–August 1823) on
'Remedy against oppression...' as a supplement to the set of
'Ministers' Checks' through which he was trying to enforce
responsibility.[71]

In the next two years he gave a good deal of attention to the
subject of 'Checks' – or, as he re-named them, 'securities for
appropriate aptitude' – not only in the Administrative but in the
Code as a whole. It is likely that he did most of his basic thinking
on the subject in relation to the Judiciary, but it is clear that he
saw the securities operating in the several branches as interdepen-
dent, and that he saw the arrangements in both Judiciary and
Administrative as subordinate to those in the Legislature which
made all functionaries subject to a general power of recall. His
first draft of 'Ministers' Checks' was pretty thin, just a few
articles. He revised it substantially in April and June 1824.[72]
He then incorporated in it many devices of indirect legislation,
similar to those which he was adopting for the Judiciary, and
some of which he had foreshadowed in 'Thoughts on Official
Economy'. They included Office Calendars listing information
about the officials, merit and demerit registers, deportment tables
(rules for conduct or deportment), the rights of the Public Opinion
Tribunal and the responsibility of Ministers for their subordinates'
conduct. He later gave it some more devices, notably the 'Extra
Despatch Book' which he had introduced as an antidote to abuses
in his new system of honorary reward.[73]

While he was changing his treatment of 'Checks' in this way, he was paying a smaller but not insignificant amount of attention to 'Remedy against oppression...' He changed its status more than once, reducing it for a time to a sub-section of his discussion of recruitment and dismissal, but then making it an independent section again.[74] He strengthened some of its provisions by confining the power of dislocation (as distinct from suspension) to 'a Minister or the superordinate authorities', and by finding a place for the Judiciary in the process of appeal against allegedly oppressive action. Finally, in the middle of 1826 he began to rethink the whole subject of official misconduct and the securities against it. It was at this point that the considerations relating to responsibility interacted with those relating to the situation of the organization within its environment.

In his revision of 'Ministers' Checks' in June 1824, Bentham had indicated that there would be rules and printed tables concerning the deportment of 'visitors' as well as of functionaries. His additions to the functions of government, and the increasingly outward-looking stance that he imposed on it, enhanced the status of these visitors in the system. More of them became involved in the processes of administration, and there were more roles for them. He described their roles in language derived from the judicial system: they might be 'suitors' or 'evidence-holders' or 'inspectees' (a special class of evidence-holders).[75] The adoption of this terminology amounted to more than economy in the use of language. It indicated how occasional or part-time participants might function in the system and how their roles might be prescribed and regulated. Like the comparable groups in judicial hearings, they might frustrate the proceedings; and they in turn might have reason to fear oppression on the part of the full-time functionaries. Bentham dealt with these matters in a characteristically legalistic fashion. Besides making provision for the 'Rules of deportment for non-functionaries' he invented the concept of 'quasi-insubordination' to cover obstruction or refusal to cooperate by those who were called on to provide information, to submit to inspection or to help the administrators in other ways authorized by law. He made quasi-insubordination an offence, with penalties, like the insubordination of the full-time employees. At the same time he felt obliged to extend the range of remedies against oppression, in order to provide protection for non-functionaries against functionaries in the same way as he was providing it for subordinate functionaries against their super-ordinates and co-ordinates. And this re-examination of the remedies coincided with and contributed to a more careful con-sideration of the nature of the conduct against which the remedies must be directed. Bentham now added to the general category of 'oppression' three other and more particular types of misconduct to be prevented or discouraged, namely extortion, insubordination, and peculation.[76]

This classification of misconduct provided the final structure for his treatment of 'securities' and 'remedies'. He abandoned the old 'Remedy against oppression...' and substituted for it four new sections – 'Oppression Obviated', 'Insubordination Obviated', 'Extortion Obviated' and 'Peculation Obviated'. He covered in each of these whatever parts of the conduct of either functionaries or non-functionaries seemed relevant to the proper functioning of the system. He retained the re-titled section dealing with 'Securities for Appropriate Aptitude', but re-arranged it slightly in order to clarify its relationship with the new sections and to make it more systematically a summary of and a complement to the securities which were provided in those four sections and in other parts of the two chapters IX and XI of the Code.

The core of those securities was of course the system of physical relationships and communications – architecture, records, in-spection and publication – which he wanted to function as both a counter to misconduct and an aid to good management. This was the aspect of the Code for which he had the largest body of com-pleted material available to be drawn on. It lay ready to his hand in the Panopticon essays, in his works on the Poor Law and preventive police, in his regulations for the office of Timber Master, and in his writings on the Judiciary. But even here he did not find it easy to choose an approach or to settle a text at the first attempt: his drafts show the same sorts of changes of mind and repeated amendments as appear elsewhere in his work-ing papers.

He covered these matters in one section of chapter VIII on the Prime Minister (§11, 'Publication System'), and five sections in chapter IX dealing with, respectively, registration or statistics, requisition, reporting, inspection and architectural arrangements.

The principal issues that troubled him concerned the location of the material on architecture, the balance between inspection and other modes of information and communication, and the internal arrangement of the material in the two complementary sections on requisition and registration.

The origin of the section on architecture was a 'Note to Ch. IX or Ch. X, §12' dated September 1823.[77] ('Ch. X, §12' was the section on conflicts of authority, which took its final shape as §14 of chapter XI.) It provided clearly for the housing of all the Departments under the same roof, the centrality of the Prime Minister's office, and the use of 'conversation tubes' to achieve 'speed of communication between office and office'. Its use of the Panopticon's devices was in some respects paralleled by the material on Judiciary Apparatus and Justice Chambers which he began drafting at about the same time.[78] In his usual fashion, he kept thinking of new points that he wanted to include. Some of his working papers suggest that he became particularly anxious in 1827 to promote the receipt of anonymous information (one of the original forms of indirect legislation).[79] He did so ultimately by providing for private interview-rooms attached to the Minister's Office.[80] For these and other reasons his treatment of architecture became too extensive and acquired too many objectives to be fitted into an appendix to the section on co-ordination and he made it the final section in chapter IX.

Inspection was one of the oldest and most familiar of Bentham's devices of indirect legislation, but he did not place much weight on it in his system of internal control. As he pointed out, its function in the system was largely performed in governmental establishments by the 'universal registration and publication system'.[81] It was therefore required within the system only as a supplementary and irregular form of supervision. Its appearance in a separate section in chapter IX was the product of the more outward-looking stance that Bentham was attributing to the Administrative, and which accounted for its inclusion among the basic 'functions in all'. While not losing all significance for the prevention of administrative misconduct, the section therefore became rather a harbinger of the typical nineteenth-century use of inspection and the inspectorate, namely the supervision of private and other establishments outside the structure of the central government. It was most applicable to them because they were less subject to registration, publication and 'the light of publicity'.

The officially-informative (report-making) function was more clearly an innovation in Bentham's thinking but it was also one that entered his calculations at a later stage in his drafting. He recognized it as a separate function in 1825, but seems not to have allocated a definite section to it until early in 1827.[82] He was then able to give it substantially the content that appeared in the published text. Its purpose was to fill an apparent gap in the system of communications, a gap relating to information that would not normally be 'registered' or that, if registered, might not be quickly transmitted. He pointed out that the volume of such information would depend on the completeness of the registration system, but he seemed to believe that there would always be some of it and that a definite obligation must be imposed on all functionaries to make it available to any of their colleagues who needed it.

The requisitive and statistic functions were concerned with two different stages of the administrative process; the former with enabling things to happen through the securing of access to resources, the latter with the recording of events after they had happened. But each had an obvious and well-developed model in earlier schemes and each seems to have presented Bentham with a similar problem or temptation before he decided on the approach that he finally adopted.

The model for the requisitive function was the scheme that Bentham and his brother had devised for the Timber Master in the dockyards. They had provided that timber (and other materials) should be made available only in response to written requests or requisitions. In the Code, Bentham generalized this procedure into a form of budgeting covering all resources. In his first draft of the section (October 1824), he placed the emphasis on *procurement*, which was the process corresponding most closely to that occurring in the dockyards.[83] But his reasoning led him to the conclusion that decisions about procurement belonged to the Legislature and must take the form of permission (or, more technically, *instructions*) to procure. Such decisions, he now felt, must be preceded by another process consisting in *requests* to procure. The making of such requests constituted the requisitive function. In later drafts he shifted the emphasis to this antecedent function and the documents (requisitions) through which it must be per-formed.[84] At the same time he eliminated material relating to the *objects* of procuration and requisition which he now saw was cluttering up his draft.

His fundamental model for the statistic function was the original system of book-keeping that he had constructed for the National Charity Company. But he took a considerable time to re-adopt that model in something like its original form, and some of the work that he had done in the intervening period seemed to distract him rather than to clarify things for him. His first draft of the section, prepared in July or August 1823, was a short one which merely imposed on Ministers and their subordinates a general responsibility to keep records and make reports.[85] In the following year he drafted a much longer and more complex text.[86] Sub-headings and notations on the papers suggest that at that time he was particularly conscious of the relationship between records and evidence, especially pre-appointed evidence, and that he was trying, not very successfully, to incorporate the relation-ship into his argument. Whether for that reason or some other, his draft devoted most attention to 'Registranda' (the things to be recorded) and less to the books in which they were to be recorded. He abandoned that approach in 1826 and adopted substantially the pattern of the published section.[87] Although he continued to make changes after that time, his 1826 amendments to his draft of this section provided him with the effective form of the centre-piece of his system of communications, around which his other securities could then be deployed.

In many respects the drafting of the *Constitutional Code* must appear as something of an anti-climax. So many of its components had been in preparation and often more or less complete for so long in Bentham's mind, its fundamental themes – influence, responsibility, aptitude, economy and the like – had been re-hearsed so often, and some of its particular parts such as the electoral system, the Judiciary and recruitment had been fore-shadowed in such detail, that the process of putting the materials into a single document must seem a relatively simple and automatic one, a process that went ahead almost as a matter of course. That judgement or expectation has not been contradicted by the preceding account of the theory of government, which has turned up few points at which Bentham changed his ideas in a significant way and many more in which he merely proceeded systematically to work them out more fully. Yet the judgement is unfair to Bentham, and it underrates the magnitude of this achievement of his old age.

The sheer bulk of the document and the complexity of its structure – its thirty-one chapters with up to twenty-six sections in a chapter – make the systematic working out of the ideas and the systematic building of them into the structure a very considerable achievement. It is known, of course, that Bentham did not perform the work entirely single handed or without recourse to the ideas or examples of others. The use that he made of Thompson and other military men in the composition of ch. X, and of J. S. Buckingham in the development of his ideas about education, have been mentioned; he at all times employed secretaries (Colls, Doane, Moore) to copy and revise, and was able to draw from time to time on the services of others (for example, Chadwick, John Neal, George Bentham) for these and for more intellectually exacting tasks; he freely consulted acquaintances such as the American diplomats Richard Rush or John Adams Smith or the Frenchman d'Argenson about institutions and practices in their respective countries;[88] he studied closely other constitutions such as those of Spain, Greece,[89] and New York;[90] he modelled some of his offices or administrative devices pretty closely on existing foreign examples, for example the Local Headman on the French maire[91] and the Office Calendar on the United States' official Register of Officers and Agents.[92] But I at least am convinced that nearly all the drafting and all but a negligible amount of the thinking were done by Bentham himself, and that where others supplied ideas he did not simply purvey them but used and shaped them in a way to make them his own. Properly speaking, then, the *Constitutional Code* was not an anticlimax, it was a consummation.

8

CONCLUSION

It is now possible to answer the questions posed in the introduction, to show how Bentham was able to develop his very detailed and in many respects prescient programme for the reform and re-arrangement of British government, and to show how he was able to develop the sophisticated theory of administrative processes and other matters which accompanied his programme. But, as was also foreshadowed in the introduction, the answers must be lengthy and complex.

Their starting point is that many elements in both Bentham's programme and his theory were borrowed from others. He was immersed in a certain kind of thinking about politics and government that was common in the eighteenth century. Its fundamental feature was that it brought together in a particular way the two great themes of modern political thought, individualism and the modern sovereign state. It respected and tried to preserve individualist notions and values, especially the beliefs that individual interests should have moral priority, that individuals are naturally autonomous and that social and political institutions are artifacts. At the same time it recognized the fragility of groupings composed only of autonomous individuals and held together only by their interests, and it offered the state, that is the central government, as an additional and decisive source of cohesion and discipline. It therefore aspired to make the government the effective master of the community in which it was located, and it sought to do so by equipping the state with institutions and instruments which would render the community responsive to its wishes. Yet it did not allow its concern with the state to displace its commitment to individual wills and interests. It sought to protect them and their role by making them the constituents of the state, either through the notion of consent or – increasingly –

by representing them as the masters and judges of the state's actions. For these multiple purposes it accumulated, and was still accumulating when Bentham began to think about society and social problems, a body of ideas, slogans and practical devices which it could offer to governments for their guidance and use. These included the principles that the public happiness should be the object of public policy and that government should be conceived as a trust; the beliefs that legislation and the legislature were central to the work of government, and that uniformity, clarity, order and consistency were essential in both law and administration; and the many devices of preventive police.

Bentham adopted both the fundamental values and many of the slogans, ideas and devices that figured in this body of thought. He shared the ambition to complete the work of providing a blueprint for the modern state, and yet to do so without encroaching on the moral claims of individuals or on their psychological autonomy. He adopted the view that government was a trust conferred for the benefit of the state's subjects. He was convinced of the importance of regularity and clarity in all of government's operations, and he devoted much thought to the devices and institutions of preventive police and to the codification of the law. But he found many of these ideas unsatisfactory in the forms in which he first encountered them. He felt that the more abstract and theoretical ones – those dealing with individuals' behaviour, with the role of the government in the community, and so on – needed to be stated more sharply than had yet been done, and needed to have their claims defended more vigorously against their competitors. He felt, too, that the theoretical links between principles and devices or recommendations must be established more completely and systematically. He tried, in his own work, to meet both of those criteria. His reasoning was therefore an adaptation and a development of what his contemporaries were saying, not a simple reproduction of it.

The course of his reasoning led him to focus his attention first, and fundamentally, on law and jurisprudence. His starting point here was supplied by his utilitarianism, and by his attempt to give that an individualist cast. He believed that it was entirely proper for self-willed individuals to pursue their own interests, and that the only legitimate grounds for interfering with or frustrating them in that activity were the requirements of utility or of the happiness of the community, which was his own version of the public happiness or public interest. He did not doubt that utility was a real object or that it required and justified some redirection of individuals' energies and actions. He conceded that they might themselves supply some of this redirection in the form of what he called moral sanctions, but he thought that these would be too meagre to promote utility. He therefore agreed that some form of social control must be supplied by a sovereign. He believed that, in a world of individual wills, the sovereign's contributions to social order must also take the form of expressions of will – commands – backed up by sanctions to bend others to its will. In other words, for Bentham as for many of his contemporaries, the essence of sovereignty must be legislation, and the primary instruments of social control must be law and the legal system conceived in a positivist or legal-rationalist way. But it was above all in relation to these basic notions about law and its social functions that he found his contemporaries' ideas inadequate. He was as anxious as they were to see a satisfactory code of laws enacted in every state, and to see an efficient and incorruptible judiciary established everywhere. He felt, however, that before either of these objects could be attained, it would be necessary to achieve a better understanding of the nature of law and of judicial proceedings, of the means by which law operated in society, and of the proper limits which the sovereign should recognize to its own activities. This belief dictated the sequence of his studies. It obliged him to deal firstly with abstractions – with jurisprudence and with ethics in a quite rigorous sense – and then to proceed through the derivation of principles of action (punishment, reward, judicial procedure and evidence) to the concrete provisions of a code and the concrete plans for a judiciary and for other legal institutions.

Those legal topics occupied him for long periods spread over his whole working life. His early work – of which the *Fragment on Government* and the *Introduction to the Principles of Morals and Legislation* were detached instalments – was concentrated mainly on the theory of the nature and the form of law. It was succeeded by the series of important studies on reward, punishment and other applications of his fundamental theory, many of which he failed to complete but which were rescued and brought to light by Dumont. These were followed, some years later, by a number of works dealing with the organization and procedure of the courts. The last major work that he published – the first volume of the *Constitutional Code* – was the first instalment of the code *in terminis* that he had always hoped to produce and for which his essays in jurisprudence were intended to be the prolegomena.

It is probable that he would have been happy to devote himself entirely to works of this kind, and happy to conceive them and the legal system in the narrowest way. But the further course of his thinking, together with his personal experience of law and politics, repeatedly forced him to take a broader view and to put his mind to other subjects. The boundaries of the legal system itself soon proved to be vague or indefinite, and he found that the functioning of the system could not be understood except in relation to the environment in which it operated. In order to complete his theory of the legal system, and his programme for it, he had to expand it into a theory of and a programme for government in all its aspects.

The most obvious source of this expansionary pressure was his recognition that the enforcement of the law – the bending of others to the sovereign's will – must involve much more than the work of the courts. It would involve also the administration of punishment or reward, and the supplementary processes of surveillance and the detection of offenders. So at an early point in his thinking he saw that the judges' work must be complemented by that of a vaguely-defined body of 'judges' assistants'. This view crystallized in attempts, from 1778 onwards, to consider and construct penal institutions and other bodies designed to carry on the work of preventive police. One of these, the Panopticon, came to dominate his life for several years to an extent that was disproportionate to its place in the structure of his thought; but it remains true that his concern with the Panopticon, like his concern with police forces, followed directly from his interest in the legal system. It illustrates a general tendency in his thinking to move outwards from the judicial to the executive branch of government through the notion of judges' assistants.

This tendency did not, however, stand alone in encouraging him to look closely at the Executive. It was complemented by others which had deep roots in his assumptions about and his attitudes to the law and the sovereign. His very notion that governing was essentially an exercise of will encouraged him to look beyond purely legal questions. As he interpreted it, it implied that the sovereign and its institutions must be adapted to the making of decisions and the concentration of decision making in one person or place. He was here echoing familiar eighteenth-century demands and propositions about sovereignty, about the importance of information or 'intelligence' to governments, and about the curbing of both judicial interpretation and the independence of the Executive. But he was not content to repeat those demands. He felt obliged to consider how they might be satisfied, obliged to establish facilities for the gathering and assimilation of information, and obliged to define the scope of judicial and executive action in precise terms and ultimately to provide the institutional means of ensuring that those limits were not exceeded. He was not, of course, unique in thinking about these problems. Montesquieu, Turgot and others had discussed or were discussing various aspects of them. But he perhaps set higher standards for himself in the matter of devising operational schemes and in considering all aspects together. He could not, at the outset, meet those standards but he could and did keep them in mind and he soon began to accumulate material bearing on them.

These considerations converged with the consequences of other circumstances and assumptions. One of those assumptions was incorporated in the ideal of codification that he espoused. It was that a code should be complete and comprehensive. From it he drew the subsidiary requirement that the code should cover and account for all legal phenomena and indeed all social phenomena other than those that rested on the (few and weak) moral or religious sanctions. This meant that the powers, activities, rights and structures of government must be found places within it: there must be a constitutional branch of the law, or a constitutional code, along with the several other particular codes which might exist within the general or universal code.

This might have remained a formal point, or it might have been satisfied by the statement of a few general propositions about governments and their powers, if it had not been reinforced and given content by some other assumptions and beliefs. The first of these was again an aspect of his understanding of codification. He saw as the core of a code the *offences* that it defined, the acts which should not be performed or the omissions which should not be tolerated. A code could never be drafted unless the list of offences could be settled; it could never be given even a preliminary shape unless the scope and contents of the list could at least be indicated in some way. He did not suppose that a final or definitive list could ever be drawn up, and he agreed that a sovereign might designate any act or omission as an offence. But he believed that the principle of utility could be used as a criterion for the creation of offences as for any other aspect or exercise of sovereignty, and that one could say a good deal in general terms about the sorts of things that should be classed as offences. In practice, however, this could only be done through a consideration of the acts and activities that governments should or should not promote, or in other words through a consideration of the functions of government. So the shaping of the penal code implied the simultaneous or prior determination of some of the content of the constitutional code relating to government.

While his view of the proper functions of government fluctuated from time to time, he was never able to confine them within very narrow limits. He had, in the beginning, no desire to multiply needless interferences with individuals' pursuit of their interests, or to override their judgements about the nature of those interests, but he nevertheless shared some of the prejudices of the contemporary writers on police. These included a somewhat *dirigiste* approach to national wealth, and a more marked willingness to regulate, guide and find occupations for the population in order to deter and distract them from criminal activities and criminal associations, and in order to prevent dangers to public health or other calamities. His closer acquaintance with the works of Adam Smith and other market-economists moderated but did not altogether remove his readiness to countenance intervention in economic life. He became enthusiastic about the market as a utilitarian device. But his enthusiasm was qualified in two important ways: he believed that there remained some parts of the economy, notably the field of money and banking, which must be regulated in order to maintain economic stability; and he believed that at best the market was a device for promoting *abundance*, one of the four 'subordinate ends' into which he decomposed utility. The significance of the second point was that any concrete economic institution or activity might affect, and might be subjected to any of the tests relating to, any of the other three subordinate ends and in particular the end of *security*. On this ground he was able to justify numerous departures from a purely market situation in many parts of the economy, including the trade in second-hand goods, those parts or aspects of economic life having a bearing on health (including the health of employees in certain industries), and the provision of education. He was also consistently in favour of government support for the poor and the impotent. It followed that the institutions of government, and especially of the executive branch, must be correspondingly extensive. They must include not only the courts, the penal institutions and the police forces concerned with the enforcement of law in the narrow sense; they must include also establishments concerned with health, education, poor relief and trade, as well as with foreign affairs, revenue and defence which were the traditional interests of governments.

The second source of enrichment for the constitutional code initially drew his attention away from the executive branch to the legislative branch of government, although in the end it required him to think very carefully about the Executive. It was his espousal of the notion that government was a trust and was bound to follow the dictates of utility. From these points he inferred that the complete code, and more particularly the constitutional branch of it, must include provisions for enforcing the terms of the trust. As early as the 1770s he seems to have favoured parliamentary elections and some use of the tribunal of public opinion for this purpose. He was then thinking of the trustee as primarily the sovereign-legislator, and his programme was not very different from that of the Whigs, although it is possible that his personal views were already more radical. (It is doubtful whether, except for a time in the 1790s, he was ever during his adult life the 'Tory' that, in the nineteenth century, he represented himself to have been.) At the time of the French Revolution he unequivocally adopted a more radical position and committed himself clearly and explicitly to the idea that the sovereign-trustee must be disciplined through 'dependence' on (accountability to) the beneficiaries of the public trust, primarily through a reformed electoral system. This was followed by the 'Tory' phase in his thought when he moved away from the programme of parliamentary reform, although not necessarily from the idea of dependence. But that phase was in its turn soon replaced by another. His disappointments and frustrations concerning the Panopticon and other reforming projects, and the similar experiences of his brother at the Navy Board, prompted him to adopt stricter standards of accountability, to move towards a still more radical electoral programme, and above all to identify more obstacles, and more serious obstacles, to the consummation of accountability. His awareness of those obstacles was expressed in the increasing prominence that he gave to the notion of 'influence' in his thoughts and his writings from 1800 onwards.

This notion was present in his arguments in the 1780s, and it was one of his linguistic debts to the Whigs. But almost from the beginning he used it in a distinctive way. It meant for him extralegal power, interference with individual wills by persons other than the sovereign and by means other than rational argument; it was the overpowering of one will by another, and thus of one individual interest by another, without the aid of legal sanctions. Its manifestations ranged from the influence of a servant over his master, to the influence of the Crown (or the 'administrative power') denounced by the Whigs, and beyond that to the 'influence of property'. From his experiences during the 1790s and beyond, Bentham drew the lesson that this form of power had infiltrated the whole of government and society and was sustained by some of their most important institutions and arrangements. He identified the Church, the corporation of lawyers and the linguistic practices of these and other groups in the community ('mischievous fictions', 'delusions' and 'fallacies') as the most important of those pernicious practices and arrangements, but he later absorbed all wielders of influence into a more general category of 'aristocracy' with many branches. Influence was by its nature hostile to accountability, because it provided an alternative system of dependence which would enable its possessors to evade, confuse, buy off or coerce those to whom they were supposed to be accountable.

It was the challenge presented by influence to good government which directed his thoughts back to the Executive and ensured that his constitutional provision for it should be at least as thorough and generous as his provision for the Legislature or the Judiciary. It was a challenge that could not be effectively met through the perfection of the electoral system or the machinery of the courts; on the contrary, influence could vitiate the most formally perfect electoral or judicial machinery. In order to counter it, he judged that one needed to adopt two other lines of attack. The first was to move outwards from the electoral system to society itself, and to eliminate from it those conditions on which influence fed. These included not only the existing forms of religion and education and existing usages of language, but also more diffuse beliefs, fears and loyalties which might tend to tie one person to another and might inhibit or prejudice his judgement of the other's capacities or conduct. In this respect the attack on influence confirmed the inclusion of education among the functions of government – and the exclusion of religion from them – and therefore confirmed the need for some corresponding establishment within the Executive. His second line of attack was to excise all the sources of influence that existed, in the form of patronage or discretionary power, within the machinery of government. Some of these were in the Judiciary but many were in the Executive. In the campaign against influence the latter were just as important as the former. The campaign, and thus the constitutional code, had to encompass all parts of the government – every single post and aspect – and it had to subject all of them to a common set of measures directed against influence and to build them all into a single system of accountability. The notion of the government as trust had correspondingly to be broadened to include all official posts within its scope.

For several compelling reasons, then, the constitutional code had to be more than an empty box in his intellectual stock, and it had to pay an unusual amount of attention to official establishments. Inevitably, most of its content would be contributed by or from his jurisprudence. Since he saw all legitimate political phenomena, including those of government, as essentially legal phenomena, he had to describe and regulate them in legal terms. This meant that he treated all institutions as 'political societies' in miniature, and the arrangements to be made for them had therefore to be analogous to those of society at large and had to embrace command, obedience, reward, punishment and deterrence. But in practice jurisprudence did not settle everything nor was it his only resource. He was forced and he was able to draw on two other sets of ideas, his theory of language and the theory of production-economics.

The relevant parts of his theory of language were the fruits of his attempts to cope with certain tensions in his methodological thinking. His individualist approach to society was matched by and based on a more general individualist (nominalist) logic and ontology. But he wanted to construct his jurisprudence around abstractions (such as powers and rights) and to recognize and distinguish numerous *classes* of phenomena. He had to find some devices for making the transition between the particulars which he recognized in his logic and the universals that he wanted to employ in his theory. The two devices which he adopted were fictions and the principle of uniformity in terminology. By labelling abstract notions 'fictions' he felt able to use them without sacrificing the convictions that they could be reduced to particulars and that they functioned as a mere aid to discourse. Similarly he was able to account for classification and classes in terms of uniformity in terminology, and to represent the latter as part of the general eighteenth-century drive towards clarity in language in which he was participating. These devices provided the foundation for his procedure throughout his jurisprudence, and they had some more particular applications in his theory of government.

His other supplement to his jurisprudence, that is his theory of production-economics, has been a relatively-neglected aspect of his thought, but it is the clearest example of one side of his utilitarianism, namely a concern with the careful and systematic adaptation of means to ends. He derived a good deal of it from standard works on political economy and on related subjects (notably accounting), but here as elsewhere he made something more of these borrowed materials than was in them originally. He was aided here by the knowledge of industrial and mercantile processes and practices that he obtained through his brother and perhaps from some members of Shelburne's circle, and by his own direct experience gained in the dealings concerning the Panopticon. His thinking about this subject was conducted mainly with an eye to industry, but he was always willing to look for other applications of it and in the end it too was reflected in his constitutional arrangements.

When he attempted to apply all of these economic and linguistic ideas to government, and to analyse it in detail, he focused on the offices of which it was composed. He interpreted these as similar to – and therefore to be treated in the same way as – the private 'conditions' (legal statuses) that he recognized in civil law. The model provided by civil law covered the means of acquiring the condition or status, the means of losing it, and the rights and duties and the incapacities attached to it. This proved to be quite a useful and convenient way of describing the phenomena of politics and government; thus, even so apparently specialized a set of arrangements as those for the election of members of Parliament could be treated as the means for acquiring the condition of membership. But it soon became clear that the civil-law model must be added to and varied in a number of ways in constitutional law, because public offices and private conditions were not the same in all respects.

They differed firstly in their relations with the environments in which they were located. A private condition was (as Bentham viewed it) a more or less isolated and self-contained situation (or aspect of a relationship), and it was of interest mainly to the person or parties involved. The most important task for private law was to prevent invasion of the condition and its rights. But a public office had to be part of a system and to occupy a definite place in the system. Moreover the public interest required that useful offices should be occupied and their duties performed. So public – constitutional – law would pay less attention than private law to rights and the invasion of rights (which would exist at all within the constitution only as being subservient to the performance of duties), and it would place more emphasis on the arrangements for occupancy of the office, on the duties and the conditions of their performance and on its relationship with other offices.

The working-out of Bentham's ideas on these subjects became as complex as most of the other projects to which he turned his mind during his long working life. He was able to make some progress in dealing with each of the separate aspects of an office by pursuing more or less abstract arguments. But he found repeatedly that beyond a certain point he needed to move to more concrete terms, and that in order to complete his account of any one aspect he had to absorb points made in relation to others, and sometimes to pay attention to wider considerations such as the functions of government. The frequent cross-references and similar instructions to the reader that are scattered through the relevant parts of the *Constitutional Code* reflect the darts, turnings and re-turnings of his own thinking as he sought to cope with these complications.

If one aspect of offices was more fundamental than another, it was that which concerned their duties. Here he characteristically made use of two approaches – starting, one might say, at opposite ends – in order to arrive at a comprehensive view. One approach was derived from his analysis of legal powers, which formed one of the most abstract (and original) parts of his jurisprudence. This was his first method of tackling the problem and he persevered with it for many years. His second and later approach was more empirical, proceeding from a consideration of the duties that he was disposed to attach to particular offices and kinds of offices.

His analysis of powers was an attempt to find a more precise and serviceable classification than that based on the orthodox classification of the *branches* of government. His objection to the orthodox scheme was partly political and partly intellectual. The political part was based on a fear that if a distinct set of 'executive' powers could be located, the Executive branch would be able to claim them exclusively and could claim to be independent of the Legislature in exercising them. The intellectual basis of his objection was his belief that in practice each branch exercised more than one sort of power, and that to represent any one sort as essentially legislative or essentially executive was quite misleading. His own scheme treated all powers and activities as legislative in the sense that all were commanding or directive, but it recognized a distinction between imperative power directed to the wills of persons, and contrectative power concerning the *use* or *disposal* of things or of persons (for example, persons in custody or under sentence). Within the imperative power he recognized a further distinction between commands expressed in terms of classes of persons or objects and those (which he called accensitive) concerning particular individuals and their allocation to a class. His first distinction provided the basis for a more elaborate account of the 'elementary political powers', and finally for his definitive framework for the classification of activities according to whether they related to persons, things, occurrences or arrangements. His second distinction, or rather the second branch of it, directed attention to activities occurring frequently (though not exclusively) in administrative situations, such as appointment and the issuing of instructions.

Before he had finished his account of the elementary political powers, he was already noting some of the more specific 'duties of office' that would have to be fitted into a general scheme. This was the beginning of his second approach to the problem of duties. He did not, however, make any serious effort to classify or even list such duties or activities until the final stage of his work, the drafting of the *Constitutional Code* itself. When he did so, he was able to go ahead quite quickly to the point where the task was almost complete. He was then in possession of a theory of administrative activity, in the form of an exhaustive classification of its varieties and components. But he did not see it in quite those terms; it was, for him, an exercise in language, a successful attempt to meet the criterion of uniformity in terminology which was one of his methodological guidelines.

He would not have been able to carry very far his listing and classification of functions or duties if he had not previously settled most of the arrangements for keeping each incumbent of an office to his duty, for many of the specific obligations that he assigned to offices were concerned with the maintenance of discipline. This problem was one which occupied him for a long time and occasioned some of his most imaginative and systematic thinking, to a point where he quite transcended his original conception of it.

His interest in the problem and his characteristic methods of dealing with it emerged in the second wave of his writings on jurisprudence, those that were concerned with the further exploration and application of the ideas that he had set out in *Of Laws in General*. He showed in these supplementary essays an interest in preventing 'misrule' or 'abuses of authority' through deterrence or, in his terminology, through indirect legislation. This preference for deterrence did not imply any intention to dispense with direct legislation, that is the definition of offences and the prescription of sanctions and the mechanisms for applying those sanctions. He always expected that those things would be present in any system of discipline, but he turned to indirect legislation as a means of reducing the *occasions* for the application of direct sanctions in official establishments. His original essay on indirect legislation proposed many devices and principles for use in such establishments. His proposals were, like the rest of the techniques of indirect legislation, adaptations of the well-known devices of preventive police, and were concerned with such objects as taking away the power or the temptation to commit an offence, facilitating knowledge of the fact of an offence, increasing the offender's liability to punishment and, in the most general terms, 'uniting interest with duty'. Perhaps the most important of all were those concerned with facilitating knowledge of the fact of an offence, for they served as one of the processes of direct legislation as well as a form of indirect legislation.

His first conclusions about indirect means of preventing misrule were fairly general and tentative, but they were available as a guide when he began seriously to draw up plans for large and complex (but usually specialized) institutions and structures late in the 1780s. Those plans covered a considerable range of institutions, some penal (the Panopticon), some judicial (the French and, much later, the English and Scottish courts), some industrial or commercial (the National Charity Company and the proposed banking and insurance ventures), some regulatory (the police forces, and the control of the bank-note issue) and some revenue-raising (the office of the Escheator). They provided him with an opportunity to make his proposals for curbing misrule more concrete and operational, and then to extend his aims beyond this negative task to the securing of efficiency and of economical working in a positive sense. He managed to re-orient and augment his approach in that way by combining the theory of indirect legislation with two other sorts of thinking, his theories of reward and production-economics. When they were put together, they yielded something quite new in his armoury of ideas about government, a theory of management.

He carried his theory to the point where he recognized management as a distinct activity in a productive or administrative establishment, and where he was able to express its conclusions in terms of principles – or, in other versions, rules – of management. These principles included some, such as the ample-scale and piece-work principles, which were derived from speculation about industrial activities, while others, such as unity of authority and uniform management, were the fruits of thinking about administrative situations. Bentham's first achievement was to bring them together as the framework of a single 'line of good management' which would be available and applicable to any sort of enterprise, even (as he reluctantly admitted) those belonging to government. His second achievement was to develop, and to incorporate in his plans or his supporting descriptions, some highly sophisticated accounts of how the principles might be applied, and some quite detailed prescriptions for applying them.

Some of his most interesting work in this field concerned the application – and the limits to the application – of the piece-work and ample-scale principles and of others drawn from production-economics or the theory of reward. But the most fully worked-out sections of his programme were a pair of topics that had a closer connection with the part of his jurisprudence that dealt with the rules of evidence. These were, as he viewed them, the separate topics of inspective-architecture (the Panopticon-principle) and book-keeping, but they amounted to a single programme of *communications* in an establishment, a programme that rested on a precise and original system of records and statistics together with the Panopticon-principle and the conversation-tubes and other devices that he proposed to install in the Panopticon-penitentiary. And his appreciation of the importance of communications both contributed to and drew some of its significance from the widening of his horizons from the negative task of preventing misrule to the positive task of securing good management; it was not only an element in the system of discipline (which was the purpose for which Bentham first developed it), but it was also an aid to the system of decision making. These dual functions were already present in the account of the Panopticon; they were perceived and described much more fully in the crucial scheme of book-keeping that Bentham devised for the National Charity Company, and they were fully preserved in the later schemes for the Timber-Master in the dockyards and for the Court of Lords' Delegates.

The theory of management was capable of contributing the bulk of the material that he needed for his account of offices, but it did not cover everything. It left unsettled some particular issues to which it had itself directed attention, notably the quality of the human resources that were to be employed in the offices. More importantly, it had to be supplemented by information about the framework into which particular offices would have to be fitted or which would determine their existence and their relationships.

He filled these gaps in his theory by the same attention to detail that he displayed in other parts of his argument.

He was always worried about qualifications and the specification of qualifications for particular posts. He habitually treated 'talent' as a variable and unequally distributed set of qualities, and he recognized that it was necessary to decide between candidates for office on some objective grounds if efficiency were to be promoted. His intellectual prejudices were reinforced here by the particular difficulties experienced by his brother in securing official employment suited to his talents and qualifications, and by his own general hostility to 'influence' in political life. In some of his eighteenth-century essays he showed a willingness to accept formal or conventional qualifications as grounds for appointment: scientific qualifications for appointment to his projected Board of Shipbuilding; experience in legal practice for appointment to the French Judiciary. After 1802, his growing sense of the need to counteract influence and to deprive it of its base in patronage gave him a stronger incentive to find a reliable objective test of suitability for employment. The timely emergence of the movement in favour of public examinations seemed to provide him with the device that he needed. He soon convinced himself that open, competitive examinations were suitable and practicable. The use of examinations as a selection test did not prove easy to reconcile with the pattern of responsibility and the forms of remuneration that he favoured, but he worked out precise and complex arrangements for 'location' which he hoped would achieve and preserve economy, objectivity and responsibility.

The unsettled questions about the structure and arrangement of offices could not be answered so easily. In order to find answers he had to draw on three main sets of ideas, each of which we have encountered elsewhere in his thought. The first flowed from his political aims of making the Legislature the supreme element in government and of making all offices and officials accountable to the beneficiaries of the public trust. The second consisted of certain principles of management, or more generally principles of indirect legislation, which had implications for organization. The third was the simple application of general utilitarian criteria to the structure of government. When he put them together they persuaded him to modify, though not to jettison, the conventional classification of government into the three branches of

Legislature, Judiciary and Executive, and to propose much more substantial changes in the prevailing arrangements *within* the several branches, at first in the Judiciary and finally in the Executive.

He might have achieved accountability most simply by prescribing that all offices, in all branches of government, should be filled by popular election. This would have eliminated the need for many (though not all) of his detailed disciplinary arrangements as well as simplifying his plan of organization. He was attracted by that course, but could not persuade himself that it was practicable. He thought that proper electoral judgements about so many offices, dispersed so widely and handling so many different and possibly technical subjects, would require a body of information that most members of the community would not have the time or the opportunity to acquire. The better system, he concluded, would be to allow them to elect deputies – members of the Legislature – who would surpervise the remaining functionaries, and to allow the electors themselves to report and publicize whatever evidence they could collect about the functionaries' performance. So the accountability of the non-legislative officials had to be 'unimmediate' or indirect. In practice, this meant the existence of a hierarchy, because the non-legislative officials were themselves not an undifferentiated mass, but fell naturally into different grades and kinds between which relationships of authority and accountability properly existed. He first worked out such a hierarchical pattern in relation to the Judiciary, where it was facilitated and partly dictated by the process of appeal, and where the final stage – the relationship with the Legislature – could easily be established. He later generalized this pattern as the 'chain of subordination', the links of which would be determined by whatever needs for authority and subordination were thrown up in the performance of tasks. The chain of subordination thus became the backbone of accountability and it provided him with the grounds for his principal modifications to the conventional account of the major branches of government. These amounted to the transformation of the conventional distinctions into a hierarchical structure, in which the Legislature was subordinate to the 'Constitutive' or electorate, but was superordinate to both the Judiciary and the Executive (Administrative), which were in turn co-ordinate to each other. He ensured the co-ordinateness of the two non-legislative branches, and their subordination to the Legislature, by giving each of them a ministerial head – a Minister of Justice and a Prime Minister – who were likewise co-ordinate and were separately but wholly responsible to the Legislature for whatever went on in their respective branches.

The existence of those two offices, and the range of authority allocated to them, were the product not only of broad political considerations relating to accountability but also of the principles of indirect legislation and management. These principles dictated what form the hierarchical structure should take in order to make accountability most certain. The vital points here were the principles of individual responsibility and unity of authority. In organizational terms these meant 'single-seatedness' (the rejection of all forms of collegiate administration), and a single directing point in each distinguishable part of the whole structure. They applied equally to the Judiciary and to the Administrative: single judges rather than a bench of judges, a Prime Minister exercising something like presidential authority over Ministerial subordinates rather than a Cabinet System, and a single figure supervising and directing the work of judges, their assistants and their colleagues.

The kinds, and where possible the number, of those subordinates, assistants and colleagues had to be determined mainly by the third and least precise component of Bentham's ideas about structure, his general utilitarian criteria. These manifested themselves as a determination to match structures systematically to functions, to create a structure (which might be a single post, or a group of posts) for every function, and to avoid duplication and redundancy. In his treatment of the Judiciary this led him to identify a wide range of subordinate officials, including prosecutors, defenders, judges' deputies and bailiffs, all of whom had some part to play in the judicial process as he described it. In the same branch it led him to sweep away the existing structure of courts, and equally to reject the system of 'functional' courts proposed early in the French Revolution, in order to build up a primarily geographical system. In relation to the Executive, he was able to provide a less complete account of the kinds of subordinate offices, and he was disposed to accept for much longer the existing set of departments and Ministers. But here too, when he finally faced up to the nature of the functions that he was assigning to governments – the kinds of legislation that he was expecting or endorsing – he quickly discarded the established set of departments and produced a new and more rational one. And he pursued the matching of structures to functions beyond the Legislature, the Judiciary and the Executive as these were ordinarily understood. He felt obliged to confer a legal status on citizens' observations and reports about the functioning of government, and he dignified them as the Public Opinion Tribunal. He recognized (as others had recognized before him) that some functions might be of primarily local interest and others might be of primarily national significance and that the two might be provided for separately. To handle the former, he proposed the creation of a system of local authorities, each of which could be a microcosm of the central government except in the abridgement of its judicial functions. These local authorities might also act on behalf of the central government, but the latter would require in addition its own network of offices, penetrating into the localities, in order to perform fully its national functions. In eighteenth- and early-nineteenth-century Britain, the clergy of the Established Church did some of the work that he wanted to see performed, but his campaign against influence required the 'euthanasia' of the Establishment. To fill the gap in the nation-wide structure, and to manage other tasks of co-ordination and supervision, he invented the additional offices of Local Headman and Local Registrar.

His conclusions about structure not only identified some of the offices that a government would need; they served also to bind the individual offices together into a coherent system. Moreover they, together with his proposals for recruitment, fed back into his understanding of duties and activities and permitted him to complete his account of those topics. With both sets of ideas at his disposal, he was at last able to lay out his whole programme for government in the *Constitutional Code*, specifying what governments ought to do, what range of activities they must undertake, what powers they ought to possess, how they ought to be organized for their tasks and to what constraints they ought to be subject. The unprecedented amount of detail in the programme rested on a depth of reasoning and a range of inquiry that no other constitution-maker had ever matched.

Perhaps the best key to an understanding of Bentham's treatment of government is to be found in Max Weber's famous remark that the 'purest type of exercise of legal authority is that which employs a bureaucratic administrative staff'.[1] Bentham was writing at a time when, as he and many of his contemporaries sensed, the modern legal–rational state was more than an aspiration and was coming within reach. He saw, however, that if it were to complete its structure and to perform the task of ordering and disciplining a mass of self-interested individuals, it needed to add to its legal resources a great body of servants. He also saw that, if self-interest were so widespread as to require the sovereign-state to create social order, it must prevail also among the state's servants, and that they must be ordered and disciplined through the same processes and devices of legal-rationalism as were to be employed in the community as a whole. The legal–rational order could be fully established in the community only if it were first imposed on the sovereign in the form of a 'bureaucratic administrative staff'. The logic of the situation – or, more accurately, the logic of the individualist and rationalist interpretation of the situation – dictated that the state should complete itself in that way. It also required that the bureaucratic staff should be subjected to another form of rational control which Weber also recognized, namely the systematic drive for efficiency in the deployment of human and other resources through the application of the principles of management.

Bentham reached these conclusions ahead of most of his contemporaries. But many of them might have worked to the same point, for they shared his assumptions about sovereignty, individualism and legal modes of social control. What enabled him to get ahead of them was his greater readiness to accept the challenge of those ideas, his unequalled willingness to work within their terms, and his unequalled tenacity in following through an argument to its conclusion however distant that might be from its original starting point.

These considerations suggest that our original question and its detailed answer have a significance beyond Bentham's intellectual history. The answer reveals him to be, in important respects, a representative as well as a creative thinker in his espousal of bureaucracy. His theory of government was not entirely the product of his own special talents and he was not an isolated precursor of later ideas. In developing his theory, he was the bearer of an established and influential kind of thinking whose implications he explored and exposed. This has a bearing on the subsequent history of thought and institutions, and on other aspects of Bentham's stance and outlook. In order to explain the growth of bureaucracy, or the simultaneous presence of apparently democratic or liberal and apparently authoritarian elements in Bentham's own thought, we do not need to resort to historical discontinuities after the fashion of A. V. Dicey,[2] or to theoretical dichotomies after the fashion of Elie Halévy or Gertrude Himmelfarb.[3] All of these things have common roots in the single theoretical structure of individualism, and in the acceptance of individualism as an accurate account of the world. In particular, bureaucracy can readily be seen to be generated by efforts to make a democratic constitution fully effective, to establish and preserve positive rights for individuals, and to maximize and universalize the responsibility of officials within a world of autonomous individuals.

At the outset Hobbes argued that modern individualism was an ambivalent body of thought, pointing at once towards the expansion of individual rights or liberty and the enhancement of the authority of a sovereign. Bentham's derivation of and adherence to a bureaucratic programme serve to confirm the truth of that perception.

NOTES

Notes to chapter 1

1 This is Book II of the *Constitutional Code* as it appears in *Bowring* ix. The first volume (of Book II) covering the first nine chapters, was published in London in 1830; the tenth chapter was also printed and circulated in the same year. The programme for the Executive is set out mainly in chs. 8–11 and 24, and that for the Judiciary in chs. 12–22. Chs. 25 and 26 dealing with local government are also relevant.

2 For a thorough and comprehensive summary of the *Constitutional Code*, see T. P. Peardon, 'Bentham's ideal republic', *Canadian Journal of Economic and Political Science*, XVII (1951), 184–203. See also A. Dunsire, *Administration: the word and the science* (London, 1973), pp. 5–8 and 58–64, where Bentham's administrative ideas are set out at some length; and G. K. Fry, 'Bentham and public administration', *Public Administration Bulletin*, 24 (August 1977), 32–40.

3 A number of people helped Bentham while he was drafting the Code. But they functioned mainly as copyists (e.g. Richard Doane), research assistants (e.g. John Neal, Edwin Chadwick and George Bentham), or friends commenting on particular drafts or supplying particular facts (e.g. Leicester Stanhope). Some of their specific contributions are described in ch. 7. All were working to Bentham's plans and were applying his conceptions.

4 cf. Peardon, 'Bentham's ideal republic', p. 200, and Dunsire, *Administration*, p. 59.

5 These are the 'Functions in all [Ministers]', set out in *Bowring* ix, pp. 219–26. The functions of particular officials might be much more limited, but would be selected from this list.

6 H. Fayol, *General and industrial management*, trans. by C. Storrs (London, 1949), pp. 19–20.

7 L. Gulick, 'Notes on the theory of organization' in *Papers on the science of administration*, ed. by Gulick and L. Urwick (New York, 1937), pp. 13–14.

8 *Bowring* ix, p. 225.

9 C. Babbage, *On the economy of machinery and manufactures* (London, 1832).

10 M. Weber, *Economy and society*, ed. by G. Roth and C. Wittich (2 vols., Berkeley, 1978), I, pp. 220–3.

11 D. S. Pugh in his set of readings *Organization theory* (Harmondsworth, 1971), p. 99.

12 W. Hazlitt, *The spirit of the age*, World Classics edition (London, 1960), pp. 5–6.

13 cf. N. L. Rosenblum, *Bentham's theory of the modern state* (Cambridge, Mass., 1978). Professor Rosenblum is concerned, however, with the final content rather than the sources of Bentham's thinking about the state.

14 For an account of the English legislation and literature, see L. Radzinowicz, *A history of English criminal law and its administration from 1750* (4 vols., London, 1948–68), especially vol. III, *Cross-currents in the movement for the reform of the police* (1956).

15 Most of these works appeared first in French, ed. by Etienne Dumont in *Traités de législation civile et pénale* (3 vols., Paris, 1802) and *Théorie des peines et des récompenses* (2 vols., London, 1811). Dumont's version of the sketch of a general code appears as 'Vue générale d'un corps complet de législation' in *Traités de législation*, I, pp. 141–370.

16 On the Panopticon, see my article 'Bentham's Panopticon: an administrative history' in *Historical Studies*, XV (1973), 703–21, and XVI (1974), 36–54.

17 As was his custom, Bentham was experimenting with alternative versions of the title – 'Thoughts on official economy', 'Thoughts on pecuniary economy as applied to office' etc. U.C. clx, fols. 38–46, especially fol. 41, and U.C. cxiii, fols. 1–24.

18 E. Halévy, *The growth of philosophic radicalism*, trans. by M. Morris (London, 1928), pp. 403–4.

19 See ch. 7 below. The relevant papers are scattered widely through the Bentham Mss. at University College London and elsewhere. The printed Catalogue to the University College collection (compiled by A. T. Milne, 2nd edn, London, 1962) lists material for the Code in Boxes 26, 33–4, 36–42, 44, 69, 83, 97, 106, 112, 113, 139, 149, 158 and 160. For samples of the process of re-drafting, one might consult U.C. xlii, fols. 130–651, where the bulk of the material relating to chapter 12, 'Judiciary collectively', is assembled in sections in which the chronological evolution of the drafts can be seen pretty clearly.

Notes to chapter 2

1 Until comparatively recently, this aspect of eighteenth-century political thought was not often noticed or discussed. Particularly valuable in directing attention to it was G. Parry's article on 'Enlightened government and its critics in eighteenth-century Germany' in *The Historical Journal*, VI (1963), 178–92. Later works which deal with it include: P. Legendre, 'Evolution des systèmes d'administration et histoire des idées: l'exemple de la

pensée française', *Annali della Fondazione Italiana per la Storia amministrativa*, III (1966), 254–74; M. Raeff, 'The well-ordered police state and the development of modernity in seventeenth and eighteenth-century Europe', *The American Historical Review*, LXXX (1975), 1221–43; C. Tilly (ed.), *The formation of national states in Western Europe* (Princeton, 1975); M. Walker, 'Rights and functions: the social categories of eighteenth-century German jurists and cameralists', *Journal of Modern History*, I (1978), 234–51; K. M. Baker, 'French political thought at the accession of Louis XVI' in *ibid.*, pp. 279–303; and M. Krygier, 'State and bureaucracy in Europe: the growth of a concept' in *Bureaucracy: the career of a concept*, ed. Eugene Kamenka and Martin Krygier (Melbourne, 1979), pp. 1–33. Further information about it is also provided in several more detailed works referred to below in the present chapter, viz. those by J. F. Bosher, J. Norris, H. E. Strakosch, H. C. Johnson and N. Baker. One of the most useful parts of Parry's article is his insistence that this body of ideas forms part of a movement towards 'enlightened government' not 'enlightened despotism', for this relates it directly to the theory of the modern state.

2 Thomas Hobbes, *Leviathan or the matter, forme and power of a commonwealth ecclesiasticall and civil*, ed. by M. Oakeshott (Oxford, n.d.), ch. 6, cf. *ibid.*, p. 104.

3 *ibid.*, chs. 17–18.

4 *ibid.*, pp. 117 and 176.

5 *ibid.*, chs. 23–6 and 30.

6 *ibid.*, pp. 227–30.

7 *ibid.*, pp. 179–81.

8 *ibid.*, p. 161.

9 *ibid.*, pp. 156–7.

10 *ibid.*, p. 163.

11 *ibid.*, pp. 217 and 209.

12 *ibid.*, pp. 216–17.

13 See H. E. Strakosch, *State absolutism and the rule of law* (Sydney, 1967), ch. 1, for a clear account of the obstacles to central power. Strakosch is writing only of Austria and its diverse possessions, but the same problems appeared in the other monarchies. Cf. W. Hubatsch, *Frederick the Great of Prussia: absolutism and administration* (London, 1975), pp. 7–9, for a succinct statement of hindrances that Imperial law set to centralisation in the scattered Prussian territories.

14 On the relations between governments and their servants, see G. E. Aylmer on 'Bureaucracy' in vol. XIII of the *New Cambridge modern history* (Cambridge, 1975), pp. 164–200, esp. 170–1; H. C. Johnson, *Frederick the Great and his officials* (New Haven, 1975); and J. F. Bosher, 'French administration and public finance in their European setting' in vol. VIII of the *New Cambridge modern history* (Cambridge, 1965), pp. 565–91.

15 Strakosch provides, in *State absolutism and the rule of law*, a case-study of the way in which obstacles to 'modernisation' generated elaborate programmes and theories.

16 I am dissenting here from a commonly-held view, shared e.g. by Charles Tilly in *The formation of national states in Western Europe*, p. 35, that 'England survived into the nineteenth century with a rather low level of stateness'. That view seems to me to be based on external criteria of 'stateness', such as monarchs' claims to be absolute or the size and complexity of official establishments, and to pay too little attention to the question of how far and how certainly the central government was able to reach into the lives of its subjects, e.g. by taxing them and by enacting and enforcing legislation. On this standard I think that in the eighteenth century England had reached a rather high level of stateness as compared with its Continental rivals. Cf. the opinion of Tilly's co-authors W. Fischer and P. Lungreen in *The formation of national states*, p. 478, that 'the state-building process in England was carried much further in late medieval and early modern times than on the Continent'.

17 Similarly, I think that J. A. La Palombara was wrong when he concluded in *Political and administrative development* (ed. by R. Braibanti, Durham N.C., 1969), p. 206, that the Northcote–Trevelyan Report represented 'the first extensive effort on the part of the British to move toward the bureaucratic state'. Reforms with a bureaucratic tendency were almost continuous from the 1780s onwards, and the Northcote–Trevelyan proposals were a mopping-up operation, not the start of the campaign.

18 C. Beccaria, *A discourse on public oeconomy and commerce* (London, 1769), pp. 9–10; Beccaria, *On crimes and punishments*, trans. by H. Paolucci (Indianapolis, 1963), p. 12.

19 William Blackstone, *Commentaries on the laws of England*, 1st edn (4 vols., Oxford, 1765–69, reprinted London, 1966), 1, p. 48.

20 J. F. von Bielfeld, *Institutions politiques*, [2nd] edn (4 vols., Paris, 1762), 1, p. 81. (The original in French.) Cf. Beccaria, *On crimes and punishments*, p. 13.

21 Instruction 19 in *Documents of Catherine the Great*, ed. by W. F. Reddaway (Cambridge, 1931), p. 217. Catherine was here paraphrasing the opening paragraphs of ch. 4 of Book II of Montesquieu's *Spirit of the laws* on the 'intermediate powers' in a monarchy. But she was giving a new direction to Montesquieu's argument.

22 Blackstone, *Commentaries*, 1, p. 49.

23 Bielfeld, *Institutions politiques*, 1, pp. 83–4.

24 J. Locke, *Second treatise of government*, ed. by J. W. Gough (Oxford, 1946), pp. 66–7 (s. 134). This conclusion follows from the absence in the state of nature, of 'an established, settled, known law' (p. 62, s. 124).

25 Montesquieu, *The spirit of the laws*, trans. by T. Nugent (2 vols. in 1, New York, 1949), Book XI, ch. 6 (vol. 1, pp. 151–62).

26 John Adams, *A defence of the constitutions of government of the United States of America, against the attack of M. Turgot in his letter to Dr Price*, New edn (3 vols., London, 1794), I, p. 362.

27 cf. R. Derathé, *Jean-Jacques Rousseau et la science politique de son temps* (Paris, 1950), pp. 406–10; C. W. Hendel, *J.-J. Rousseau, moralist* (2 vols., Oxford, 1934), I, pp. 100–3; and J. McDonald, *Rousseau and the French Revolution* (London, 1965), pp. 88–9.

28 *Institutions politiques*, I, p. 225. (The original in French.) But he also spoke elsewhere (I, pp. 56–7) of the 'union of wills' in the state, and suggested that the laws might be 'deemed the will of all'.

29 Blackstone, *Commentaries*, I, pp. 39–40 and 52.

30 *On crimes and punishments*, p. 15.

31 Denis Diderot, *Oeuvres politiques*, ed. by P. Vernière (Paris, 1963), p. 353. (The original in French.)

32 *ibid.*, pp. 40–1.

33 *The spirit of the laws*, p. 152 (Book XI, ch. 6).

34 *On crimes and punishments*, pp. 14–15. This was not new doctrine; N. de Lamare had confidently asserted, more than thirty years earlier, that only the sovereign had the authority to interpret the laws. See his *Traité de la police*, 2nd edn (4 vols. in 2, Amsterdam, 1729), I, p. 241.

35 *On crimes and punishments*, p. 13.

36 *Documents of Catherine the Great*, Instructions 148 and 152–4, pp. 235–7.

37 W. Eden, *The principles of penal law*, 2nd edn (London, 1771), p. 318.

38 J. W. Gough, 'Political trusteeship', the seventh of the eight studies in his *John Locke's political philosophy*, 2nd edn (Oxford, 1973).

39 *The spirit of the laws*, I, p. 17 (Book II, ch. 4); Instruction 24, *Documents of Catherine the Great*, p. 218.

40 *ibid.*, p. 217, Instruction 22.

41 *On crimes and punishments*, p. 15.

42 See Diderot, *Oeuvres politiques*, pp. 37, 41 and 222.

43 *ibid.*, p. 363.

44 *The works of the Right Honourable Edmund Burke*, World's Classics edn (6 vols., London, 1906–07), III, p. 60. (From the speech on Fox's East India Bill.)

45 Montesquieu, *The spirit of the laws*, I, pp. 6–7.

46 C. A. Helvétius, *De l'esprit, or essays on the mind and its several faculties* (London, 1807), p. xlviii. This is part of the summary, in the Table of Contents, of ch. 27 in Essay III of the work. Such summaries often convey a clearer idea of Helvétius's meaning than his full argument does.

47 See R. Shackleton, *Montesquieu: a critical biography* (Oxford, 1961), pp. 316–17.

48 Montesquieu, *The spirit of the laws*, I, p. 299 (Book XIX, ch. 14). Catherine's paraphrase was in her Instruction 60, *Documents of Catherine the Great*, p. 222.

49 Diderot, *Oeuvres politiques*, p. 372. (The original in French.)

50 *De l'esprit*, p. 123.

51 *ibid.*, p. 125.

52 See *Hume's theory of politics*, ed. by F. Watkins (Edinburgh, 1951), p. 136.

53 J. L. De Lolme, *The constitution of England, or an account of the English government* (first published in French, 1770), Bohn's Standard Library (London, 1853), p. 24.

54 Blackstone, *Commentaries*, IV, p. 404.

55 *Oeuvres de Turgot et documents le concernant*, ed. by G. Schelle (5 vols., Paris, 1913–23), IV, pp. 568–628. Cf. D. Dakin, *Turgot and the Ancien Régime in France* (London, 1939), pp. 272–8; and K. M. Baker, 'French political thought at the accession of Louis XVI', pp. 295–8 and 302–3.

56 *Oeuvres de Turgot*, IV, p. 576. (The original in French.)

57 *ibid.*, p. 607.

58 *ibid.*, p. 576.

59 *ibid.*, p. 572. For a somewhat different view of the Memorandum, and a review of the extensive literature on it, see G. J. Cavanaugh, 'Turgot, the rejector of enlightened despotism', *French Historical Studies*, VI (1969), 31–58. Cavanaugh's discussion is focused on despotism and democracy, not 'enlightened government' or the form of the modern state.

60 *Institutions politiques*, I, p. 229.

61 *On crimes and punishments*, p. 98. The enthusiasts for education included Turgot (in the Memorandum on municipalities) and Helvétius, especially in his *Treatise on man*, trans. by W. Hooper (2 vols., London, 1810), which was his sequel to *De l'esprit*.

62 L. Radzinowicz, *A history of the English criminal law*, III, pp. 1–8.

63 N. de Lamare, *Traité de la police*, I, p. 2; Bielfeld, *Institutions politiques*, I, ch. 7, s. 2, pp. 276–7.

64 This outlook is not expressed in so many words in any one place; rather it supplies the rationale for the extraordinarily close and comprehensive regulation of sources, commodities and markets that the theorists of police contemplated and that Lamare described (*Traité de la police*, II, pp. 565–1029). Lamare himself repeatedly stressed the continuity between contemporary and medieval attitudes, by trying to find medieval precedents for modern practices. Cf. Raeff, 'The well-ordered police state', p. 1235.

65 *Documents of Catherine the Great*, pp. 295–9.

66 *ibid.*, p. 300 (Instruction 567).

67 *ibid.*, p. 308 (Instructions 646–9).

68 *ibid.*, pp. 304–5 (Instruction 613).

69 *Lectures on justice, police, revenue and arms*, ed. by E. Cannan (Oxford, 1896); *Lectures on jurisprudence*, ed. by R. L. Meek and others (Oxford, 1978).

70 *Lectures on jurisprudence*, pp. 333–4 and 486–7.

71 *Society and pauperism: English ideas on poor relief* (Melbourne, 1969), pp. 33 and 39–44.
72 cf. Strakosch, *State absolutism and the rule of law*, ch. 1; and, on the early steps towards the re-casting of law and the judicial system in Prussia by Frederick II and his Chancellor of Justice Cocceji, see H. C. Johnson, *Frederick the Great and his officials*, ch. 4, especially pp. 107–8.
73 Helvétius, *De l'esprit*, p. 135; and cf. *Memoirs of the House of Brandenberg by Frederick III [sic] the present King of Prussia* (London, 1757), 4th supplementary dissertation on 'the reasons for the enacting and repealing of laws', supplement, p. 62.
74 D. Barrington, *Observations upon the statutes*, 2nd edn (London, 1766), pp. 431, 433, 435–6.
75 *ibid.*, p. 433; Eden, *The principles of penal law*, p. 328.
76 Diderot, *Oeuvres politiques*, pp. 224–5.
77 *The spirit of the laws*, II, pp. 165–9 (Book XXIX, ch. 16).
78 Beccaria, *On crimes and punishments*, ch. 5, 'Obscurity of the laws'; Eden, *The principles of penal law*, ch. 24, 'Of the composition and promulgation of laws'; *Documents of Catherine the Great*, pp. 282–5, 'Of the composition of the laws'.
79 Blackstone, *Commentaries*, III, p. 328; J. Necker, *A treatise on the administration of the finances of France*, trans. by T. Mortimer (3 vols., London, 1785), I, p. lxxxvi.
80 *On crimes and punishments*, p. 16.
81 *ibid.*, p. 12.
82 Especially in Book VI – 'Consequences of the principles of different governments with respect to the simplicity of civil and criminal laws, the form of judgements, and the inflicting of punishments.'
83 *On crimes and punishments*, p. 99. See also L. Radzinowicz, *A history of the English criminal law*, I, chs. 9–10, where the ideas of Montesquieu, Beccaria and Eden are discussed in much more detail than here.
84 *Discourse on public oeconomy and commerce*, p. 9.
85 *On crimes and punishments*, ch. 41, 'How to prevent crimes'. The passage quoted in the text is the opening sentence of the chapter (p. 93). Catherine made it her Instruction 240, and provided a summary of most of the substance of the chapter in the following eight Instructions (*Documents of Catherine the Great*, p. 255). A preference for prevention over punishment is also one of the main themes in Jonas Hanway's *Defects of police* – see note 103 below.
86 Beccaria, *Discourse on public oeconomy and commerce*, p. 15.
87 Hobbes, *Leviathan*, ed. by Oakeshott, p. 122.
88 Helvétius, *De l'esprit*, p. xlvii; Hume, *Theory of politics*, ed. by Watkins, p. 136; Catherine, *Documents of Catherine the Great*, p. 220, Instruction 43; *The works of Edmund Burke*, World's Classics edn, II, p. 376; Necker, *A treatise on the finances of France*, I, p. xxv. Catherine, Burke and Necker all wrote in terms of a relationship between interest and *duty*.

89 Locke, *Second treatise of government*, s. 136, p. 68.

90 N. de Lamare, *Traité de la police*, I, p. 241. Cf. Blackstone's argument that a 'municipal' (i.e. domestic) law must always be a rule, in his *Commentaries*, I, pp. 44–5.

91 *Institutions politiques*, I, pp. 239–40; *The spirit of the laws*, II, pp. 79–80 (Book XXVI, ch. 24).

92 Instructions 440–6, *Documents of Catherine the Great*, p. 282.

93 *Institutions politiques*, II, p. 15 (the original in French); cf. *ibid.*, III, pp. 171–2, where he made substantially the same points about the Department of Foreign Affairs.

94 *Oeuvres de Turgot*, IV, p. 620.

95 Necker, *A treatise on the finances of France*, III, p. 363.

96 *Institutions politiques*, IV, ch. 4, especially p. 255.

97 *Oeuvres de Turgot*, IV, p. 620; *Treatise on the finances of France*, III, p. 359.

98 *Institutions politiques*, I, p. 255. (The original in French.)

99 For a contemporary account of Frederick's scheme, see *The King of Prussia's plan for reforming the administration of justice* (London, 1750). See also Hubatsch, *Frederick the Great*, pp. 211–20.

100 Eden, *Principles of penal law*, ch. 16.

101 Blackstone, *Commentaries*, III, pp. 266–9.

102 W. Mildmay, *The police of France: or an account of the laws and regulations established in that kingdom for the preservation of peace and the preventing of robberies* (London, 1763).

103 J. Fielding, *Account of the origin and effects of a police set on foot by His Grace the Duke of Newcastle in the year 1753* (London, 1758); J. Hanway, *The defects of police the cause of immorality and the continual robberies committed, particularly in and about the metropolis* (London, 1775).

104 W. Mildmay, *The police of France*, pp. 48–9, 89–90, 103–4, 120–1; Bielfeld, *Institutions politiques*, I, pp. 288–90, 343–5; Radzinowicz, *A history of the English criminal law*, III, pp. 539–52.

105 *Institutions politiques*, III, p. 118.

106 But cf. N. Baker, 'Changing attitudes towards government in eighteenth century Britain' in *Statesmen, scholars and gentlemen*, ed. by Anne Whiteman and others (Oxford, 1973), pp. 202–19. Baker sees a real shift in attitudes in the 1780s. I see a new sense of urgency and a greater sophistication at that time, but little change in approach.

107 cf. Parry, 'Enlightened government and its critics', pp. 182–4; and J. F. Bosher, *French finances 1770–1795: from business to bureaucracy* (Cambridge, 1970), pp. 133–5 and 296–7.

108 *Institutions politiques*, II, p. 9. Bielfeld was writing here specifically of the Ministry of Finance, but was making a point of general application.

109 S.-J.-L. Bonvallet des Brosses, *Moyens de simplifier la perception et la comptabilité des deniers royaux* ([Paris], 1789), p. 32.

110 Paymaster-general's Act (22 Geo. 3, c. 81), s. 7.
111 Bonvallet des Brosses, *Moyens de simplifier*, p. 33.
112 *Institutions politiques*, III, ch. 1, pp. 35–41, and ch. 2, pp. 111–27.
113 cf. H. C. Johnson, 'The concept of bureaucracy in cameralism', *Political Science Quarterly*, LXXIX (1964), 399–400.
114 *Letters and papers of Charles, Lord Barham*. Publications of the Navy Records Society, Nos. 32, 38 and 39 (London, 1907–11), II, pp. 236–7, and III, pp. 76–8.
115 *Institutions politiques*, III, p. 191. The defence of individual responsibility appears at II, p. 5, and III, pp. 44–5.
116 *A treatise on the finances of France*, III, p. 186.
117 See, for example, the inconclusive discussion 'de la ferme et de la régie' in Diderot's 'Observations on the Nakaz' in *Oeuvres politiques*, pp. 415–16. The indirect source of the argument was Montesquieu's *Spirit of the laws*, Book XX, ch. 13. Even the forthright Bielfeld wanted to 'leave to the reader the choice between the alternative systems', although he pointed out that the effect of farming was to place a share of the 'sovereign power' in the farmers' hands (*Institutions politiques*, II, p. 171).
118 See R. Dorwart, *The administrative reforms of Frederick William I of Prussia* (Cambridge, Mass., 1953), pp. 199–211.
119 *Fourteenth report of the Commissioners appointed to examine, take and state the public accounts*, p. 29 (*Lambert* XLIV, p. 225).
120 Hume, *Theory of politics*, pp. 142–3; Necker, *Treatise on the finances of France*, I, p. cx.
121 *ibid.*, pp. lv and lxi.
122 *ibid.*, pp. lxxiii and cv–cxii; Bielfeld, *Institutions politiques*, II, p. 182.
123 *ibid.*, III, p. 111.
124 The Ministry of Finance in vol. II, chs. 1 and 2; Foreign Affairs in vol. III, ch. 3; the Council Office in vol. III, ch. 2, especially s. 8.
125 C. Davenant, *The political and commercial works* (5 vols., London, 1771), I, pp. 178–83; Bielfeld, *Institutions politiques*, III, pp. 145–57 and 201–2; Necker, *Treatise on the finances of France*, I, pp. xlvi–l.
126 *Institutions politiques*, III, pp. 156–7.
127 *Treatise on the finances of France*, I, p. li.
128 *House of Commons papers* (1812–13), vol. X, pp. 3–18. Wellesley's despatch was dated July and August 1800.

Notes to chapter 3

1 See the 'Outline of Bentham's life to 1780' in *Correspondence*, vol. I (*C.W.* ed. Sprigge), pp. xxiii–xxv. See too Mary P. Mack, *Jeremy Bentham: an odyssey of ideas 1748–92* (London, 1962), which also treats 1768–69 as marking the end of Bentham's intellectual apprenticeship and the beginning of his serious work.
2 The turning point is recorded most precisely in his letter to Lord Ashburton (John Dunning) dated 3 June 1782, in which he

explained what he had done and what he hoped soon to do. See
Of laws in general, (*C.W.* ed. Hart), pp. 304–11.

3 On the tradition of esteem for jurisprudence, see D. R. Kelley,
'*Vera philosophia:* the philosophical significance of Renaissance
jurisprudence', *Journal of the History of Philosophy*, XIV (1976),
267–79.

4 U.C. xxvii, fol. 144. This comes from one of two related and
similar documents – fols. 95–116 and fols. 117–75 – which are very
informative about Bentham's methodological ideas and attitudes.
They appear to be drafts for a Preface to the *Introduction to the
principles of morals and legislation*, but their exact purpose and
date of composition are uncertain. (The date must be, on internal
evidence, not earlier than 1779, and before Bentham decided not to
submit the *Introduction* for the prize offered by the Oeconomical
Society in Berne, probably at the end of 1780.) I think that they
probably represent a reservoir of points jotted down by Bentham in
the hope that he might include them, in differing forms, in a series
of covering letters to be addressed to the Society in Berne and to
other possible recipients such as Catherine the Great. Fols. 1–5 in
U.C. xcix record some abortive attempts to re-order the materials
into a coherent form. The two other writers whose influence
Bentham acknowledged on fol. 144 were Helvétius and Beccaria.

5 J. Le R. d'Alembert, *Preliminary discourse to the Encyclopédia of
Diderot* (1751), trans. by R. N. Schwab and W. E. Rex (Indianapolis, 1963). D'Alembert gave a more extended account of his
own philosophic views in his *Essai sur les elémens de philosophie ou
sur les principes des connaissances humaines*, in *Oeuvres complètes
de d'Alembert* (5 vols., Paris, 1821–22 – reprinted Geneva, 1967),
I, pp. 115–348.

6 *Preliminary discourse*, Introduction, p. xxxii.

7 *ibid.*, p. 50.

8 *Of laws in general*, p. 284.

9 See the references to Bergman in *Correspondence*, vol. II (*C.W.* ed.
Sprigge), especially p. 405, and vol. III (*C.W.* ed. Christie), p. 207.

10 U.C. xxvii, fol. 154.

11 *Of laws in general*, p. 284.

12 *ibid.*, p. 251.

13 Cf. d'Alembert, *Preliminary discourse*, pp. 32–3 (language) and
45–55 (classification); and *Oeuvres complètes*, I, pp. 234–60.

14 U.C. xxvii, fol. 117.

15 *ibid.*, fols. 140–1 and 144.

16 *ibid.*, fol. 141.

17 *ibid.*, fol. 164. His long argument on exhaustive analysis at this
point is closely related to his critique of the conventional classification of the powers and functions of government in *A fragment on
government*, ch. 3.

18 U.C. xxvii, fol. 154.

19 *ibid.*, fol. 165.

20 *ibid.*, fol. 132.
21 *An introduction to the principles of morals and legislation* (*C.W.* ed. Burns and Hart), p. 300 (p. 299n).
22 *ibid.*, pp. 8–9.
23 U.C. xxvii, fol. 160.
24 *ibid.*, fol. 164.
25 In Montague's edition of *A fragment on government* (Oxford, 1891), p. 59.
26 *A fragment on government* (*CW*. ed Burns and Hart, London, 1977), pp. 428–9.
27 *ibid.*, p. 484.
28 *ibid.*, pp. 429–31 (429, note o).
29 *ibid.*, p. 428.
30 *ibid.*, p. 495 (494, note b).
31 See H. L. A. Hart, 'Bentham on sovereignty', *The Irish jurist*, II (1967), 327–35, and J. H. Burns, 'Bentham on sovereignty: an exploration', *Northern Ireland legal quarterly*, xxiv (1973), 399–416. See also M. H. James (ed.), *Bentham and legal theory* (Belfast, [1974]).
32 *A fragment on government* (*C.W*. ed. Burns and Hart), p. 432.
33 *ibid.*, p. 429.
34 *ibid.*, p. 431, note p.
35 See, for example, *An introduction to the principles*, p. 12 (the fictitious character of the community), and p. 97 (the fictitious character of motives such as avarice and benevolence).
36 *ibid.*, p. 11. Ch. 10, 'Of motives', develops and illustrates his point in greater detail.
37 *Of laws in general*, p. 253.
38 *A fragment on government* (*C.W*. ed. Burns and Hart), p. 429, note o.
39 *An introduction to the principles*, p. 119n. The reference to association brings out the fact that Bentham was trying throughout to treat habit as Hume had treated causality.
40 *A fragment on government*, p. 431, note p.
41 *ibid.*
42 *ibid.*, p. 496, note b.
43 He concluded his discussion of the family with a cross-reference to a passage (*ibid.*, p. 433) in which he introduced some of his qualifications concerning sovereignty.
44 For an analysis of those writings (drafted apparently in 1772–74), see J. Steintrager, 'Morality and belief: the origin and purpose of Bentham's writings on religion', *The Mill Newsletter*, vi, 2 (1971), 3–15. The point is that they expressed hostility to the Church as an institution and as a source of and buttress to power (*ibid.*, pp. 5–6). The significance of these writings for Bentham's political stance is discussed further in ch. 4.
45 *A fragment on government*, p. 484. See also his references 'to the auxiliary force of the [moral and religious] sanctions' in *Of laws in*

general, p. 133, and to them as the 'allies' of the legislator in *ibid.*, p. 245.

46 U.C. xxvii, fols. 153–4. His marginal note on the passage (U.C. xcix, fol. 4) is 'Ethics why comprehended in my plan'.

47 U.C. xxvii, fol. 100. In *A fragment on government* (p. 415, note v) he traced the principle back to Aristotle's *Nicomachaean Ethics*, for the benefit of those 'who like the authority of Aristotle better than that of their own experience'. This passage is one where he came close to offering a positive justification of the principle, in the form of a morality of 'ends'.

48 *Of laws in general*, pp. 232–3.

49 *ibid.*, p. 246.

50 This was the famous diagnosis of George Wilson. See *Correspondence*, vol. III (*C.W.* ed. Christie), p. 526.

51 *Of laws in general*, p. 233.

52 *ibid.*, p. 252. Cf. p. 237, where the list of offences generates the 'catalogue of the laws'. In a recent work, *In the interest of the governed* (Oxford, 1973) David Lyons has argued that Bentham also recognised the existence of 'permissive' laws which did not include any restrictions or imply any offences. But as Lyons remarks (p. 133), Bentham found it possible to view a body of laws *as if* there were no such permissive laws; he allowed no place for them in his account of a code.

53 See *A fragment on government*, pp. 415–17.

54 Ch. 16, which occupies nearly one third of Bentham's text in the volume.

55 *An introduction to the principles*, p. 190.

56 *Of laws in general*, p. 137.

57 *ibid.*, pp. 137–9.

58 *ibid.*, p. 142. Bentham explained that his terminology was derived from the notion of enclitic particles employed in Greek and Latin grammar.

59 *ibid.*, p. 234 (pyramids); *An introduction to the principles*, p. 299n ('mechanisms').

60 *Of laws in general*, p. 236. This passage is of special interest because of its bearing on the practice of interchangeable parts in factory production, which Bentham's brother Samuel was one of the first to adopt at the end of the century. Bentham is treating it here as an *established* principle.

61 This conclusion was vital to the *development* of Bentham's jurisprudence. It provided the principal stumbling-block to the completion of his *Introduction to the principles* and stimulated him to draft the chapters that became *Of laws in general*. See Professor Hart's Introduction to the latter work, especially pp. xxxiv–xxxv.

62 *Of laws in general*, pp. 196 and 247.

63 *ibid.*, p. 199.

64 *ibid.*, p. 234.

65 e.g., *ibid.*, p. 248.

66 *ibid.*, pp. 135–6 and 245–6.

67 *ibid.*, p. 308.

68 Students of Bentham who are interested in him primarily as a philosopher are accustomed to treat these chapters as an elucidation or extension of his moral theory. That approach is legitimate, but it does not reflect Bentham's own reasoning or his motives for writing the chapters. They were his attempt to elucidate his theory of sanctions.

69 *Of laws in general*, p. 149.

70 *ibid.*

71 *ibid.*, p. 151.

72 See *A comment on the Commentaries* (*C.W.* ed. Burns and Hart), pp. 38–43, for his critique of Blackstone on laws as rules.

73 *Of laws in general*, p. vii (summarising the contents of pp. 4–8). He retained, however, a distinction between legislation and administration in terms of the permanence or transience of the measures taken: see *ibid.*, pp. 3–8 and *An introduction to the principles*, p. 283.

74 *Of laws in general*, p. 80.

75 *ibid.*, pp. 82–3.

76 *ibid.*, pp. 83–91.

77 *ibid.*, pp. 137–9 (p. 137, note h).

78 *ibid.*, p. 271. Cf. *An introduction to the principles*, pp. 205–7 and 238–9.

79 *Of laws in general*, pp. 245–6.

80 *Correspondence*, vol. III (*C.W.* ed. Christie), pp. 26–7. This is the letter sent to Shelburne. An earlier draft, printed at p. 28, was a little more explicit about constitutional law.

81 e.g. in *An introduction to the principles*, p. 14 (a footnote added to the 1823 edition); *A fragment on government* (*C.W.* ed. Burns and Hart), pp. 508 and 516 ('Preface intended for the second edition'); 'J.B.'s quondam arguments against reform', (8 Jan. 1810), U.C. cxxvi, fols. 98–104, and 'Government as viewed at 27 and 70' (1817–18), U.C. cxi, fols. 1–55.

82 Cf. Mack, *Jeremy Bentham: an odyssey of ideas*, pp. 125–7.

83 *Of laws in general*, p. 271. Cf. p. 293.

84 *ibid.*, p. 86.

85 *ibid.*, p. 249.

86 Bentham's references to these points are scattered through a number of places in *Of laws in general*, e.g. pp. 139 (p. 137, note h), 64 and 249–50.

87 Significantly, in defining indirect legislation for the benefit of Ashburton in 1782, he pointed out that it might be used against either 'delinquency' or 'misrule' (*ibid.*, p. 308).

88 *An introduction to the principles*, pp. 260–1 (p. 260 note r4).

89 *A fragment on government* (*C.W.* ed. Burns and Hart), p. 485. He was writing here not explicitly in terms of breach of trust, but of the distinction between a 'free' and a 'despotic' government. But

cf. U.C. xxvii, fols. 121 and 143, where he justified his demand for 'the giving of reasons for laws' as 'a control on the sovereign'.

90 *An introduction to the principles*, p. 189.

91 *ibid.*, pp. 196 and 260–4 (p. 260, note r4).

92 *ibid.*, p. 262.

93 *Of laws in general*, p. 81.

94 *Of laws in general*, p. 80.

95 He set out most clearly his purposes, and the connections that he perceived between the different topics, in the *Fragment on government*, ch. 3, especially pp. 462–4.

96 *Of laws in general*, p. 21.

97 *ibid.*, pp. 232 and 239–41; and *A comment on the Commentaries*, pp. 89–117.

98 Cf. Bielfeld, *Institutions politiques*, I, ch. 8, s. 43, 'Représentations permisses aux magistrats de la police', and II, ch. 1, s. 6, 'Liberté de faire des remonstrances accordée aux subalternes'.

99 *Of laws in general*, p. 140.

100 *An introduction to the principles*, pp. 260–4. He referred specifically to institutions for care of the sick, the insane and the poor, and for educational purposes etc., but did not make it clear whether these should be maintained or merely supervised by the government.

101 *Of laws in general*, p. 140.

102 U.C. xcix, fol. 103. This paper was a brouillon or set of preliminary notes, prepared in the course of drafting *Of laws in general*, but not incorporated directly in that work.

103 *Of laws in general*, pp. 308–9.

Notes to chapter 4

1 *A view of the hard-labour bill*, London, 1778 (*Bowring*, iv, 1–35); U.C. cvii, fols. 5–13 (Office of Intelligence); U.C. clxix, fols. 6–12 (Board of Shipbuilding); U.C. v, fols. 1–32 (religion).

2 *Traités de législation, civile et pénale* (3 vols., Paris, 1802); *Théorie des peines et des récompenses* (2 vols., London, 1811).

3 See J. Norris, *Shelburne and reform* (London, 1963), esp. pp. 292–3.

4 D. Jarrett, *The begetters of revolution. England's involvement with France, 1759–1789* (London, 1973), pp. 133–4.

5 *Correspondence*, vol. III (*C.W.* ed. Christie), p. 118 (Shelburne to J.B., 1 Nov. 1781).

6 Some of the details of what he did for Samuel in Russia are recorded in *ibid.*, esp. pp. 496–508 (Dec. 1786) and 577–91 (Oct.–Nov. 1787). He had also acted for Samuel before going to Russia, seeking labour and equipment for him, and the correspondence about these matters involved the exchange of a good deal of information on technical matters and economical modes of working. See *ibid.*, pp. 271–82 (June–July 1784). Bentham's own interest in

science had been partly an interest in the design of scientific apparatus. Some notes he made on Samuel's enterprises (apparently for Samuel's guidance) are on fol. 7v, U.C. cxlii. They are characteristically realistic in tone and content. But his choice of subordinates on Samuel's behalf – his judgement of character – was not very good.

7 This work has a rather unusual history of publication because, although Dumont put it into the *Traités de législation* (1st edition, vol. I, pp. 141–370), neither Hildreth nor Atkinson included it in his translation of the *Traités*, perhaps because it had already been translated for Bowring's edition of Bentham's *Works* (vol. III, pp. 155–210).

8 Most of the relevant brouillons and chapter headings are in U.C. xcix, fols. 53–60, 142–62 and 190–1, and U.C. xxxiii, fols. 72 and 99. The title quoted in the text is on fol. 156 of U.C. xcix.

9 *General view of a complete code of laws*, in Bowring iii, pp. 157–8. Cf. U.C. xxxiii, fols. 115 and 131. The fundamental division into civil, penal and constitutional applied properly only to *national* law; there was, in addition, international law ('droit des gens').

10 U.C. clxx, fol. 201.

11 See, for example, the Preface that he added to *An introduction to the principles of morals and legislation* on its publication in 1789 (*C.W.* ed. Burns and Hart), p. 6.

12 *Bowring* iii, pp. 199–200; cf. U.C. xxxiii, fols. 79–80.

13 *ibid.*, fol. 77, and U.C. clxx, fol. 182.

14 *Bowring* iii, p. 192. Cf. U.C. xxxiii, fol. 60.

15 *ibid.*

16 *Bowring* iii, p. 199. Cf. U.C. xxxiii, fol. 79.

17 *Bowring* iii, pp. 197–8; U.C. xxxiii, fols. 77–8. Cf. *A fragment on government* (*C.W.*, ed. Burns and Hart), p. 463, note b.

18 *Bowring* iii, p. 197; U.C. xxxiii, fol. 78.

19 *Bowring* iii, p. 199; U.C. xxxiii, fol. 76.

20 Significantly in the draft Preface or covering letter for *An introduction to the principles* to which I referred repeatedly in ch. 3, he grouped Adam Smith with Beccaria and Montesquieu among the most distinguished and recent writers on the principles of legislation (U.C. xxvii, fol. 132). The inclusion of his discussion of political economy in the 'Projet' is itself compelling evidence that he regarded the subject as a branch of jurisprudence.

21 *The theory of legislation*, trans. by R. Hildreth (London, 1911), p. 96. Cf. U.C. xxxiii, fol. 102.

22 The surviving evidence for the existence of this manuscript consists principally of two marginal summaries, fols. 149 and 190–1, in U.C. xcix. The material was probably used by Dumont, not for his version of the 'Vue Générale', but when he was preparing the *Théorie des peines et des récompenses*, vol. II, Book IV, ch. 13 'Des moyens d'accroissement de la richesse'. In the same box, fol. 160 shows the analysis at an earlier stage of development,

fol. 152 is a brouillon indicating how Bentham intended to develop some parts of his argument, and fol. 158 records the decision to eliminate the material from the 'new plan' for Projet.

23 *ibid.*, fol. 191. The marginal summary does not reveal how Bentham intended to treat infant industries.

24 U.C. lxxxvii, fols. 29–39 and 134; U.C. xcix, fol. 111.

25 Ch. 28, *Bowring* iii, pp. 203–4.

26 *Bowring* iv, p. 12. He found the principle in the draft Bill on which his pamphlet was a critical commentary. As a close reader of Beccaria and Catherine, Bentham must have been acquainted with the phrase and the concept before he encountered them here. He employed a variant of the concept in the Shipbuilding plans, which he probably drafted a little earlier than 1778.

27 This became Book iii of the second volume of the *Théorie des peines et des récompenses*. Bentham's Mss. are in U.C. cxlii, fols. 239–56.

28 'Indirect means of preventing offences', Part iv of 'Principles of the penal code' in *The theory of legislation* (pp. 358–472 in Hildreth's translation).

29 See, for example, ch. 10 'To facilitate knowledge of the fact of an offence', ch. 12 'To facilitate the means of recognising and finding individuals' and ch. 4 'To change the course of dangerous desires and to direct the inclinations towards amusements conformable to the public interest'. In drafting the material for what became ch. 10 (U.C. lxxxvii, fols. 10–15 and 31–5), Bentham seems to have considered measures more rigorous than those that actually went into the chapter.

30 J. Steintrager, 'Morality and belief', pp. 5 and 8.

31 The most complete guide to the chapter is a marginal in U.C. xcix, fol. 148. This represents a planned revision, not the chapter as originally drafted. Some of the draft material is in U.C. clxx, fols. 191–207.

32 U.C. clxx, fols. 199–200.

33 *ibid.*, fol. 199.

34 *ibid.*, fol. 200.

35 *Theory of legislation* (trans. Hildreth), pp. 449–52; U.C. lxxxvii, fols. 102–3.

36 *ibid.*, fol. 117.

37 *ibid.*, fol. 38.

38 U.C. clxx, fol. 168 and U.C. xcix, fol. 133.

39 U.C. lxxxvii, fols. 110–11.

40 *ibid.*, fol. 124.

41 *ibid.*, fols. 107–8 and 119–21.

42 U.C. xcix, fols. 133 and 148, and U.C. clxx, fol. 189. The references to 'Secret dans les suffrages' do not reveal whether he had in mind voting by the *electors*, or voting by members of Parliament.

43 U.C. xcix, fol. 133.

44 *Of laws in general*, p. 259.

45 U.C. xxxiii, fol. 72.
46 U.C. xcix, fol. 133.
47 *ibid.*, and fols. 17–19.
48 *Bowring* iv, p. 29.
49 *An introduction to the principles* (*C.W.*, ed. Burns and Hart), p. 300 (p. 299, note b2).
50 U.C. xcix, fol. 190. (The original in French.)
51 *ibid.*
52 The rules are in ch. 10 of Book i ('Of rewards in general') and chs. 2–7 of Book ii ('Of salaries'). The relevant Mss. (which Dumont sometimes used very freely) are in U.C. cxlii, fols. 77–90, 164, 179, 184–5 and 187. Bentham was distinguishing in the conventional way between salaries, in the sense of a fixed periodical payment, and day or piece-wages.
53 U.C. cxlii, fol. 80.
54 U.C. clxix, fols. 8–9 (remuneration for the Shipbuilding Board's officials); *ibid.*, fol. 7 and U.C. cvii, fol. 6 (the system of records in the Board and the Office of Intelligence).
55 U.C. cxlii, fols. 188–92 (venality) and 195–6 (farming). *Théorie des peines et des récompenses*, ii, Book ii, chs. 9 and 11.

Notes to chapter 5

1 *Defence of usury* (London, 1787). He sent the Panopticon letters to his friend George Wilson, asking for Wilson's help in getting them published, in a letter dated 19–30 December 1786. See *Correspondence* vol. iii (*C.W.*, ed. Christie), pp. 513–15.
2 The public response to the *Defence of usury*, and Bentham's new thinking on the occasion of the second edition, are described by Werner Stark in his Introduction to the first volume of his *Jeremy Bentham's economic writings*, pp. 26–30 and 34–8.
3 B.L. Add. Mss. 33 541, fol. 133, Lansdowne to J.B., June 1790, making arrangements for the first meeting with Parnell. The negotiations continued into 1791. They included suggestions that Parnell should become a partner in the Panopticon enterprise; he contributed money towards the printing of the essays (*ibid.*, fols. 164–5, Parnell to J.B., 3 Sept. 1790).
4 See my article, 'Bentham's Panopticon: an administrative history – I', *Historical Studies*, xv (1973), 703–21, especially p. 708 to the end.
5 He discussed his intentions with Lansdowne at that time: B.L. Add. Mss. 33 541, fols. 1–4, Lansdowne to J.B., 3 Jan. 1789.
6 He was corresponding with André Morellet (who acted as a link between Lansdowne's group and the moderate French reformers such as Mirabeau and Necker) from February 1789. See *Bowring* x, p. 199. A substantial body of material was in Morellet's hands by May – B.L. Add. Mss. 33 538, fols. 184–7, Morellet to J.B., 8 May 1789.

7 *Essay on political tactics...being a fragment of a larger work* (London, 1791); *Draught of a new plan for the organization of the judicial establishment of France* (London, 1790).

8 For differing accounts of the cycle, see: (i) M. P. Mack, *Jeremy Bentham: an odyssey of ideas*, pp. 407–42; (ii) J. H. Burns, 'Bentham and the French Revolution', *Transactions of the Royal Historical Society*, 5th Series, XVI (1966), 95–114.

9 S. Bentham, *Services rendered in the civil department of the Navy* (London, 1813), pp. 1–44.

10 *Correspondence* vol. III (*C.W.*, ed. Christie), p. 527, George Wilson and James Trail to J.B., 26 Feb. 1787.

11 They are in U.C. v, fols. 33–9 and 63–86. Fols. 84–6 seem to belong with 33–9 but may be part of a separate work. The papers are undated, but, from the nature of references to the eighteenth century (fol. 82) and to what I take to be the publication of *An introduction to the principles of morals and legislation* (fol. 63) and Richard Watson's *Letter to Archbishop Cornwallis* (fol. 65), I judge them to be products of the early 1790s.

12 Cf. J. R. Poynter, *Society and pauperism*, pp. 117–44 and 200–7.

13 His copy of the summary of the Bill is in U.C. cli, fols. 47–60. Some of his early comments are in U.C. cliii, fols. 369–71.

14 U.C. cliii, fols. 21–54. Essay III is incomplete in this version; the missing sections are in U.C. clii, fols. 196–7 and 215–18. Other copies and drafts of the essays are scattered among the papers in these two boxes.

15 U.C. cxxxiii, fol. 10 (31 May 1796). There are related papers, drafted in the same month, at fols. 5–9 and 12, and in U.C. cliii, fol. 78.

16 Colquhoun introduced himself to Bentham. See B.L. Add. Mss. 33 542, fols. 373 and 377; and U.C. ix, fol. 20, which suggests that the acquaintance was partly prompted by Richard Clark, the former Lord Mayor, who had known Bentham since the 1760s.

17 The memorandum is in U.C. cli, fols. 40–3. Colquhoun's covering letter, dated 20 Jan. 1797, is in B.L. Add. Mss. 33 542, fol. 444; see also fol. 423, in which he undertook to tell Bentham about his ideas on the poor, and acknowledged the receipt of some of Bentham's drafts on the same subject. This last circumstance makes it difficult to establish whether Colquhoun did or did not hit on all the ideas in his memorandum independently of or before Bentham.

18 London, 1796. The 'Advertisement' is dated 15 Feb. 1796 in the first edition and 25 July 1796 in the second. Colquhoun's scheme is set out more fully in the second edition, for which the first seems to have been a rather incomplete draft. For a more complete and detailed account of his work on police, see L. Radzinowicz, *A history of English criminal law*, II, pp. 384–8, and III, pp. 211–312.

19 Colquhoun set out his matured scheme in his evidence to the

Select Committee on Finance in 1798; see Appendix C, p. 48, to the Committee's 28th Report (*Lambert*, cxii, p. 50). Another version, apparently drafted by Bentham, is in U.C. cl, fols. 126–9. Copies of the earlier papers, dated 1794, are in U.C. cxlix, fols. 12–35, and cl, fols. 296–300. An intermediate stage is represented by a copy of a submission from Colquhoun to the Duke of Portland (Home Secretary), divided between U.C. clii, fol. 565 and U.C. cxlix, fols. 147–8.

20 J. H. Burns, 'Bentham and the French Revolution', p. 104.

21 *Anarchical fallacies, Bowring* ii, p. 523. For a different perspective on this work, see the two articles on 'The contemporary significance of Bentham's *Anarchical Fallacies*' by W. Twining and M. T. Dalgarno, *Archiv für Rechts- und Sozialphilosophie*, LXI (1975), 325–56 and 357–67.

22 *Bowring* ii, pp. 522–3.

23 U.C. clxx, fols. 47 ('Constitution' brouillon) and 174 ('Constit. law heads'). There is a chance that this distinction had been in his mind for a decade or so, in the form of a contrast between 'le souverain' and 'le prince'. See *Of laws in general*, p. 64, note 1.

24 U.C. cxxvii, fol. 2, brouillon on 'Constit.'

25 U.C. clxx, fol. 47.

26 U.C. cxxvi, fol. 1. Cf. Mack, *Jeremy Bentham: an odyssey of ideas*, p. 458, where the passage is transcribed a little differently. This is one of the places where Bentham offered different versions of his own sentence without deciding between them.

27 *ibid.*, p. 458.

28 *ibid.*, pp. 460–1; U.C. cxxvi, fols. 4–5.

29 U.C. clxx, fol. 183.

30 U.C. cxxvi, fol. 12.

31 U.C. cxxvii, fol. 5.

32 U.C. clxx, fol. 168.

33 U.C. xliv, fol. 4, where these are listed among advantageous points in the British constitution. This is one of a set of papers (fols. 1–5) where Bentham ran through his anti-democratic arguments, but it is not always easy to see whether they were intended seriously or ironically or as Aunt Sallys to be subsequently refuted. Fol. 1 seems to me to include (in its column 5) some 'Aunt Sally' material which is answered systematically in U.C. cxxvii, fols. 13–14. But I think fol. 4 must be accepted at face value.

34 This is the title of one of the principal essays in which he set out his constitutional theories, and which have been quoted already above. It is in U.C. cxxvi, fols. 1–7, and is reprinted by Mary Mack (with some omissions) as Appendix F in *Jeremy Bentham: an odyssey of ideas*, pp. 457–61.

35 U.C. clxx, fol. 154 (Part III of Bentham's most substantial draft constitution). There were similar provisions in the French Constitution of 1791, Title III, ch. III, s. 1, articles 2–3.

36 This was the point highlighted in the part of the 'Essay' that was

originally published in London in 1791. As the plan for the work then stood, this was intended to be ch. 6 'On the mode of proceeding in a political assembly in the formation of its decisions'. But the facilitation of decision making set the standard for the argument of the whole work.

37 U.C. clxx, fol. 164 (Part IV of the draft Constitution).

38 His *Draught of a new plan for the judicial establishment*, and his detailed critique of the French draft for which his own was intended to be a substitute.

39 *Bowring* iv, pp. 328–38 (the geographical principle); and pp. 325–8 (single-seatedness).

40 *ibid.*, p. 289.

41 *ibid.*, pp. 289–90 and 300–1.

42 *ibid.*, pp. 287–8 and pp. 312–16.

43 U.C. clxx, fol. 155 (draft constitution).

44 U.C. cl, fols. 758–67 ('Preliminary observations to the Board of Police Bill').

45 U.C. clii, fol. 196.

46 *Stark* III, p. 323.

47 In his and Colquhoun's police scheme, the Police Revenue Board was to be made fully and exclusively responsible to the Treasury in financial matters. The Treasury's authority was to extend to the appointment of officers handling the Board's financial transactions: U.C. cl, fol. 203 (Police Revenue Bill, s. 8).

48 *ibid.*, fol. 477 ('Notes on the Police Bill').

49 *ibid.*, fols. 203–4 (Police Revenue Bill, ss. 8 and 9).

50 U.C. v, fol. 63 (a draft 'Preface' to a work on the church).

51 *ibid.*, fol. 39 (brouillon related to 'Principles of ecclesiastical polity').

52 U.C. cl, fols. 270–1 (Police Revenue Bill, s. 47).

53 See *Stark* III, pp. 303–80. The first of his introductory works was the 'Manual of political economy', in *ibid.* I, pp. 219–73.

54 *ibid.* III, pp. 310–11.

55 *ibid.*, p. 322n.

56 See Stark's discussion of the development of his attitudes between the first and second editions of the *Defence of usury*, in *ibid.* I, pp. 36–7.

57 See *ibid.* I, p. 29 and III, pp. 524–5 which deal with Bentham's projected 'Letters to Mirabeau' and related writings in which he discussed 'saving measures'. His own best summary of the measures is in U.C. clxvi, fol. 24, 'Saving measures recapitulated', forming a part of the paper 'Views of economy: written for the use of the French nation...'

58 U.C. v, fol. 85.

59 *ibid.*, fol. 63.

60 In his 'Defence of a maximum', in *Stark* III, p. 301. The circumstances were those of excessive population growth and dearth.

61 U.C. clxvi, fol. 24.

62 These form the category 'Noscenda' in the 'Institute of political economy', in *Stark* III, pp. 378–80.

63 See Bentham's summary of the Thames Police Bill in *Bowring* x, pp. 331–3 (J.B. to Abbot, 8 June 1799). In the more general Police Revenue Bill (U.C. cl, fols. 179–289), the appointment of police officers (to be called Surveyors, and to have the authority of constables) and the line of authority back to the Home Office were covered in Part II of the Bill, and the Gazette and Calendar of Delinquency in Part VI.

64 *Stark* III, p. 361 ('Institute of political economy').

65 U.C. cliii, fol. 25, Essay II, 'Fundamental positions in regard to the making provision for the indigent poor', 28 April 1796.

66 *ibid.*, fol. 26.

67 *Bowring* viii, p. 370. See note 69 below.

68 U.C. cliii, fol. 29.

69 This is the scheme described in the 'Outline of a work entitled *Pauper management improved*', first published in Arthur Young's *Annals of Agriculture*, xxx–xxxi (1798), and reprinted in *Bowring* viii, pp. 369–439.

70 U.C. cliv, fol. 155, which appears to be an early draft for the third essay on the Poor laws. Cf. the similar argument in U.C. clii, fols. 164–83, which is an advanced draft for the same work.

71 *U.C. cliv, fol. 156.*

72 *ibid.*, fol. 155.

73 *Stark* III, p. 361 ('Institute of political economy').

74 *ibid.* II, p. 12. See generally Stark's comments on Bentham's draft pamphlet 'A plan for the augmentation of the revenue', *ibid.*, pp. 8–14.

75 *Bowring* viii, pp. 414–17 ('Outline of *Pauper management improved*').

76 U.C. clxvi, fol. 23.

77 *Bowring* viii, pp. 395–7 and 422–4. What Bentham envisaged was less formal learning than apprenticeship, combining productive labour with useful learning. (He often referred to the young paupers as 'apprentices', and their labour was to be an important economic resource for the system of Industry Houses.) In a draft note on the economics of the scheme he described what he had in mind as 'a great system of national education' (U.C. cli, fol. 284), but in the published 'Outline' his language was more guarded.

78 *Stark* III, pp. 338n and 361 ('Institute of political economy'). The projected lectures in midwifery were to be part of some versions of the pauper-management scheme, e.g. in U.C. cliii, fols. 52–4 (third essay on the Poor laws).

79 *Stark* III, p. 338n.

80 The prospect of general bankruptcy was the theme of his pamphlet 'The true alarm', printed in *ibid.*, pp. 65–216. See especially ch. 20, 'Propositions concerning the effects of paper money'.

81 *ibid.*, pp. 143–4; cf. *ibid.* II, pp. 286 and 302 ('Circulating annuities') where the point is made still more clearly.

82 *ibid.* III, p. 338 ('Institute of political economy' – joint-stock companies); I, pp. 260–5 ('Manual of political economy' – patents legislation).

83 *ibid.* II, p. 213 ('Circulating annuities').

84 U.C. cxlix, fols. 36–46 ('Mode of disposing of old stores').

85 *Stark* II, pp. 117–49. This is a pamphlet whose full title sets out clearly its theme: 'A plan for the augmentation of the revenue: by the establishment of a traffic on government account in life annuities and every other branch of money dealing where adequate security can be obtained upon a plan adapted to every modification of demand.' He took up the question of a note-issue more directly in two other pamphlets, 'Proposal for the circulation of a species of paper currency' (*ibid.*, pp. 153–200) and the 'Abstract or compressed view of a tract intituled circulating annuities' (*ibid.*, pp. 203–423).

86 *Stark* III, pp. 339–40 ('Institute of political economy'); and I, pp. 265–8 ('Manual of political economy').

87 This was the principal argument in his 'Defence of a maximum', in *Stark* III, pp. 249–302. He added a new defence of magazining (pp. 296–8) on the interesting ground that Britain could no longer feed its population from its own agricultural output and, 'population having no limit', could never hope to do so; but he was more sanguine on this occasion that magazines could be run as a commercial enterprise.

88 *Bowring* viii, pp. 398–9 (employment-exchanges and *Gazette*), 417–18 (remittance-facilities, 'frugality-inns' and 'frugal-conveyance stages').

89 U.C. clii, fols. 94–120 (third essay on the Poor laws, dealing with 'collateral uses').

90 The possibility of managing the note-issue was the point of ch. 14 of 'Circulating annuities' – 'Rise of prices – how to obviate', in *Stark* II, pp. 282–7.

91 *ibid.* III. p. 175 ('The true alarm').

92 *ibid.*

93 U.C. cl, fols. 179–289.

94 *ibid.*, fols. 182–99: Part I, ss. 1–6 of the Bill.

95 *ibid.*, fol. 246.

96 *ibid.*, fol. 248.

97 *ibid.*, fols. 249–50.

98 *ibid.*, fols. 232–5.

99 *Bowring* viii, pp. 369–72.

100 *ibid.*, p. 369n. As Bentham indicated there, these matters were covered in some of the later chapters of his 'Outline', entitled respectively 'Prospect of success', 'Management, why in one company, not several' and 'Management, why in a company, not Government'. He did not, however, publish those chapters, although

he drafted versions of them. He discussed some of the issues again in his unpublished work, 'Pauper systems compared', and occasionally in his economic writings.

101 U.C. clii, fol. 554 (from 'Pauper systems compared').
102 U.C. cli, fol. 325 (from the draft chapter 'Prospect of success').
103 *ibid.*, fol. 353 ('Prospect of success').
104 U.C. cliii, fol. 317 (from the draft chapter 'Management, why in one company').
105 U.C. cli, fol. 312 ('Prospect of success'). The argument on Steadiness extends over fols. 309–14.
106 *ibid.*, fol. 309.
107 *Stark* ii, pp. 146–7 ('Plan for augmentation of the revenue').
108 U.C. cliii, fols. 278–80 ('Management, why in a company').
109 U.C. cli, fol. 313 ('Prospect of success').
110 U.C. cliii, fol. 278 ('Management, why in a company').
111 U.C. cli, fol. 358 ('Prospect of success').
112 U.C. cliii, fol. 267 ('Management, why in a company').
113 U.C. cliv, fol. 547 ('Prospect of success').
114 *ibid.*
115 U.C. cl, fol. 286 (s. 53 of the Police Revenue Bill).
116 U.C. clii, fol. 359 ('Management rules').
117 U.C. cvii, fols. 116–47 ('Table of trades and earnings', 15 April 1797).
118 U.C. cli, fol. 380 ('Prospect of success').
119 U.C. cliv, fol. 554 ('Prospect of success').
120 U.C. cliii, fol. 209. This is the basis of Book ii, ch. 3, s. 2 of the published 'Outline of *Pauper management improved*'.
121 These matters are discussed in the *Panopticon postscript; part I* (London, 1791) chs. 9–16. His recommendations on all points were designed to promote discipline as well as economical production.
122 U.C. cli, fol. 474 ('Management rules'). Bentham was writing specifically here about paupers, some of whom might be sick or partly disabled and might be left idle on that account. Part of his argument was that work and occupation were therapeutic.
123 U.C. cliii, fol. 198 ('Management rules').
124 *ibid.*, fol. 194.
125 *ibid.*, fol. 195.
126 U.C. cli, fol. 475 ('Management principles').
127 *ibid.*, fol. 478.
128 *Bowring* iv, pp. 289–90.
129 U.C. cliv, fol. 557 ('Prospect of success'). Cf. *ibid.*, fols. 562 and 571, where he discussed 'want of competent education' in terms that suggest the importance of technical knowledge rather than a liberal education.
130 U.C. cli, fol. 390.
131 See *Bowring* iv, pp. 290–1 and 372–8.
132 *ibid.*, pp. 293–4, 296–7 and 368–70.
133 *ibid.*, p. 290.

134 U.C. cliii, fol. 318 ('Company, one').

135 *ibid.*, fol. 168 ('Management rules').

136 *Bowring* viii, p. 384. Cf. U.C. cliii, fols. 157–9 and 165–7.

137 *ibid.*, fols. 168–70.

138 U.C. cl, fol. 204 (Police Revenue Bill, s. 9). In his 'Notes to the Police Bill', *ibid.*, fols. 480–2, he also canvassed the idea of awarding titles to the Commissioners as a form of non-pecuniary remuneration.

139 *Bowring* viii, p. 384.

140 *ibid.*, p. 387.

141 *ibid.*, p. 384.

142 The escheators were to be the officials concerned with 'escheat', the lapsing of property to the Crown in cases of intestacy or where there was no surviving close relative of the deceased. See *Stark* i, p. 71. For the pay of the police, see U.C. cl, fol. 204.

143 *Bowring* viii, p. 381.

144 *ibid.*, p. 386.

145 *ibid.*, p. 383.

146 *ibid.*

147 U.C. cliii, fol. 160 ('Management rules').

148 U.C. clxx, fol. 179 ('Constitutional articles' – a brouillon or preliminary draft of part of his Constitution).

149 *Bowring* iv, p. 290.

150 *ibid.*, pp. 289–97 ('Title iii, s. 1 Appointment..., power and rank, s. 2 Pay, s. 3 Attendance, s. 4 Oath of office, s. 5 Deputes'); and pp. 368–70 and 378–81 where Bentham defended several of these provisions. His mastery of detail is illustrated by the fact that in the section on attendance (pp. 291–2) he provisionally prescribed both the hours of business for the courts (8 a.m. to 8 p.m., with one hour for lunch) and the judges' annual vacations (thirty days).

151 U.C. cl, fols. 200–3 (ss. 7–8 of the Police Revenue Bill). In his 'Notes' (*ibid.*, fols. 467–8), Bentham explained that he could not predict the real (and possibly changing) needs of the institution accurately enough to cover all matters in the Bill.

152 *ibid.*, fol. 209 (s. 11 of the Bill). Similar obligations were to be imposed on the escheators and those dealing in Annuity Notes.

153 *ibid.*, fols. 246–50 (ss. 33–5 of the Bill). In his note on this part of the Bill, Bentham congratulated himself (fol. 537) that he was defining the conditions of search more stringently than was usual in contemporary statutes.

154 *Bowring* iv, p. 294.

155 U.C. cl, fol. 209 (s. 11). Bentham's 'Note' on the arrangement is at fols. 489–93.

156 *Bowring* iv, p. 292.

157 U.C. cl, fol. 203 (s. 8 of the Bill).

158 *ibid.*, fol. 478.

159 *ibid.*, fol. 207 (s. 10). Cf. fols. 483–6, Bentham's 'Note' on the proposal.

160 The subtitle to the original essay on the *Panopticon or the inspection-house* (Dublin & London, 1791). For a different approach to the Panopticon, which nevertheless stresses its ties with earlier thinking and the multiplicity of its applications, see M. Foucault's *Discipline and punish* (London, 1977), pp. 195–228.

161 *Panopticon: postscript; part I,* p. 75.

162 *ibid.*, pp. 75–6.

163 *ibid.*, p. 45.

164 *Bowring* x, p. 331 (J.B. to Abbot, 8 June 1799, Head 2).

165 U.C. cl, fol. 496. He was commenting here on s. 14 of his Bill.

166 *Bowring* viii, p. 386.

167 *ibid.*, p. 392.

168 U.C. clii, fol. 360 ('Management rules'). Tabular-statement was a generalised version of – or a new name for – the simple statistical technique that Bentham had always wanted to apply to criminal and legal data. Cf. *Of laws in general*, p. 242, on 'a sort of universal harmony of the laws'.

169 *Encyclopaedia Britannica*, 3rd edition (Edinburgh, 1797), vol. III, pp. 367–91. For the resemblances between Hamilton's book and the scheme criticized by Bentham, see L. Goldberg, 'Jeremy Bentham, critic of accounting method', *Accounting Research*, VIII (1957), 218–45.

170 U.C. cviii, fol. 109.

171 U.C. cxxxiii, fol. 65.

172 *Encyclopaedia Britannica*, vol. III, p. 391.

173 U.C. cxlix, fol. 19 ('Explanatory observations on a Bill...against embezzlement...', 1794).

174 U.C. cl, fol. 147 ('Heads of the draught of a Bill...'). The relevant part of the Bill is s. 27, in *ibid.*, fols. 233–5.

175 *Bowring* viii, p. 393.

176 *ibid.*

177 His working papers are in U.C. cxxxiii, fols. 61, 62 and 65.

178 *ibid.*, fols. 61–2.

179 'On the accounts proper to be kept by farmers', *Annals of Agriculture*, xxviii (1798), p. 56.

180 U.C. cliv, fol. 33, J.B. to A. Young (draft), Sept. 1797.

181 *Bowring* viii, p. 393.

182 See 'Further proceedings on the Finance reports – Navy Board – Attachment K', pp. 19–25, in *Lambert*, cxiv, pp. 499–505. I assume that the Instructions printed there were substantially drawn up by the Benthams, and principally by Jeremy. They follow closely the argument submitted by Samuel to the Finance Committee in 1798; see the Committee's 31st Report, Appendix pp. 34–6 (*Lambert*, cxiii, pp. 36–8). And their style resembles that of Jeremy, whose letters sometimes refer to his participation in the preparation of Samuel's schemes, e.g. B.L. Add. Mss. 33 542, fol. 65 (J.B. to S.B.), and 33 543, fols. 488 (J.B. to St Helens), and 584–5 (J.B. to S.B.).

183 Instructions 5–7, 13–14, 17, 26–7, 29.

184 *P.R.O.*, Adm. 1/3526, S.B. to E. Nepean, 26 Dec. 1801.

185 'Further proceedings on the Finance reports – Navy Board – Attachment K', p. 25, Instruction 33.

186 *Bowring* viii, pp. 391–2. Cf. his comment that 'book-keeping *rationalised*...is one of the main pillars of my system' (U.C. cliv, fol. 34, J.B. to A. Young, Sept. 1797).

187 U.C. clxix, fol. 164, draft of J.B. to Morellet, probably April 1789. What appears to be Morellet's reply, dated 8 May 1789, is in B.L., Add. Mss., 33 538, fols. 184–7.

188 U.C. cl, fol. 100.

189 U.C. cli, fol. 369 ('Prospect of success').

190 Instruction 32, 'Further proceedings on the Finance reports – Navy Board – Attachment K', p. 25.

191 *ibid.*, Instructions 2–4 (p. 19), 8 (p. 20), 19–20 (pp. 22–3), 25 (pp. 23–4).

192 U.C. cli, fol. 352 ('Prospect of success').

193 This is based on a list in U.C. cix, fol. 6. Cf. *Bowring* viii, pp. 380–6, where some additional points are introduced (e.g. the 'wholesale purchasing principle').

Notes to chapter 6

1 I have given a fuller account of the death and burial of the scheme, and of Bentham's behaviour, in 'Bentham's Panopticon: an administrative history – II', *Historical Studies*, xvi (1974), 36–54.

2 e.g., in letters to Samuel in 1804, Bentham instructed him to insist to some Russians that he was inaccessible to outsiders; but his reason was an unwillingness to see these particular visitors who, he feared, would pick his brains and give nothing in return. See especially B.L. Add. Mss. 33 544, fols. 109–12, 22 Sept. 1804.

3 U.C. cxx, fols. 464 ('Incapacity') and 470–591 ('Dispensing power'); U.C. cxxi, fols. 253–8 ('Despotism'). There is much more in U.C. cxxi on dispensing power, in the form of discarded drafts and marginal outlines.

4 U.C. cxx, fol. 582 includes an explicit appeal to 'the principles of the Revolution' of 1688; and fol. 586 contains further references to Hampden and Ship money.

5 *ibid.*, fols. 570–1.

6 *ibid.*, fol. 583.

7 *ibid.*, fol. 586.

8 B.L. Add. Mss. 33 544, fol. 198, J.B. to S.B., 24 July 1806. In this period Bentham seems to have been concentrating on the rules relating to the *exclusion* of evidence, which he wanted to see greatly modified in the interests of full disclosure. *Ibid.*, fol. 202 (J.B. to S.B., 20 Aug. 1806) contains more information about his progress. Many of the relevant papers are in U.C. clviii, fols. 1–51.

9 See *Bowring* v, pp. 55–60. The work, as planned, was to consist of seven or eight chapters each with its usual apparatus of basic text, reasons and explanatory notes. The *Summary view* deals more or less adequately with most of the planned chapter on 'Organization', but hardly at all with the two chapters on 'Functions', or with the material on 'Advantages to the Public' where Bentham introduced some of his most important arguments about his objectives.

10 'Law versus arbitrary power', U.C. cvii, fols. 193–343; W. Paley, *Principles of moral and political philosophy*, 8th edn (2 vols., London, 1791), II, pp. 274–80.

11 Bentham's intentions for these works can be traced through the papers in U.C. xxvi, fols. 1–65. The most illuminating are fols. 2–11 (marginal outlines for the code) and 12–50 (marginals for essay on the press and libel laws).

12 *The elements of the art of packing as applied to special juries, particularly in cases of libel laws*, London, 1821. Many of the relevant marginal outlines, dated 1809, are in U.C. xxvi, fols. 66–136. The argument is clearly connected at numerous points with that in the works on the press.

13 U.C. cvi, fol. 162. This passage occurs in an important 'Essay on judicial injustice' which Bentham drafted in 1807. It seems to have been intended originally for *Scotch reform* but to have been re-allocated to the introduction to the *Court of Lords' delegates*.

14 *Introductory view of the rationale of evidence*, Bowring vi, p. 7. The passage is from ch. 2, entitled 'Relation of law to happiness – of procedure to the main body of the law – of evidence to procedure'. A large part of this work (including ch. 2) was drafted, and printed, in 1810 or 1811, but it was not completed until the 1820s.

15 U.C. xlvi, fol. 155; lxxxix, fols. 61 and 99; xci, fols. 199–204; xcii, fol. 5; and *The elements of packing*, p. 245.

16 U.C. xc, fol. 36; lxxxix, fol. 61; xci, fol. 199.

17 U.C. lxxxix, fol. 131.

18 U.C. xc, fols. 49 and 90.

19 On the relationship between the rules of evidence and sinister interest, see especially the *Introductory view of the rationale of evidence*, ch. 11, s. 6 and Appendix B, s. 4 (*Bowring* vi, pp. 42–4 and 178).

20 *ibid.*, p. 12. See also note 8 above.

21 *ibid.*, chs. 10 and 11, pp. 30–44.

22 *ibid.*, chs. 14–18, pp. 60–86.

23 The equation of a right to pardon with the dispensing power is a recurrent theme in 'Law versus arbitrary power', e.g. in fols. 194, 196, 214 and 236 in U.C. cvii.

24 U.C. cvi, fol. 163.

25 This was the title of a section of one of the chapters of *Court of Lords' delegates*. The draft is in U.C. lxxxix, fols. 560–76.

26 U.C. cvi, fol. 165.

27 U.C. lxxxix, fol. 23.

28 *ibid.*, fol. 146.

29 *Court of Lords' delegates*: (a) Ch. 'Organization: 4 Recordation' in U.C. lxxxix, fols. 417–18 and 454–85, (b) Ch. 'Functions supplementary: I Statistics' in *ibid.*, fols. 137–88 and 201–68. *Scotch reform*: (a) 'Registration', in U.C. xciii, fols. 133–5; (b) 'Establishment of an Inspector-general's office', *ibid.*, fols. 219–31.

30 In an informative letter to Romilly (June–July 1807), Bentham enclosed a summary of his plans for *Scotch reform*, and explained his dealings with Dumont, who was acting on behalf of Lord Henry Petty and (Bentham now believed) Grenville. (U.C. clxxiii, fols. 7–9). See also B.L. Add. Mss. 33 544, fols. 269–72 (J.B. to S.B. 9 April 1807), which contains additional information about *Scotch reform* and his attempts to use Romilly and Dumont to promote it.

31 The drafts for the proposed petition and its attachments are in U.C. lxxxii, fols. 150–264. Fols. 162–5 set out his intentions most clearly.

32 The most thorough, recent discussions of this issue are J. R. Dinwiddy's article, 'Bentham's transition to political radicalism, 1809–10', *Journal of the history of ideas*, xxxv (1975), 683–700; and ch. 4 in *Bentham* by James Steintrager (London, 1977).

33 *Summary view*, *Bowring* v, pp. 55–6. Cf. U.C. lxxxix, fols. 377–411.

34 *ibid.*, fol. 397.

35 *Bowring* v, p. 56.

36 B.L. Add. Mss. 33 544, fol. 269, J.B. to S.B., 9 April 1807.

37 *ibid.*, postscript, fol. 272: '(lack a day!) the majority is against us. . . [and] the new Ministers continue in their places'.

38 These reports dealt with, respectively, the Pay-Office; the Bank of England and the management of the Public Dept; Pensions and Sinecures; and the Commissioners for Prizes. The first three were printed in *House of Commons Paper*, 1807, vol. II, at pp. 313, 379 and 423. The third was revised and the new version was printed in the *Papers* for 1808, vol. III at p. 257. The Supplement to the 3rd Report and the 4th Report are in *ibid.*, 1809, vol. III, at pp. 61 and 103. The Committee sat until 1812 and produced a total of 13 reports. Some of the later ones were very valuable, but they seem to have made less impact on Bentham than these early ones.

39 See the Report, *House of Commons Papers*, 1808, vol. III, p. 259.

40 As is related in the text below, Bentham soon afterwards wrote critically on the legislation concerning the disposal of the proceeds of naval prizes, and proposed a new scheme.

41 Third Report, *House of Commons Papers*, 1808, vol. III, pp. 270–2; Supplement, *ibid.*, 1809, vol. III, p. 62. More of his ideas appeared in the second part of the Fifth Report (*ibid.*, 1810, vol. II, p. 381), which had a good deal to say about the need for individual responsibility, general control or superintendence in financial and

other agencies, and uniformity in procedures. But by the time that report was presented, Bentham had already committed himself to new positions.

42 Select Committee on Sinecure Offices: *House of Commons Papers*, 1810, vol. II, p. 591; 1810–11, vol. III, p. 961; 1812, vol. II, p. 191. Commissioners on Saleable Offices in the Courts of Law: *ibid.*, 1810, vol. IX, p. 125. The Select Committee's reports were rather an anti-climax, for the possible savings that they revealed were relatively small.

43 Bentham's line, following from his general approval of 'venality', was 'Gift worse than sale' (U.C. cxlvii, fols. 319–27). He was generally critical of the way in which the Select Committee on Sinecure Offices presented and interpreted the evidence before it, arguing that its work was much inferior to that of Abbot's Committee in 1797–8 (*ibid.*, fols. 271–427, passim).

44 cf. the argument of J. Steintrager in 'Morality and belief: the origin and purpose of Bentham's writings on religion', that after 1800 Bentham did not change his views but became more forthright in his expression of them as the apparatus of the state appeared more threatening but the public appeared more receptive to his views. See especially p. 9 of Steintrager's argument. See also the same author's *Bentham*, especially pp. 51–4.

45 He produced five different (but to some extent over-lapping) essays in criticism. The most important of his remonstrances were 'J.B. to Mallet' (J. L. Mallet, the Secretary to the Commissioners for Audit), in U.C. cxxii, fols. 36–41, 93–100, 238–76 and 284–99; and 'Arrangements humbly suggested to the Commissioners of the Audit Board, in the character of remedies to certain supposed defects in the practice of that judicatory', in *ibid.*, fols. 277–83, 300–19 and 332–[338]. (Fols. 334–8 in this box were numbered wrongly, as 324–8.)

46 Bentham traced the origins of this work to the prosecutions of authors, printers and publishers that were prompted by the published allegations concerning the Duke of York, Mary Anne Clarke and the sale of army commissions, especially those in Denis Hogan's (fairly circumspect) *An appeal to the public and a farewell address to the Army* (London, 1808); and to the account given by Sir Richard Phillips, in his *Letter to the Livery of London* (London, 1808), of the opposition that he encountered from members of the Judiciary when, as Sheriff, he tried to bring about changes in the methods of jury-selection. See *The elements of packing*, pp. 1–5. His references to Phillips and his *Letter* may be somewhat disingenuous; there is some evidence that he was cultivating Phillips at that time, partly because he found some of his views (on prisons as well as the courts) sympathetic, and partly because Phillips controlled the *Monthly Magazine* through which Bentham hoped to publicize some of his own ideas: B.L. Add. Mss. 33 544, fols. 362–3, J.B. to S.B. [June 1808].

47 The list of 'sacrifices', dated 9 Aug. 1807, is in U.C. xv, fol. 2; the list of 'grievances', dated 4 July 1809, is in U.C. cxxvii, fol. 117.

48 Fols. 114 and 116, in U.C. cxxvii, brouillons headed 'Parliamentary reform' and bearing various dates in June 1809, imply that he had taken the decision in or by that month. A note of 2 July 1809 on fol. 116 implies that he had not yet decided how to proceed, but fol. 114 has references to 'Necessity' which became one of the two major themes in his central work on reform. I think that fol. 117 (see Note 47) was probably a product of the same line of thought and was probably the source of a projected section or chapter on 'Grievances' in that work.

49 The first part is outlined in U.C. cxxviii, fol. 49, the second in *ibid.*, fols. 5–6 and U.C. cxxvi, fol. 105, and the third in U.C. cxxix, fol. 25. It seems that the 'Plan' was to consist of a set of 'articles', and a commentary on each article. But some of Bentham's drafts envisage a different scheme, in which the material would be divided into at least nine books.

50 *Sinecures*: U.C. cxlvii is entirely devoted to this topic. *Admiralty Prizes Acts*: U.C. cxxix, fols. 653–74 and B.L. Add. Mss. 33 547, fols. 1–444. *Official economy*: U.C. cxxviii, fol. 1 (1809); cvi, fols. 230–5 (29 July 1810); and cix, fols. 57–8 (Oct. 1810). These papers are fragmentary, but in the published work Bentham pointed out that he did write the two pieces in 1810, and that they were written as sequels to a third entitled 'Hints towards economy' – a heading which occurs in fol. 1 of Box cxxviii. *Influence*: three different but incomplete plans for 'Influence', in U.C. cxxv, fol. 1 (June 1810–May 1811), suggest that this part of the original work was being expanded to absorb some of the material previously allocated to 'Necessity'. *Reward*: U.C. cxlii, fols. 14 (14 Sept. 1809), 15 (3 Oct. 1809), 17 (27 Jan. 1811). These papers are lists of 'Books' and 'Chapters' in which Bentham was trying to fix upon a suitable structure for the material. The last bears a cross-reference to the 'Defence of economy'.

51 Dumont had been consulting him about the 'Peines' part of the work since the beginning of the year. See B.L. Add. Mss. 33 544, fols. 404–7, Dumont to J.B., 12 Jan. 1809, and 21 Jan. 1809.

52 cf. J. R. Dinwiddy, 'Bentham's transition to political radicalism, 1809–10', p. 691 and *passim*; and D. P. Crook, *American democracy in English politics, 1815–50* (Oxford, 1965), pp. 16–17.

53 For a practical application of the notion, see his reference to the obsequiousness of special juries in *The elements of packing*, pp. 109–17.

54 U.C. cxxv, fol. 42 (7 May 1811). This is one of a series of 'J.B.'s propositions' relating to influence (fols. 42–53), in which he summarized many of his ideas on the subject.

55 U.C. cxxvi, fol. 110 (12 Dec. 1809) designed for 'Parliamentary reform, Book I, Necessity'. Cf. U.C. cxxv, fols. 54–7 (8 May 1811).

56 U.C. cxxv, fols. 47–52. Cf. James Steintrager, *Bentham*, p. 119.

57 U.C. cxxviii, fol. 129 (18 Sept. 1809); drafted for the 'Recapitulatory conclusion' to 'Parliamentary reform, Book I, Necessity'.

58 'Defence of economy against the late Mr. Burke', *The Pamphleteer*, IX (1817), p. 12.

59 U.C. cxxvi, fols. 77–8 (8 Aug. 1809); seems to have been drafted for 'Parliamentary reform, Influence'.

60 *ibid.*, fols. 51–62 (20–28 Nov. 1809); seems to have been drafted for 'Parliamentary reform – Necessity'.

61 *ibid.*, fols. 79–84 (24–27 Dec. 1809); drafted for 'Parliamentary reform – Necessity'. Cf. other versions of the same arguments in U.C. cxxviii, fols. 51–61 (8–9 Oct. 1809), and in U.C. cxxv, fols. 24–6 (7 June 1810) on 'bands subjugated by reference to the subjugation of their leaders'.

62 U.C. cxxvi, fols. 372–8 (6 Nov. 1810), drafts for 'Parliamentary reform'.

63 U.C. cxxvii, fols. 102, 105 (Aug. 1809), drafts for 'Parliamentary reform – Necessity'.

64 His analysis here ran parallel to that in his theory of reward. He was asking what was the 'matter of corruption', and finding that it was much the same as the matter of reward, with some admixture of the matter of punishment.

65 U.C. cxxx, fol. 102 (3 Dec. 1809), draft for 'Parliamentary reform, Book II, Influence'.

66 Cf. the titles of draft chapters for 'Parliamentary reform – Necessity', in U.C. cxxvi: 'Tests – their use in the propagation of immoral dependence', fols. 19–23 (1 Sept. 1809); 'King – interest he has in depraving the morals and understanding of his subjects', fols. 24–47 (24 Sept. 1809); and 'Parallel relation between the imposition of tests and the enslavement of the press', fols. 48–50 (27 Sept. 1809).

67 U.C. clviii, fol. 69 (23 June 1813). This was a marginal outline, employed in the drafting of *A table of the springs of action*.

68 U.C. cxxv, fols. 152–7.

69 U.C. xv, fols. 3–83.

70 U.C. cxxv, fols. 158–410. Many of these papers relate to the published *Plan (or Catechism) of parliamentary reform*, but there seem to be parts of two distinct works here.

71 U.C. cxi, fols. 1–55.

72 *ibid.*, fols. 60–137, and U.C. cxxviii, fols. 8–9.

73 U.C. cxxxii, fols. 1–513, and cxxxvii, fols. 1–24.

74 U.C. cxxviii, fols. 334–465.

75 U.C. clx, fols. 117–47.

76 U.C. cxxviii, fols. 313 and 325–6 (May 1818); the Resolutions drafted for Burdett.

77 *Church of Englandism and its catechism examined* (London, 1818). There are four different series of page-numbers in the volume – (i) for the Preface on Publication; (ii) for the Preface and plan of the work; (iii) for the Introduction; and (iv) for the Body of the

work and Appendices. The Body of the work occupies 86 out of a total of nearly 800 pages.

78 The surviving Mss. for *Church of Englandism* are mainly in U.C. vii and clviii. Those relating to the earlier plan(s) are mainly in U.C. vi. But the division between the two sets of Mss. is not absolute, and they share many topics, arguments and purposes. Another precursor of the published work was a set of 'Propositions on parish priests, how to improve their education and make them useful', which were apparently drafted 'on the occasion of General Miranda's expedition': U.C. xxi, fol. 75 (20 Aug. 1810).

79 J.B. to Mora, 22 Sept. 1820, B.L. Add. Mss. 33 551, fol. 32.

80 *Church of Englandism*, p. viii of 'Preface on publication'.

81 *ibid.*, pp. x–xi.

82 U.C. clviii, fol. 157 (8 May 1816), marginal for 'Plan of the work'.

83 Although this was one of his principal complaints against the Church, he did not argue it coherently at any point in *Church of Englandism*. Some of it is to be found in Appendix i, a good deal more is in Appendix iv, 9, 'Vices of excellent Church recapitulated' (especially in s. 3 'Vices having relation to discipline'), and more is scattered throughout the work. See, e.g., Appendix v on Lord Harrowby's 'pretended reform', pp. xlviii–xlix of the 'Plan of the work', and pp. 169–72 of Appendix ii which refer to the representations made by the Dean of Canterbury on behalf of a brewer charged with adulterating his product, and the suspension of the prosecution by Vansittart despite the strength of the evidence. Bentham had intended to set out his views more systematically, in a section 'As to government' in an extended treatment of the 'Effects produced' by the Church, but decided to drop the whole discussion of 'Effects' (Appendix i, p. 196). The best guide to his position is the set of marginals for 'Effects' in U.C. clviii, fols. 184–95, especially fols. 194–5 (28 Aug. 1816) 'As to government'. He also intended to deal separately with Dean Andrewes, Vansittart and the brewer – see U.C. vii, fols. 8–80.

84 *Church of Englandism*, Appendix iv, pp. 369–70.

85 *ibid.*, 'Preface on publication', pp. xxi–xxii.

86 *ibid.*, Appendix i, p. 89. The phrase 'prostration of the understanding and will' had been used approvingly by the Bishop of London in a charge to his clergy about the evils of Unitarianism, which Bentham examined and disputed at length in his Appendix i.

87 Internal peace, tranquillity and rational obedience were the objects that the politician should seek through the educational system, he argued in his Introduction to *Church of Englandism*, pp. 52–3.

88 *ibid.*, 'Preface on publication', p. ix.

89 U.C. clx, fol. 146. This paper (in a copyist's hand) is dated vaguely '1820 or 1822'.

90 U.C. clviii, fol. 69 (23 June 1813).

91 *ibid.*

92 *Bowring* v, p. 74 (*The elements of the art of packing*).

93 *Bentham's theory of fictions,* ed. by C. K. Ogden (London, 1932), p. 97.

94 *ibid.,* pp. 14–18. His belief in the possibility of reducing necessary fictions to real entities is brought out still more clearly in a draft chapter on the subject in B.L. Add. Mss. 33 550, fols. 4–47. (A few of the papers in this set are dated 1807–08, but 1814 seems to mark the real beginning of the work.)

95 cf. D. N. Winch, *Classical political economy and colonies* (London, 1965), pp. 36–7.

96 *ibid.* The first title was 'Emancipation Spanish', and the drafts for it were written generally in 1820. Bentham adopted the later and more extensive plan of 'Rid yourselves' not later than August 1821 (U.C. viii, fol. 63), although that was still not the final scheme. The most complete list is in *ibid.,* fol. 64 (8 Feb. 1822). John Colls recorded in his diary the distribution of some of the completed letters (apparently in Ms.) in April 1822 (B.L. Add. Mss. 33 563, fol. 100). Part I of the work dealt with the position of Spain, Part II with that of Ultramaria.

97 U.C. clxiv, fol. 74 (12 July 1820). He argued the point at some length in fol. 60 of U.C. clxii (1 June 1820).

98 U.C. viii, fol. 2 (11 July 1818).

99 U.C. clxii, fol. 151 (15 May 1820).

100 *ibid.,* fol. 166 (20 May 1820).

101 *ibid.,* fols. 160–4 (20–25 May 1820).

102 U.C. viii, fol. 3 (11 July 1818).

103 *ibid.,* fol. 68 (9 Feb. 1821); and U.C. clxii, fols. 254–5 (6 Feb. 1821). He had offered a preliminary sketch of this kind of analysis in his drafting of 'Emancipation Spanish', in U.C. clxiv, fol. 102 (20 June 1820).

104 For the footnote, see *Codification proposal* (London, 1822), p. 39 (*Bowring* iv, p. 558). The drafts of the essay are in U.C. lxxxiv, fols. 1–72 (Nov. and Dec. 1821). Its apparent title was 'Sinister interest and interest-begotten prejudices particularised and delineated'; this indicates how far Bentham was aiming at a generalised account of interests in society. It was designed at first as part of, and then as an Appendix to, what became s. 7 of his *Codification proposal.* But before it was finished, Bentham was conscious that it was growing too long and might have to be abandoned (U.C. lxxxiv, fol. 91, 28 Dec. 1821).

105 *ibid.,* fol. 1 (22 Dec. 1821).

106 *ibid.,* fol. 2 (22 Dec. 1821).

107 *ibid.,* fol. 21 (5 Dec. 1821).

108 *ibid.,* fol. 1 (22 Dec. 1821).

109 *ibid.,* fol. 91 (28 Dec. 1821).

110 *ibid.,* fol. 146 (5 Feb. 1822).

111 *Church of Englandism,* Appendix IV, pp. 192–392, entitled 'Remedy to all religious and much political mischief – euthanasia of the Church'. 'Euthanasia' was a term that attracted him at this time.

He found it in David Hume's essay on 'Whether the British government inclines more to absolute monarchy or to a republic', and he made it the informal title of his own 'Essay on the British Constitution' of 1815.

112 U.C. cxxxii, fol. 242 (20 June 1819); draft of Letter 7 to Lord Erskine.

113 *ibid.*, U.C. cxxviii, fol. 230 (9 Dec. 1818), preparatory matter for the Radical Reform Bill.

114 U.C. lxxxiv, fol. 22 (5 Dec. 1821).

115 U.C. xiii, fol. 201 (2 July 1821), J.B. to Carvalho.

116 The three are joined together, for example, as the subject-matter of the projected chapter 6, 'Obstacles to good government' in 'Political deontology', U.C. xv, fol. 79 (10–12 July 1816).

117 His plans for the Church are discussed in the text below. He set out his plans for schools in *Chrestomathia* (*Bowring* viii, pp. 1–191), especially pp. 46–54 which cover his 'notes to the principles' of school-management.

118 U.C. lxxxiv, fol. 2 (22 Dec. 1821).

119 *Bowring* vi, p. 72 (*Introductory view of the rationale of evidence*).

120 *ibid.*

121 U.C. xc, fol. 46 (26 Sept. 1807).

122 *Church of Englandism*, Appendix iv, p. 149: 'As for trade, so for religion…the best thing that a government could *now* do would be not to meddle with it.' For his pamphlet on Spanish economic policy, see *Stark* iii, pp. 381–417.

123 *Bowring* vi, p. 84.

124 'Defence of economy against the late Mr Burke', *The Pamphleteer*, ix (1817), p. 4.

125 He summarised his proposals in *Church of Englandism*, Appendix iv, pp. 386–92.

126 *ibid.*, pp. 369–85. He envisaged a still more thorough treatment of these matters in his discarded plan for the study of the Church. So, in U.C. vi, fol. 27 (6 Sept. 1813) he outlined a prospective analysis of 'Discipline ecclesiastical' under ten headings: duties; qualifications at large; qualifications – declarations of opinion; power inter se; power in omnes; dignity and dignities; pay; appointment; removal; responsibility other than by removal. Much of this did not appear explicitly in *Church of Englandism* although it conditioned his approach there. Cf. K. A. Thompson, *Bureaucracy and church reform: the organizational response of the Church of England to social change, 1800–1965* (Oxford, 1970), pp. 15 and 67–8. Thompson classes Bentham as a spokesman for the 'instrumental values' that he sees as one of the two main tendencies in the reform movement.

127 *Church of Englandism*, Appendix iv, p. 289.

128 U.C. cxxviii, fol. 318 (May 1818); one of the Resolutions drafted for Burdett. He used the point there specifically as an argument against the device of 'recall'. But cf. U.C. clxiv, fol. 263 (23 Aug.

1820): 'it is not to the filling of every official situation [by election] that a promiscuous multitude can in respect of appropriate information be competent'.

129 U.C. xxxviii, fol. 102 (5 Aug. 1820); a marginal on 'Corruptive influence' designed for 'Emancipation Spanish'.

130 *Bowring* viii, pp. 47–9 (*Chrestomathia*).

131 *Bowring* vi, pp. 72–9, especially p. 75.

132 U.C. lxxxix, fol. 146 (Oct. 1807).

133 These papers are scattered in U.C. lxxxix and xc. The basic prescriptions are in the sections dealing with the statistic function (U.C. lxxxix, fols. 201–6) and 'recordation' (*ibid.*, fols. 417–18). The commentary (in the form of 'Notes' and 'Reasons') is in the same box, fols. 137–88, 207–68, 274–7, 454–85 and 613–24, and in U.C. xc, fols. 44–8. But the discussion covers the general, public uses of legal statistics as well as the managerial uses.

134 U.C. lxxxix, fol. 207 (2 Oct. 1807); cf. U.C. xc, fol. 44 (28 Sept. 1807).

135 *Bowring* vi, pp. 75–6 (*Introductory view of the rationale of evidence*).

136 U.C. cxi, fols. 111–25 (21 Sept. 1818), 'Factitious dignity', a section of the 'Picture of misrule'.

137 U.C. cxlvii, fols. 468–85 (17–18 April 1810); 'What the prospect for official emolument?', drafted for the work on Sinecures.

138 *The Pamphleteer*, ix (1817), pp. 45–6. For Burke's hostile reference to the auction of public offices, see *The works of Edmund Burke* (World's Classics Edition), ii, p. 361 (Speech on economical reform).

139 U.C. cxxx, fol. 17 (17 Jan. 1810); a draft for 'Parliamentary reform'.

140 On this movement generally, see R. J. Montgomery, *Examinations: an account of their evolution as administrative devices in England* (London, 1965); and (for a later period) J. Roach, *Public examinations in England 1850–1900* (Cambridge, 1971). Montgomery (pp. 19–20, 32) refers to Bentham's views, mainly as they appeared in the *Constitutional code*.

141 U.C. clviii, fol. 167 (Sept. 1816). This was one of a set of so-called 'Graduate's maxims', a version of which appeared in *Church of Englandism*, Appendix iv, pp. 234–9. He gave them that title because at one time he intended to publish the work as 'by an Oxford Graduate', and he drafted some of it as a debate between 'Graduate' and 'Zealot'. His interest in examinations and the University reforms went back at least to 1813 – see U.C. vi, fol. 142, dealing with 'remedies' in the Church.

142 U.C. cxxviii, fol. 485 (13 Dec. 1819); part of a remonstrance that he proposed sending to Castlereagh on the insufficiency of the abolition of sinecures as a measure of reform. In the same argument (fol. 484) he explicitly linked the topic with Samuel's difficulties in the 'Marine Department'.

143 U.C. clx, fols. 6–29. The title in the text appears on fol. 28.

144 U.C. xxxi, fol. 260 (14 July 1818). At some point the heading 'Government...science' was crossed out, and 'Civil code' substituted.

145 Fols. 31–4 in U.C. clx are dated 4 Mar. 1820 and are headed 'Official economy or necessity of reform'.

146 His hopes were probably at their peak in November and December 1820, when he was in touch with the Spanish Embassy, was corresponding with Mora (whose journal he was trying to subsidise and to prop up in other ways with Walter Coulson's help), and was getting information and encouragement from Blaquiere and Bowring (who had just entered his life, as a supposed expert on Spanish affairs). His state of mind is best seen in his letters to Samuel in B.L. Add. Mss. 33 545, fols. 453–4 (24 Nov. 1820), 455–8 (29 Nov.–18 Dec. 1820), 491–4 (22 Feb. 1821) and 497–502 (Feb. 1821). By the last of these he had been somewhat disconcerted by Mora's arrest on political charges, but he remained fundamentally optimistic.

147 That title is in U.C. xxxvii, fol. 4 (3 April 1821). The bulk of the surviving and readily identifiable 'First lines' material is in that box, and U.C. xxxvi. But the position is obscure, because Bentham converted some of his drafts to other uses.

148 U.C. xxxvii, fols. 15 (27 April 1821) and 393 (28 April 1821). The main sequences relating to the Constitution are in this box, fols. 8–16, 58–62, and 391–3; and in U.C. xxxvi, fols. 53–61.

149 U.C. xxxvi, fols. 17–38 (Apr.–June 1821) and 62–70 (9 July 1821), and U.C. xxxvii, fols. 69–70 (27 May 1821).

150 U.C. clx, fols. 38–46 (17–18 Feb. 1822) employ these titles. Fol. 41 looks like an intended beginning – but that does not imply that it was the first piece drafted. Bentham's usual short title for the work was 'Economy as to office' or simply 'Economy etc.'

151 In U.C. xxxviii, fol. 11 (9 May 1822) he envisaged these and two more parts – 'III Things as they are in England' and 'IV Things as they ought to be and are in the Anglo-American United States'; but he questioned whether the material for the last two parts should not be fitted into the first two. I have not found many Mss. relating to Parts III and IV as separate topics.

152 U.C. cxiii, fol. 30 (10 June 1822); draft on the theme 'legal responsibility universal'.

153 He argued this at length in U.C. clx, fols. 240–310 (June and July 1822).

154 U.C. cxiii, fol. 28 (26 June 1822).

155 This and the next point were substantially the titles of sections in 'Aptitude maximized', listed e.g. in U.C. cxiii, fols. 34–5 (25 May 1822).

156 U.C. clx, fols. 58–62 (April–May 1822).

157 U.C. cxiii, fol. 106 (9 June 1822).

158 *ibid.*, fol. 107 (9 June 1822).

159 *ibid.*, fols. 156–9 (16 May 1822).

160 U.C. clx, fol. 56 (28 April 1822).

161 U.C. cxiii, fol. 7 (11 May 1822).

162 *ibid.*, and fols. 91–2 (19–20 May 1822) where the case for total subordination is argued at length.

163 *ibid.*, fol. 2 (25 April 1822).

164 *ibid.*, fol. 3 (25 April 1822).

165 *ibid.*, fol. 5 (27 April 1822).

166 *ibid.*, fol. 19 (26 June 1822).

167 *ibid.*, fol. 12 (17 June 1822).

168 *ibid.*, fol. 5 (27 April 1822).

169 U.C. clx, fol. 61 (5 May 1822).

170 U.C. xxxviii, fol. 53 (27 June 1822); this is the marginal summary of fols. 19–24 in U.C. cxiii.

Notes to chapter 7

1 Mora's arrest on political grounds in January 1821 destroyed his usefulness as an agent, but it did not convince Bentham that his own projects would be set aside. He continued to write about Spanish affairs, including the Spanish Penal Code in his *Letters to Count Toreno*, and early in 1822 told his brother that he still hoped that the draft Code would be thrown out and 'thus room will be left for mine'. See B.L. Add. Mss. 33 545, fol. 539, J.B. to S.B., 18 Jan. 1822.

2 *Codification proposal*, p. 77. The invitation to work on the Paper Money proposal had been formally issued to Bentham by Diego Colon, the Secretary to the Spanish Embassy in London, before Mora's arrest: U.C. lx, fols. 55–6 (7 Dec. 1820). Bentham's puzzlement at that development emerged in a letter that he drafted but did not send to O'Higgins, the President of Chile, in *ibid.*, fols. 66–7 (1821). Cf. B.L. Add. Mss. 33 545, fol. 456, J.B. to S.B. (18 Dec. 1820).

3 U.C. xxxiv, fol. 9 (26 April 1822 – brouillon), and fol. 12 (30 July 1822 – 'Constitutional code, heads proposed'); U.C. xxxviii, fol. 3 (13 May 1822 – 'Constitutional code – rudiments'). Cf. *Bowring* ix, p. iii, where Richard Doane suggested in his editorial note to the *Constitutional code* that the invitation from Portugal was decisive in encouraging Bentham to set to work.

4 U.C. xii, fol. 141, J.B. to Leicester Stanhope (21 Oct. 1823).

5 U.C. lx, fol. 66, J.B. to O'Higgins, and fol. 94, J.B. to Boyer of Haiti (Dec. 1822). He had in mind particularly Article 13 of the Spanish Constitution which, in the translation published in *The Pamphleteer* in 1823 (vol. xxii, No. 43, p. 63), reads: 'The object of the Government is the happiness of the nation; since the end of all political society is nothing but the welfare of all individuals of which it is composed.' But Bentham had access to Spanish-

speaking friends, such as Bowring and Sarah Austin, who may have provided him with a different translation.

6 U.C. lxxx, fols. 43–8 (July 1821).

7 *Codification proposal*, pp. 4–5 and 75 (Letter to the Cortes, 7 Nov. 1821).

8 U.C. clxxiii, fol. 19, J.B. to Bowring (1 Nov. 1820).

9 *ibid.*, fols. 66–72, entries for period Feb. to April 1822.

10 They probably met first in June or July 1822. See B.L. Add. Mss. 33 545, fols. 572–4, D'Ghies to J.B. (6 July 1822).

11 *Bowring* viii, pp. 555–600.

12 U.C. xxiv, fol. 43, J.B. to D'Ghies ('Facienda by government') 14 Aug. 1822.

13 Bowring had sent him (through Walter Coulson) information about the Greek insurrection in August 1821, as John Colls reported in his diary (B.L. Add. Mss. 33 563, fol. 84, entry for 7 Aug. 1821). Bentham had taken the matter seriously enough to entertain Nicolo Piccolo and another Greek to dinner (*ibid.*, fol. 86, entries for 22 and 23 Aug. 1821). He continued to correspond with Piccolo, as in U.C. xii, fols. 42–5, 47 and 84 (15 Sept. 1821–30 June 1822).

14 *ibid.*, fols. 100 (Louriottis to J.B., 14 Feb. 1823) and 101–2 (J.B. to Louriottis, 16 Feb. 1823). Louriottis called in person at Queen's Square Place on 19 February, as Colls reported (B.L. Add. Mss. 33 563, fol. 119).

15 U.C. xii, fol. 99, 'Le Métropolitain Ignace' to Bowring (18 Aug. 1822). Fol. 98 in the same box indicates that Bowring had been in touch with the Provisional Government of Greece since at least April 1822.

16 'J.B.'s observations on particular articles in the Greek Constitution', U.C. xxi, fols. 180–212 (9–23 Feb. 1823), and U.C. cvi, fols. 327–94 (Feb.–March 1823); 'Principles of legislation as to Constitutional Law exhibited summarily but in order', U.C. xxi, fols. 237–56 (19 Feb. 1823).

17 The tangled and unedifying story of the London Greek Committee, and the participation in its affairs of Bowring, Blaquiere, Stanhope and Joseph Hume, has been recounted by W. St Clair in *That Greece might still be free* (Oxford, 1972). See also the essays by D. Dakin and A. Dimaris in *The struggle for Greek independence*, ed. by R. Clogg (London, 1973).

18 U.C. xii, fol. 103, J.B. to Blaquiere (2 Mar. 1823).

19 B.L. Add. Mss. 33 563, fol. 126, Colls's diary, entries for 26 Aug. 1823, 10 Oct. 1823 and 14 Oct. 1823.

20 U.C. xxxvi, xxxvii and clx contain large amounts of material which, as the cataloguers of the collection have established, was used by Doane. A good deal of it originated in 'First lines' or Bentham's other contemporary writings.

21 Many of the papers relating to these chapters are so headed, e.g. U.C. xlii, fol. 53, 'Enactive, Ch. 4 Executive' (31 Mar. 1823 etc.),

and U.C. xli, fol. 457, 'I Enactive, Ch. 7 Judiciary, Justice Minister' (9 April 1823). That scheme seems to have been abandoned before August 1823, when Stanhope received the first set of eight chapters that he was to take to Greece.

22 So he told Stanhope in a letter accompanying the last of the chapters despatched to him for the Greeks (U.C. xii, fol. 193, 19 Feb. 1824). This and all the previous chapters related only to the Enactive part.

23 *Extract from the proposed Constitutional Code entitled 'Official aptitude maximized, expense minimized'* (London [1826]), pp. 14–17.

24 U.C. xxxviii, fols. 9–10, n.d., but with annotations dated 17 Feb. and 30 Mar. 1824. This list of the Code's contents was evidently prepared for Stanhope's use. It seems that he was given the text of only 14 of the 23 chapters, but that Bentham supplied this list and some marginals to cover the rest.

25 The new chapters were to deal with Appellate Pursuers-General, Appellate Defenders-General, and Appellate Registrars. They did not in fact appear in the published text as separate chapters.

26 *Extract from the proposed Constitutional Code*, p. 18; and Bentham Mss., U.C. xii, fol. 192, J.B. to Stanhope (19 Feb. 1824).

27 The intended contents of the Law Amendment proposals (1827–28) are set out in U.C. lxxxv, fol. 3, and U.C. lxxxiii, fols. 120 and 124. These arguments are connected at some points with the renewal of his critique of Blackstone in 1828–31, collected in U.C. xxx and xxxi.

28 He set out most of his presuppositions and objectives in brouillons for the abortive introductory chapters to the Code, especially in U.C. xxxiv, fol. 18, n.d., 'Ch. 1, Ruling principles', fol. 25 (15 Feb. 1824), 'Fundamental or leading principles', and (most valuable of all) fol. 26, 'Leading features of the proposed Constitutional code' (22 April [1824]).

29 U.C. xxxviii, fol. 86 (17 Aug. 1822) marginal, 'Ch. 2 Interest junction'. Cf. U.C. clviii, fols. 337–8 (27 July 1822) marginals, 'Securities against misrule'.

30 U.C. xxxviii, fols. 85–6 and fols. 22–8 (13–21 July 1822) marginals, 'Securities – moral counterforce – Public opinion tribunal'.

31 U.C. xxxvi, fols. 228–34 (16–18 April 1823) draft, 'Ruling principles – means here employed – Efficiency and undangerousness of these means demonstrated by American experience'. The corresponding marginals are in U.C. xxxviii, fols. 153–5.

32 U.C. xxxiv, fols. 18 and 26.

33 *ibid.*, fols. 29 (24 Feb. 1824) and 64 (15–16 Jan. 1824), brouillons.

34 These were among the 'leading features' of the Code summarized in U.C. xxxiv, fol. 26.

35 U.C. xxi, fols. 252 and 309 (Feb. 1823). These papers belong to, respectively, the 'Principles of legislation as to constitutional law' and the 'Arrangements' that he drafted for the use of the Greeks.

See also U.C. xxxvi, fols. 228–30 (16–18 April 1823), draft of 'Ruling principles – means here employed'.

36 The whole pattern of 'subordination as between authority and authority, individual and individual functionary' is set out in 'enactive' form in U.C. xxxvi, fols. 221–2 (30 Mar.–14 April 1823).

37 U.C. cvi, fol. 339 (26 Feb. 1823); a page in a detailed comparison of the Greek and Spanish constitutions.

38 The character of Bentham's thinking when he began the Code is well illustrated by some remarks on security and abundance, drafted in 1821 apparently for 'First lines' but used by Doane for his 'Book 1'. Their tone is hostile to government's intervention in the economy, but they do not commit him to Say's Law and they emphatically recognize the prevention of calamities as a proper task for governments: U.C. xxxvii, fols. 50–4 (14 April 1821).

39 As late as June 1820, Bentham expected the construction of the school to start 'in about three weeks': B.L. Add. Mss. 33 545, fol. 418, J.B. to S.B., 6 June 1820. But in a subsequent letter to his brother (29 Nov.–18 Dec. 1820) he said that he had put aside the project in the expectation of receiving a commission from Spain: *ibid.*, fol. 456. Most of the correspondence and the records of negotiations about the school are in U.C. clxv.

40 U.C. xlii, fol. 71 (28 Sept. 1823), 'Ministers severally–Education Minister', draft. Cf. *Bowring* ix, p. 442.

41 So he argued in a draft for the supplement to s. 17 of ch. 9 of the *Constitutional code*, in U.C. cxiv, fols. 125–7 (23 Mar. 1826).

42 U.C. x, fols. 166–74, consists of a set of papers supplied to Bentham by Buckingham in 1824, and some of Bentham's comments. The related correspondence is in U.C. clxxiv, fol. 91 (23 Mar. 1824), and B.L. Add. Mss. 33 546, fols. 39–40 (1824) and 102–3 (1826).

43 Bentham wrote to his brother that Hill 'knowing nothing of Chrestomathia, to his astonishment...finds that the Chrestomathia principles coincide throughout with the practice they had arrived at thro' long fumbling'; B.L. Add. Mss. 33 545, fols. 575–6 (n.d., but shortly after June 1822 when he first entertained a Hill at Queen's Square Place). Several of Bentham's protégés and acquaintances, including Stanhope and D'Ghies, were sent to Birmingham to inspect and be impressed by Hazelwood.

44 Bentham introduced this material not later than May 1824. See U.C. lxxxiii, fol. 6 (5 May 1824), 'Locable Who, Number of scholars in each school maximized', marginal outline.

45 U.C. xxxvii, fol. 234v (25 Mar. 1823), draft. This paper was intended for his earlier scheme and is marked 'Ch. 4 Executive/ 3 Administrative collectively'. But his first drafts for the several departments are also dated March 1823.

46 E.g. in the material relating to the Interior Communication Minister, the shift in emphasis is recorded in two places. The original Article 1 related the Minister's functions to such of 'the instruments of communication...as are at the disposal of Govern-

ment'; in the revision this became 'all ordinances of the legislature as to the means employed by Government for facilitating the communication between one part and another of the territory of the state'. The original Article 5 had authorised the exercise of the 'statistic and melioration-suggestive functions' in relation to non-government instruments; as revised, this read 'the inspective, statistic, recordative and melioration-suggestive functions'. See U.C. xlii, fols. 60 (29 Mar. 1823) and 61 (27 Sept. 1823), drafts.

47 *ibid.*, fol. 73 (May and June 1826) draft. Cf. *Bowring* ix, p. 442.

48 U.C. xlii, fols. 104–6 (29 Sept. 1823), draft. These pages represent the second 'layer' of drafts for the Ministry, added to the first layer of April 1823 (fols. 99–100).

49 These are the dates suggested by the surviving drafts in U.C. xlii, fols. 77–80 (Health) and 94–6 (Trade). They are confirmed by the absence and appearance of the departments in lists and summaries. Health appears first as an afterthought in U.C. xxxviii, fol. 249 (10 May 1824) and Trade is still missing from fol. 4 in U.C. xlii (16 June 1826).

50 U.C. xlii, fol. 3 (20 May 1824) lists at least 9 sub-sections for 's. 3, Army Minister'. He set out the new scheme, and the related re-numbering of chapters, on fol. 417 in U.C. iv. The paper is dated 14 June 1824, but the list was probably written a little later than that. Fols. 422–4 in the same box (29 July 1824) were drafted with the new scheme in mind.

51 Some of the contributions of these men are scattered through U.C. xl, e.g. at fols. 1 (Neal), 6–10 (Young and Stanhope). See also B.L. Add. Mss. 33 546, fols. 416–17 (J.B. to G.B., 18 May 1830) which focuses on Thompson's role, but refers also to Samuel's and Young's.

52 U.C. xxxviii, fols. 287–90 (11 Mar. 1826) and 295 (17 April 1826), marginal outlines. The new section drew to some extent on three earlier drafts for sections which did not survive in their original form: on 'subordinates' term of service', 'responsibility of subordinates', and 'subordinates'.

53 U.C. xlii, fol. 656. (This paper was dated 14 Oct. 1823, but that date related to material on 'Judge's night attendance' for which the page was first used.)

54 B.L. Add. Mss. 33 549, fol. 170 (19 June 1823), 'Preliminary explanations' – draft.

55 *ibid.*, fols. 14–15 (9 Mar. 1823), 'Preliminary observations', draft. This is an expansion of part of fol. 16 in U.C. xxxix (7 Mar. 1823 – 'Constit. code rudiments').

56 B.L. Add. Mss. 33 549, fol. 165, n.d., 'Preliminary explanations', draft. Another version of the argument is in Add. Mss. 33 549, fols. 264–5 (28 July 1826 – 'Constitut., Penal code and procedure. 1 Form – rudiments'). There are related papers in Add. Mss. 33 551: fols. 67–8 (8 Oct. 1824 – 'Preliminary explanations'), and fol. 297

(n.d. – probably part of the paper to which fol. 165 in 33 549 belongs).

57 U.C. lxv, fol. 12 (18 Sept. 1823), 'Rudiments – functions collected from different functionaries'.

58 Some of his efforts are preserved in U.C. xlii, fols. 289–92 (5 Oct. 1823), 293 (Nov. 1825), 294 and 297 (10 May 1827), 295–6 (20 Aug. 1828), and 303 (26 Sept. 1831).

59 *ibid.*, fol. 294.

60 U.C. xxxiv, fol. 64, 15 Jan. 1824 (inspective function) and fol. 71, 15 June 1826 (information-elicitative and officially-informative). These papers contain the tables of functions derived from fol. 12 in U.C. lxv. There is an intermediate table, dated 3 April 1826, on fol. 68 in U.C. xxxiv.

61 U.C. xxxviii, fol. 224 (1 Sept. 1823 marginal) summarizes the eliminative, the statistic and the melioration-suggestive sections. The section on the reparative function is provided for in a revision of the chapter's contents in *ibid.*, fols. 9–10, March 1824.

62 'Inspective' appeared in a new table of chapters and sections dated February 1825, in U.C. xxxviii, fol. 220. The first drafts of 'Information-elicitative' seem to date from July 1826 (U.C. xxxviii, fol. 321, marginal); and the drafts of 'officially-informative' from August 1826 (*ibid.*, fol. 332, marginal).

63 U.C. xxxix, fol. 19 (29 July 1823), draft. This section was part of a scheme in which the chapter would contain one set of sections dealing with the conditions of Ministers' employment, and another set dealing with the employment and discipline of their subordinates. The scheme seems to have been abandoned soon afterwards, perhaps in the following month.

64 These were added to the marginal summary in U.C. xxxviii, fol. 225 (2 Aug. 1823); the uncorrected marginal corresponds to the text in U.C. xxxix, fol. 19.

65 U.C. xxxviii, fols. 263–6 (Nov. 1824), revised marginal, and U.C. xxxix, fols. 113–48 (April–May 1824), text.

66 *Bowring* ix, pp. 267–8.

67 He stated the problem, and took the first steps towards finding a solution, in an early draft on 'Subordinates, choice of': U.C. xxxviii, fol. 194 (14 May 1823), marginal outline.

68 U.C. xxxix, fol. 18 (29 July 1823), draft.

69 *ibid.*, fol. 23 (31 July 1823), draft.

70 *ibid.*, fol. 24 (30 July 1823), draft.

71 'Ministers' checks' is at fol. 20 (29 July 1823) in U.C. xxxix.

72 U.C. xxxviii, fols. 226–8, marginal outline.

73 The inclusion of the Extra Despatch Book is recorded (but not accurately dated) in U.C. xxxix, fol. 185 (July 1825).

74 U.C. xxxviii, fol. 272 (31 Mar. 1824), marginal outline; and U.C. xxxix, fols. 28–9 and 33–4 (April and June 1824), drafts.

75 U.C. xxxviii, fols. 319–20 (4–5 July 1826 – 'Insubordination obviated'), marginal outline.

76 *ibid.*, fols. 322 (15 July 1826 – 'Extortion obviated') and 340 (13 Mar. 1827 – 'Peculation obviated'), marginal outlines. Fols. 323–8 (18–24 July 1826) retained the old term 'oppression'.

77 U.C. xlii, fol. 122 (25 Sept. 1823).

78 *ibid.*, fols. 616 (19 April 1823) and 617 (3 Aug. 1823), fragmentary drafts.

79 U.C. xxxix, fols. 241–4 (June 1826–April 1827), fragmentary drafts.

80 *Bowring* ix, pp. 328–30.

81 *ibid.*, pp. 259–60. Cf. U.C. xxxviii, fol. 335 (24 Jan. 1827), marginal outline.

82 *ibid.*, fols. 337 and 339 (29 Jan. 1827), marginal outlines.

83 *ibid.*, fols. 283–5 (14 Oct. 1824), marginal outlines.

84 *ibid.*, fols. 282 and 286 (27 Feb.–24 April 1826), marginal outlines, amended by Bentham.

85 *ibid.*, fol. 224 (1 Aug. 1823); this is a marginal summary of several sections of ch. 9 composed at about that time.

86 U.C. xxxviii, fols. 255–61 (Sept. 1824), marginal outline.

87 *ibid.*, fols. 296–318 (May–June 1826), marginal outlines. Fol. 318 (23 May 1826) dictates an arrangement of the material into 'A Generalia All Books. B Outset Books. C Journal Books. III Loss Books'. Those headings correspond to the first 4 of the 5 parts in the published section.

88 He consulted d'Argenson about French prefectures, as he recorded in his memorandum book for 18 June 1822 (U.C. clxxiii, fol. 81). He maintained close relations with Rush and Smith over several years; one incident is recorded in note 90 below.

89 The Greek Constitution seems to have prompted some of his speculations about federalism and the place of sub-legislatures in his system, for he wanted to warn the Greeks against copying the U.S. Constitution on this point. The drafts are in U.C. xlii, fol. 838, and U.C. xxxiv, fols. 297–301 (all 27 Feb. 1824).

90 He was insistent on having a copy of the New York Constitution in 1823. He had secured one by 1822, but had passed it on to John Black of the *Morning Chronicle* (Colls's diary, entry for 18 Jan. 1822, B.L. Add. Mss. 33 563, fol. 96); Black had somehow 'annihilated' it, and Bentham pestered Rush to get him another. (U.C. xii, fol. 161, J.B. to Rush, 4 Dec. 1823; and fols. 162–3, Rush to J.B., 5 Dec. 1823 and 8 Dec. 1823.)

91 *Bowring* ix, p. 613. Bentham's draft is in U.C. xlii, fol. 656 (probably December 1824).

92 U.C. xxxix, fol. 185 (July 1825), draft.

Notes to chapter 8

1 M. Weber, *Economy and society*, I, p. 220.

2 I have in mind here, of course, the discontinuity that Dicey sees between the 'individualism' of the middle half of the nineteenth century and the 'collectivism' of its last third, in his *Lectures on*

the relation between law and public opinion in England during the nineteenth century (London, 1905).

3 Halévy's dichotomy between the 'natural identity' and the 'artificial identification' of interests which is a major theme in *The growth of philosophic radicalism*; Himmelfarb's attempts to establish an authoritarian and to refute a democratic interpretation of Bentham's outlook in 'The haunted house of Jeremy Bentham' (*Victorian minds*, London, 1968, pp. 32–81) and other writings.

BIBLIOGRAPHY

Bentham's Manuscripts

The Bentham Manuscripts in the Library of University College, London.
Catalogue of the Manuscripts of Jeremy Bentham in the Library of University College, London. Compiled by A. Taylor Milne. London, 1962.
The Bentham Manuscripts in the British Library, Add. Mss. 33 537–64.

Collections of Bentham's Works

The works of Jeremy Bentham. Published under the superintendence of his executor, John Bowring. 11 vols. Edinburgh, 1838–43.
The collected works of Jeremy Bentham. General editor, J. H. Burns. In progress, London, 1968–:
   The correspondence of Jeremy Bentham, 1752–1780. 2 vols. Ed. by T. L. S. Sprigge. London, 1968.
   The correspondence of Jeremy Bentham, 1781–1788. Ed. by I. R. Christie. London, 1971.
   An introduction to the principles of morals and legislation. Ed. by J. H. Burns and H. L. A. Hart. London, 1970.
   Of laws in general. Ed. by H. L. A. Hart. London, 1970.
   A comment on the Commentaries and A fragment on government. Ed. by J. H. Burns and H. L. A. Hart. London, 1977.
Traités de législation, civile et pénale. Ed. by P. E. L. Dumont. 3 vols. Paris, 1802.
Théorie des peines et des récompenses. Ed. by P. E. L. Dumont. 2 vols. London, 1811.
Jeremy Bentham's economic writings. Ed. by W. Stark. 3 vols. London, 1952–54.

Bentham's works quoted or referred to in other editions

Bentham's theory of fictions. Ed. by C. K. Ogden. London, 1932.
Church of Englandism and its catechism examined. London, 1818 (printed 1817).
Codification proposal addressed to all nations professing liberal opinions. London, 1822.
'Defence of economy against the late Mr Burke', *The Pamphleteer,* IX (1817), 1–47.

Defence of usury. London, 1787. 2nd edn, London, 1790.

Draught of a new plan for the organization of the judicial establishment of France. London, 1790.

The elements of the art of packing as applied to special juries, particularly in cases of libel laws. London, 1821.

Essay on political tactics...being a fragment of a larger work. London, 1791.

Extract from the proposed Constitutional Code entitled 'Official aptitude maximized, expence minimized'. London, 1816 [=1826].

A fragment on government. Ed. by F. C. Montague. Oxford, 1891.

'Outline of a work entitled *Pauper management improved*', in *Annals of Agriculture*, xxx (1798), 89–176; 241–96; 393–424 and 457–504; and xxxi (1798), 33–64, 169–200 and 273–88.

Panopticon, or the inspection-house. Dublin and London, 1791.

Panopticon: postscript, part I: relative to the plan of construction. London, 1791.

The theory of legislation. Translated by R. Hildreth. London, 1911.

A view of the Hard-labour Bill. London, 1778.

Works by Bentham's predecessors and contemporaries

Adams, John. *A defence of the constitutions of government of the United States of America, against the attack of M. Turgot in his letter to Dr Price*. New edn. 3 vols. London, 1794.

d'Alembert, J. le R. *Oeuvres complètes de d'Alembert*. 5 vols. Paris, 1821–2. Reprinted Geneva, 1967.

d'Alembert, J. le R. *Preliminary discourse to the Encyclopedia of Diderot*. Translated by R. N. Schwab & W. E. Rex. Indianapolis, 1963.

Babbage, C. *On the economy of machinery and manufactures*. London, 1832.

Barrington, D. *Observations upon the statutes, chiefly the more ancient*. 2nd edn. London, 1766.

Beccaria, C. *On crimes and punishments*. Translated by H. Paolucci. Indianapolis, 1963.

Beccaria, C. *A discourse on public oeconomy and commerce*. London, 1769.

Bentham, S. *Services rendered in the civil department of the Navy*. London, 1813.

Bielfeld, J. F. von. *Institutions politiques*. [2nd] edn. 4 vols. Paris, 1762.

Blackstone, William. *Commentaries on the laws of England*. 1st edn. 4 vols. Oxford, 1765–69. Reprinted London, 1966.

Bonvallet des Brosses, S.-J.-L. *Moyens de simplifier la perception et la comptabilité des deniers royaux*. [Paris], 1789.

Burke, Edmund. *The works of the Right Honourable Edmund Burke*. World's Classics edn. 6 vols. London, 1906–07.

Catherine II of Russia ('the Great'). *Documents of Catherine the Great*. Ed. by W. F. Reddaway. Cambridge, 1931.

Chastellux, F. J. de. *An essay on public happiness.* 2 vols. London, 1774. Reprinted New York, 1969.

Colquhoun, P. *A treatise on the police of the metropolis.* 1st edn, London, 1796. 2nd edn, London, 1796.

Colquhoun, P. *A general view of the national police system recommended by the Select Committee of Finance.* London, 1797.

Colquhoun, P. *A general view of the causes and existence of frauds, embezzlements, peculations and plunder, of His Majesty's stores in the dockyards…with remedies humbly suggested.* London, 1799.

Colquhoun, P. *A treatise on the commerce and police of the River Thames.* London, 1800.

Coxe, W. *An account of the prisons and hospitals in Russia, Sweden and Denmark.* London, 1781.

Davenant, C. *The political and commercial works.* Ed. by C. Whitworth. 5 vols. London, 1771. Reprinted 1967.

De Lolme, J. L. *The constitution of England, or an account of the English government.* Bohn's Standard Library. London, 1853.

Diderot, Denis. *Oeuvres politiques.* Ed. by P. Vernière. Paris, 1963.

Eden, W. (Lord Auckland) *The principles of penal law.* 2nd edn. London, 1771.

Encyclopaedia Britannica. 3rd edn. 18+3 vols. Edinburgh, 1797. Article on 'Bookkeeping', vol. III, pp. 367–91.

Fielding, J. *Account of the origin and effects of a police set on foot by His Grace the Duke of Newcastle in the year 1753.* London, 1758.

Frederick II of Prussia ('the Great'). *The King of Prussia's plan for reforming the administration of justice.* London, 1750.

Frederick II of Prussia ('the Great'). *Memoirs of the House of Brandenberg by Frederick III [sic] the present King of Prussia.* London, 1757.

Halhed, N. B. *A code of Gentoo laws, or ordinations of the Pundits.* London, 1776.

Hanway, J. *The defects of police the cause of immorality and the continual robberies committed, particularly in and about the metropolis.* London, 1775.

Harris, James. *Hermes: or a philosophical inquiry concerning language and universal grammar.* London, 1751.

Helvétius, C. A. *De l'esprit, or essays on the mind and its several faculties: with critical observations by W. Mudford.* London, 1807.

Helvétius, C. A. *Treatise on man.* Translated by W. Hooper. 2 vols. London, 1810.

Hobbes, Thomas. *Leviathan or the matter, forme and power of a commonwealth ecclesiasticall and civil.* Ed. by M. Oakeshott. Oxford, n.d.

Hogan, Denis. *An appeal to the public and a farewell address to the army.* London, 1808.

Howard, John. *State of the prisons in England and Wales.* 2 parts. Warrington, 1777–80.

Hume, David. *Hume's theory of politics*. Ed. by F. Watkins. Edinburgh, 1951.

Lamare, N. de. *Traité de la police*. 2nd edn. 4 vols. in 2. Amsterdam, 1729.

Locke, J. *Second treatise of government*. Ed. by J. W. Gough. Oxford, 1946.

Middleton, C. (Lord Barham). *Letters and papers of Charles, Lord Barham*. Publications of the Navy Records Society, nos. 32, 38 and 39. London, 1907–11.

Mildmay, W. *The police of France: or, an account of the laws and regulations established in that kingdom for the preservation of peace and the preventing of robberies*. London, 1763.

Montesquieu, C. L. de Secondat, Baron de. *The spirit of the laws*. Translated by T. Nugent. 2 vols. in 1. New York, 1949.

Necker, J. *A treatise on the administration of the finances of France*. Translated by T. Mortimer. 3 vols. London, 1785.

Paley, W. *Principles of moral and political philosophy*. 8th edn. 2 vols. London, 1791.

Phillips, R. *Letter to the livery of London relative to the views of the writer in executing the office of Sheriff*. London, 1808.

Smith, Adam. *Lectures on justice, police, revenue and arms*. Ed. by E. Cannan. Oxford, 1896. Republished New York, 1956.

Smith, Adam. *Lectures on jurisprudence*. Ed. by R. L. Meek and others. Oxford, 1978.

Spain: *Constitution of 1812. The Pamphleteer*, xxii (1823), 62–87.

Steuart (or Denham), James. *An inquiry into the principles of political oeconomy*. 2 vols. London, 1767.

Turgot, A. R. J. *Oeuvres de Turgot et documents le concernant*. Ed. by G. Schelle. 5 vols. Paris, 1913–23.

Young, A. 'On the accounts proper to be kept by farmers', *Annals of Agriculture*, xxviii (1797), 47–64.

Commentaries and other works by later authors

(This is not a complete or a select bibliography of writings on Bentham. It includes only those works that I found directly useful in preparing the present volume.)

Baker, K. M. 'French political thought at the accession of Louis XVI', *Journal of Modern History*, L (1978), 279–303.

Baker, N. 'Changing attitudes towards government in eighteenth century Britain', in A. Whiteman and others (eds.), *Statesmen, scholars and gentlemen* (Oxford, 1973), pp. 202–19.

Bosher, J. F., *French finances 1770–1795: from business to bureaucracy*. Cambridge, 1970.

Braibanti, R. (ed.) *Political and administrative development*. Durham N.C., 1969.

Burns, J. H. 'Bentham and the French Revolution', *Transactions of the Royal Historical Society*, 5th Series, xvi (1966), 95–114.

Burns, J. H. 'Bentham on sovereignty: an exploration'. *Northern Ireland Legal Quarterly*, XXIV (1973), 399–416.

Cavanaugh, G. J. 'Turgot, the rejector of enlightened despotism', *French Historical Studies*, VI (1969), 31–58.

Clogg, R. (ed.). *The struggle for Greek independence*. London, 1973.

Crook, D. P. *American democracy in English politics 1815–50*. Oxford, 1965.

Dakin, D. *Turgot and the Ancien Régime in France*. London, 1939.

Dalgarno, M. T. 'The contemporary significance of Bentham's Anarchical Fallacies', *Archiv für Rechts- und Sozialphilosophie*, LXI (1975), 357–67.

Derathé, R. *Jean-Jacques Rousseau et la science politique de son temps*. Paris, 1950.

Dicey, A. V. *Lectures on the relation between law and public opinion in England during the nineteenth century*. London, 1905.

Dinwiddy, J. R. 'Bentham's transition to political radicalism, 1809–10', *Journal of the History of Ideas*, XXXV (1975), 683–700.

Dorwart, R. A. *The administrative reforms of Frederick William I of Prussia*. Cambridge, Mass., 1953.

Dunsire, A. *Administration: the word and the science*. London, 1973.

Fayol, H. *General and industrial management*. Translated by C. Storrs. London, 1949.

Foucault, M. *Discipline and punish: the birth of the prison*. Translated by A. Sheridan. London, 1977.

Fry, G. K. 'Bentham and public administration', *Public Administration Bulletin*, No. 24 (Aug. 1977), 32–40.

Goldberg, L. 'Jeremy Bentham, critic of accounting method', *Accounting Research*, VIII (1957), 218–45.

Gough, J. W. *John Locke's political philosophy*. 2nd edn. Oxford, 1973.

Gulick, L. 'Notes on the theory of organization', in *Papers on the science of administration*. Ed. by L. Gulick and L. Urwick (New York, 1937), pp. 1–45.

Halévy, E. *The growth of philosophic radicalism*. Translated by M. Morris. London, 1928.

Hart, H. L. A. 'Bentham on sovereignty', *The Irish Jurist*, II (1967), 327–35.

Hazlitt, W. *The spirit of the age*. World's Classics edn. London, 1960.

Hendel, C. W. *J.-J. Rousseau, moralist*. 2 vols. Oxford, 1934.

Himmelfarb, G. *Victorian minds*. London, 1968.

Himmelfarb, G. 'Bentham scholarship and the Bentham "problem"', *Journal of Modern History*, XLI (1969), 189–206.

Himmelfarb, G. 'Bentham's utopia: the National Charity Company', *Journal of British Studies*, X (1970–71), 80–125.

Hubatsch, W. *Frederick the Great of Prussia: absolutism and administration*. London, 1975.

Hume, L. J. 'Bentham's Panopticon: an administrative history'. Part I, *Historical Studies*, XV (1973), 703–21; Part II, *Historical Studies*, XVI (1974), 36–54.

Hutchison, T. W. 'Bentham as an economist', *Economic Journal*, LXVI (1956), 288–306.

James, M. H. (ed.). *Bentham and legal theory*. Belfast [1974].

Jarrett, D. *The begetters of revolution. England's involvement with France, 1759–1789*. London, 1973.

Jeremy Bentham Bicentenary Celebrations: Bicentenary Lectures. London, 1948.

Johnson, H. C. 'The concept of bureaucracy in cameralism', *Political Science Quarterly*, LXXIX (1964), 378–402.

Johnson, H. C. *Frederick the Great and his officials*. New Haven, 1975.

Kamenka, Eugene and Krygier, Martin (eds.). *Bureaucracy: the career of a concept*. Melbourne, 1979.

Kelley, D. R. '*Vera philosophia*: the philosophical significance of Renaissance jurisprudence', *Journal of the History of Philosophy*, XIV (1976), 267–79.

Legendre, P. 'Evolution des systèmes d'administration et histoire des idées: l'exemple de la pensée française', *Annali della Fondazione Italiana per la Storia amministrativa*, III (1966), 254–74.

Lyons, D. *In the interest of the governed*. Oxford, 1973.

McDonald, Joan. *Rousseau and the French Revolution 1762–1791*. London, 1965.

Mack, M. P. *Jeremy Bentham: an odyssey of ideas 1748–1792*. London, 1962.

Montgomery, R. J. *Examinations: an account of their evolution as administrative devices in England*. London, 1965.

The new Cambridge modern history
  vol. VIII: *The American and French Revolutions*, ed. by A. Goodwin. Cambridge, 1965.
  vol. XIII: *Companion volume*, ed. by P. Burke. Cambridge, 1979.

Norris, J. *Shelburne and reform*. London, 1963.

Palmer, R. R. 'Turgot: paragon of the Continental Enlightenment', *Journal of Law and Economics*, XIX (1976), 607–19.

Parry, G. 'Enlightened government and its critics in eighteenth century Germany', *The Historical Journal*, VI (1963), 178–92.

Peardon, T. P. 'Bentham's ideal republic', *Canadian Journal of Economic and Political Science*, XVII (1951), 184–203.

Poynter, J. R. *Society and pauperism: English ideas on poor relief, 1795–1834*. Melbourne, 1969.

Pugh, D. S. (ed.). *Organization theory*. Harmondsworth, 1971.

Radzinowicz, L. *A history of English criminal law and its administration from 1750*. 4 vols. London, 1948–68.

Raeff, M. 'The well-ordered police state and the development of modernity in seventeenth- and eighteenth-century Europe', *The American Historical Review*, LXXX (1975), 1221–43.

Roach, J. P. C. *Public examinations in England 1850–1900*. Cambridge, 1971.

Robbins, L. C. *Bentham in the twentieth century*. London, 1965.

St Clair, W. *That Greece might still be free*. Oxford, 1972.

Shackleton, R. *Montesquieu: a critical biography*. Oxford, 1961.

Small, A. W. *The Cameralists*. Chicago, 1909.

Stark, W. 'Jeremy Bentham as an economist', *Economic Journal*, LI (1941), 56–79.

Steintrager, J. *Bentham*. London, 1977.

Steintrager, J. 'Morality and belief: the origin and purpose of Bentham's writings on religion', *The Mill Newsletter*, VI 2 (Spring, 1971), 3–15.

Strakosch, H. E. *State absolutism and the rule of law: the struggle for the codification of the civil law in Austria, 1753–1811*. Sydney, 1967.

Thompson, K. A. *Bureaucracy and church reform: the organizational response of the Church of England to social change, 1800–1965*. Oxford, 1970.

Tilly, C. (ed.) *The formation of national states in Western Europe*. Princeton, 1975.

Twining, W. 'The contemporary significance of Bentham's Anarchical Fallacies', *Archiv für Rechts- und Sozialphilosophie*, LXI (1975), 325–56.

Walker, Mack. 'Rights and functions: the social categories of eighteenth century German jurists and cameralists', *Journal of Modern History*, L (1978), 234–51.

Weber, M. *Economy and Society*. Ed. by G. Roth and C. Wittich. 2 vols. Berkeley, 1978.

Winch, D. N. *Classical political economy and colonies*. London, 1965.

Zepos, P. J. 'Jeremy Bentham and the Greek Independence', *Proceedings of the British Academy*, LXII (1976), 293–307.

INDEX

The Political Works of James Harrington, edited by J. G. A. Pocock
Selected Writings of August Cieszkowski, edited and translated with an introductory essay by André Liebich

Studies

1867: Disraeli, Gladstone and Revolution: The Passing of the Second Reform Bill, by Maurice Cowling

The Social and Political Thought of Karl Marx, by Shlomo Avineri

Idealism, Politics and History: Sources of Hegelian Thought, by George Armstrong Kelly

The Impact of Labour 1920–1924: The Beginnings of Modern British Politics, by Maurice Cowling

Alienation: Marx's Conception of Man in Capitalist Society, by Bertell Ollman

The Politics of Reform 1884, by Andrew Jones

Hegel's Theory of the Modern State, by Shlomo Avineri

Jean Bodin and the Rise of Absolutist Theory, by Julian H. Franklin

The Social Problem in the Philosophy of Rousseau, by John Charvet

The Impact of Hitler: British Politics and British Policy 1933–1940 by Maurice Cowling

Social Science and the Ignoble Savage, by Ronald L. Meek

Freedom and Independence: A Study of the Political Ideas of Hegel's 'Phenomenology of Mind', by Judith Shklar

In the Anglo-Arab Labyrinth: The McMahon–Husayn Correspondence and Its Interpretations 1914–1939, by Elie Kedourie

The Liberal Mind 1914–1929, by Michael Bentley

Political Philosophy and Rhetoric: A Study of the Origins of American Party Politics, by John Zvesper

Revolution Principles: The Politics of Party 1689–1720, by J. P. Kenyon

John Locke and the Theory of Sovereignty: Mixed Monarchy and the Right of Resistance in the Political Thought of the English Revolution, by Julian H. Franklin

Adam Smith's Politics: An Essay in Historiographic Revision, by Donald Winch

Lloyd George's Secretariat, by John Turner

The Tragedy of Enlightenment: An Essay on the Frankfurt School, Paul Connerton

DATE DUE